Joy Packer writes:
'It was in response to innumerable kind and friendly letters from readers of *Pack and Follow* that the impulse was born to write *Grey Mistress*.

They asked me 'What did the war do to you?' They made me weigh and consider many things it might have been easy to take for granted.
And for this I thank the writers of those letters.

What did the war do to me? What did if inflict of suffering, and what bestow of mirth and adventure? What new facets of life's prism were caught in its lurid glow? *Grey Mistress* is an answer to these questions, and it is a story of human beings, and human feelings, and the three ships who were my rivals.'

Also by Joy Packer

Fiction
THE HIGH ROOF
NOR THE MOON BY NIGHT
THE GLASS BARRIER

Non-Fiction
PACK AND FOLLOW
APES AND IVORY

and published by Corgi Books

Joy Packer

Grey Mistress

CORGI BOOKS
A DIVISION OF TRANSWORLD PUBLISHERS LTD

GREY MISTRESS

A CORGI BOOK 0 552 09449 8

Originally published in Great Britain by
Eyre & Spottiswoode (Publishers) Ltd.

PRINTING HISTORY
Eyre & Spottiswoode edition published 1949
Eyre & Spottiswoode edition reprinted nine times
Corgi edition published 1974

This book is set in 10pt. Plantin

Corgi Books are published by
Transworld publishers Ltd.,
Cavendish House, 57–59 Uxbridge Road,
Ealing, London W.5.
Made and printed in Great Britain by
Cox & Wyman Ltd., London, Reading and Fakenham

For my husband

Contents

FOREWORD

It was in response to innumerable kind and friendly letters from readers of *Pack and Follow* that the impulse was born to write *Grey Mistress*.

They asked me 'What did the war do to you?' They made me weigh and consider many things it might have been easy to take for granted. And for this I thank the writers of those letters – so many of them unknown to me.

What did the war do to me? What did it inflict of suffering, and what bestow of mirth and adventure? What new facets of life's prism were caught in its lurid glow?

Turn the prism this way and that. See England's green dreaming meadows and tortured cities; her grey North Sea, and the stone hamlets of Scotland; South Africa's silver beaches and golden veld; house-boats drifting down the Nile; the soaring mountain villages of Italy; Trieste with the Borina filling the sails of a naval yacht; and the pale battlements of Malta brooding over warships at anchor in the Grand Harbour. In each facet are faces and figures – British, African, Egyptian, Italian, and many from the lost world of Europe as once we knew it. There is grief, gaiety and romance. And, always in the background, is the ghost of the Grey Mistress, who haunts the life of every sailor's wife.

In peace-time it is possible for a woman to share her man with his ship. But in time of war the Grey Mistress takes full possession. Her needs are inexorable. Women yield her their men – not readily or easily – but with the courage of understanding; and, while her lean grey form is a shadow over their lives, her exploits are a glory in their hearts.

What did the war do to me?

It gave my happiness into the iron hands of the Grey Mistress, and matched the Stranger's step with mine. It gave me great anguish and some bitter-sweet joy. It enriched my life with new places and people, it salted experience with tears and seldom forgot the leaven of laughter, it taught me a new sense of gratitude and changed my standard of values.

How these things came about is told in this book, which is a story of human beings, and human feelings, and the three ships who were my rivals.

Chelsea, London
1949

JOY PACKER

Part One

CHAPTER ONE

THEN IT WAS SUNDAY

THERE was something poignant about those last uneasy days of peace. To me, as to thousands of other women at that time, every word, gesture and look of husband or child seemed disproportionately significant. Even Nature held her breath. Suspense was the master note of our existence – for existence it was. Life had ceased to be. It was held in abeyance – waiting.

The late summer clasped this island in a lingering embrace, as if loth to leave her to an unknown fate. The very leaves clung overlong to their parent trees; and there was that same helpless clinging between human beings, only too well aware that when the wind should rise they would be driven apart, powerless to resist its fury.

My husband and I had just returned from the Balkans, where he had been serving as Naval Attaché to Greece, Turkey and Yugoslavia. He was due for two and a half months' foreign service leave and we had bought a racy-looking wine-coloured S.S. Jaguar with a little chromium-plated sailor at the helm, and we had planned a motor tour of the Scottish Highlands. Our twelve-year-old son, Peter, was home for the summer holidays, and we felt that our timing had worked out pretty well.

'Home', that August in 1939, was a service flat in Chelsea taken by the week. Like most naval people we had learned to live without roots.

Above London, whose threatened beauty lay closer to my heart than ever before, swam a shoal of barrage balloons.

'Like those funny swollen fish that glower at one through the glass in aquariums,' I said to Piet.

My son did not agree. 'Like blue-bottles,' he said.

He was right. They resembled nothing more than the silver-blue cellophane bladders washed up on our white South African beaches after a south-easter. Children tread on them to hear them pop and see them deflate, but they tread gingerly, for 'blue-bottles' trail long stinging threads behind them. The balloons were the same; the sting was in the tail, in the slender wires between earth and sky, traps for unwary aircraft. They were a sign of our times, shining, sinister portents in the summer sky.

Early one morning a telegraph boy came to our flat. It was 24th August.

'Name of Packer?' he asked.

'Name of Packer,' I said, and for the last time in five years took a thin orange envelope and opened it without fear.

It was from the Admiralty. My husband was to go to his war station. He was to take command of H.M.S. *Calcutta*, a small twenty-one-year-old cruiser, till now in the Reserve Fleet. He was to bring her forward in readiness for active service.

We had flown from Athens with only a suit-case each, and all our luggage was still on the high seas.

'I haven't even a uniform,' he said. 'I must get a reach-me-down from Gieves.'

The reach-me-down didn't fit, but there was no time for alterations. By eleven that morning he and Piet were in the Jaguar on their way to Hull, and I was left to pack up the flat and join them by the afternoon train. Leave was forgotten and the glory of the Highlands is still unknown to me.

So there it was. One day a joyous reunion with our little son and the bright prospect of a long holiday together, the next the rustle of an orange envelope and darkness on the mirror of the future.

Things went fast after that. The sands ran out unchecked like lifeblood from a severed artery. It was the end of August. Midnight at the Station Hotel in Hull and I waited for my husband. Piet slept soundly in the bed beside mine, his face turned away from my reading-lamp. There was the sound of the key in the door and he woke and sat up blinking away sleep.

'Hullo, Dad!'

'Hullo, my bold warrior.'

The boy stared at his father with speculative over-observant eyes, and the drowsiness fell from his voice.

'You look awfully tired.' Odd for a child to notice that, I thought.

'We've been pretty busy getting ready for sea.'

Bertie sat on my bed and I slipped my hand under his.

'We sail tomorrow afternoon,' he said.

'Gee! So soon, Dad!'

'Then you mean this is good-bye,' I said. The words rode thinly on a swell of despair.

'Yes,' he said. And his voice and eyes were troubled. 'I hate leaving you both – with no place to go, no plans, nothing . . .'

'We'll manage,' I said. And added, 'Will there be war?'

'Who can say? Even now it may all come right—'

I felt his arms tighten about my shoulders, and for the first time in my life knew the bitter pang of the parting that holds no promise of the next meeting.

'*Auf wiedersehen*,' he said as he left us, and we echoed the words that many a German woman was whispering to her man. '*Auf wiedersehen* . . .'

Next day we saw him sail.

As the little cruiser drew away from the pier Piet stood to attention and saluted. The Captain, on his bridge, returned the compliment. Beside him, smiling down at us, was a dark-bearded officer with a white cockatoo upon his shoulder. We did not know it then, but they, like their ship, were setting out to keep a date with destiny. Yes, even Cocky, the white cockatoo, was soon to be a bird-of-war with a rendezvous to keep in the best traditions of the Service to which he now belonged.

We spent the next few days with our good friends Group-Captain Tommy Elmhirst and his wife Katharine.

Tommy was in command of a Bomber Station outside Hull, and Piet was in his element there with the constant roar of aero-engines to rejoice his ears and the blissful sight of the long-winged monsters thick as flies on the ground or in the summer air.

Katharine and I packed up the house in readiness for any emergency. The great migrations had begun from danger areas to safety zones, and Katharine's turn might be forced upon her at any time. Already the two children, Caroline and Roger, were in Scotland with their grandmother.

It was a crisp bright morning when Piet and I drove into Hull to get our mail at the Station Hotel. I waited in the car while he plunged into the packed station. A sea of little heads swayed this way and that. The children of Hull were being evacuated. They carried their gas-masks and their iron rations and wore identity discs round their necks. A policeman stopped Piet and asked him to which party he belonged. He replied with indignation that he was not 'an evacuating child' but was trying to get into the hotel. The policeman smiled and piloted him through the throng.

In the streets the newsboys were crying 'Speshul! Speshul! Poland invaded – Poland and Germany at war!'

A band of ice closed round my heart.

'Paper, please!'

A newsboy handed one through the window of the car and pocketed his copper. A naval officer, passing by, stopped to speak to me.

'Looks like this is it!' he said. 'If you want to keep your car in commission you'd best lay in a store of petrol. It won't be long now before that's rationed.'

He sounded exuberant.

We took his advice and bought three five-gallon drums and loaded them into the back of the Jaguar.

'Will it be war?' asked Piet, his green eyes sparkling, keen for it.

'Looks like it,' I said.

Then it was Sunday, 3rd September, and that inexhaustible, monotonous radio voice told us to stand by for an important announcement. At 11.15 a.m. the Prime Minister, Mr. Neville Chamberlain, would address the nation.

Tommy Elmhirst was out on the aerodrome somewhere; Piet said he would listen in the kitchen with the cook (it was always his principle to be on the best possible terms with the cook in any household). So Katharine and I sat alone in the living-room to hear the words that would disrupt our lives and destroy our peace of mind for the next five years.

She was painting her nails a frivolous red, and I watched her doing them, delicately and steadily, while Mr. Chamberlain informed us in his flat pulpit-sounding voice that Great Britain and France were at war with Germany. There was no sense of drama or climax to the announcement. It was merely an obvious and rather dreary *dénouement* too long postponed.

'So now we know,' said Katharine, switching off the radio, careful not to damage her newly applied varnish.

Piet popped his head through the door.

'War!' he said. 'Oh gee, I hope this war lasts long enough for me to be in it!'

In the grey mists of Scapa Flow His Majesty's Warships received the Admiralty signal 'TOTAL' (War) and were ordered to 'commence hostilities against Germany'.

The Captain of the *Calcutta* had his new ship's company piped aft and spoke to them. He told them that the old qualities of their race would win this war, doggedness, perseverance, determination, and the capacity to endure discomforts uncomplainingly – snow, ice, tropical suns and rough weather – for one, two, three, or even five years. They listened cheerfully, and at 'five years' they had a good laugh. He told them to remember what he had said when they found themselves getting fed up in the long struggle ahead, and always to bear in mind that the enemy was in a worse state than they were. Guts and endurance had won the last war and would win this. He added that many had left their homes in haste, that some were Active Service, R.N.R., R.N.V.R., R.F.R. and Pensioners, but that now they were all the same. They were the ship's company of the *Calcutta* – and 'Good luck to you all!'

They needed good luck. Seventy per cent of the seamen were men from the London Division of the Royal Naval Reserve, and most of them had never been to sea in their lives. But the 'old qualities of their race' were strong within them – and experience would come. That, at least, was sure.

CHAPTER TWO

ENTER – THE STRANGER

I ONCE had a very young and immensely vital friend who was determined to live every moment of her life to the full. 'Sleep is a waste of time,' she'd say, bright eyes and eager lips avid for experience.

I understood the sentiment, for I, too, love living.

And now life was suspended. There was only time to mark while the process of readjustment took place.

I began this marking time in Robin Hood's Bay. Piet and I

had chosen to go to this North Country seaside village near Scarborough in the way old ladies choose the horses they intend to back – because the name pleased us. It sounded like a winner.

Have you heard starlings in the trees and chimneys of the City of London at sunset? A high-pitched piercing mass-voice rising and falling, insistent and almost deafening as the birds swarm like bees in the boughs with the remorseless restlessness of all winged creatures. The beach below our hotel was like that now with the city evacuees yelling, running, fighting and playing, unstable as the grey North Sea that lapped the strand. Somewhere in their midst were the rough shaggy donkeys of the gypsies, straddled by the shrill wizened gnomish youth of the great industrial heart of a threatened island.

Robin Hood's Bay was a pretty village, with the scent of sea and moorland mingling in the strong windy air. The honeycombed cliffs reminded us of the Greek mountains where Piet had spent other summer holidays with us. There, every cranny and yawning cave had once been the habitat of some fearsome mythical monster; here, in factual England, no dragons or many-headed serpents dwelt in the cliff face. No, these caves had been smugglers' lairs – and might still be. Oh, boy, if we explore we might find a spy in hiding – anything!

Robin Hood's Bay was a good choice for a holiday, but to me it was never quite real. There are blind times in one's life when the touch and sight of outside things is no more than a puff of wind on closed eyelids because all one's seeing and feeling seems directed inwards. It was thus with me that summer vacation, and I have often wondered how much the boy with me was aware of the new aching pre-occupations I strove to conceal from him. Children are peculiarly sensitive to the moods of those they love. They suffer actual physical discomfort in their chests and behind their eyes because some dear grown-up is in distress, and long with all their might to help and heal. My son was very companionable those first difficult days of the war – solicitous in the touching way that marks the formless helpless sympathy of the very young.

'What'll you do, Mom, when I go back to school? You've nowhere to go. It's a pity we've never had a home.'

'Oh, something'll turn up – and I'm glad I'm not tied.'

'Good,' he said, and put on his gas-mask to clown a bit and make me laugh.

When I nagged him, womanlike, I believe he was pleased. There was something reassuringly everyday about being told not to talk so fast or wolf his food. While my own gullet felt packed with damp shoe leather at meal-times, Piet ate with the gulping rapidity of a greedy puppy. Remembering that my husband had told me that a boy learns his lessons at school and his manners at home, I felt it necessary to remonstrate.

'You boys all gobble and gabble as if your lives depended on it. You swallow your words without saying them and your food without chewing it.'

'We have to at school,' said Piet at high speed.

'But why?'

'Well, if you're telling a story and you don't tell it fast the other chaps drift away before you're finished. And if you don't eat fast the other chaps have finished before you've started.'

'Sounds crazy, put that way. Now, honestly, did you taste one mouthful of what you've just shovelled into your face?'

'Not much. But who wants to *taste* rabbit stew?'

We stayed in a 'Family Hotel' – 'Homely, you'll find it', we had been told – and we shared a very homely bedroom with an even more homely black-out contrived out of an old bedspread lined with newspapers. It took close on half-an-hour to pin it up with safety-pins and, once up, there it remained till those acquainted with its eccentricities chose to take it down.

As an extra precaution against showing lights our single electric bulb had been removed and was replaced by a tallow candle. Thus the wrath of that nocturnal prowler, the Air Raid Warden, was kept at bay in company with the glory of the night.

The manager was a genial soul, who lent us a spare pair of binoculars and a spare dog 'to make your walks more interesting'.

The dog was a thin little wire-haired fox terrier at the leggy age of adolescence, and her name was Dinah. At low water she scampered along the beach with us under the cliffs, honeycombed with smugglers' caves and white with the droppings of sea-birds; and, when the tide was in, we trod the heights aquiver with windswept grass and unpretentious field flowers.

When we sat down to rest Dinah crept up to us, and, flattening her ears well back against the sides of her narrow little head, she'd thrust it gently under Piet's hand till he spoke to her and stroked her with absent-minded patronage.

And while the manager's little dog-for-sale wheedled her way into our affections we gazed through his binoculars at the slow convoys passing daily up and down the coast.

'The *Calcutta*!' cried Piet. 'That's her out there! I'm sure it is . . . nearly sure, anyway . . .'

'Let's see, quick! Oh, yes, that's her, sure enough!'

So, as humans do, we saw what we most desired to see.

In point of fact, the *Calcutta* was somewhere between Iceland and the Shetlands, on contraband control in an area infested with submarines.

In Robin Hood's Bay my son was able to indulge a lovable weakness for giving me presents. All along the beaches were 'moss-agate' pebbles which, when polished, held the grey-green of a northern sea shot with sunlight. These he gathered for me and the best we took to Scarborough on one of our walks, and there they were fashioned into plain stud earrings and a brooch for me to wear with country clothes.

'And we must have a tie-pin for Dad – for luck!' said Piet.

For luck? Oh, yes, he'd need something for luck.

So the keen autumn days went by on the breath of the salty wind.

At night, while Piet slept with his dark head a smudge on the pillow in the bed beside mine, I read by the small uncertain flame of the candle. Often as not, the words I read meant no more to me than a pattern of newsprint – no more than an unacknowledged excuse for me to keep alive the thin stiletto of light with which I fought the Stranger.

For now a Stranger had come to dwell by my side, and, when darkness fell, he laid cold hands over my heart.

Somewhere at sea my husband wrote to me:

> 'You must live like a soldier now, from day to day, even hour to hour. And you must try to believe what we all believe – whether we are soldiers or sailors – *it's always the other chap who gets it . . .*'

He must have known about the Stranger who had entered my life that September – that faceless Stranger whose name was Fear.

I am South African, and many years of wandering in the wake of a sailor husband have failed to wean me from my birthplace.

Piet, too, is South African, in spite of his English father, for he was born, like me, in the house under the violet buttress of Table Mountain. And, in his early childhood, when we were stationed in the Far East, he was cared for by my mother and the coloured folk who serve her so faithfully – Cookie and Teena and Arend, to whom she never refers as 'servants' (hateful word!) but always as 'my domestics'. Mother's domestics were part of the feudal system which obtained in the gabled house that was never very far from our thoughts, and which Piet always used as an unconscious yardstick for measuring the loving kindness of every other hearth and home. So whatever happened, not only in our home but in our homeland, was always of the closest interest to us. Thus, when we heard over the radio that South Africa had declared war on Nazi Germany, we looked at each other in amazement.

'I thought she'd be in it, anyhow!' said Piet. 'How could there even be talk about it?'

I shook my head. Yet there had been much talk – sad and bitter talk – before the decision had been reached.

For six years General Smuts, the firm supporter of Commonwealth policy, and General Hertzog, with his narrower Nationalist views, had sunk their differences and combined to form the United Party. But now, with a great world issue at stake, it seemed that they could no longer agree upon the course of action.

On Monday, 4th September, General Hertzog, the Prime Minister, asked the Cape Parliament to support him in a policy of neutrality, albeit neutrality 'friendly to the Commonwealth'. I could imagine him well, for my father had often brought him home to lunch in the days of my girlhood – a hollow-cheeked, sincere, spectacled man, who in all things followed his conscience, no match for the shining brilliancy of his old comrade in arms of forty years ago and for many years his relentless adversary. Hertzog had never really succeeded in envisaging world trends and the inevitable shrinking and vulnerability of a globe linked by air travel and wireless. Even now South Africa still appeared to him as an ark which could ride the flood of universal upheaval in divine isolation till the waters should subside.

Smuts rose to oppose him – the aged, ageless Magi, with a world view and a world reputation for far-seeing wisdom. This man was more than a statesman and a strategist, he was also a legal expert. Under International Law, said Smuts, there was no such thing as the benevolent neutrality suggested by General Hertzog. South Africa must declare herself friend or foe, and it was in her own best interests to take a firm stand against Hitler Germany. This issue was no British quarrel dragging in a reluctant Commonwealth, it was the beginning of a mighty struggle to arrest a madman's dream of world domination. This was no case of putting Britain first and South Africa second. South Africa herself was in peril. If the Union meant to keep her independence she must take the only courageous and honourable course and declare herself. She must wage war against Hitler.

Smuts won his case by a majority of only thirteen votes.

Next day General Hertzog resigned the Premiership and Smuts formed his Cabinet.

Great events have personal repercussions, and presently I received a sorrowful letter from my cousin Maisie te Water, the wife of Charles te Water, who had served ten years in London as High Commissioner for South Africa. Charles had felt compelled to resign when his old Chief had been defeated, and Smuts had accepted that resignation. They would be sailing for South Africa shortly with deep regrets.

'Would you like us to take Peter back?' Maisie wanted to know. 'I am sure your mother would want to have him – and there are hard times ahead in Europe.'

I showed Piet the letter. Much as he adored 'Tees Lodge' he could not bear the idea of being sent into safety. He sought my face anxiously. 'You don't want me to go, do you? You *need* me here . . . and there's Dartmouth . . .'

I put my arm about his shoulders. 'I should hate you to go. I need you very much – and, of course, you must take your Dartmouth entry this autumn. You and I will stick together whatever happens.'

Speech and sentiment are embossed upon our lives. They form the pattern and intensify the colour. Sometimes the pattern goes awry, but it can never be unravelled. These words of mine, 'We'll stick together, whatever happens', spoken on the impulse and from the heart, paid no heed to circumstances. The day was to come when they would be taken in evidence against me. I had no premonition of such a day. Already we were learning to live 'like soldiers . . . from hour to hour . . .'

Maisie te Water's letter filled me with a deep sense of personal loss. For ten years, whenever we had returned to England, usually on Foreign Service leave, the house in Prince's Gate had been open to us with its atmosphere of friendly bantering hospitality. The te Waters' departure severed a strong link with my home in South Africa.

But, as if to offset this blow, the afternoon post brought a warm-hearted letter from our dear friend, Hillie Longstaff, who offered us a home with her in Southsea for as long as we might need it. It was, had she known it, an offer of more than sanctuary; it meant breathing space in which to decide how best to tackle this new life wherein there seemed so little save anxiety to be shared with my husband.

All over the world women were facing up to this same problem – the adjustment of their lives to the uncertainties of war.

When we went south Dinah went with us.

'We're fools,' I said to Piet, as she flattened herself down between us. 'It's lunacy to saddle oneself with a dog – and a girl dog at that – when one hasn't even a home.'

He grinned as he fondled her absurd collapsible ears.

'She'll be company for you when you're lonely.'

'All the same, I'm an idiot.' I was cross with Dinah, Piet, the manager of the hotel, and most of all with myself. Life is the more unpredictable to me because I seldom know what I'll do next. Impulse is my master. Thus a rash and frivolous Joy Packer frequently 'lets herself in' for things which her sensible self deplores. The acquisition of Dinah was a trifling example of this unfortunate tendency.

In Oxford we bought her a basket and a packet of Spratt's Ovals, and deposited Piet at his preparatory school. It was his last term before taking his entrance examination for Dartmouth, and he was filled with bold resolutions. The sooner he could be in the Navy the sooner he would be in the war!

It was evening when I drove over Cosham Bridge and through Portsmouth Town to Southsea.

Here, fourteen years ago, a young naval officer had married a girl from Cape Town, who knew little of England and less of the Navy. The month had been February, the year 1925, and the girl was the present writer.

The great naval arsenal, sprawling between the Portsdown Hills and the wintry sea, with its history and tradition of

Nelson and the Royal Navy, meant no more to me then than 'a muddly sort of place where I'll never find my way!'

My parents had brought me to England to see me 'safely married and settled' – ridiculous to apply the word 'settled' to a naval alliance! – and a month later we had bidden them good-bye at Southampton. Daddy, usually so full of little jokes and chuckles, had been irritable as he always was when his emotions threatened to get the better of him, and Mother had taken refuge behind a laager of 'final bits of advice for the child'. I alone wept without restraint, for I had not yet learned to part from those I loved.

We had had a terrier then, too – a wedding present – an irksome animal called John, with a delicate stomach and subject to fits. I used to walk him along Southsea Front, where he soon demonstrated an unbridled passion for the ocean. He was like those people who feel impelled to fling themselves off heights. He could not behold water without striving to plunge into it. For a naval dog this was a pity, and when presently circumstances forced my husband to take him to sea, the beast, seized by his peculiar mania in the middle of the Bay of Biscay, leapt from the quarter deck some thirty feet into the sea. He did this not once, but constantly, and the Ship's Company became expert in 'Man Overboard' drill. And while John was establishing a reputation in the Mediterranean Fleet as the 'diving dog', I was back home in Cape Town in the House under the Mountain preparing for the arrival of our son.

Now, as I drove through the darkened streets, disfigured with military strong points and civilian shelters, it occurred to me that the six thousand miles of ocean between England and South Africa would no longer present an easy way home. Civilian transport would get less and less until it ceased altogether; and, with that reflection, the old nostalgia for my childhood's home welled up anew as it had done so often those fourteen years ago. Daddy was no longer there with his kindliness and merriment, but his memory bloomed on in the carnations that had been his pride and delight and that were tended now by my mother and Arend, the coloured chauffeur-gardener who had loved his 'ole Baas' so well.

September. It would be Spring now in the Cape Peninsula, with the scent of mimosa on the breeze. Old Cookie would be buying spring vegetables from the Indian 'green man' who came daily to our back door. Teena, her sister, and Chrissie, her daughter, who were as much part of our family as of hers, would be moving all the furniture through the French windows on to the sunny side stoep to give 'de house an extra speshul brighten up now de fine wedder is here', and David, Arend's deaf boy, would be mooning at his work, dreaming, in his silent world, of imagined laughter and words of love spoken in the high-pitched giggling Taal.

How many Springs would come and go before I would see them again – those at home?

The little chromium sailor, standing at his wheel on the Jaguar's radiator cap, was a gleam in the black-out as I turned into Craneswater Park and drew up outside Hillie's sturdy Edwardian house. Roses bloomed in the garden. I was aware of them though the night withheld their beauty. Then I heard her voice – that young alive voice belying the years – and saw the forbidden beam of light as the door opened, and knew that here, too, was a house of welcome.

CHAPTER THREE

NAVAL OCCASIONS

THE comfort of Hillie Longstaff's home had not yet been whittled away by the war. She still had her excellent cook and a charming little maid called Iris, both of whom adored her and would not willingly leave her, for she was one of those who, by the very nature of their personality, unconsciously call forth devotion. Her collection of Dresden and Copenhagen china stood, as before, upon their specially lighted shelves in the lounge, and everything was as I remembered it, from the porcelian pheasants over the fireplace to the heavy carved Spanish chest in the bay window. There was always a jigsaw puzzle on this chest, and, as soon as one was completed, Hillie changed it for another at the puzzle library. She had done this ever since the death of her husband, 'Cuddy' Longstaff, had left her bereaved and broken-hearted. The puzzle was a narcotic.

Hillie and Cuddy had known Bertie longer than I had, and

for his sake they had befriended me with warmth and the generosity characteristic of both of them. In those early days of my marriage they had lived in considerable luxury in a beautiful mansion in Craneswater Park; then one of those 'depressions' with which our times are afflicted forced them to move into a smaller house quite near their erstwhile home. Their aura of goodwill and hospitality went with them to enhance the atmosphere of 'Hanaker'. But then if Hillie were to live in a garret it would somehow become a garret with glamour.

Her friends took their troubles to Hillie, and Hillie took her troubles to God. Like my mother, she had been educated in a Roman Catholic convent-school, and some afterglow of the innocent serenity of a rapt and happy girlhood with the nuns she held in such affectionate esteem lingered with her to defy the inevitable disillusionment of the years.

Hillie loved God and her fellow man, and she also loved luxury, frivolity, the pleasures of the palate, worth while books, good perfume and a naughty story. But if the last-named lacked humour or point to justify it her pretty face assumed a cool little air of 'We are not amused', and she instantly changed the subject in her clear firm voice.

I had thought of putting Dinah into kennels, but Hillie assured me that this was not necessary.

'But I don't think she's properly house-trained,' I said.

'Well, you must train her. The only carpet she has to respect at all costs is the green one in the lounge. It's just been cleaned.'

So, at the first hint of danger, I used to rush at Dinah and carry her upside down into the garden.

'What about Suzette?' I asked.

'She won't go for a puppy,' said Hillie, who knew all about dogs. 'They'll be all right together.'

Thus Dinah learnt her few good manners from Hillie's Sealyham, Suzette, who performed miracles of combining perfect obedience with immense independence.

Every day I took the dogs for a walk along the Front to the great rusty old anchor of the *Victory* bearing its inscription, 'Ready, aye ready'. It was much the same walk as I had been wont to take fourteen years earlier with dog John; only now the esplanade and the piers were mined against invasion and the beaches fanged with iron and concrete teeth, and the Pied Piper of War had called away the laughing yelling hordes of children who had once played and quarrelled on Southsea Common or round the Canoe Lake. The 'safety areas' held them now, and Southsea was deserted.

At nights we listened in to the wireless, and quite often we tuned in to 'Lord Haw-Haw' to hear 'their latest propaganda'. Propaganda is most effective when there is truth in it. Thus one night we were shocked to hear the Irish-American traitor announce in his nasal bleat that we had lost the aircraft-carrier *Courageous*.

We looked at each other. 'It can't be true!'

'Then the B.B.C. will deny it,' said Hillie.

In a naval port the loss of any ship is always a dire grief and calamity, but this was particularly terrible news – the loss of a carrier with a complement of some twelve hundred men! Our hope that the B.B.C. might contradict the German report was a vain one, and presently we heard the confirmation, and, for the first time, I was chilled to the heart by the words that were to haunt the lives of women at home, 'The next of kin have been informed'. They had, but, in this case, not in time. Haw-Haw's announcement had forced the hand of the B.B.C. and the news was put out before those flimsy orange envelopes could reach over a thousand English homes with their messages of good or ill.

'*Courageous* is sunk . . . *Courageous* . . . *Courageous* . . .'

The words, so impersonally spoken over the radio, were taken up and echoed round the port. They were cried aloud by the newsboys, and whispered in homes bereaved; they were keened by the gulls and moaned by the wind; and, for every woman who wept that night, there was one who went down on her knees to give thanks that it was not *her* man, but 'the other chap' – God rest his soul – who had paid the ultimate price of service.

On 21st October the B.B.C. gave us heartening news of a victorious sea-air battle off the north-east coast. Some seventy ships, steaming in slow convoy, had been attacked by waves of Heinkels that had been driven off with heavy casualties to the raiders and little harm to the convoy.

That night the Captain of the *Calcutta* wrote:

'You'll have heard of our adventures over the wireless. It's been a wonderful day, really most exciting, with things happening all the time. My inexperienced crew were magnificent, jumping about like cats to man the guns. It was a grand way of spending Trafalgar Day!'

Soon afterwards I received a telephone call from Grimsby. It was the first time I had heard my husband's voice since those days of intolerable suspense before the declaration of war.

'Joy-Joy, could you come to Darley's Hotel at Cleethorpes? It's part of Grimsby – a long way – but it would be fun if you could bring Jaggy. I don't know how you stand for petrol.'

'I'll manage. I laid in a store – not much, but enough to get me to you. When d'you want me to come?'

'As soon as you can.'

'Piet has his interview and his medical for the Navy on Thursday. I've arranged to meet him in London, and we are going to Philip Rhodes for the night.'

'Good luck to him, bless him! I only wish I could take him myself. Tell him not to bother too much about the interview. They aren't out to catch him, and it won't be as bad as he thinks.'

'I'll tell him. Shall I come on up north from London on Friday?'

'Yes, do that. Friday then—'

'I can't believe it!'

'Nor can I. And, darling . . . if by any chance I'm not there to meet you, don't worry. Just wait. It may even be a day or two. You'll understand.'

'I'll understand; Darley's Hotel, Cleethorpes. I'll be there.'

I met Piet in London on Wednesday afternoon, and saw at once that he had made one of his 'leaps ahead'. Except in a physical sense children do not grow up gradually. Events precipitate sudden moments of mental and emotional advancement. My haphazard Piet, my arch-dawdler, seemed to have crystallized without warning into a firm brusque lad with a most determined lift to his chin. Upon the result of tomorrow's ordeal depended his entire future.

We spent the night at Philip Rhodes' house in South Audley Street. Philip was Bertie's oldest friend. They had been cadets together at Osborne and Dartmouth, and no one could have known better than he what this interview meant to all of us.

During the 1914–18 war Philip – one of the most restless and vital of human beings – had been incarcerated for three years in German prison camps. On his return he was invalided out of the Navy and went into the Stock Exchange. Now World War Two was the signal for him to abandon temporarily a most successful career in the City and get back into uniform, and before long he was one of the leading spirits in the vast secret escape organization which enabled so many of our prisoners to get safely out of Europe.

His housekeeper, Mrs. Homes, a cherished family retainer, gave us one of her delicious dinners, with all Piet's favourite dishes, for she and my son were fast friends. Philip's quick wit kept us entertained all evening, so that the overwhelming import of the morrow was almost forgotten. It was his way to tell the latest Stock Exchange stories with such brevity and rapidity that there was never any danger of his hearers 'drifting away' before he had finished. If the more slow-witted missed the point he didn't care and passed on to something else. Philip never 'boiled his cabbages twice'.

We tucked Piet up early, and he slept soundly under the white polar-bear rug that was the joy of his heart.

Next day our host took us in his Bentley to the Admiralty, thereby gratifying Piet, who loved the Bentley even more than the polar-bear rug. 'Good-bye,' said Philip. 'and don't worry. You'll probably enjoy your interview. I know I did!'

We said good morning to the statue of Captain Scott, and were then swallowed by the labyrinthine corridors of the cold and musty Admiralty. A Wren, who, like the legendary Ariadne, must have had some secret device for finding her way, led us up and down and round about till we came to a wooden hat-stand adorned with raincoats, woollen scarves and those extraordinary little caps that distinguish one mass-produced schoolboy from another.

'They're writing their essays,' said Ariadne, with a casual wave of the hand at the laden hat-stand. She turned to me. 'If you'll wait through there I'll take him along. Or perhaps you'd rather go away and come back? He'll be about an hour all told – possibly even longer.'

'I'll wait,' I said, and threw my son what I believed to be an encouraging smile as he was taken away to the Monster's lair.

It is the myth-established habit of Monsters to ask heroes riddles, and only by giving satisfactory replies can the heroes preserve themselves from perishing ignominiously. Thus it was quite in keeping that Piet should now find himself in the presence of no less than five salty Minotaurs who plied him with questions, ending up with the most important one of all: 'Why do you want to go into the Navy.'

The hero stood to attention and told them.

'I've loved sea-things all my life, and I want to serve my country and follow my father.'

When he rejoined me it was already past midday.

'What about lunch?' I asked.

'After the Medical,' he said. 'Then we'll be able to enjoy it. Let's have juicy steaks.'

We made our way to a grim grey building in Pall Mall, where an aged porter whisked Piet into a lift and left me to cool my heels in one of those cold inhuman waiting-rooms with nothing to read but an out-of-date *Financial Times*. A scholarly man with a wooden leg was seated in a leather armchair, and I discovered that he was a schoolmaster acting in *loco parentis* for another father who, like Piet's, was at sea. Presently a snub-nosed lad with freckles appeared.

'How did it go?' asked the man, levering himself out of his chair with the aid of a stick.

'Seemed all right, sir,' said Freckles.

'Good. And now for some lunch.'

'Is it awful?' I asked the boy.

He grinned. 'Not so bad.'

I was left alone.

The hands of the clock crawled round. One o'clock. . . . One-thirty. . . . What could they be doing all this time? Surely they must be finished soon!

At last I heard my son's step on the uncarpeted stair. The step of one you love – how much it tells! I did not need to look at his face for my heart to be choking me.

His eyes were dilated and the tell-tale pulse I knew so well was beating visibly in his throat above the little soft grey collar of his school shirt. It was clear that he had been shaken to the core of his whole eager healthy being.

'What's wrong?' My stomach seemed to have dissolved. What *could* be wrong?

'They've done me in,' he said. 'I'm no good. Colour-blind.'

'Colour-blind! Nonsense!'

'I am. They said so.'

'What happened?'

He told me at Fuller's, staring down at an untouched 'juicy steak', twisting his handkerchief in his hands.

'The eye-man showed me a book with patterns in it and asked me what numbers I saw. When I'd told him, he went into another room and I heard him say, "This boy's hopeless – not a clue – colour-blind"—'

'You've misunderstood.'

'I haven't misunderstood. After I'd heard him say I was hopeless he came back with somebody else and they both gave me a lantern test . . . lights flashing. I know I made a mess of it . . . my heart was hammering so hard, right in my head . . .'

I could see the dark room, the flashing points of light. 'What colour is this? And this? And *this*?' Pin-points blurring before the tear-filled eyes of a boy who had heard the word 'hopeless'.

He said: 'I have to go back after lunch so that they can finish me off . . . but it's no good now . . .'

The waitress said brightly, over his shoulder, 'Don't you want your steak, Sonnie?' Then she caught a glimpse of his face, and, with a glance at me, removed that 'juicy steak' untouched.

We went back to the grey building – the lair of the Medical Minotaur – and they 'finished off' my Piet. I took what was left to a cinema to while away the time before his train left for Oxford. The film was Disney's 'Pinnocchio'. The colours were beautiful, and it seemed strange that I had never guessed that they might not appear to my son exactly as they appeared to me. There was a horrific sea-monster too, but how much less deadly was his fearsome roaring than the quiet penetrating voice of the white-coated man who had said, 'This boy's hopeless!'

It was dark when I put Piet into the train at Paddington. In the corpse-blue light of the darkened third-class compartment the boy, alone in his corner, looked small and forlorn. Gone were the high hopes of yesterday, the resolute lift of the chin; gone was the quiet confidence of this morning.

'There's surely been a mistake,' I said, as the train began to move. 'Keep your pecker up, Piet!'

He turned his eyes upon me with the large dilated pupils.

'They've done me in,' he said for the second time. 'Tell Dad when you see him . . . it wasn't my fault.'

When the train had gone the little figure, solitary in its corner, was still before my eyes, alone with its suffering.

'All my life I've loved sea-things.' I remembered a little spindly boy clinging to my shoulders as we rode the pounding South African surf before he was six years old; and the thin hardy ten-year-old sailing by himself in the 'wine dark seas' of Homer, gibing and overturning, and his father's voice, 'You're never a sailor till you've been over and in—', and the same little lad being taken in the battle-cruiser *Warspite* on a gunnery exercise, and the pride in his father's eyes afterwards 'Didn't turn a hair – not even for a fifteen-inch salvo – mad keen on everything! Just the type we want for the Navy.'

Just the type, maybe, but somewhere tonight, on the road between London and Oxford, the dear sea-dreams and ambitions of a short lifetime would have to be thrown overboard, and presently it would be my task to 'tell Dad' . . .

CHAPTER FOUR

SECRET WEAPON

It was a night of surging wind and rain and splintering hail when I checked in at Darley's Hotel with dog Dinah. The stormy darkness outside smelt of fish and rope and tar, while inside there was the clean odour of linoleum and furniture polish mixed up with the sour emanations of the longest bar in Grimsby Port.

Cleethorpes was to Grimsby what Southsea was to Portsmouth, only infinitely less inviting. Narrow streets and identical grimy brick dwellings fanned out from Grimsby Fish Market, which, apart from being the peace-time hub of the Humber area, was now also the Naval Headquarters. The people of this rather isolated part of England were like none I had ever met before. Their heavy features were good-natured, yet informed with sly obstinacy and an air of lurking suspicion. There was a marked lag between their thinking and their speaking. If you asked a native of Grimsby the way to anywhere you had given up all hope of a reply by the time the slow rounded syllables had expressed his total ignorance of what you wanted to know. The men of the port were men of few words, but those few were effective and freely used. Basic English was the verbal currency of the locality.

There were only a handful of guests in the hotel – a couple of 'commercials', one other naval wife, leaving on the following day, and two naval officers on shore duty in the port. One of these was Lord Monsell, a former First Lord of the Admiralty, now acting as Naval Officer-in-Charge of the Humber with the rank of Commander.

After dinner he stopped at my table and made himself known to me.

'Your husband should be back about lunch-time tomorrow,' he said, with his remote and charming smile.

'Thank you,' I said, longing to bombard him with questions, but warned off by the detached and guarded expression of his careworn intellectual face.

Next day, just before lunch, a small naval car drew up outside Darley's, and Bertie sprang out. A few moments later we were alone together in my small single room with its uninspiring view of endless rows of chimney-pots in quadruplet.

He carried a breath of the sea with him, as sailors do – a sense of wild invigorating weather and strong salt air. He was thinner and his eyes were swollen and sore, gale-tortured and heavy for lack of sleep, yet alive with an immense eagerness, which was a look I came to know throughout the succeeding years. It was the look of a man who is getting on with a job in which he ardently believes.

I touched Bertie's swollen lids. 'Your eyes, darling! What's wrong with them?'

'It's nothing. Only a bit of strain. The weather and the black-out. My bridge has very little protection and we've had north-easterly gales for the past fortnight.'

'Can't you wear goggles?'

He shook his head and smiled. 'Steaming in and out of the Humber one has to be on the look-out all the time. It's quite a performance.'

He didn't mention that the Humber was known as 'the Graveyard of Ships', because every night there were new wrecks piled up on the treacherous mud-banks – ships that had been mined or had collided with others in the black-out, made more deadly by a seven-knot current at the ebb. Neither did he tell me that U-boats were reported at the river mouth, nor even the small domestic fact that he was suffering constant pain from an injured back. He had been conditioned by an earlier war to a stoical acceptance of every form of discomfort and danger, and the less you thought or talked about them the better, in his opinion.

'How long will you be ashore?' I wanted to know.

'A few hours. I go back to the ship at nine o'clock this evening – then, with luck, I'll be back about this time the day after tomorrow.'

'When did you get into port?'

'About midnight. But never mind the cycle we work on, I'll tell you all about that afterwards. I want to hear about Piet. What happened in his interview?'

I found the tears streaming down my face as I told him, for he, like his son, had contemplated no other future than the Navy for that eager boy whose first and most enduring love was for the sea. Incredulous indignation gave way to shocked horror in those sore eyes of his.

'But if it really *is* so, surely something can be done about it?' he said, biting off the words.

'I believe not . . .'

'I'll find out. There must be some mistake! I've taken Piet to sea with me – I've had him reading the flags – and there was that night in the Corinth Canal in "Landfall", he had no trouble with the lights!'

I was silent. It was clear that he had not accepted the medical verdict, and I knew by the tightening of his lips that within the greater war a small personal campaign would be waged. It was not his way to let go easily.

After lunch we went for a walk along the deserted seashore with its odour of sewers and rotting seaweed. Dinah scampered ahead of us chasing gulls or making hoydenish advances to the scurvey mongrels who hung about the beach in gangs demonstrating the lengths of depravity to which the friend-of-man can sink in the absence of a master.

The sulky greyish sea was lashed by the wind, and in the distance we could see the tall tossing masts of the trawlers turned minesweepers. The sky was heavy with storms passed and to come. Yet, listening to my husband's voice, raised against the wind, I forgot the cold and the bleak dreariness of our setting.

'We pick up our convoy at dawn,' he said. 'That may mean several hours of steaming through the dark to reach the rendezvous; then we stay with it all day to protect it from air attack. At sunset we creep back into the Humber. We may get in at nine or ten, or nearer midnight, depending upon where we leave the convoy. When we're safely anchored I snatch a few hours' sleep. Then, in the morning, I have my routine work of the ship to do, and after that I can come ashore till after dinner. Then off and away again.'

Never a full night's sleep. It was a merciless routine.

My husband was now senior officer of three anti-aircraft cruisers. It was his task to organize their work, their play, their gunnery, and such matters as anchor-berths and drifters to take the men ashore for liberty. His staff consisted of one paymaster midshipman of ten months' experience and two young lieutenants, who had all they could do to hold down their ordinary ship's jobs. But his motto – one which he shared with his mother – was Disraeli's 'Never complain, never explain.'

I learned many things on those walks we used to take along the beach, or in the deserted sea-gardens where the wind in the reeds was a ghostly echo of the hoarse or high-pitched shrieks of vanished children who, like those of 'Pompey', had been spirited away into a 'safety area'.

No woman can ever really envisage life on board a warship going about its appointed tasks, either in peace or war. But every now and again some word or phrase or sentiment may flash a torch for an instant on the obscurity of that essentially masculine picture. Such a glimpse had been vouchsafed me once when I had heard my husband make a speech in which he told of life in the Navy. A small portion lingered in my mind long after the rest had gone.

He was speaking to a civilian audience which knew and loved his ship, and had contributed generously to the comforts of the men on board her.

'Take a cruiser like the *Calcutta*,' he had said. 'Some five hundred men are thrown together for better or worse. We literally sink or swim together, and pass through the same dangers and share our pleasures. We are a large company and close packed with very little individual privacy ...' He'd smiled then. 'We are in an iron box with the lid down. In fact, there's every human reason for discord among us. But we've learnt the art of getting along with each other. It's essential to do so – and there's no mystery about how it's done. It's just a bit of give and take, and seeing the other chap's point of view. It's a matter of good fellowship. A great Englishman once said, "Good fellowship is life, bad fellowship is death" . . .'

There was always plenty of evidence of good fellowship in the life of the *Calcutta,* and there was more, there was a stout-hearted faith in her fortune and in the future. Between decks she was known as 'the lucky *Calcutta*'.

'That's a good way to feel,' said Bertie. 'When men feel that way about their ship they'll be on their toes for anything.'

He was thrilled, too, when one day his secretary – that very young paymaster midshipman – brought him the first copy of the ship's magazine, a thin little rag run off on a jelly. It had as its cover a crude picture of the *Calcutta* firing off at an enemy aircraft with gay abandon. It was full of topical rhymes, and jokes in simple salty taste, and nostalgic illustrations with a Vie Parisienne flavour, and scraps of honest sentiment – a cheerful family affair, alive with that peculiar English gift for picking out something which is no laughing matter and laughing at it.

That his men should have had the initiative, and made the time, for this small extra voluntary effort over and above their gruelling tasks meant a great deal to the Captain of the *Lucky Calcutta,* for such things are not without significance, and he recognized them for what they were – the outward and visible signs of that inward and spiritual grace which is the soul of a 'happy ship'.

A little before nine o'clock Bertie went back on board, refreshed by two hours' deep sleep after our walk. Already we had fallen into the routine which was to regulate our lives during the next fortnight. Lunch together on alternate days, a walk, and then, while Bertie slept for a couple of hours, I curled up in a chair with a book, and my dog and I kept guard. I had not known how deep could be the sleep of mental and physical exhaustion – 'fathoms deep', as he put it. Throughout the war lack of sleep was a torment to the men at sea, especially those in command, yet there were times when, rather than snatch a brief doze, my husband would deliberately force himself to remain awake. 'It's less painful than dropping off and having to stir out again.' Fortunately for him he had the power to defy fatigue and the gift of being able to fall asleep at any time and in any position if his sense of responsibility permitted him to take that greatest and most precious of all luxuries.

Grimsby – what a sinister-sounding name! As bad a *Grimm's Fairy Tales*, and even more frightening and veined with haunting melancholy. There was mystery, as well as the odour of fish and tar and mild and bitter in the air, and there were ominous undertones to the harsh voices of the fishermen that drifted up to my room from the Long Bar. Uncanny things were afoot that November turning the screw of fear a little tighter on many a bolder heart than mine.

There was a certain moon-silvered night when for a space the wind was lulled, and I went with Bertie to the Fish Market where the *Calcutta*'s boat throbbed alongside waiting to take him across the harbour to Grimsby Roads. We could see the ship out there, a swaying silhouette, tall and stately by virtue of comparison with the squat high-masted minesweeping trawlers.

'*Aug wiedersehen*,' said my husband, and smiled at me.

'So long, darling.'

There was the slight shake of the boat as he sprang in, the sudden roar of the engine, a foaming bow-wave and a shining wake. Then he was gone.

An hour later the moon-pale surface of the Humber was broken by mysterious parachutes dropped from audacious low-flying aircraft. Next day the whole port knew that merchant ships and escorting warships had been seen to explode in the shallow coastal waters for no apparent reason. One moment they were steaming in convoy in the swept channel, the next there was a roar and burst of flame as splintered wreckage soared into the air. What was this invisible death that could elude the patient vigilance of our minesweepers?

At lunch I saw Lord Monsell. As he went out he said: 'Your husband's ship is still in port. He may be ashore this afternoon.'

'That's grand news,' I said. And wondered at the pale troubled silence with which he went his way.

Rosie, the manageress, came over to me, with the tiptoe air of one who enters a sick-room. Her ample contours seemed to quiver with unspoken suspicions and every golden hair on her head prickled in the dark shadow of its roots. Her broad peony face, usually as placid as that of the Persian cat asleep in the big flat basket she carried, was now informed with mystery as her glance round the empty dining-room confirmed that we were alone. She inclined towards me.

'Did Lord Monsell tell you what happened last night, loov?'

'No,' I said. 'But I've heard that the Gerries dropped something in the Humber—'

'Do you know what that soomthin' was?'

The palms of my hands crawled as I pushed away my plate of apple pie.

'What?'

Her whisper came as the beat of distant wings – the dark wings of death.

'It was Hitler's Secret Weapon!'

I said, 'No, Rosie, no!' And added, 'What is it? What *is* Hitler's Secret Weapon?'

She uttered a sigh, long-drawn with awe. 'You ask your 'oosband, loov. His guess'll be better than mine.' The cat in the basket stirred with a pitiful *miaow*.

'Poor lad,' she said, her North Country voice going practical and everyday once more. 'He's got the rheumatics soomthin' awful. Can't move without crying. Poor Doozoo, doozems den!'

When Bertie came back to tea, as Lord Monsell had suggested he might, I followed Rosie's advice. But I learned little, for he assumed a certain blank look with which he always shuts a gently padded door against feminine curiosity. He told me only what was already common knowledge in the port – that the aircraft of the night before had dropped mines in the Humber by parachute.

'They'll need to sweep a channel before we can sail,' he said. 'That gives me a breather – a day off and a night ashore!'

'That's grand ... but these mines ... I heard there was something queer about them. Rosie said they were Hitler's Secret Weapon.'

'*Women!*' There was his sideways smile. 'Hell's delight! Women can think up anything!'

'Then it's all right?'

'When the channel's swept it will be.'

Next night he went back to the ship as usual, and in the

morning the tall *Calcutta* was no longer with the trawler family in Grimsby Roads.

In the afternoon I took Dinah for her run.

Storm clouds were massing above the grey foam-flecked sea, and there was grandeur and beauty in the long daggers of light that pierced them. The beach was, as usual, almost empty, save for the presence of the members of the Mongrel Club in the vicinity of the main sewer, and an ancient beachcomber digging for cockles and mussels near a heap of stranded seaweed.

At first sight this bowed figure appeared sexless, for it was clothed in a hybrid assortment of male and female garments. Its feet and ankles were bare, despite the cold, and its form was enshrouded by a shapeless threadbare coat which had evidently once been black and was now weathered to a mouldy green. Between a solid red muffler and a battered peak cap was a wizened window of face, blotched with cold and sparsely bearded.

At the heels of this apparition scavenged a shaggy animal in the final stages of decay. It was only when the window of face was opened a slit to emit a shrill command to the Shaggy One that I realized that my beach companion was a human female.

Her decrepit dog, to do him justice, was not without his fair share of animation, and, as my little Dinah's virginal charms frisked merrily into his orbit, he slowly raised a moth-eaten head in which a rheumy eye kindled with the memory of dog-days gone by, and presently his hoary limbs were galvanized into activity as he set off in shambling pursuit.

Dinah, fully conscious of the effect she was creating, cast him a provocative glance over her thin little snow-white shoulder, and, with shrill mockery, scampered round him in a semicircle, evidently intent upon attacking him from the rear. The Shaggy One, aware of his limitations, made no attempt to counter her lightning sorties, but contented himself with giving a masterly demonstration of the canine art of 'lying doggo', and then suddenly, as her increasing boldness brought her within range, he made an unexpected move and nipped her neatly on the posterior. Dinah fled with a shocked indignant yelp and the aged warrior at her heels.

'Will they fight?' I asked the old beachcomber, who had straightened her bowed back. A toothless grin opened wide the window of face.

'Fight? With a pooppy? Bless you, no; my Laddie wouldn't do such a thing! And he wouldn't be disgoostin' with her neither – not like soom!' She threw a hostile look in the direction of the Cur's Club, and spat with feeling. 'No, loov, 'e's a daicent dog, is Laddie – always 'as been – even in his youth. So don't you woory.'

While the 'daicent dog' disported himself with Dinah the crone told me that her son was a fisherman. From him she gleaned the rumours of the port as diligently as she sought shell-fish at low tide.

'You know the Gerries bombed the lightship last week – noothin' left of those poor lads but blood and bones and bits of 'air! Well, joost afterwards, my boy's trawler picked two Gerries out of the ditch, and, when they brought 'em in, the women was waitin' dahn by the Fish Market with boat-'ooks to shoov 'em in again! Fair mad they were! If they 'adn't 'ad a naval guard those Gerries wouldn't be alive today.'

'My husband's in the Navy,' I told her.

'Is he, loov? Well, I hope he's safe ashore today.'

'Why do you say that?'

' 'Cos o' them new mines they dropped night afore last.'

'Oh, they'll be swept by now.'

'They will *not*!' said the Ancient with conviction. 'Those new mines is 'Itler's Secret Weapon. Listen to me, loov, an' I'll tell you soomthin'.' She put her toothless face close to mine, and her whisper rose above the wind and the cry of the gulls and the moan and beat of the sea.

'You *can't* sweep them mines! *There's no way to sweep 'em!* They're still there . . . there *now* . . . waitin' for ships . . .'

'Did your son say that?'

'I 'eard it . . . an' they say that ships is blowin' oop everywhere arahnd this coast – and in the 'Oomber too – withaht so mooch as toochin' the mines! It's the Secret Weapon . . . that's what the fishermen say. . . . 'Ere, Laddie, coom 'ere this minute! Noon o' that, nah!'

I walked back to Darley's conscious that the cold beauty had gone out of the day. The Stranger was back beside me, matching his relentless step to mine.

It was thus, by a word here and there, by the grave faces of the silent naval officers, snatching a hasty meal before going back to their offices, by a young waitress's foolish echoes of trawler-men gossip in the Long Bar, that I knew all was far from well round our coasts. It was thus that I became aware of the existence of the dreaded magnetic mine which was to cause such havoc before the scientists found the answer. But it had no name then. It was the 'Secret Weapon' – the unpredictable death.

Next day I waited in vain for my husband's return. And the day after. Fog came down and blanketed the Humber. I walked down to the Fish Market and strove to pierce the grey curtain, seeking the ghost of a tall ship among the phantom trawlers tossed by the heavy swell. But night fell, black and starless, the blind fog-horns moaned in Grimsby Roads, the terrible unsweepable mines strained seawards in the swift Humber ebb, while at the river's mouth the hungry U-boats prowled, lean sea-wolves stalking the slow convoys.

The Stranger now was no faceless shadow, he was a foe with cold hands upon my throat. But I fought him hard.

It was a poet of the 1914 war who wrote: 'There's wisdom in women, of more than they have known. And thoughts go blowing through them are wiser than their own . . .' Thus it may have been one of those 'wiser' thoughts that helped me through the bad days of waiting. For it seemed to me that if the Stranger beat me down and forced me to cry out the belief that my husband's ship might be lost, in that moment my living fear would go forth upon some dreadful hidden wave-length potent to destroy. Will-power must hold it in leash – it must not burst the bonds of faith!

After dinner I sat alone in the lounge. The 'commercial' had gone his way, the naval officers were at Headquarters, for convoy casualties had suddenly soared, and, if there were other naval wives in Grimsby, they were not at Darley's.

There was a tap on the door, and Rosie came in carrying her flat cat-basket with Doozoo in it, purring under the soft weight of her knitting.

'It's snug here by the fire,' she remarked complacently. 'I thought I'd bring Doozoo in for a warm through – good for his rheumatics.'

'Do,' I said gratefully. 'I'd be glad of company.'

Fire or no fire, it was not Rosie's custom to bring her cat and her knitting into the visitors' lounge. The real kindness of her intentions was transparent, and my heart warmed towards her. She was closely followed by the hotel dog, Tangles, an appropriately named animal who looked as if he might have been sired by a sheep. He suffered severely from halitosis, and, whenever he approached Dinah, she drew away from his fishy middle-aged greetings and flattened her ears against the sides of her narrow nervous little head.

'What breed is he?' I asked Rosie, as he sighed gustily and flung himself down on the hearthrug in an attitude of dejection, while Dinah relaxed.

'Wire-haired fox,' alleged Rosie, somewhat offended. 'You can see that!'

I hastened to make amends. 'Yes, of course, but his ears rather put me off – the way they stick straight up; and he *is* a bit on the big side . . .'

'He *is* a well-developed dog,' conceded Rosie. 'And as for his ears – that's noothin'.' She cast an affectionate glance at the stiff diabolical appendages protruding from his woolly head like those of a satyr. 'When he was a pooppy he got a terrible fright, an' his ears stood straight oop an' never came down!'

Rosie regaled me with fragments of her life story that evening by the fire, while the three animals slept unheeding of human cares and suffering; and I was struck anew by the unexpectedness of people. Rosie, who looked the very incarnation of placid good sense, was, in fact, as webbed about with superstition as Hitler himself. In common with the Führer, she had her oracles and astral advisers, and the pattern of her life was woven upon their ambiguous precepts and warnings. Yet perhaps this was not so astonishing, after all, for anyone who could accept Rosie's version of the origin of Tangles's upstanding ears in all good faith could believe in anything from horoscopes to spooks. All the same, I was curiously comforted when, as she bade me good night, she paused in the doorway to say: 'Don't you fret, loov. He'll be back tomorrow. You'll see!'

Next day a watery sun was shining, and at lunch time Lord Monsell's genial assistant advised me, with a smile, to 'go over to Immingham late this afternoon. It may be worth your while!'

CHAPTER FIVE

GREY MISTRESS

THE winter sun was low when I came to the marshes of Immingham. Destroyers and minesweepers lay in the river with a depot ship or two; and there, moored at the end of a long wooden pier, was the *Lucky Calcutta* herself!

The tide was out and gulls hovered round the ships with their harsh insistent mewing; the shallows were opalescent in the evening light, feathered by a cold sunset breeze; and the smooth mud-whorls clear of the ebb were scarred by the delicate imprints of innumerable bird feet. Here was desolate sanctuary for ships and men of war.

Leading Seaman Corney, my husband's coxswain, was at the end of the pier to meet me. He was a powerfully-built Isle of Wight man with a clear eye and complexion that were no doubt partly due to the fact that he neither drank nor smoked. His slow smile revealed sparkling teeth, and he was amply blessed with what my husband termed 'the shrewd cunning of the countryman'. He loved gardens, animals, the young lady to whom he was betrothed, the *Calcutta* and our Jaguar; and his admiration for the toughness of his mother and his Captain was such that he believed both to be imperishable.

'We knew you'd find your way here, Madam,' he said. 'And when I spotted the Jagger the Captain said to meet you and bring you on board.' To Corney the Jaguar was always the 'Jagger', to rhyme with dagger.

'Thank goodness you're safely here! I've been so worried!'

'We made it by the grin of our teeth,' said Corney, with his flashing smile. He had his own way of adding a touch of originality to hackneyed expressions.

It was the first time I had seen the ship at close quarters since that day in Hull a lifetime ago. She looked grimed and gashed, with angry red-lead scars, and her grey flanks were spattered with the small wounds of near-misses. Her indefatigable guns were canvas covered. Pacing the deck was a spare, bearded officer with a white cockatoo on his shoulder.

'That's Lieutenant-Commander Arkwright,' said Corney. 'That parrot on his shoulder is Cocky – our mascot – an old-fashioned bird, if ever there was one.'

'Wait a moment before we go on board,' I said. 'I want to look at her – at your ship. She looks wonderful to me!'

'She could do with a coat of paint,' suggested Corney modestly. 'But we don't get much time—'

I have written somewhere else that every naval wife sees in her husband's ship the 'Grey Mistress' who is her rival. The ship is the 'other love'. For her sake a naval officer will leave his wife with that look in his eyes which is something apart from the world of men and women, for her sake he will suffer and fight and die and never once use – or even think – the word 'sacrifice'. In time of war his ship holds undisputed dominion over his life, and the wife who strives to weight the scales against that greater loyalty will break her heart. There is only one course open to her. She, too, must learn to love the Grey Mistress. Now, as I stared at the *Lucky Calcutta*, battered and bruised, but ever 'ready, aye, ready', my heart swelled with pride and I thought that never would any warship be as dear to me as this little outworn cruiser, my husband's first command in the hour of his country's need. It was no effort to me to love the *Lucky Calcutta*, though it might never be given to me to sense more than the merest vicarious quickening of the full rich complex life within her. I knew only that she had a great heart and a gallant soul, and that I wished her well with every fibre of my being.

My husband was at his desk when Corney showed me into the Day Cabin, and, as I entered, he rose and took off the spectacles he wears for reading or writing, and behind the smile of welcome I saw physical fatigue deeply etched round eyes and lips.

'You've been worried,' he said. 'I'm so sorry, darling. There was no way of getting you a message, and we were really only weather-bound.'

I nodded, unable to speak.

There was a double knock on the door, and the Yeoman of Signals stepped smartly in with a batch of signals, My husband went through them quickly, drew a signal pad towards him and made out a few replies, which he handed back with an order in the quick bitten-off tone of voice he occasionally used to Piet but never to me. When we were alone again he turned to me with his crooked half smile.

'My Yeoman of Signals is a postman in private life. He always gives a postman's knock—'

I laughed, and suddenly all the tension of the past few days was eased and I was warm and relaxed and happy. But not for long.

'Darling,' said Bertie. 'I think you should leave tomorrow. It's not worth your staying any more—'

'So you're going away . . .' I would like to have asked him where, but it would have been useless. 'Then I s'pose you're very busy.'

He said, 'I've got about half-an-hour's work. Then I'll be free and we'll go ashore and find a bite of food.'

'Couldn't we come back here for the bite?'

'It wouldn't do,' he said. 'You being here at all is irregular enough.'

Irregular be damned! I thought. Naval wives are always inflicting small irregularities upon their husbands, and naval husbands – at the risk of disrupting what transitory matrimonial bliss their profession permits – exert considerable pressure to resist subtle feminine infiltration into the sacrosanct life of the 'iron box with the lid down'.

'Inhospitable—' I muttered, but Bertie was conveniently deaf. He handed me two letters, both from South Africa.

'I've just answered these – personally, of course. I was very touched.'

One was from a mother and daughter asking for names 'of a few boys on board whose parents are not in a position to send them the necessary requirements. We feel that we'd like to send them parcels to make them feel that there is somebody who appreciates what they are doing for the Empire.'

The other had arrived with a generous parcel of woollen comforts. 'There isn't much I can do to help the war along,' said the writer, 'except knit. Because, unfortunately, I am blind.'

'Then I've been trying to get hold of some rousing new prayers,' said the Captain, looking up from the report he was drafting. 'Something to put the right fighting spirit into our church services on board. I think this is the best so far – though you'd hardly call it *new*!'

On a small slip of paper was written:

'THE PRAYER OF SIR FRANCIS DRAKE'
(On entering Cadiz, 1587)

'Oh Lord, when Thou givest to Thy servants to endeavour in any great matter, grant us also to know that *it is not the beginning, but the continuing of the same until it be thoroughly finished which yieldeth the true glory* – through Him Who for the finishing of Thy work laid down His life – our Redeemer, Jesus Christ. Amen.'

The italics were the Captain's.

Presently I prowled into his Sleeping Cabin. There were photographs of Piet and me on the chest of drawers, and beside them lay a flimsy little journal with a white cockatoo on the cover – the *Calcutta* magazine. Idly I turned the pages and paused at an unpretentious little poem to a Kipling beat:

'It's thick off the Head they say tonight,
And a convoy's southward bound.
We've got to shepherd it safely in,
With neither light nor sound.

It's not much fun to crawl along
And grope your way in a fog,
And a damned sight worse when you're not alone,
(But you can't put that in the log!)

An S.O.S. from a ship being bombed,
That's fifty miles away.
Thirty knots in the blinding rain,
Drenched with the biting spray.

It's not much fun as she takes it green
And rolls like a hump-backed whale,
To plough your way full speed ahead,
In the teeth of a biting gale.

There's a nasty swell, and a steep head sea,
But the old ship runs to time.
Though it's dark as pitch and wet as hell,
The folks at home must dine.

It isn't much fun up the stick tonight,
  A four-hour spell in the dark.
Where there's mines and shoals and a lurking death,
  With never a guiding mark.

It isn't much fun, but it is our job,
  And a job that has no end.
So we're nosing out to sea tonight,
  To take what the sea may send.

We don't care what we are called to do,
  So long as the war is won.
There's a spot of work on hand tonight,
  And *Calcutta* will see that it's done.'

On the bunk was the silver jackal karross I had given Bertie in South Africa; behind the door hung his heavy hooded duffle coat; and on a chair, neatly folded, were the thick fisherman's jersey and trousers he wore at night on the bridge. Over the back of the chair was the long white scarf Hillie had knitted for him, which he wrapped round and round his chest and throat, and a warm knitted helmet.

I touched these things and strove to allow my imagination, imprisoned by ignorance, to escape through my finger-tips. Biting weather, weariness and constant danger – these were the elements of his life. Presently the ship would be 'nosing out to sea tonight – to take what the sea may send'. The cabin-hand would put away the photographs of the Captain's family, and probably someone would take a cup of cocoa on to the bridge. There would be no warm restful sleep under cover of the silver jackals; at best there might be an hour's doze in the tiny Sea Cabin up by the bridge – a sailor's sleep, banished by a sound, by an altered vibration in the ship's rhythm, by the very breath of peril.

I turned, to see my husband standing watching me.

'You're in a dream,' he said. 'Snap out of it, my sweet, and we'll go ashore.'

We found no meal ashore. The only hotel was quite literally dead. There was a wreath in the bar and a coffin in the hall.

'The foonereal's tomorrow,' said the manager gloomily. 'Me moother-in-law. Sorry, noothin' doin' tonight.'

Presently he relented to the extent of a cheese sandwich and a pint of beer, but we ate and drank fast, having no wish to linger under the white flowers of death.

How dark it was that night! 'Black as the inside of a Dutchman's hat,' said Bertie. 'Be careful driving home!'

'And what about you,' I thought, '*with never a guiding mark*—'

My little dog flitted ahead of us like a wraith as we made our way back to the river. At last we stood beside the Jaguar in the shelter of a goods shed. Dim figures came and went from the Men's Canteen; the tiny tram from Grimsby rattled into the terminus, trailing her glow-worm chain of dim blue lights. There was a confusion of voices as sailors got out and fumbled over to the jetty where the liberty boat awaited them. From the Humber we could hear the throb of a motor-boat and the clank-clank of an anchor chain being weighed. A command echoed across the water, and then the sharp aggressive bark of a destroyer announced that she was going about her hazardous business.

The sounds and smells of the sea were here on the river bank. The tang of the sea was on the everlasting north-east wind, it was in the texture of my husband's rough blue coat, in the grain of his weather-bitten cheek. The night was impregnated with it.

Then, in the moment of parting, a strange thing happened. Mild as snowflakes, soft as doves, a host of small memories came to flutter round me – memories of a thousand and one little kind things out of the past, out of the shared years of gaiety and grief. They gathered about us with a light whirling warmth which bore no relation to wind or weather, time or space, and somehow their soft gentle magic made it easier for me to send my man back to the Grey Mistress waiting, implacable and confident, at the end of the long pier.

CHAPTER SIX

CHRISTMAS HOLIDAYS

PIET spent his Christmas vacation at Hillie's. I met him at Portsmouth Town Station, where I beheld him leap out of the train welded to a package of curious shape.

'It's Sea Lion,' he explained, in answer to my query. 'A new seaplane I've designed. I've only just begun her, and I want to finish her these hols.'

Piet was a keen designer. In the preparatory school he had now left for good he had been given a hut in the garden to use as a workshop, and there, with a team of ardent apprentices, he had contrived a varied fleet of gliders, some of which had a flying distance of over five miles to their credit.

'Of course, it's going to be a bit tricky,' he added, with a feather-frown, 'having no proper place to work in.'

But he had reckoned without his hostess, who, when she had seen him consume an enormous tea as only boys can, threw out a casual remark.

'Oh, by the way, there's a potting shed in the back garden. I'd like you to come and have a look at it. It might be useful as a sort of workshop.'

Piet came, he saw, and was conquered.

'Oh, gee, Hillie! Oh, gosh! Oh, thank you!'

The erstwhile potting shed contained a carpenter's bench along the wall under the window, a vice, a motley collection of tools, electric light, a radiator, and a black-out curtain 'so that you can use it after dark'.

It was Shangri-la – a place of magic where we spent the greater part of that winter holiday, with the thin light feel of balsa wood and stretched silk under our fingers and the pungent smell of fish-glue in our nostrils. Piet was the master craftsman and I was the willing apprentice, and within the narrow walls of the shed a new intimacy was established between us, the intimacy of fellow workers.

One day I said: 'You'll be going to Wellington next term. I suppose I ought to tell you the facts of life.'

'You can if you like,' conceded Piet graciously. 'But I know most of that stuff already. Jock gave us a leavers' talk. He always does that to the chaps who are leaving.'

'Then we'll skip it.'

'Oke,' said Piet. 'Now if you'll just hold this wing steady I can draw the silk a bit tighter before glueing it.'

We took Dinah for her daily walk whatever the weather, and we usually ended up at the Canoe Lake which was to be the eventual launching-site of 'Sea Lion'.

At last one evening we put the final touches to the flying-boat. 'Tomorrow's the day!' said my son. He slept restlessly that night.

It was grey and raw when we took 'Sea Lion' down to the Canoe Lake just after breakfast. 'But the wind's right,' said the designer. 'Not too much, not too little.'

The wide shallow surface of the water was fringed by a thin layer of ice, but the centre had not yet frozen. As usual we had the place to ourselves. 'Sea Lion' was balanced delicately on her maker's outstretched right hand.

'Now for it!' He was pale with excitement and cold, almost trembling. Some two foot of silk and balsa wood was poised like a great butterfly on the back of his hand. Suddenly his arm recoiled and shot forward again with the gesture of one putting the weight. 'Sea Lion' was airborne in a beautiful curve, and gradually descended to make a perfect landing in the centre of the lake. Then, to our horror, she began to sink. In a flash Piet's shoes and socks were off and he was wading thigh-deep in the frozen water. When he came out in triumph with his water-logged plane he was blue with cold. As he dried his feet and legs with a grubby pocket handkerchief he said, between chattering teeth, 'Was it a good landing?'

'Perfect. But why ask? You saw it.'

He shook his head. 'I couldn't look. I only really saw her after she was down.'

We took her home and patched her up, and when we told Hillie of our adventures she conjured up a pair of hip-high waders for Piet. 'If you *must* paddle in mid-winter!'

The next time we launched the flying-boat the designer watched coolly and critically, no longer blind with emotion.

'That was fine, wasn't it?' I said.

He puckered his forehead reflectively. 'It was passable. But next time I'm going to build a more stream-lined body with a wider wing span – something lighter altogether.'

'You mean you aren't satisfied?'

He looked at me in genuine surprise. 'Of course not.'

Already his beloved creation had changed its character. It was no longer an end, it was merely a beginning. As we walked home, with the winter wind rising now and cutting through our clothes, it occurred to me that my son had taught me more than the elementary craftsman's art of glueing silk on balsa wood.

A few days later Southsea clothed herself in raiment of glittering white, and soon the Canoe Lake was solid ice, but the only skaters were the ravenous sea-birds. Piet loved watching them. 'See, Mom, how neatly that one takes off, retracting his undercarriage as he goes! And have you noticed how they all land, with their weight well back and putting the brake on their skids?' The flight of birds was a scientific wonder to him. His pleasure in it was purely technical. Here, under his eyes, were living gliders, exquisite working models from the hand of the great Master.

There were a few Christmas parties for the children of naval officers in the port, but I fear Piet did not enjoy them. Most of his contemporaries wore the smart uniforms of Dartmouth cadets, and, when he thought himself unobserved, he would stand apart, staring at them with hostile envious eyes and lips set in a sort of arrogant defiance.

One evening, after listening to the wireless with Iris and the cook, he came charging up to the lounge in high excitement.

'Lord Haw-Haw says the *Nelson*'s been mined and that she's lying in a Scottish lake with two anti-aircraft cruisers to guard her! That's probably Dad – *must* be Dad!'

In point of fact, Lord Haw-Haw had once again spoken the truth.

Only the day before, the little *Calcutta* had been called to the *Nelson*'s assistance – so off she'd rushed in the dark at full speed. Dawn had found her waiting to go into the heavily mined Loch. Her final orders were not encouraging. '*When entering port today approach in a line as near the western shore as possible . . . the fore part of the ship should be cleared and as few men as possible below decks. . . . Speed should be as slow as possible.*'

But the *Lucky Calcutta* made it, and soon she was standing

by the wounded battleship, already badly down by the bows.

Her Captain wrote to us in one of those letters from H.M. Ships with no stamp and no address.

'You would love this beautiful place. Only a few houses, snow-capped mountains, peaty-brown moors and gloriously clean sea-water after the flat muddy Humber. I went on deck tonight, and the sky was clear and no wind. The mountains were white and bright in the starlight and one could smell the damp heather-scent of the earth. Cold, of course, but magnificent air. There is something wonderfully freshening about this wildness and loneliness. One can see its effect on the sailors. And perhaps on oneself . . .'

But it was there, in that beautiful place, that he was to learn that he had lost his own small war, waged so tenaciously within the greater one; there that he received the letter informing him with regret that the Medical Board were unable to reconsider their decision with regard to his son's entry for Dartmouth. So among those snow-capped mountains, cradling the heather-girdled Loch, he faced the fact that his son would never stand – as he himself stood now – upon the bridge of a ship under his own command.

Early in January the *Calcutta* put into Chatham for degaussing, the antidote to Hitler's 'secret weapon', the magnetic mine. Although the 'answer' to that problem had been known for some time, it was many months before it could be put into full effect in home waters. Ships could not be spared, miles of electric cable was needed for both warships and merchantmen, and everyone had to wait their turn. The *Calcutta*'s turn enabled the men to take their belated Christmas leave. Bertie came to us in Southsea, and Hillie, with her never-failing tact and understanding, made a transparent excuse to be away for the first few days of that precious week's leave.

In that time I noticed a new and subtle constraint between my husband and his son. The talk of ships and seafaring matters, that had always been so close a tie between them, was a subject they tacitly avoided. No longer did the boy learn unconscious lessons in leadership by listening to those human stories his father always had to tell. For Bertie understood men as instinctively as a bird flies. 'I may not know the King's Regulations backwards,' he would say sometimes, 'but I *do* know ships and sailors.' He loved ships and sailors as did the boy who had spun so strong a web of dreams across the Seven Seas. And now I saw them seeking new lines of communication – these men of mine, the big one and the little one – and it seemed to me that they were groping in their search.

So, after seven days, Bertie went back to the frozen Humber; and one morning Piet woke up and dressed himself in a new blue suit with long trousers and a stiff white Eton collar, and I drove him into the Army country near Camberley.

The tall iron gates of Wellington College swung open, and we entered into the hushed isolation of a small cruel world held in the icy palm of mid-winter. The red brick college buildings rose gaunt and barren from leafless shrubberies and silent snow-gardens; the playing-fields spread their vast white carpets between the thin gallows of goal-posts; and, through the frost-spangled trees beyond them, we caught glimpses of frozen lakes, still as the heart of a dead bird. The east wind howled its bitter dirge on a high note of anguish, and here and there a midget figure, head down and huddled in its overcoat, trudged across the trackless wastes.

Piet looked upon the scene of desolation with loathing and trepidation.

'It could be lovely in summer,' I said.

His voice, not yet broken, was fragile as spun glass.

'It's very big in winter!'

Yes, I thought, it's very big and very cold, and I hate it as much as you do, my son.

I left him standing, alone and friendless, outside his School House, a little figure in a new blue suit rather too large for him. His chin was up, and his hands – the deft hands of a craftsman – twisted his clean pocket handkerchief as he watched me go. How well I knew that gesture and all that it signified!

When our little sailor piloted the Jaguar through the high iron gates, a ghost of glory departed with him – the glory of a dream of Dartmouth now finally and for ever lost.

CHAPTER SEVEN

'IT HAS REALLY BEGUN!'

BY the end of the year I knew that the time had come for me to take the initiative and make a life for myself somewhere. So I took a small flat in Chelsea, bade good-bye to generous-hearted Hillie and the hospitable home where I had found such welcome sanctuary while 'sorting myself out', and Dinah and I set off for London in the Jaguar.

England was experiencing one of those 'record' cold winters which fall upon her with unfailing regularity and for which she is never, by any chance, prepared. The English climate stands to the Englishman in the relation of a brilliant but temperamental wife. She can seduce and entrance him with her charm and glory and she can depress him beyond measure with the abominations of which she is capable, and, however well he may think he knows her, she can always astonish him.

The land lay deep in drifts of snow and London was transfigured by a dazzling white magic which blurred her form and muted her voice. Everything was frozen – earth, river and water-pipes. Only my dog was the reverse. My little Dinah sat by the electric fire in the living-room with her ears flat aback and a startled look in her eyes. She had reached the age of consent, and neither she nor I had the faintest idea what to do about it, though, within a very short space of time, we reached diametrically opposed conclusions on the subject.

I soon had the good fortune to find a reliable North Country maid to look after us. Evelyn came in daily to tidy the flat and prepare the supper. She was a woman of character, small, wiry, grey-haired, and forbidding till she smiled. She had once worked in the 'big house' of her home village near Otterburn, and she belonged to the era of Mrs. Beeton, when a household was a self-contained community, depending for its well-being upon the good management of a mistress '*whose spirit . . . as with the Commander of an Army, or the leader of an enterprise . . . will be seen through the whole establishment . . .*' When the disintegration of that era made itself felt in Otterburn, Evelyn packed her bag and came to London, where she shared a diminutive flat with her friend, Gracie, who worked for an old lady somewhere near South Kensington Tube Station.

'I like to work in a well-run Big House,' she said, with her prim yet charming smile. 'Or else to be quite on my own.'

With me she was certainly on her own, for I was out during the greater part of the day.

I had now become a scribe in the Royal Naval Depot for Knitted Comforts, and I sat at a bench with a row of other women and wrote thank-you letters to the knitters who supplied us with comforts for the men at sea. Throughout the Empire, from Hong Kong to Hammersmith, knitting needles were clicking diligently, so that, in due course, the lofty rooms of the mansion in Eaton Square, which housed the Depot, were stacked ceiling-high with heavy minesweeping jerseys, sea-boot stockings, pullovers, helmets, gloves, and enough scarves to girdle the globe.

The Depot had the peculiar girls' school atmosphere which permeates any organization entirely staffed by women. We fell into the categories of mistresses, girls, seniors and juniors, bullies, stooges and trouble-makers. There were subtle cross-currents of irritability threading an astonishing amount of good humour, and we were always aware of a powerful bond of shared anxiety, for most of us had our men at sea. On the 'Board of Governors' was Lady Pound, the wife of the First Sea Lord, whose gentle features were already shadowed by the onset of a fatal illness, and Lady Louis Mountbatten, who flashed in and out, herself as bright, keen and nimble as a flexible steel knitting needle.

Once Mrs. Winston Churchill came to inspect the Depot, slender and glamorous in snow leopard with a white turban wound about her distinguished little head.

'What ankles!' murmured my neighbour at the scribe's table. 'Really quite divine!'

And indeed, even Dinah, who lay under my chair, and who was apt to relieve the tedium of 'school hours' by pouncing out at unwary extremities, allowed those divinities to drift into her orbit and out again without so much as a hint of disrespect.

Dinah went daily with me to Eaton Square, and in the eleven o'clock break I borrowed the vast rusty iron key which enabled us to enter the sacred precincts of the gardens, where my little dog chased a ball or a twig, and where already the wand of spring was performing small green miracles.

The Easter Bertie was appointed in command of the modern cruiser *Manchester*, Flagship of Vice-Admiral Geoffrey Layton, C.B., D.S.O., and, on leaving the *Calcutta*, he was able to take a week's leave.

During that time he went to Wellington in the Jaguar to fetch Piet home for the holidays. The snow wilderness had been transformed into primrose woods and fine playing-fields of spring turf. As father and son strolled among the college buildings, Piet suddenly paused and seized his parent's arm.

'Here comes the Master!'

Bertie looked round and saw a youthful athletic figure striding towards them. The young man wore shorts and his red hair was untidy. He carried a squash racquet. Clearly the Games Master. He smiled and stopped to pass the time of day with his pupil and the officer in the uniform of a Captain in the Navy. Presently he said, 'I have a brother in the Navy.'

'Really,' said Piet's father. 'What would be his name? I'm afraid I didn't catch yours—'

He was conscious of a gasp of horror at his elbow, and observed his son's face crimson.

'Longdon,' said the other, with his amused pleasant smile.

'Hell's delight! You can't be the Head!'

They both laughed, and Piet relaxed.

'I envy my brother,' said the young man with red hair. 'This is no time to be in a safe billet.'

Bertie had to agree.

When he got home he told me about the incident. 'I disgraced our bold warrior for evermore by not knowing Longdon when I saw him. Unfortunately I hadn't got their jargon taped, so I didn't realize that at Wellington the Head is simply "the Master" in true biblical style. Poor Piet!'

'Poor Piet' didn't worry for long. In place of 'Sea Lion' he had brought home an extinct petrol engine, bought from a school mate for five shillings, and a model speed-boat made by himself in the College workshop. When he had put monkey gland into his engine he would put the revitalized result into the speed-boat. Piet would contrive a carpenter's bench in a bird's nest, if necessary, so he had no difficulty in adapting a wide window-sill for his purpose. There he laboured joyously, if not silently. When the engine gave tongue, Piet cheered, Dinah barked shrilly, and complaining heads were poked out of nearby windows.

Trials were conducted on the Round Pond in the presence of an idle crowd which assembled to advise or mock the designer. The engine was a sulky brute, which all Piet's ministrations had failed to relieve of chronic arthritis, and it seldom consented to function. On one memorable day, however, it avenged the many insults its owner had endured by charging out to sea with a strident bellow, and rounding back upon the stupefied audience, and up the sloping stone embankment into their midst, scattering them hither and thither.

'Gee!' gasped Piet afterwards. 'That was really something! Tonight I'll work on her some more, and tomorrow we'll get Dad to come and see her in action.'

'Do,' I said. 'It's his last day.'

The capricious engine, considerate for once, performed nobly upon the morrow, and Piet, flushed with happy pride and crowned with glory, watched it streaking into the midst of a flock of indignant water-fowl. Sir Malcolm Campbell never drove his 'Bluebird' with more swelling heart!

'And you see, Dad,' said Piet, on the way home, 'if I alter the mixture next time, I could get a longer run on her . . .'

That evening we saw Bertie off by the night train for the north. He was to join his ship at Scapa Flow.

Waiting for him at the barrier with the luggage was his coxswain, Corney, his cheerful grin a little self-conscious, for he had improved the short but shining hours of his leave by marrying his young lady and taking her on a honeymoon. Perhaps, in the circumstances, it was surprising that he was able to grin at all, but then he was the true professional sailor, always the same, always good-humoured and imperturbable, always keen to go into battle, but always supremely happy to come home.

When he had found his sleeper, Bertie bought an evening paper and glanced at the headlines. He uttered a quick exclamation.

'Norway and Denmark invaded! Now it has *really* begun!'

The words were bitten off, his eyes were gleaming, and we knew that already he had left us. His tremendous impatience to be gone was visible in every word and gesture; and, indeed, it was only by dint of considerable determination and ingenuity that he managed to catch his ship – and the disastrous Norwegian Campaign – at all!

'Done it by the grin of his teeth, Madam,' said Corney afterwards. 'Left the train and took to the air, while I came on with the gear.'

So it happened that when a 'Walrus' Amphibian landed him in the Flow, the *Manchester* was already weighing anchor. Her motor-boats had been hoisted, but she sent a skiff out to meet the new Captain, and, as he mounted the gangway, the departing Captain went down it. There was not even time to 'turn over' officially. In fact, he went straight up on to the bridge, ready to take his fine new cruiser into the teeth of the enemy, and there, for the next fortnight, he remained with scarcely a break. After sixteen days, he wrote, in a letter: 'All I have seen of my new Grey Mistress so far, is her noble forehead!'

Once again he had no clothes with him, other than those he was wearing, for Corney, with the baggage, was still in the Flying Scotsman when the ship sailed, and only succeeded in catching up with her several days later by devious means of his own.

I was fortunate at that time inasmuch as our good friend, Jack Borrett, was then a Duty Captain at the Admiralty, and from him I received constant, albeit guarded, news of my husband. Whatever happened, anywhere at sea, the Duty Captain at the Admiralty was one of the first to hear of it, and before very long it was evident that terrible things were happening.

The Army had been safely conveyed to Norway and landed there by the Navy, but, alas, the Air Force was grievously absent from the operation, and the *Luftwaffe* was present in strength and having things all its own way in a northern latitude where twenty hours of daylight meant twenty hours of uninterrupted bombing on troops ashore and ships approaching the coast. Only too often, over the radio, in tragic context, I heard the names of men and ships well-known to me.

One evening Jack Borrett came in to see me with his wife, Joy. He was smiling all over his face – what Joy called 'showing his teeth'. We were always glad when Jack 'showed his teeth'. It meant the war news was good.

'I wish you could have seen Winnie,' he said, 'when I gave him the signals about the Second Battle of Narvik! He was so thrilled it was wonderful to watch. He just danced for joy – quite literally *danced*!'

Winston Churchill was still First Lord of the Admiralty then, supported by Admiral Sir Dudley Pound, who was a First Sea Lord with energy and vitality to match Winston's own. Deaf and lame he might be, but, like Winston, he too 'poked his nose in everywhere' and turned night into day, sparing neither himself nor his staff.

'What a pair!' said Jack, in admiration.

'Winnie's always telephoning Jack,' said Joy, with pardonable pride. But Jack quickly disillusioned us.

'He doesn't telephone *me*, darling! He telephones the Duty Captain – and very rude he is too – just says "What are the latest signals, Boy? Let me have them at once!" *Boy* – at my age and seniority!'

As often as not, while Jack was on night duty, Joy used to come over to my flat, or I went to hers, and together we glued our ears to the radio, which gave us nothing but bad news.

Joy suffered from one of those masterful consciences which compelled her to do everything she most disliked because she believed it to be her duty. Thus she always arrived with a large bag containing sea-boot stockings, which she was knitting for the Depot.

'The *smell* of this oiled-wool!' she'd groan. 'I'll smell like a sea-boot stocking for the rest of my life, and Jack'll leave me for a brunette – I know it!'

'Why don't you knit pullovers instead?'

'Because the Navy *needs* sea-boot stockings. Anybody will knit pullovers and like it – except you, darling, you have to stick to scarves – but can you imagine anybody in their senses knitting a sea-boot stocking for *pleasure*?'

The argument was unanswerable.

Joy was excellent company, chiefly because of her conscience, which inexorable mentor had convinced her that it was 'up to' her to play an active part in rounding up the King's enemies. In queues, in buses, wherever she might be, she kept a careful look-out for Fifth Columnists, spies, and those nebulous individuals who wickedly spread 'alarm and despondency'.

'It was ghastly today,' she said, attacking the heel of her hated stocking with determination. 'Really quite ghastly! There was a man in my butcher's sausage queue *deliberately* spreading gloom all round him. A *man* shouldn't be in a sausage queue, anyway, you must admit. That, in itself, is suspicious!'

'But what type of man was he? And what did he do?'

'Working class, I suppose, you'd say. And he was muttering to himself – but so that we could all hear – that our wartime sausages are nothing but horse-meat and bread. Well, I grant you they may be – but *still*! I told him very quietly that he was extremely lucky to be getting sausages at all—'

'What did he say to that?'

She laughed. 'I couldn't *begin* to tell you! But he *also* said he'd like someone to tell him why we had to let ourselves in for a bloody war, anyway!'

'What did you do?'

'I gave up my place in the queue to go and find a policeman.'

'And did you?'

'Oh, dear no! Not a sign of the law anywhere! It's always like that. If you've parked your car in the wrong place you may be sure there'll be a *pair* of policemen with little books open, and sucking their pencils, but if there's somebody undermining the war effort and you want him arrested then there isn't a tall hat in sight!'

'So what happened?'

'I missed my place in the queue and the sausages as well.'

'And the man?'

'Oh, *he* got the very last pound of horse-meat and bread while *I* was looking for the invisible policeman.'

We were all on the watch for disguised parachutists at that time, and we had been particularly warned that the enemy favoured dressing up blond young Nazis as nuns. The result was that all nuns were looked at askance when they ventured abroad on their lawful occasions. Joy was haunted by nuns with 'men's feet'.

'Darling, those nuns! Only look at their feet – obviously men!'

'All nuns wear men's shoes – at least, that's my experience.'

'But the tall one has a moustache! I can see it from here!'

'Then, if you really think she's a parachutist, go and ask her the time and hear if she answers in the voice of a man . . . a German.'

Joy would hasten after the good religious, who invariably told her the time in agreeable – and feminine – Irish.

But one evening she came over to me with an anxious face, and she had none of her usual funny little adventures to relate. She said: 'Jack hasn't shown his teeth for days. Things must be grim.'

And indeed they were, for that night the nine o'clock news informed us that King Haakon and his family and the coffers of Norwegian State gold had been evacuated from Molde by a British cruiser. It was virtually the end of the campaign – but it was also a beginning, for, in all Europe, there was no resistance stronger than that of Norway and no Government in exile more determined in its fight for freedom.

Much later my husband allowed me to see an extract taken from the report of the cruiser in question, H.M.S. *Glasgow*, and written on 9th April, 1940:

> 'Although it may seem impertinent on my part to refer to this, I am unable to refrain from remarking on the tremendous impression made on us all by His Majesty and the Crown Prince. His Majesty had undergone the severest ordeal, he was feeling broken-hearted at the fate of his country; he had remained in his field uniform for days on end, and had been subjected to continuous bombing whilst without sleep. His embarkation and departure had taken place under the most trying conditions with night-bombing occurring for the first time; under these circumstances, his composure and dignity, his kindliness and thoughtfulness for others, his confident and ever-cheerful bearing when in public, were an inspiration to all of us and unforgettable.'

In the meantime the rest of the evacuation was still in progress under hideous conditions, and, what Jack knew – and I did not – was that the last ships to embark the shattered rearguard of our troops were those under the command of Rear-Admiral Geoffrey Layton in the *Manchester*.

In due course I learned what had happened.

The cruiser and her accompanying ships – including the *Lucky Calcutta* – steamed up the long fjord in that so limited time of darkness under frequent night-bombing attacks, during which the Captain several times found it incumbent upon him to remonstrate with the Admiral, who kept jumping on to a stool to look over the bridge every time a bomb exploded.

Geoffrey Layton was always abominably careless of his personal safety, and his language when reproved was as red as the burning towns along the shore.

Near Molde a destroyer slid away to embark the Norwegian Commander-in-Chief and his staff and take them to Tromso. On went the *Manchester*, with her destroyer screen, towards a sullen far-off glow which intensified as they approached Aandalsnes – ''Ands and Knees' the sailors called it – brightening the rugged mountains on either side of the fjord. It was caused by a town in flames – every wooden house ablaze. At two a.m. the cruiser dropped anchor off Aandalsnes where the weary troops were waiting by the bombed and burning pier. Those troops had been through hell upon earth, they could hardly walk, they hadn't washed for a fortnight and had been bombed and machine-gunned from the air unceasingly. Destroyers ferried them on board, and they collapsed in bunches on the deck, and only stirred to accept the soup that was offered them.

Next day, when the *Manchester* was well clear of the land, the Captain spent half an hour walking round and talking to the troops.

He wrote in his private log:

> 'A lot were still "out", and the real youngsters "cooked", but, generally speaking, I was very much impressed by the good condition of the elder men and regular soldiers . . . who were shaving and sprucing themselves up. They all said they would take on as many "bluidy Bosches" as they could find, but they couldn't cope with the aeroplanes which gave them no chance. We have 840 on board, and the total taken off by our party last night was 2,200. My old *Calcutta* took 740 – a big effort after twelve hours of being attacked with 153 bombs.
>
> 'In the sick-bay we have no serious wounded, but an enormous number of bad feet, swollen blue, black, blistered and bleeding.
>
> 'This party from the rearguard had entrained the night before. The train crashed in a bomb crater. The troops were already pretty well worn out, but they then had to set out and march seventeen miles to a tunnel where they could take cover during the day. . . . They rested in the tunnel and got another train on to about four miles from Aandalsnes, when they had to march the rest.

'I was delighted to see that most of them still had their rifles and equipment, and also they brought off a lot of ammunition and anti-tank guns.

'Our Admiral's drive and decision is largely responsible for the fact that there has been successfully accomplished that most difficult operation of embarking a rearguard in the face of the enemy.

'The Germans were in Aandalsnes today!

'At present we are steaming to the W. at twenty-seven knots – and *for the first time* we have some air protection – a Sunderland flying-boat and three Blenheims!'

Meanwhile, in England, the temper of the nation was rising. There must be a debate on Norway!

So it transpired that at Westminster, too, there was defeat and tragedy, as a statesman, with the hand of death already upon him, was driven relentlessly forth.

Chamberlain must go! In his speech, attacking the Premier, Mr. Amery used in the House words once pronounced by Cromwell. 'In the name of God, go!'

When the House adjourned for the division those words were taken up by the Socialists with cruel and bitter intent. As the bowed, care-worn figure of the elderly Prime Minister walked slowly out, they chanted to the measure of his flagging steps. 'In the name of God, go! In the name of God, go! In the name of God, go!' So, with that dreadful chant of condemnation ringing in his ears, an honest upright man, who had genuinely striven for peace in our time, faced the annihilation of his career. Death, not long delayed, was more merciful than his political opponents. Death, too, was an ending, but in death there was neither hatred nor humiliation, nor the blind judgment of his fellow men.

Thus Neville Chamberlain went, and Winston Churchill, with a Coalition Government, took his place. The British Commonwealth of Nations had gained the greatest and most ferocious war leader of all time, and the Navy had lost a well-loved First Lord.

CHAPTER EIGHT

BRIEF REUNION

THINKING back of those dark days when the Low Countries were invaded and France was crumbling, it stands out in my memory how remarkable an intimacy was established between the new Prime Minister and the people. It was the sort of intimacy young children naturally assume with God.

I have a little nephew, who wished to go to a Christmas Day service in Cape Town Cathedral. His mother said, 'Darling, you'll find it a very long service, you won't understand most of it, and I think you'll get extremely tired.'

'No, Mummie,' said he. 'I won't get tired, and when I don't understand, I'll just sit and talk with Jesus by myself.' He has always been on excellent terms with the Almighty, and chatting with Jesus is one of his pleasantest relaxations.

Winston, that Man of Wrath, through the medium of the radio, descended into our midst and made it possible for all of us to feel that, when the situation was beyond our comprehension and control, he was there – ready to come to us in our homes with comfort and wise counsel. God-like he saw into the warm human core of our troubles and God-like he breathed his own great fighting spirit into our heavy hearts. He knew our weakness and our strength and he loved us, so he chastened and exhorted us as Jehovah chastened and exhorted his people in the Wilderness. Tribulation we must suffer if we were to reach the Promised Land – 'sweat, toil and tears' – but it was there, ahead, 'the broad sunlit upland', and if we followed him we would achieve it.

When Joy and I had heard Winston over the wireless of an evening, we would sit silent, with our hands idle and our heads bowed. Tears might stand in our eyes and great resolves swell our hearts. *We were all in the Front Line now* ... what tremendous pride lay in those words!

But words alone cannot hold back armies, and Hitler's hosts were surging towards the Channel ports, invincible. In the faces of friends 'in the know' one read dire tidings, and an accumulation of small personal incidents pointed the way things were going.

For instance, there was Katharine Elmhirst's message one morning.

Our friends, the Elmhirsts, were now in London and had taken a charming house in Walton Place. I often went in to see Katharine for a drink and gossip round six o'clock which was their 'Children's Hour' when Caroline and Roger brought their toys into the drawing-room and allowed the grown-ups to play with them. Tommy, now an Air Commodore, used to come back from the Air Ministry grey with anxiety, but he was never too tired or too worried to read with his historically-minded little daughter, or to construct a fortress of bricks with the cherubic small war-monger making aeroplane noises on the carpet. Katharine watched them with a look on her face which mothers wore in those days – a naked yearning, thinly veiled. I knew that night after night she dreamed of a great German bomber-plane tearing through the walls of her house into the nursery, where, with a terrible cry, she flung her body across that of her still sleeping son. The cry always woke her and found her trembling, with tears pouring down her cheeks on to the pillow.

One morning she rang me up.

'I'm in bed with tonsillitis, and Tommy thinks the children should leave London at once and go to my sister Do, near Tring. Could you take them in your car?'

'When?' (*So it was as bad as that? Tommy must fear some sort of an attack on London.*)

'Today. I have the petrol for the journey.'

'Of course, I will. This evening after the Depot.'

The children were excited when I fetched them, and when Katharine tried to tell me the way to Do's, Caroline bounced up and down like a tennis ball shouting, 'Don't tell her, because I know it, I know it, I know it!'

'I think she does,' said Katharine from a very sore throat, and abstained from kissing them good-bye.

'I know it for sure,' said Caroline. 'Sure as eggs!'

So we set off, Nannie and Roger in the back, Caroline beside me, her small spectacled face wrapped in fearful concentration. 'Sure as eggs,' she might be, but had yet to learn that they were rotten eggs.

'I think this must be the fork your mother meant,' I said, about a mile out of Tring. 'Do you recognize it?'

Caroline looked hard down the road, and shook her head vigorously. 'Further on.'

We went on. But soon it was evident that the mobile sign-posts of her memory had deceived her, and quite suddenly she called out loud, weeping with mortification behind her spectacles. 'This isn't the Lammy Road – oh, what shall I do? I've *lost* the Lammy Road . . .'

'We can ask,' I said. 'Lammy Road – is that its name?'

'Lammy Road is *my* name for it – because there were l-lots of l-lovely little lambs in it last time we came here – and now I can't f-find m-m-my lambs!'

I stopped at an A.A. call-box and telephoned Do, who told me how to find her house. We went back several miles, and suddenly, at the original fork in the road, Bo-Peep dried her tears and uttered loud shouts of glee. 'This is it! This *is* it, after all!' She knew it, of course, by the cloud of dust and the flock of sheep and lambs homeward bound!

Just after the News that evening my telephone bell sounded. The exchange was Scottish, and Bertie's voice came thinly from a long way off.

'Can you make the night train for Edinburgh? You've only got an hour—'

'Yes, I can! What shall I bring?'

'Country things for a few days. Corney'll meet you at Waverley Station tomorrow morning.'

'I'll be there!'

Corney looked sun-tanned and cheerful, as if he had just returned from a pleasure cruise instead of from the tragic fjords of Norway. But then the tall Isle of Wight man had an infinite capacity for taking the rough with the smooth and everything else for granted. Nothing ever surprised or shocked him, except when he unmasked a ship-mate who hadn't 'got his heart in his work'. My husband once said that if, in the midst of that fearful evacuation from Aandalsnes, he had suddenly said to his cox-swain, 'Just lower the skiff, I feel inclined to go for a row,' Corney would have done so without batting an eyelid, though he would certainly have found cause to complain that the bowman had not stowed her away properly last time – 'doesn't seem to have his heart in 'is work, Sir . . .'

'The Captain has taken rooms for you at South Queensferry, Madam, just across the bridge. Nothing very grand, but we think you'll be comfortable there, and they'll take Dinah.'

As we drove from the station he gave me little bits of news. My husband was well, 'The Captain seems to *thrive* on excitement—' – General Paget, who had been evacuated with his troops, had been very sea-sick, 'and his feet were in a terrible state! We lent him a pair of the Captain's socks,' – and at Aandalsnes (he called it ' 'Ands-and-Knees') they'd nearly lost their cat, Leslie, 'Not much to look at as cats go, but a proper sea-going animal!' – and they'd seen Cocky of the *Lucky Calcutta* – 'in them fords – going up the rigging claw-over-claw, proper seaman-like'.

On the Forth Bridge, Corney pointed down the Firth. 'There, Madam, that's where we're lying.'

The long Firth gleamed softly between her bonnie green banks, studded with sombre stone villages. In the crook of her arm she cradled a fleet of warships come back to lick their wounds before going out again. Over Rosyth Dockyard a shoal of silver balloons floated dreamily in the clear air. How good this scene must look to men who had endured the nightmare of Norway.

During the next few days Bertie and I spent many sunny evenings walking together in the hills around the Firth after a substantial 'high tea', supplied to us by the proprietress of our inn, 'Mistress' Maconochie. And though, for the time being, I had my husband safely with me, the Stranger walked beside us, for the news from across the Channel grew more desperate every hour.

Yet, while the enemy legions pressed towards the Channel Coast, I garnered a queer little harvest of Norwegian souvenirs – Disney happenings bearing small relation to the background of burning devastation against which they had taken place.

There were the Chasseurs Alpins, the famous French mountain troops, who had not been allowed to take their mules to Norway. In vain had they thrown up their hands and cried aloud that it was *fantastique* – *incroyable* – that they should be required to campaign in Norway without their animals – Fifi, Violette *et la petite* Héloise! Their mules were their porters, their fellow-campaigners, their sisters and brothers – without their mules they would be lost.

But the Navy and remained adamant, if not unmoved. The

lesser cannot contain the greater, and already the troopships were filled to over flowing. Violette, Fifi, *la petite* Héloise and all the other relations would have to stay behind. So, with bitter lamentations, the Chasseurs had bidden their friends *adieu*. Birds without wings were mountain troops without mules. They were betrayed – *Nous sommes trahis!*

Blinking on the wharf had stood the sturdy mountain mules, oblivious of their good fortune and twitching their long ears. Little did they know that beneath the dirge of their masters lay the reedy music of the great god, Pan, patron of all furred and feathered creatures, who was caring for his own.

There were vignettes of Cocky, that old-fashioned and seaman-like bird, flying from the mast-head of the *Lucky Calcutta* like a battle ensign; and there was the unfinished symphony of Leslie, the sea-going cat.

Leslie, of H.M.S. *Manchester*, was a personality.

When the ship was building at Tyneside, in the yards of Messrs. Hawthorne and Leslie, in the year 1938, two young cats took up their abode on board and were soon known as Hawthorne and Leslie. When the ship was ready for sea and about to sail for the East Indies Station, Hawthorne, the tortoiseshell, stepped gracefully down the gangway and stood upon the quay to watch her depart, while Leslie, black-for-luck, stayed on board. The sailors cheered. It amused them to see the girl cat wave her lad farewell.

But the sailors had been fooled on a small point; for it happened that, in this case, the beautiful Hawthorne was the lad and little black Leslie was the lady – as she duly proved by producing a batch of tawny Tyneside kittens somewhere in the Red Sea.

Leslie began as she meant to go on. She selected the boiler-room as her private lying-in ward and place of safety. She took meticulous care of her babies and brought them up beautifully in sea-going ways. They caught mice and rats and paid no attention to birds, because sea-birds are too big for little cats to tackle. When the ship was doing gunnery practice the family repaired to the boiler-room. In the eyes of all, Leslie established herself as the perfect mother and the perfect sailor.

In Colombo she went ashore to sniff the spicy breezes of the Orient – intoxicating perfumes to a cat on leave – and, in due course, an exotic little tar-brush party was delivered in the boiler-room.

Then it was spring 1940, and the *Manchester* was steaming up that snowy fjord to disembark an infantry battalion at Molde. So this was Norway! Leslie slipped sinuously ashore with the soldiers and happened to fall in with a blond Norwegian Tom. Foreign he might be, but they soon found that they spoke the same language, and loud and long they spoke it before the little black cat returned to her ship.

'All the King's horses – and all the King's men—
Walked up the street – and they walked back again . . .'

ran the popular refrain of that time; and so it had been in Norway. The *Manchest*er had helped to take the King's men up the long fjords, and then she helped to bring them back again. So, once again, she'd found herself steaming up past Molde to the burning town of Aandalsnes to embark a shattered rearguard.

Leslie became puzzled and restless as strange chords of memory miaowed faintly in her pointed ears, urging her to go ashore again in search of something – someone. . . . At last she could resist her instinct no longer, and, as the final batch of exhausted soldiers was ferried over to the *Manchester* by the destroyer *Delight*, she leapt lightly down on to the destroyer's deck. But she was too late. There were no more trips to the burning pier, for the last of the King's men were safely on board. The ships cast off, and soon the glow of ' 'Ands-and-Knees' was visible only as a far-off reflection in the dawn sky. At 3.22 *Manchester* received a signal from *Delight.*

'I have a black cat in exchange for 400 soldiers discharged to you. Does she belong to you please? 03.22.'

Manchester made immediate reply.

'Please return our black cat. You can have the 400 soldiers back. 03.26. 2/5/40.'

The Molde kittens were red-heads when they arrived. Red for danger, red as the glare of flames on snow, a small feline seal on a campaign that had plunged a free and vigorous nation into five years of purgatory.

One day Bertie told me that I must return to London, and

then I knew that his fine cruiser would soon be gone from the gleaming Firth.

That same night, over the radio, we heard the translation of a rousing speech in which the French Premier, M. Reynaud, implored his countrymen to go on fighting to the bitter end, no matter what it might cost in sacrifice. But we knew, even as we listened, that the fall of the Channel ports was imminent. What we did not know, and could not guess, was that we had heard the last fighting speech from inside France. Our only ally was on the eve of destruction.

So much was happening so fast! Would I find London changed after so short a time away? The first evidence that I would, met me in the flat on my arrival at eight o'clock in the morning. It was a message in Evelyn's neat handwriting.

'Mrs. Bain-Marais telephoned. Will you ring her up as soon as you get back.' There followed the number.

I turned the slip of paper over in my hands. 'Dinkie' Bain-Marais here! Did that mean that the end had already come in France? Colin Bain-Marais, my mother's youngest step-brother, had recently been appointed South African Minister to France and the Low Countries. His wife, Dinkie, and their daughter, Shirley, had been with him in Paris. Their son, young Colin, was still at school in South Africa.

I called up the number at once and learned that Dinkie and Shirley were in London – refugees – swept out of France with the rest of the Diplomatic Corps, that they had been severely bombed in crossing the Channel because the Germans had evidently believed that the French Government was on board; that Colin was likely to arrive at any time now and would remain in England pending further orders from Smuts; but that Dinkie and Shirley would sail for South Africa within a few days.

I went to see them at the hotel. They looked exhausted. Dinkie's attractive heart-shaped face was hollow under the high cheek-bones, and she had the vague distracted manner of one who has been through a shocking ordeal. Shirley was pale but calm, a lovely girl with eyes like blue agate in a face too compassionate for her nineteen years.

Before I left, Dinkie said, 'I feel I must get back to South Africa to see young Colin again before he joins up. He's nearly seventeen, you know, and he wants to leave school and go into the Air Force—' She passed a hand across her eyes and her small pointed chin was trembling. 'We thought perhaps you might like us to take your Piet back . . .'

I said, slowly, 'Thank you very much, Dinkie – but no, not yet.'

'Well, it's up to you,' she said. 'Your Mom would want him, I expect.'

'Yes,' I said. Letters from home, wonderful in their understanding, were in my desk at the flat.

> 'I don't want to influence you my darling, but the doors of Tees Lodge are open, wide open, to receive you and your beloved boy at any time you wish to return.'

Perhaps that time might come – but not now – not yet!

In Eaton Square I found changes, too. A few doors down from us the W.V.S. had set up a Clothing Depot for refugees; across the road was a Reception Bureau for them; and almost next door to us the flag of the Netherlands flew from a tall old mansion which now housed the Dutch Royal family, safely evacuated by a British destroyer. From our windows we could see Princess Juliana playing in the gardens with her two chubby little girls.

In the Depot women with sons and brothers in the B.E.F. were silent and drawn. One morning Lady Pound said, as she paused at our table, 'King Leopold has surrendered—' The woman beside me turned pale. 'Then the B.E.F. is trapped?' she asked, in a low voice, thinking of her son. Lady Pound shook her head helplessly.

Soon the news came through about Dunkirk – the epic of the 'little ships'. Yachts, ferry-boats, pleasure steamers, even the Cowes paddle-steamer, *Gracie Fields*, pride of her fleet, went to and from Dunkirk to take off the weary troops who waded out to meet them under a rain of bombs from a roof of fierce air conflict. Many strange and moving signals went out that summer's day – my husband, on anti-invasion duty, off the north-east coast, followed them all. '*It is such a remarkable evacuation*,' he wrote at the time, '*that very soon we shall regard it as a victory!*' And, grim though the news might be, he had to smile when the Yeoman solemnly handed him a signal intercepted from *Gracie Fields* – 'Making water fast!' *Gracie*

Fields was lost to the Cowes paddle fleet, but like many another 'little ship', she saved countless lives before she gave up her own.

'Two-thirds of the B.E.F. back!' said Jack Borrett, over a pink gin in my flat. 'It's a ruddy miracle!'

And that was what they called it, 'The Miracle of Dunkirk'.

But a few days later, as we looked out of the Depot windows, we saw that Princess Juliana and her children no longer played in the gardens of Eaton Square; and presently we heard that they had sailed for Canada, thus striving to ensure the future of a dynasty. While, in the tall mansion, flying the Dutch flag, an aged Queen, lonely and sick at heart, waited for whatever the fates might bring.

CHAPTER NINE

HOUR OF DECISION

I THINK it was when those little Dutch children disappeared from the gardens that the Stranger seriously began to force my hand.

'Invasion' was the word of the moment. From sea and air we expected it. Our wireless and our papers told us how to behave 'in the event of invasion' just as they had prepared us for 'the event of war' only last autumn. The popular Press published readers' suggestions about what to do if parachutists were to appear on the doorstep. 'Don't ask them in for a cup of tea, throw pepper in their faces, and, while they collect themselves, telephone your nearest police point.' Small boys invented ingenious booby-traps and tried them out on friends and relations; they armed themselves with bows and arrows, slings and water-pistols in the name of Home Defence. The Home Guard drilled with pikes and broom-sticks, and Winston made his finest speech of the war. Never would we give up our island. We would fight in the fields and in the hills, street by street and house by house; in the dreaming meadows of England and the grey hamlets of Scotland; in the gracious squares and crescents of London herself. Oh, yes, we would fight to the death!

'But if we fail,' whispered the Stranger. *'What then?'*

Grim tales had filtered through of the German occupation of Poland. 'Extermination' was no longer a word applicable only to vermin. Ought I to have thrown up that opportunity of sending Piet home with Dinkie?

But fate sometimes offers a second chance. One morning, in Lady Pound's troubled features, I read a knowledge of evil tidings. She said, 'Have you thought of going to your home in South Africa?'

I looked up at her as she stood leaning across the table, and suddenly there was a stinging behind my eyes. South Africa! Would I ever again see the gabled house under the mountain, and my silver-haired mother with the pearls gleaming at her throat, and her brown retainers who were part of my childhood, and of Peter's?

Lady Pound went on. 'I wondered – because my friend, Betty Waterson – you know, the wife of your High Commissioner – is sailing tomorrow with a number of children. She's taking her own boy, who's about Peter's age, and her little girl. I'm sure she'd willingly include another—'

'Thank you,' I said, 'but there's hardly time now—'

'Enough, if you hurry,' she said quietly, and moved on.

When she had gone I took my dog down into the gardens for her usual break.

The June day was one of haunting loveliness. All that summer it was like that, as if our threatened island were pouring forth the fullness of her beauty before it was too late. The sky had never been so rich a blue nor the earth such radiant green. London lay entranced, fairest of cities savouring the last of her glory on the eve of disfigurement. It was odd – that contrast between the heavenly tranquillity of nature and the tempestuous conflict of man.

When grief must be faced and contemplated it is good to be alone in a garden. As a girl, when I was unhappy, I went with my dog into the woods on the slopes of Table Mountain, and there, among the fresh-scented pines under the bright indifferent eyes of the grey squirrels, a moment of anguish might have its being before the cool hands of resignation folded over it. Now, in the gardens of Eaton Square, another such moment was born.

I did not go back to my scribe's table that morning. I went instead to South Africa House in Trafalgar Square.

Betty Waterson was in her huge modern office surrounded by women sorting and packing gifts and comforts for the Springboks. Ordinarily I would have been glad to hear the sing-song South African accents and the laughter and little jokes called across the room in Afrikaans, I would have felt a pang of pleasant nostalgia at the sight of tins of Rhodesian tobacco and packets of Springbok cigarettes, I would have welcomed the old school-friend from up-country who greeted me with pleased recognition. 'Why, if it isn't Joy Petersen! I'd have known you anywhere! We used to be in the same class at St. Cyprian's ...' Today none of these things signified. A step must be taken – the hardest yet – nothing else mattered ...

'Certainly, I'll take him,' said Betty Waterson. She looked up from a pile of papers awaiting her signature. Pretty, with a kind smile. When she stood up I saw that she was no taller than a child – no taller than our Queen. But her air of authority was more queenly than childish and there was determination in the set of her lips and in her eyes. Here was a force to be reckoned with – an extremely competent woman with a will of her own and a strong sense of duty.

'I want to take as many children as possible to South Africa,' she said. 'I'm coming back for more when this lot are settled. There's no trouble in finding them homes, people out there are longing to have them. Of course, your Peter is specially lucky because he's going to his own Grannie – his own home, really.'

'You honestly think it's – *right* – to send him away ...?'

She looked straight at me, and her expression softened.

'Don't take it so hard – you're doing the best thing for him. We wouldn't be sending our own two home if we didn't think that. There'll be child casualties in this country soon. Now you'll want to see about his passport. I'll get hold of someone to help you with all that ...'

When I got back to the flat Evelyn said, 'What's wrong, Madam? You look ill.'

'There's nothing wrong,' I said. 'I'm sending Peter home to South Africa.'

Evelyn pursed up her lips in silent disapproval. 'I'll get you some tea,' she said.

I telephoned Piet's Housemaster at Wellington. 'Please get

him all packed up and send him to London tonight. He sails tomorrow.'

Then I went to Gieves and bought him a safety waistcoat. A boy's – one that might have fitted a cadet. If only he had been at Dartmouth all this could never have happened. He would have been in the Navy now. If only Bertie would telephone me and share this burden of responsibility.

And then, as if in answer to my need, there was a long distance call from Immingham and my husband's voice on the line.

'Quick!' I said. 'Before they cut us off – there's something terribly important! I've got it all set to send Piet home with Mrs. Waterson – she's taking her own children back and some others. Should he go? It isn't too late yet—'

There was no hesitation from the other end of the line.

'Great work, Joy-Joy! He must go. And what about you? Shouldn't you go with him?'

'That doesn't arise. But what shall I tell him? He'll break his heart—'

'Tell him he has his sailing orders from me. He has to take them – like all of us in time of war. Tell him that!'

An hour later Piet arrived, all excitement.

'We're going home!'

I answered him slowly, with a heavy heart.

'*You* are, darling. I'll follow later – when Dad's had his leave.'

He stood quite still, with his dark blue overcoat on his arm and his little attaché case clasped in his hand. The colour drained out of his face, and he looked as he had done the day he came into the waiting-room of a grim grey building in Pall Mall, and said, 'They've done me in!'

I gave him his father's message. But he only said: 'You promised we'd stick together, whatever happened. You promised that in Robin Hood's Bay . . .'

He set down his things and went over to the window where his speed-boat waited for him. He touched it without seeing it. He said: 'What about you? What about if there's an invasion? You wouldn't even know how to change Jaggy's tyre if you were trying to get away . . . if they were after you. You trusted me for all that . . . Dad said to look after you – and *now* . . .'

He broke off, and I put my arm round his shoulder and said, 'Listen, darling – *please*—' But my throat ached so heavily that words refused to come to my aid. The pictures I wanted to paint – of the welcome awaiting him in the House under the Mountain, of the faithful friends, white and Coloured, who had helped to bring him up and who longed for his return, of his dog, of days on the seashore or in the country – remained imprisoned by that heavy pain.

Then Jack and Joy came in, and Philip Rhodes. They were very bright and cheerful and they made Piet blow up the little safety waistcoat, and he even clowned a bit in it, so that things seemed better while they were there.

When they were gone, I said, 'Let's make scrambled eggs.'

He loved making scrambled eggs. So we went into the kitchen and he tied a dish-cloth round his waist. He melted the margarine and cracked in the eggs, he added milk and began to stir the mixture over the stove. I cut the bread for toast, and then, as I looked at my son, I saw that great tears were falling into the scrambled eggs.

'Salt,' he choked. 'I forgot the salt—'

Darling, I thought, *you won't need it – oh, darling—*

He wiped his eyes with the dish-cloth apron.

After supper he said, 'You must come with me to the lock-up. You must know how to change a wheel! You were counting on me, and now you'll be alone ... escaping alone ... and not really knowing anything about Jaggy ...'

'You can show me,' I said. 'Come and show me now.'

So we went up the road to the lock-up where our car lived. There was no electric light, but Piet stood over me with a torch.

'See, Mom, this is how the jack works – this is the little hammer you'll need ...'

I changed that wheel for the first time in my life, according to instructions delivered in a boy's voice choked with tears. It seemed to me, as he stood there in the dark, leaning against the wall, that this was the worst that had ever happened to him and me.

'Can you see what you're doing, Mom? Shall I bring the torch closer?'

'It's done,' I said. 'It's done now, Piet.'

Next morning Evelyn's stern little face was grimmer than usual as she made Piet's bed.

'His sheets are twisted into a rope,' she commented, dryly. 'He must have tossed all night!'

Victoria was swarming with children and parents. We found Betty Waterson and her son and daughter in the crowd; with them was the tall aesthetic figure of the High Commissioner, Sydney Waterson. Strain was etched on his pale narrow features. Betty seemed as unconcerned as if she were going to Le Touquet for a peace-time week-end. There'd be a gamble, of course, but she fancied her chances. Their boy, who was Piet's age, and his little sister were laughing and rosy, obviously thrilled to be going home – so different from the tense set face of the boy at my side.

'Piet,' I said, at the last. 'You'll help Mrs. Waterson, won't you? Some of her party are very small—'

'Yes,' he said. 'I'll try.'

'Give my love to Gran – and Cookie and Teena – and everybody at home . . .'

'Get in, Peter,' said Betty briskly. 'This is our compartment. . . . Good-bye, Sydney, take care of yourself. . . .'

The young Waterson's Coloured Nannie was on the platform. Peter opened the door of the compartment for her.

'After you—' he said. And then, as the plump brown body clambered in, I felt his arms flung tightly and suddenly about my neck, and wondered dimly if the rising tide within me could be stemmed just till the train was out of sight.

'All seats, please!'

Doors were banging in a sardonic *feu de joie* down the length of the long train that was going to some port we knew not where. And now the wheels were turning, the windows flashing past with their bouquets of young faces, singing, 'Roll out the barr-ull – roll out the barrel of fun!' Now their song was lost in the rhythm of the wheels gathering speed – and now that refrain, too, was fading, absorbed in the swelling symphony of a great terminus . . .

Less than a week later one of the first bombs to fall on a Home County landed on Wellington College. The brilliant young man with red hair, who so much disliked being in 'a safe billet', insisted upon leaving the school shelter to see what damage had been done and what measures should be taken. As he stepped into the courtyard the second bomb whistled down.

'You'll be sorry,' I wrote to Piet. 'I know you admired the Master – but at least it was instantaneous.'

The letter was an air-mail. It arrived in Cape Town on the same day as Piet.

CHAPTER TEN

ALONE

AMONG our friends in London was Beverley Baxter, who had been my boss in 1931, when he was editor of the *Daily Express*, and I was a very junior news reporter on the same paper.

Mrs. Baxter and the two children were in Canada, so 'Bax' shared his substantial Georgian house in St. John's Wood with a succession of other temporary bachelors. It was always a pleasure to go there. In the long summer evenings the French windows of the beautiful drawing-room were left open to the garden, where vegetables had been planted in the erstwhile herbaceous border. For Bax, from the moment he entered Westminster as Member of Parliament for Wood Green in 1935, had felt it incumbent upon him to compress a naturally rebellious temperament into the severe limitations which hem in the behaviour of a satisfactory citizen. His life was graced with small, law-abiding gestures most cheerfully made but only too often abortive. The planting of vegetables where flowers had been was just such a gesture, and encouraging his chauffeur-gardener to go into essential industry was another; but unfortunately the latter cancelled out the former, so most of the vegetables died. Thus, at his hospitable table in the panelled dining-room looking upon a broad avenue of magnificent plane trees, we ate, more often than not, the products of the greengrocer's shop rather than those of the ex-herbaceous border.

There was always good conversation at Bax's table – most of it admittedly supplied by the host, who was an excellent and amusing raconteur. But, though Bax could hold an audience spellbound, he could also, when the spirit moved him, listen well, for, in common with all born journalists, his mind was as much a receiving station as a transmitter, accepting and recording all and any human signals that might come in useful for future re-editing and re-distribution. Mostly he was the genial host, but his guests were never entirely safe from the barbs of his ruthless wit – the saving disgrace of a nature so warm and kindly that it might otherwise have leaned towards sentiment.

I was dining at his house the night we knew that France had fallen after receiving the final 'stab in the back' from Italy.

'Bill' Mabane, then Parliamentary Under-Secretary for Home Security, was there, and so was General Critchley, at that time in charge of Air Training. I had naturally expected to find the party downcast, but, instead, the atmosphere was one of relief, almost elation. Even Bill, whose fine Roman features could crease themselves into a mask of unbelievable pessimism, looked cheerful. He stood with his long lean back to the empty grate and, probably for the first and only time in his life, became the involuntary mouthpiece of the entire British nation.

He said, 'Now we know where we stand!' And he said it with the sort of conviction that is akin to satisfaction.

In the days that followed I heard those words a thousand times. They were spoken by Evelyn in my flat, by my fellow workers at the Depot, by bus conductors and shop assistants, by soldiers and sailors and airmen. And, in those words, which acknowledged a bitter blow and recognized the fact that now we stood alone, Britain showed her mettle.

'Yes,' said Critch. 'Now we know where we stand. And we can stop pouring aircraft into France. Whatever comes now, we'll handle it our own way!'

Bax's Buddha eyes narrowed as he picked on the core of the situation.

'What about the French Fleet in North Africa?'

Critch made an impatient movement.

'We ought to sink the lot!'

'Not a pleasant decision,' said Bill, 'to sink the ships of a defeated ally!'

'I doubt we'll have the guts,' said Critch.

At that I felt a sudden blaze of anger leap up in me.

With France out and Italy in, the Mediterranean would be what my husband would describe as 'hardly an attractive proposition'! This was no time for politicians' talk, it was a time for naval action – and naval action there would surely be!

'I bet you a fiver we sink their Fleet unless they do as they're told!' I challenged him.

Critch looked slightly taken aback, but recovered quickly. Bets were always flying at Bax's, and tempers, too, upon occasion.

'I'll take you,' he said. 'I'll give you a fiver to half-a-crown and I hope you win!'

Bill was right. The decision to sink the French Fleet, *if it had to be*, was not a pleasant one; still less was it pleasant for those who had to put it into effect. The tragic task fell to the lot of our friend, Admiral Sir James Somerville, at Mers-el-Kebir on 4th June.

We knew James well. In the Navy he was regarded as something of a magician. Just before the war, as Commander-in-Chief of the East Indies Station, he had been invalided out of the Service, much to his fury, and told that, with his delicate chest, he should never go to sea again. When the war came he was recalled for duty at the Admiralty, but the Admiralty was about as likely to hold him as a milk bottle with a tin-foil lid could hold a genii. And very soon he was back at sea in command of the famous task force known as Force H. Throughout the war he had as arduous sea-service as ever fell to the lot of any senior officer. But he, in common with many others, 'liked a bit of excitement – seemed to thrive on it—' People were afraid of James. His humorous tongue and lightning repartee could be slashing, and, perhaps because he was a man of little personal ambition, he did not hesitate to use them where and how he pleased. His naval signals were legendary both for their levity and their brevity.

But there was no humour in the drama of Mers-el-Kebir. In all his long naval career he had known no sadder task.

A letter from my husband gave me the naval angle on that distressing operation.

'I am delighted that the Cabinet's decision about the French Fleet at Oran was unanimous, and, whatever odium we may incur, it at least shows that we are in earnest and *can* act with vigour and decision. The only thing that succeeds now is force. The French Fleet was given every opportunity to join us, or to sail to some port outside the British Empire, but the French Admiral would not even see our envoy – "Hooky" Holland, who'd been Naval Attaché in Paris before the war – so there was nothing for it but to sink the ships and so make sure that they would not fall into German or Italian hands. This James did, with two casualties to us and God knows what to the French. It was a terrible thing to have to do, but there was no alternative. The French ships at Portsmouth, Plymouth and Alex. all gave in – very wisely, for France will get them back eventually . . .'

In the evening, after the Depot, I took Dinah to the park and, during those walks, I had time to think.

The flower-beds were planted out with vegetables; sheep grazed under the trees; anti-aircraft gun emplacements and Army huts disfigured the green lawns of yesterday; and quite often the barrage balloon came to earth and squatted on the bowling-green to allow competent-looking young women to darn it. Girls and young men in uniform lounged on the grass down by the Serpentine or rowed up the silver stretch of water where Piet and I had rowed in the last days of peace less than a year ago. Water-fowl sailed on the Round Pond side by side with the white wings of model yachts, and there were still folk feeding bread to the stately swans or throwing crusts to common sea-gulls who swooped and grabbed them with hoarse cries of triumph.

I felt curiously detached as I observed the faces and bearing of these English people whose plight, as a nation, had grown so desperate. They showed no trace of despair, or even apprehension; just a stolid doggedness when they thought about it. Hitler was trying to 'muck them about' and they resented it. Let him come and try it over here! The English can take a lot of 'mucking about' from a Government of their own choosing, but let old So-and-So from across the Channel have a go, and they roll up their sleeves.

Perhaps the act of sending my son back to South Africa had brought home to me the fact that, although I was married to an Englishman, I was, after all, not English. My roots were not here in this threatened island; these people, facing their hour of tribulation, were not mine. I found myself wanting to know about them, wondering about them.

As a child in South Africa I had absorbed the tradition of British might – 'Might is always right' I was told sardonically – and, to many of us, the tiny island off the coast of Europe was a cornucopia of military strength, always ready to pour out armies into any part of the globe where they might be required to enforce Imperial rights and privileges. Our Afrikaner people, the Boers, had matched their obstinacy and cunning with the big battalions of the Red-Coats and had been crushed. Yet, in 1914, South African boys – Springboks – had gone to the slaughter of France to do their share towards the survival of their erstwhile conquerors. There were those who said the dead in Delville Wood had given their lives in 'England's war'.

Thus Empire was a word not all South Africans liked. It savoured too strongly of the compulsion to stand or fall with the Mother Country. Smuts's term, Commonwealth of Nations, had a better ring to it, but it had still to come into popular usage. We, in the Dominions, had made our own decisions to fight with the Mother Country – but in our own defence and only to protect out own borders. How far flung would be those 'borders' we had yet to learn. Canada had conceded an anti-invasion force for Britain, which she recognized as her own front line, but it was not to cross the Channel! South Africa, with the entry of Italy into the war endangering her northern limits, was standing by to defend her desert frontier. Australia and New Zealand would presently play their part, and so would turbulent India. But, in the meantime, the heart of the Commonwealth was exposed to grave and immediate peril. What was the true strength of that heart? What power kept it so high and bravely beating?

'Now we know where we stand,' was one thing they said. The other was 'Let 'em come!' And they said that pugnaciously, clenching their fists. Yes, the heart was strong and stubborn. And it was loving – above all, loving.

Perhaps because the Englishman is, like all maritime races, a natural settler and pioneer, one is apt to forget what his own island means to him. Those not of his blood are inclined to resent him as a grabber, hungry for luscious corners of the earth where he may live more comfortably and profitably than at home. Yet, for the few who emigrate, the many remain. And the love they bear their island is an abiding love.

Such thoughts came to me as I studied these people faced with disaster. The greater the threat, the greater grew the spiritual strength to meet it. '*The strength of a Fleet is not in its ships but in its men*,' said Nelson, in another age of strife, and now, once again, that strength could be seen to grow throughout the entire nation. Slow, substantial, infinitely menacing was that life-force born of adversity. But it was nursed and fanned by leadership. In her hour of need, Britain, weak and unprepared, had one inestimable blessing. She had Winston Churchill. It was Winston who interpreted her to herself, to the Commonwealth and to the New World across the Atlantic. Churchill was the soul of the Empire as Hitler was the soul of Nazi Fascism. Winston allowed his countrymen no illusions, he told them all that might befall, because he knew them as a man knows himself. They could take it.

He was right. There was no panic, nor yet patriotic hysteria, just a little more acid in the music-hall jokes about 'Mr. Schikelgruber' and 'Goring' and 'Gobbels' and 'Haw-Haw'. And there was an unwonted tenderness in eyes that saw, for the first time, the meadows and quiet reaches of shining water, the mediaeval towns and sleepy village greens that were part of the English scene and that hitherto had been taken for granted. When the mother of a household is sick the family realize to the full their need of her, their devotion for her, the familiar beauty and sweetness that were hers, even when she goaded them; and thus the English looked upon their land now that she was sick unto death.

Young airmen flew over the handkerchief fields and great trees, that, in all the world, have no equal, over deep thatched roofs and dreaming spires, and they said, in their hearts, 'This is worth fighting for!' And sailors, going ashore to humble homes, went back to sea ready to give their lives that those at home might live in peace and freedom.

'Perhaps I will come to know them,' I thought. 'Perhaps one day I will understand these English.'

On Sundays I usually spent the day with my sister-in-law, Marion, at her Ruislip bungalow.

Marion was the junior of Piet's two 'spinster aunts'. She was in charge of the personnel of a great chemical industry in Middlesex now given over to war production and expanding steadily to meet new calls upon its resources. So the thin little 'spinster aunt' had a family of some two thousand under her surveillance – to say nothing of The Fritz. The Fritz was a dachshund, sleek as a seal and about as self-effacing as a film star. Winifred, the senior 'spinster aunt', who, as Head-Mistress of a girl's school, was also blessed with a large vicarious family, had bestowed the boon of The Fritz upon her sister, and for this lapse the rest of the family frowned upon her, especially my mother-in-law, who lived in a hotel in Heswall, Cheshire, where 'that sausage' had failed to endear himself to the management.

Dinah and The Fritz approved of one another, and, while they played imbecile games in Marion's little garden, she and I lounged in the sun and won the war.

Marion's garden was as neat and English as she was herself, a cottage garden with a lawn and a herbaceous border, a lily of the valley bed against a shady wall, roses and larkspur, columbine and love-in-a-mist; and already honeysuckle was clustering over a tiny concrete excrescence outside the kitchen door: her two-bunk shelter.

'It'll do for Piet later on,' she said. 'When he wants to come and stay and bring a friend.'

My sister-in-law had 'green fingers', like her mother. Anything would grow for Marion.

Being with her always did me good. Her tolerance, her immense humanity, her sense of proportion, and even her chuckle that invariably turned into a violent fit of coughing because she smoked too much, were as reviving to me as the tranquillity of her garden, drowsy with honey-bees, bird-song and flower fragrance.

Tiny, she was; nothing to her except a great heart and a pair of wise twinkling eyes in a little sallow face; always brisk, with a quick jaunty walk on a pair of funny feet that gave her hell with every step. She'd spent a month in a hospital once, having them 'taken to pieces and reassembled', and after that she always said they were splendid, but then she'd said the same before, so none of us put much faith in the tarnished splendour of our Mary Ann's feet. Except for a few matters (such as her feet) – which she elected to ignore – nothing escaped her shrewd observant glance, not so much as a shadow in the eyes of a friend – or a dog. So one Sunday she said to me: 'Joy-Joy, what are you doing for Dinah's eyes?'

'I bathe them with poppy-seed tea,' I said. 'The dog-book says so. The right one's been troublesome ever since we got back from Scotland – I think she hurt it rabbiting in the bramble woods – but now the left one has begun to discharge a bit in sympathy.'

She lifted Dinah's narrow little white head in her strong

hands, roughened by gardening, and looked attentively into my dog's eyes. Presently she said:

'I wouldn't worry – but I would take her to a vet.' Then she change the subject.

A hint from Marion was as good as a lecture from anyone else, and next day I went upstairs to Lady Louis Mountbatten's little office in the Depot.

She was sitting at her desk with her Sealyhams at her feet. They were always as beautifully groomed as she was herself. She raised her too thin face with the haunting dark blue eyes that were now so often troubled, for her husband, too, was at sea and having no easy time.

I said, 'I hope you don't mind my bothering you, but I'm worried about my little terrier's eyes. Do you know of a good vet? Your dogs always look so healthy—'

She said, 'Of course I do.' And wrote down the name and address of a man in Elizabeth Street. 'He's just round the corner.'

As I went out her lips smiled while her magnificent eyes remained sad. She said, 'I hope your little dog will soon be better.' Then, once again, she bowed her head over her papers.

How different was this energetic woman, with responsibility written all over her rather haggard features, from the society beauty who had appeared in Malta with her naval husband soon after I was married. 'Lord Louis' had been in the same ship as Bertie, and on Sunday mornings his wife had come to Church Service on the quarter deck – soignée and glamorous, with her lips a little redder and her skirts a little shorter than anyone else's. Now she, too, seemed charged with the same all-pervading spirit of determination which characterized the nation from Churchill to the char.

The vet was a big man, with crisp dark hair going grey and the sort of masterful gentleness that all animals trust.

He looked grave when he had examined Dinah. Then he gave me a lotion and he said: 'This will relieve the discharge and it may soothe the irritation – but I'm afraid her condition is serious. Bring her back to me in a fortnight's time – or sooner, if you wish.'

After that, as the days passed, I noticed that when I threw a ball or a stick for her she ran eagerly after it and then seemed to lose her way. She'd stand hesitant and worried, ears flattened, and would presently come back to me with a puzzled look that caught at my throat. She developed a habit of brushing a paw across her eyes, as if trying to brush away a cobweb. Then one evening in the flat she stumbled against a chair. When that happened my heart stood still. I called her, and lifted her on to my lap and buried my face in the roughness of her coat. I knew then that now if I threw a ball for her it would leave my hand and be lost in the night.

When I took her back to Elizabeth Street the vet gave me a very honest opinion. 'But if you'd feel happier to have it confirmed you might like to take her to someone else.' He suggested a specialist in Harley Street. It seemed incongruous to take my thin little terrier to an address in Harley Street, but I gathered that her trouble was one more frequently found in humans than in animals.

The specialist was an oldish man and his business was with people and not with dogs, but he was very kind and careful in examining Dinah. He told me that soon she would be quite blind.

I cried out, 'But she's only a young dog – scarcely more than a puppy!'

He said, 'This is a very rare disease. A film is moving up over her eyes like an eclipse. It must take its course, and it's painful. In time it may pass over and she may recover a glimmer of sight – no more. Have you a home she need never leave – somewhere she can learn to know by instinct? If so, blindness may not be such a handicap.'

I shook my head. We had no such home. We lived 'like soldiers' – my dog and I – from day to day.

I took her into the Park, and I noticed, as she played with other dogs, how thin she had grown, how poor and starting her coat. 'It's painful,' the specialist had said. I called her, and watched how she came to me – not to my figure, but to my voice – how she blundered into a tree coming at full tilt, and stood dazed for a moment. *The night is drawing on, my little Dinah, it's dark in your world already!*

'Yes,' said the vet, when I took her back to him. 'I'm sorry; but you've decided on the kindest course. Let me take her now. In a few minutes I'll bring her back to you.'

When he brought her to me he carried her as one carries a tired child.

'There, Dinah, go to your mistress.'

He laid her on my lap and she looked up at me with those trusting eyes, so nearly sightless, and pressed her hot nose against my shoulder. I stroked the narrow little head and said her name, and soon I felt her grow strangely heavy in my arms . . .

Back in the flat my ghosts haunted me – Piet's abandoned speed-boat still on its window-sill, my little dog's empty basket in the corner of my room, a tin of chocolate biscuits side by side with a packet of Spratt's Ovals . . .

I rang up Marion.

'Dinah – Mary Ann . . . she would have gone blind—'

I could say no more. But there was no need. Marion said, 'I was afraid so, Joy-Joy. You did the best thing for her. Come on Sunday as usual – the bluebells are out in the woods, we'll go bluebell picking.'

But we didn't go bluebell picking, because next day I received a message through the ever-helpful agency of Jack Borrett.

'Go to the Eversfield Hotel at Southsea the day after tomorrow. Apply for supplementary petrol to join your husband. It may be for a week, it may be a month.'

When I left the flat in Evelyn's charge, she said, with that unexpectedly sweet smile of hers:

'There, now, Madam, the sun is shining again!'

CHAPTER ELEVEN

SUSPENSE

I HAD to show my Admiralty pass to the sentries on Cosham Bridge, which connects the great naval arsenal of Portsmouth with the hinterland, and, as they signed me through, I drove on with a strong feeling of excitement mingled with awe. Here was a First Line of Defence in case of sea-invasion, and a straggling island-fortress which might well be sealed off and besieged in the event of invasion from the air. On Portsdown Hill the old forts stood guard, as they had done a century ago lest the winds blow too fair from France, filling the sails of yet another invader.

It was no good allowing my little sailor mascot to turn the Jaguar's helm towards Hillie's, for Hillie had let her house to naval people and was living with friends just outside the Hampshire village of Liphook. Her absence impressed upon me still further the sensation that the whole port was now one vast deck cleared for action.

The Eversfield Hotel on Clarence Parade was a homely residential hotel run by Miss Heyward, with whom I had often played tennis in the early days of my marriage. I remembered her as an unspectacular, but forceful, player with an infinite capacity for astonishing her more brilliant opponents by beating them soundly. They had the strokes, but she had the determination. Very British! She was grey-haired now, but as energetic as ever, even if somewhat less nimble.

'I've reserved you one of our best sitting-rooms on the first floor,' she said. 'I'm sure you'll like it.'

I did. The room was gay with flowers, and sunshine streamed through the great bay windows looking over the common towards the sea.

'But why a single room?' I wanted to know, as she showed me the bedroom.

'It's what Captain Packer booked,' she said. (*So the Grey Mistress was going to be exacting!*) 'These are queer times,' she added, with a smile and a sigh. 'Anything might happen.'

On the polished table lay a leaflet – '*INVASION INSTRUCTIONS*'. Across the Channel 'Operation Sea-lion' (*See Loëwe*) was in course of preparation. If the enemy could gain sea-air supremacy he would launch it. Landings would be made all along the South Coast. So the citizens who remained in the threatened areas had their instructions. The first leaflets issued by Home Security told civilians to 'stay put'. Then the modern American term was altered in favour of an ageless English one. The hand of a great War Leader was at work.

'I don't like this phrase,' Mr. Churchill had growled. 'Strike out "stay put" and write in its place "stand firm"!'

Thus, too, this master of the national tongue and sentiment refused to allow the 'Wailing Banshee' to be called the 'Alarm'. 'Let it be known as the "Alert"!' he decreed. So, as the situation worsened, innumerable tiny strokes of genius from a natural leader fortified the pride of every man and woman in the land.

Attacks on shipping, both from the air and from E-boats, had increased in violence during the past month. The *Manchester* was standing by in case of sea invasion, or for whatever other purpose she might be required, and, in the meantime, her guns reinforced the shore batteries and Coastal Command in attacking the air-raiders who came regularly over the port.

Desolate in the harbour lay the French ships, with only a few British sailors manning their close-range armament. There was also a Dutch ship – a fine new cruiser which had been in course of construction at the time of the Occupation. Somehow her Commander had got her away to England before the enemy could lay hands on her. She was in commission, ready to carry on the fight – a heartening contrast to the French. That Commander, whose name was Van Holthe, survived the war and rose to be the Chief of the Netherlands Navy.

To evoke the particular atmosphere of that time one must remember that, as in the days of Napoleon, not only England, but the entire world, expected the British Isles to be invaded. Only, in those days, there had been 'the British Moat' – less of an obstacle now to an enemy with wings!

This expectancy had its local rhythm in Portsmouth. At a certain time of the month there occurred what was known as the 'critical period of moon and tide' when conditions for invasion would be most favourable to an enemy. There was no secret about it. We all knew when this time approached with its almost unbearable crescendo of suspense. We began to wish they'd come. 'It'd give the Navy something to bite on,' said Bertie, who craved action.

He used to come ashore in the afternoons, but we had to keep within the perimeter of the port lest he should suddenly be recalled to the ship. At nightfall the Grey Mistress claimed him, and I was shaken by a new sense of relative values. What happened to him and her was important – they might influence the course of a battle, the trend of history. What happened to me, and to millions like me, was of no significance. With the suspension of our private lives we were nothing.

There was a sound we listened for in those days.

The whole country listened – so intently that we seemed to hear a chiming faint and far away on the pure air of the incredible summer – an echo of peaceful Sundays gone by, of our church-bells that had fallen so sadly silent. If now they should peal we would know that somewhere the invader had set foot on English soil. Have you ever awaited footsteps with nerves so taut that the pulsing of your own blood has marched across the frontiers of the mind with the tramp-tramp of feet? Have you stood outside a room drumming with the sound of many voices and sought to distinguish one ... *and heard it when it was not there because memory, harnessed to anticipation, has echoed it*? It was like that with the church-bells. It seemed to me sometimes that we moved and had our being in a vacuum ringing with intangible imagined chimes, as a fine goblet, lightly struck, gives out a high delicate note till a quick hand touches the glass to silence it, because 'while a glass rings a sailor drowns!'

I used to lie in bed at nights listening through the sound of the sea for those pealing bells.

Thus, as a child, I had lain awake in my small white bed in the room that looked towards the mountain, and I strained my ears for the first dreaded breath of the south-easter that might rise within an hour to ruin a longed-for picnic by the sea upon the morrow. Was that it? Was that a faint dry scutter of leaves along the *stoep* – a rustle in the overhead trellis of the grape-vine? Was that a swelling murmur in the foliage of the trees, or was it the distant sea? My eyes, wide open in the dark, would reluctantly seek the billowing of the chintz curtains at the French windows. *Dear God, please don't let it blow and spoil tomorrow!* But, hush, the great throat begins its moaning, and now I know the cloud battalions are massing on the summit of the mountain to launch themselves over the grey buttress into the upper town, to invade our very fig orchard! And along the silver coast the fine sand must be blowing inland in a stinging mist, piling up on the dunes, while at sea the Centaurs of the Wind ride the galloping rollers with flying white manes. *Please God ... dear, dear God ... make the south-easter go down again before everything is ruined! Let us have a fine day tomorrow!*

So now, in my maturity, I lay awake in the night as I had done in my childhood, listening for the wind, for the first whisper of the hurricane that might tear my life to pieces.

Things happened in the 'vacuum' in which we had our being. But even those that lent the most normality twisted the occasion a little in conformity with the threat across the water.

We played tennis on the United Services courts, and one afternoon a weird peach-coloured fog crept up from the sea, and we looked at one another and said, 'There's never been a fog like that in Portsmouth – it must be synthetic!' But it was not a screen of Hitler's making, masking a fleet of flat-bottomed boats, it was only old Dame Nature calling 'Wolf! Wolf!' We played golf at the Municipal course, and I complained that I could smell gas. My husband laughed as he glanced at the huge gasometers looming over us. 'It would be very odd if you couldn't!'

Once Winston visited the cruiser, and the sailors, who hung upon his every word, cheered him loud, long and spontaneously. He smoked his cigar in the hangar against all rules and only removed it to ask pertinent questions about the aircraft. At his heels strutted a gnome carrying a black dispatch case. His secretary, no doubt. Then Winston turned to the gnome and said tersely: 'Make a note of that, Max!' And Beaverbrook, the Minister of Aircraft Production, replied, with asperity, that he had already done so.

On another occasion the King honoured his ship *Manchester* with an inspection. He looked young, fit, and in excellent heart.

One evening I was allowed to go on board for half-an-hour to meet a new member of the Ship's Company.

'A Free Frenchman,' said my husband. 'Rather a personality. I know you'll like him. He has quite a story. He came off in a destroyer during the Dunkirk evacuation, and he's been living on board her till recently. But, when we came alongside, he decided that he'd sooner live in a big ship, so he's joined us.'

'Does he speak English?' I asked. 'It's ages since I've talked any French.'

'He understands English fairly well,' said my husband. 'But why not try him in his own language? He won't be particular about your accent. His own is a bit shaky.'

Corney said, smiling, as he ushered the Free Frenchman into the Captain's quarters. 'He's very French in his manners, Madam. Excitable-like.'

He was certainly excitable. He came in like a bolt from the blue, glanced round with a distracted air, gave my husband a hasty greeting, ignored me completely, and rushed out again as if the devil were after him. A few moments later he evidently remembered that he owed his Captain a certain courtesy, and, having duly composed himself, he returned and acknowledged my presence for the first time by graciously kissing my hand, albeit with damp and undue fervour.

'We haven't been properly introduced,' I complained. 'I don't know his name.'

'We call him Shrapnel,' said Bertie. 'Ordinary Dog Shrapnel.'

Strapnel was only an Ordinary Dog in a naval sense, as you find Ordinary Seamen, however improbable they may be in actual fact. He was an animal of most unusual appearance – long, strong, black-and-white, with a predominance of hound in his make-up, and a snaky expressive hound tail. In his home port of Dunkirk he had pulled a milk cart, and the marks of his harness had worn his coat a trifle thin over the shoulders. He was, in common with the Latin race, an individualist, and he possessed considerable charm, though there was in his character a certain unscrupulous egoism. This egoism he had displayed in deserting from the destroyer which had succoured him in order to join a larger and more comfortable ship. But the simple sailors of the *Manchester* forgave him such disloyalty in the mistaken belief that he was merely proving himself to be a dog of rare discrimination. Even Leslie – when she found that his intentions towards the current kittens were strictly honourable – accepted him without demur.

Like everybody else on board Shrapnel had his duties. And, while Leslie occupied herself with the war against rodents, he kept a vigilant anti-aircraft look-out and opened up a rapid fire of Free French barking at any stray sea-bird who appeared likely to make a tip-and-run raid on the quarter deck. Like all good seamen, he detested the contempt shown by gulls to newly scrubbed decks, and the things he said to them and they said back to him are unprintable. I heard such an exchange going on as we left the ship.

'As Corney says, he seems rather excitable-like,' I murmured to Bertie.

'He's a good dog,' said the Captain of the *Manchester* in a professional sort of voice. 'He shows a very fitting respect for the quarter deck.'

Then, one day, the vacuum of suspense was shattered by the dull rumble of bombs falling on the gasworks where only yesterday we had played golf on that malodorous little municipal course. No longer shipping alone, but the port itself, was under attack. From my bedroom window I saw for the first time the sight that was to become part of that extraordinary summer – the white vapour trails of fighters writing the story of battle in the blue sky, and the headlong spiral fall of an enemy plane with smoke pouring from its tail.

When my husband saw his cook next day, he said: 'Good morning, Hogg, I hope you found everything all right at home after yesterday's air battle.'

Hogg grinned. 'Yes, Sir, quite all right. Only when I reached 'ome I found an 'Einkel 'ad got into our garden. The police was round in no time!'

Heinkels, Junkers and Messerschmidts were trespassing freely on a great deal more of our island than the garden of Leading Cook Hogg. Within a few days their wreckage littered the land, while parachutes opened over hill and vale and sank gently into hedgerows and haystacks. It was 8th August, and the Battle of Britain had begun.

On the 11th the *Manchester* had to go into dry dock for a week, and Bertie and I went on leave to London, driving up the familiar Portsmouth Road between the bracken-covered beech woods and the heather purple dales, past formal parks flanking, every here and there, a rise where stood a noble mansion above its grazing-lands.

Notices, 'ALERT IN PROGRESS', met our eyes on the southern roads, and overhead the vapour trails told of youth defending the land it loved.

> 'I count myself lucky and honoured to be the right age and fully trained to throw my weight into the scales. . . . However long time may be, one thing can never be altered – I shall have lived and died an Englishman. Nothing else matters one jot, nor can anything ever change it . . . I have no fear of death – only a queer elation. . . . I would have it no other way—'

Thus wrote one young airman to his mother in a letter only to be given to her should he fail to return.

When she opened that letter she knew that her boy, like so many of his generation, had learned how to die before he had had time to learn how to live. Up there, in an element strange to our earthbound spirits, he and his comrades were fighting out the first great air battle known to history.

At last we came to the river, shining beneath her mirrored willows, and then the tang of London was in our nostrils – dear London, whose hour of trial was at hand.

That five days passed in as many seconds, or so it seemed, and then Bertie was bidding me good-bye as he looked for the last time upon London unscathed and the little flat where we had known happiness and some grief.

'Take care of yourself,' he said.

They were only words to tide over a bad moment. Soon they would be a mockery.

CHAPTER TWELVE

SHOCK

EARLY in September I spent a week-end in the country with the Watersons and Colin Bain-Marais, my mother's step-brother, who had now been appointed South African Minister to the Governments in Exile of the Low Countries.

Betty Waterson had returned to England and was preparing to take another large party of sea-vacuees to homes in South Africa. She rang me up to say:

'What about coming down to our cottage in Hertford next week-end – the week-end of the seventh – it's been a noisy week and a couple of days' quiet would do us all good. Colin's coming, too, and a young Rhodesian bomber pilot....'

I accepted eagerly. It had indeed been a 'noisy week' with the not yet familiar *whoomph* and *swish* of falling bombs drawing ever nearer the heart of the capital. In fact, I had suggested to Evelyn that she would be well advised to go back to her home in Otterburn while the going was good. But she had said, in her blunt North Country way:

'I couldn't evacuate and leave Gracie.'

'Couldn't you take Gracie with you?'

'Gracie can't leave her Old Lady,' said Evelyn, looking surprised and a little reproachful. Gracie's Old Lady was still quite literally embedded in her fifth floor flat overlooking South Kensington Tube Station, which had already become a dormitory for the dwellers in the flimsy little houses of the vicinity.

'But oughtn't the Old Lady to go away?' I persisted. 'She's not very mobile and it would be difficult to shift her in an emergency—'

'It would be impossible,' admitted Evelyn, with a smile. 'But she won't budge. She doesn't want to leave her cat—'

I felt that the conversation was beginning to assume the characteristics of a roundel, and it seemed quite fitting when Evelyn added firmly, 'In any case, we couldn't leave our flat.'

Much the same theme was being sung in a very much higher key, at no less a place than Buckingham Palace itself. There were many who urged that the Princesses be sent into safety to one of the Dominions. But the Queen said: 'The Princesses can't go without me, and I won't leave the King, and the King won't leave the country – so that settles that.'

The flat Evelyn shared with the indomitable Gracie – a thin anaemic-looking spinster, making up in high spirits what she lacked in red corpuscles – was the symbol of her independence. It was her justification for the step she had taken in leaving Otterburn and coming to the Great City. There, in an attic in Walham Green, was Evelyn's kingdom, wherein she reigned supreme with her co-ruler, Gracie. There was the fount from which she drew her self-esteem.

I realized that Evelyn would not easily be dislodged.

At six o'clock on Friday evening I went up to Colin's imposing office in South Africa House. Betty and the Rhodesian pilot were already with him.

'Sydney's just coming,' said Betty. 'He's had rather a heavy day.'

The Rhodesian was a restless frustrated young man who seemed unable to keep his eyes off the sky. He stood at the window, staring at the pigeons circling round Nelson's Column, and listening to the evening twitter of sparrows and starlings – a high, fluted accompaniment to the roar and mutter of the city. He was a bomber-pilot and he loathed bombers. He wanted to fly 'Spitfires'. He longed for the sharp thrill of the 'dogfight' and the sense of personal combat that lifts a fighter-pilot above fear. But he was past it – too old, they said – too old at twenty-seven!

Colin handed me a cable. It was from his seventeen-year-old son. 'Need your written permission join Air Force. Please send it air-mail. Colin.'

'What have you done?' I asked.

'Sent it, of course,' said Colin, with a certain pride in those transparently blue eyes of his. He was a magnificent looking man, and anybody with any knowledge of the Dominions would have said at once, on seeing him, 'That must be a South African!' He seemed to keep his tan as a souvenir of an outdoor life, and his very fair eyebrows and moustache were sun-bleached. His crisp fair hair was grey on the temples. He had lived much in London and Paris and had remained impervious to sophistication. Colin believed in God and loved his family and his mother, and didn't care who knew it.

'I couldn't refuse,' said Colin. 'After all, I did the same at his age. Your old Granddad had to give me his consent ...' He grinned as he recalled the somewhat cynical attitude taken up by his step-father – a formidable six-foot-five of patriarchal authority. 'The Old Dad said, "My boy, it's up to you. If you want to go and be killed by bloody Germans you have my blessing. But I think you're a damned fool".'

With that off-hand benediction he had sailed for England and joined the Coldsteam Guards, with whom he saw some of the toughest fighting on the Western Front. When he returned to South Africa in 1918 he was a wreck, a gas casualty. He owed much of his final return to health to 'Dinkie' Cullinan, the girl he was fortunate enough to marry, the daughter of that Cullinan whose name has been given to a famous South African diamond in the Crown Jewels.

The door opened, and the High Commissioner came in.

'Everybody ready?' he asked. 'Then let's be off.'

The Waterson's cottage was near the river, so that Sydney could indulge in his favourite pastime of fishing. The drowsy peace of a summer afternoon on the river bank and the pleasant hypnotism of flowing water was the ideal relaxation for his highly strung temperament. The rest of us played golf on a switchback country course. It was Sunday afternoon.

'There go the sirens,' said Betty comfortably, as we reached the fifteenth. 'Your drive, Colin.'

'But look!' I cried. 'I've never seen so many!'

They were flying high, straggling rather, like a cloud of starlings.

'Must be well over a hundred,' said the Rhodesian. 'Bombers with fighter escort – going towards London.'

They passed on, and we continued our game.

We had a late supper that evening and sat out of doors in the long twilight. At about eleven o'clock Colin and the Rhodesian, who had been for a stroll, called to us.

'Come and look at this!'

We sauntered up the hill to meet them, and then stood transfixed at the top of the rise. The sky to the south was blood-red, overhung with a murky pall of smoke.

'London!' said Sydney. 'My God! Look at that!'

Our 'starlings' of the afternoon had ringed the target with incendiaries; then, as night fell, their bombers had come in strength to drop high explosive on the blazing city.

'So London is really for it,' said Colin. 'Poor old London!'

And *we* are for it! I thought with a shiver.

Thus, for the third time, the Stranger came to me in a new guise. That night, as I saw the glow of burning London, I knew that now I was afraid for myself.

On Monday morning we went back to the scene that, with an infinity of variations, was to become monotonously familiar during the next eleven months.

First the canopy of smoke and the dry acrid smell, then the heaps of rubble sprawled across once busy streets; great yellow notices 'UNEXPLODED BOMB' and 'TRAFFIC DIVERSION'; men, women and children, expressionless with shock, prodding about in the ruins of their homes in search of salvage; windows splintered over pavements and red-eyed women stolidly sweeping away the glass as if they were sweeping fallen leaves from their doorsteps; tangled hose-pipes, and begrimed firemen still fighting the flames of the night before; demolition squads struggling to disinter the living and the dead from beneath mountains of wreckage. It was always the same aftermath. It got worse, of course, because there was more of it; conversely we grew accustomed to it.

Joy rang me up that morning.

'Thank heaven you were away for the week-end! It was terrible – past description! Jack says we must go to my people in Hereford. He says Bertie would never allow you to stay in London—'

'But your parents have Nannie and your children there already!'

'Mummie would always find a corner for you. You don't know what it's been like! Fifty people were killed last night in the Beaufort Street shelter, just a few steps from your block. You don't imagine I want to leave Jack, do you? But he's made up his mind, and you know the Borrett obstinacy.'

'You owe it to your children to get out. But I think I should hang on.'

'There's nothing at the Depot now. You aren't needed in the least.'

'I know, but I've just promised Alice Hopkinson to give a hand in a mobile canteen she's driving. When are you going?'

'On Friday. I've got to pack up this flat – and that's no small job. I wish you'd think it over.'

'It's awfully sweet of you, but I'm going to stay – for the time being anyway . . .'

Evelyn came to work with the peaky exhausted look which was soon to characterize Londoners.

'Captain Borrett telephoned while you were away. He wants you to evacuate with Mrs. Borrett.'

'I know.'

'Will you go?'

'Not for the present.'

She smiled through her tiredness. 'May I ask why not, Madam?'

'Certainly. I value my independence. My flat probably means as much to me as yours does to you. How are Gracie and her Old Lady?'

'Gracie sleeps in now. She can't leave the Old Lady alone at nights.'

'How does the Old Lady take it?'

'She's deaf,' said Evelyn simply. 'So it's all right for her.'

For those of us who were not deaf it was pandemonium.

As a child I was afraid of storms because the elements in Africa display a violence seldom known in Europe. Thunder, reverberating in the mountains or echoing over the veld, is the wrath of Almighty God; lightning strips giant trees of life, leaving them blighted for evermore among their fellows; hail destroys flocks of sheep or cattle; rain brings rivers down in flood with their dead upon their bosoms; wind sends roofs and chimney-pots hurtling through space; and I well remember the night when the hand of storm smote down an entire avenue of pines. It was the avenue leading to Piet's school, Diocesan College, on the lip of the Cape Flats. My mother grieved at the felling of an avenue beneath which her brothers in their time had walked to and from 'Bishops'.

'A landmark gone,' she lamented. 'It looks so bare without those tall pines. They were so lovely against the sky.'

It was thus with London now. The storm we called 'the Blitz' razed many a landmark that had been 'so lovely against the sky', and day by day we watched a new skyline come into being – a silhouette of towers and lighthouses riding a sea of desolation.

Now a strange thing happened to me.

I began to fall in love. To fall in love is to discover the beloved, to find, with amazed delight, a thousand endearing qualities and lovable faults and an intimacy of spirit wherein all laughter and tears are shared.

This new love – this curious affinity – came upon me almost imperceptibly. Yet I think I was first aware of its quickening on those early autumn mornings when I drove with Alice Hopkinson and the two 'electric women' down to the School for the Blind in Stepney, where we collected our mobile canteen, the donation of a certain Electrical Association. The School for the Blind had been turned into a communal kitchen, and it was there that we stacked up with dinners for the dock-workers whose eating-houses had been swept out of existence overnight.

Alice, very jaunty in her FANYS' uniform, drove the unwieldy van down to the Albert Dock, where we took up our station. The 'electric women' were very patient with me and taught me how to whack out meals in record time and wash up hundreds of knives, forks and coffee-cups afterwards in one small bowl of water. 'Fair gives me the 'eaves,' I said, and tried to look as if I didn't mean it. The 'dockies', in their good-natured queue, barracked me when I handed their plates of food through the van window.

'H'y, Gracie? 'Ere, chum, we got Gracie Fields waitin' on us 'and an' foot!'

'Give us a song, Gracie!'

They were disappointed when I was unable to comply.

I got to know them well. There was old 'Green Hands', who

worked with camouflage, 'Sweet Tooth', who liked a bit of extra sugar in his coffee ('Me mate don't use it, Miss; can you give me 'is?'), and 'No Teeth', who had trouble with his meat ('Bit gristly today M'm'), and the saucy ones and the hungry ones and the humble ones. When they brought back their empty plates and cups they hung round the little window and told us about their bombs and their babies, boasting a bit about both.

Back in the Blind School yard we cleaned out our van before going home through the terrible wastes of West Ham and the devastation of Whitechapel. Squalid interiors gaped at us theatrically. 'Slum clearance by Hitler,' said the younger electric woman, piloting her car expertly past gashes in the Mile End Road. She knew her London like a taxi-driver. The great mass of the London Hospital wore a banner across its pock-marked façade, 'THE LONDON CAN TAKE IT!' I felt an ache in my throat. Here my brothers had studied medicine and here they had delivered their first babies – children of the Ghetto, squawling brats who had by now reached a war-troubled maturity.

Round St. Paul's and the river the twisted iron guts of great offices and warehouses hung limp as cooked macaroni. Further west exclusive clubs and private mansions exposed an Adam fireplace, a carved staircase, a panelled hall, or the shamelessness of a bath-tub riding the debris. Sometimes the shattered delicacy of a crystal chandelier caught rainbow gleams of sunshine hitherto unknown to it.

All these things moved me. There was a melting within me, a yielding to this agonized untidy city with its multiple wounds. London, I thought, dear London, you have always charmed and thrilled me, but now I think I love you. Now, for the first time in my life, I feel that I belong to you – I am yours!

Joy Borrett did not go to Hereford on the Friday. She made excuses to stay on until one day all the windows of her flat blew in.

'I'll have to go after the week-end,' she said over the telephone. 'On Tuesday. I wish you'd come.'

I have known Joy's wishes to have a flick of 'The Monkey's Paw' about them. Remember the gruesome tale of the Paw that could grant wishes, but how evilly it twisted them? They came true – *but . . .*

On Sunday I went to Addington Golf Club with Bax and Charles Graves and an airman called Clarence.

Bax and Charles played a blood match, while Clarence and I walked round admiring their strokes.

On the first tee we heard that faint throbbing to which we had by now grown accustomed.

'One of theirs,' said Charles, teeing up his ball.

'Ours,' said Bax, who contradicts him on principle.

Clarence, who was musical, but rather deaf, said: 'Is it a rich contralto or a measly mezzo?'

'Mezzo,' said Bax.

'Theirs,' said Clarence.

'Of course,' said Charles.

By the time we had reached the green the sirens of Croydon and its environs were confirming their opinion.

Bax, who was about to putt, stopped to listen. He, too, thinks in terms of music and he was enchanted by the symphony echoing over hill and vale. The fierce concentration he expends upon his unpredictable golf had given way to beatific rapture and he began to conduct the Siren Song with a narrow sensitive hand.

'A magnificent orchestral effect!' he said. 'Those chromatics, rising and falling, taking up the motive, one from another, all in different keys, the crescendo and diminuendo—'

'Your putt,' said Charles, who had money on the match and was growing impatient.

Bax, spellbound by the notes now dying into silence, holed a ten-foot putt like a man in a trance.

On the third tee we saw the enemy formation flying high – about fifty of them – and then, with a sudden deep-throated roar, a dozen Hurricanes swept into view in hot pursuit, swift and lovely as the flight of birds against the pale apricot sky.

On Monday evening Jack and Joy were coming in for a drink with me. But before they could arrive two rude and uninvited guests descended upon our building. These were announced by the urgent rat-tat-tat of machine-gun fire and a mighty whistling as they plunged into the north wing, disembowelling it with neat precision. Two thousand pound bombs.

In the south wing I clung to my heaving walls and wondered whether they would collapse and crush me. The slow roar of falling masonry sounded in my ears like the breaking of a monstrous wave on some outcrop of my own surf-girdled peninsula. Into the silence that followed filtered the dry powdery smell of destruction, the Guy Fawkes odour of fireworks.

I rushed out on to the landing and found the lift installation in flames. A flying figure whisked past me, calling out, 'Come this way! The stairs are behind these big doors!' It was a female figure in a dressing-gown and curlers. 'I was having my bath – going to a cocktail party,' she gasped. 'Always knew I'd be caught in my bath! I wonder what happened?'

We soon saw. A tip-and-run raider, interrupted, no doubt, in an intended attack on the nearby power station, had jettisoned his load and we had caught it. The north wing was now a smoking, open cross-section of the building. The Jaguar, parked near it, was partially buried, but the little sailor still had his head above water. Firemen were already playing their hoses on a number of small potential conflagrations.

Then I saw Joy Borrett picking her way through the debris, white-faced and shaken.

'I was on my way here . . . they told me the block had been hit. I didn't know what I'd find . . .'

'Our things,' I said. 'All Bertie's civilian clothes and everything I didn't actually need is under there.' I pointed to the heap of rubble. 'That's the box-room, under there.'

'It might have been worse,' said Joy drily. 'It'll be a week before they dig it out. You'd better come home with me tomorrow.'

Although my flat was little harmed, it was now without light, water, cooking facilities, or windows, and an A.R.P. Warden said, 'You'll need to get out for a few days. The building may not be safe.'

'Joy,' I said. 'I'd be glad to go with you if you think your parents could do with me.'

'Of course,' she said. 'I always hoped you would.'

Somewhere that invisible Monkey's Paw must have given a little flicker of triumph.

CHAPTER THIRTEEN

OUT OF THE WAR

We had no difficulty getting petrol to evacuate. It was now clear that the enemy wished to isolate the capital and destroy all systems of communication with the rest of the country. Non-essentials were urged to go, and to use their own transport wherever possible. The main railway stations had suffered severe damage, and the overloaded trains bearing London's second great exodus were subjected to machine-gunning by terror-raiders like those who swooped down on busy streets to shoot up the shopping queues. Curious how those terror-raiders improved the morale they were out to destroy. Anger is a fighting force, and it was anger, more even than fear, that they engendered.

We left late next afternoon, having arranged that Evelyn should get in touch with Jack at the Admiralty in a day or two to hear our plans. She refused to accompany us, although Joy assured her that she could pull her weight at Hereford by helping in the house.

It was a strange drive. The shock, excitement and weariness of the past fortnight had stripped away all the mental and physical snubbers that ease our everyday lives. Always of the thin kind, I now felt down to the bone – light and over-receptive. Chill autumnal moonlight bathed the Cotswolds serenely remote from the sound and fury of war.

I said to Joy: 'What is that psalm about the hills?'

'I lift up mine eyes unto the hills from whence cometh my help . . .'

I seemed to understand those words now, for the hills are of God. The London Blitz would pass into history, but the Cotswold hills would endure to the end of the world.

It was after ten o'clock when we turned into the drive of Joy's parental home some five miles out of Hereford. I was aware of the waning moon drowned in a willow-fringed pond; of orchards and great trees; of silvered grass whereon the ragged leaves danced lightly; of a rambling creeper-covered house with a verandah, in a corner of which stood a child's tricycle and a push-cart. And then Joy's lame old father was holding his daughter in his arms and they were both too moved to speak.

There was a flutter as her slim white-haired mother drew us into the hall.

'Thank goodness you're here at last! We've been so worried, and it's so late! Have you had dinner?'

'Yes, darling, we had a meal at Tewkesbury.'

A square resolute figure hastened up from the nether quarters behind a baize-covered door.

'You'll be wanting some coffee, Mrs. Borrett—'

'Oh, Ada, how wonderful!'

Ada, the cook, was the last of the lost legions of Mrs. Beeton's era. And, as her stalwart back vanished once again into the realms of the kitchen, Joy's mother whispered despairingly: 'She's given notice again! Isn't it ghastly?'

Joy laughed. 'She'll stay, darling. She always does.'

'But we haven't anyone to help her except a girl from the village. It's appalling these days. . . . We're putting you in with Daphne tonight. I hope you don't mind sleeping with your daughter for once – and Joy's to sleep with the boiler. We're expecting Cherry and Elizabeth tomorrow, and when they come, Elizabeth will go in with Daphne, and Cherry can have the boiler, and you two girls can have beds over at the Manor House and all your meals here, of course . . .'

'You'll want to put your car away,' said Joy's father.

We unloaded the Jaguar and stabled her under the apple loft. *You'll be safe here, little sailor, I thought, there's no war here.*

When Joy's mother bade us goodnight, she said to me:

'I hope the boiler won't keep you awake. It groans and gurgles like a live thing – really makes shocking noises! It's in that cupboard.'

I had to laugh. 'Nothing could keep me awake tonight. And, anyway, we're used to shocking noises—'

'Oh, yes, of course, you poor children! By the way, there's something else you'd better know. Daddy has absolutely *banned* war talk. He won't have it.'

Joy cast me a look so expressive that it groaned aloud. But I found myself saying with genuine relief, 'Thank goodness for that!'

Joy's father, the Colonel, had the gift of closing his eyes to what he did not wish to see. He had lost one son in the last war, and his remaining son was at sea in this one. He read *The Times*, noted the progress of the war, did all in his power to help the war effort, and then strove to put the thing from him, just as he strove to ignore the increasing pain in his game leg and the growing deafness of his sweet wife. He had been a Cambridge rowing blue in his time, and his house bore upon its friendly walls gilded oars, photographs of boat's crews, and many other associations of those happy days. In his home there lingered decorum. We dressed for dinner, there was grace before meals, shining silver and sparkling glass adorned the polished table as did a bowl of flowers exquisitely arranged by the pale fluttering hands of my hostess. 'Mum doesn't understand the rations,' Joy would say. But it was clear that Ada did, and her beautifully cooked meals were adequately served by the 'girl from the village'. Fruit and vegetables were supplied from the garden, and the Colonel took particular pleasure in his delicious sugary hot-house melons and juicy peaches.

We spoke of apple-growing and cider-making, of the clover-fed bees that produced the clear amber honey that was the pride of the Colonel's heart; or we discussed the history of Hereford and the Welsh Border. Nobody mentioned the 'Mercy Ship' torpedoed in mid-Atlantic, or the bodies of sixteen frozen children found clinging to one another in a drifting lifeboat. We did not even hurry to hear the nine o'clock News. If we wanted to talk about the war we would have to do so furtively – like naughty children talking smut, for the Colonel, despite his kind geniality and twinkling eyes, had authority, and he imposed his wise *tabu* upon his household.

Joy's children, Daphne, aged ten, and Kingsley, aged four, had nursery meals in charge of one of those intimidating Nannies who regard grandparents as their natural enemies.

'Mum upsets Nannie by spoiling the children,' Joy would say over her sea-boot stocking.

I did not agree. 'Nannie bullies your Mum. If training children was like knitting a sea-boot stocking Nannie would feel convinced that your Mum was unravelling it as fast as she made it. But it would be an illusion. Your mother contributes lovely things to their training – the right ideas of thoughtfulness and good manners . . .'

As I spoke, memory carried me back to another grandmother, who had brought up a little restless boy whose parents had sailed for China and left him in the house under the mountain. No doubt she had spoiled him, but what loving kindness she had taught him!

'Possibly,' Joy admitted. 'And I must say Nannie nags Daphne. They always seem to lose interest in older children. I must think out some plan for living within reasonable distance of London and getting Daphne to a day school.'

When Joy's sister-in-law, Cherry, arrived with her little girl, Elizabeth, Daphne's boon companion, we were given sleeping accommodation at the Manor House nearby.

Our hostess was as beautiful as Anna Neagle in the part of the aged Queen Victoria. Spun glass, you might think her, brittle as icing sugar, and as sweet, but she was strong as tempered steel. I have learned by experience that the frail little old ladies of England have iron in their veins.

While we stayed in the Manor House, among the suits of mail that stood in the wide hall, and the stuffed birds and beasts in glass cases on the landing, we conformed to the rules laid down by its mistress.

'There's hot water on Mondays and Thursdays, from six till ten in the evening,' she said. 'We don't feel justified in lighting the boiler more often these days. One has to remember that there's a war on!'

She sat in a wicker armchair with a fleecy rug over her knees. Her Persian cat dozed on her lap and an ancient dog, heavy with fat, rested his chin upon the embroidered footstool at her feet. Canaries shrilled in a large cage, and a green parrot clawed his way up and down the bars of his prison. I thought of a white cockatoo in the rigging of a little anti-aircraft cruiser, 'climbing claw-over-claw, proper seaman-like', and of Ordinary Dog Shrapnel of H.M.S. *Manchester*, and his friend, Leslie the cat, who'd combined love and war on the shores of a burning Norwegian fjord, and I wondered where they were now – those seafaring animals. I remembered a letter from my husband:

> 'I was going round with a torch, inspecting between decks, when suddenly the beam fell on a queer little party. You'd have loved it. A tiny hammock was slung with two even tinier ones on either side of it. Leslie and the four Norwegian kittens were tucked up snug as you please. The sailors had

made the little hammocks for the cat family and taught them to sleep in them . . .'

When Joy asked our hostess for a latch key 'so that we don't disturb anyone when we come in after dinner,' she received a charming refusal.

'That's quite unnecessary, my dear. I wouldn't dream of burdening you with our fearful heavy old key and the responsibility of bolting the door and putting up the chain . . . my maid always does that herself. And, in any case, we don't have prayers till a quarter to ten, and naturally you'll be back in time for prayers.'

The Lady of the Manor was interested to hear that I came from South Africa, for her late husband, a great hunter of wild things, as the cases on the landing bore witness, had, in his time, shot birds, beasts and Boers in my country. It was remarkable, she said, how little ill-feeling had been left by the Boer War. Just look at General Smuts. We looked at General Smuts, and, for once in my life, I refrained from dispelling a popular British illusion by telling her that the Boer War hang-over still eats like a sickness into the head and heart of the greater part of the Dutch Afrikaner population. If she thought South Africa was all good-will towards the Mother Country, let her keep that happy belief.

'General Smuts understands the Empire,' she said.

'Yes,' I agreed. 'He sees the importance of the Commonwealth of Nations. So does Mr. Churchill.'

That evening both statesmen were included in the family prayers.

On Sunday morning we all went to the lovely little village church, and the vicar prayed specially for those in the Battle of London. Afterwards, in the porch, people greeted Joy, as his neighbours must once have greeted Lazarus when the chill of the tomb still lay upon him.

'It must be dreadful in London,' they said. 'Do you hate talking about it?'

But, if she tried to tell them about it, their eyes went blank.

'They don't understand,' she said afterwards. 'It's like it was when I came back from the Yangtse. One's experienced something it isn't possible to pass on . . . and people aren't really interested anyway, they'd much rather talk about the apple crop, or Mrs. So-and-So's affair with the grocer. They used to say "How was it in China?" like they say "How is it in London?" but, if you try to tell them, you're a bore.'

In the afternoon we went to tea with Great Aunt Mary, who had very nearly scored up her century. Daphne and Elizabeth came with us, but not Kingsley.

'He's too young,' explained Daphne with elder sisterly patronage. 'We took him once, but he screamed when he saw Great Aunt Mary and she was upset.'

Great Aunt Mary was stone deaf, but her eyes were still as sharp as gimlets in the crumpled vellum of her small shrunken face, and it was clear that she enjoyed being At Home to the younger members of the family. She was particularly fond of her septuagenarian nephew, the Colonel, whom she regarded as a very promising lad. Her manner of holding court was reminiscent of a game of Consequences. Her visitors were grouped about her in a semi-circle and supplied with paper and pencils, and then, while Great Aunt Mary bestowed 'nods, becks and wreath'd smiles' upon their bowed heads, they scribbled furiously, with the exception of those who stared into space and sucked their pencils as if hypnotized. Upon them the old lady concentrated her gestures of encouragement, thereby depriving them of their last vestiges of coherent thought. The messages were presently collected and passed to Great Aunt Mary, who scattered some far and wide, ignored others entirely, and read the remainder with the aid of a lorgnette. When she was entertained, she repeated what she had read, laughed shrilly, and added a few trenchant comments. Finally she swept all the papers off her lap into a wastepaper basket, and the audience, realizing that the game was now at an end, dispersed, leaving their venerable relative to snooze in her high velvet chair by the fire.

'What did you write?' I asked Daphne on the way home, for she had seemed in no wise afflicted with pen-paralysis.

Daphne said: 'I wrote, "Dear Great Aunt, it is my birthday next week. I am very fond of painting but have no paint-box. Do you like painting?" '

I laughed. 'What did she say?'

'She didn't read it,' said Daphne. 'It was one of the ones she spilt. It's always that way when they're important.'

Two days later Jack rang up from the Admiralty.

'Evelyn has been bombed out. She's getting a train to Hereford some time tomorrow . . .'

So next evening a ramshackle car crunched up the drive with Evelyn sitting bolt upright in the back.

Already the 'No War' magic of Hereford had withdrawn us far out of range of London. But now, as Evelyn stepped out of the car and smiled at us wearily, we saw the face of the city we had left. Pale it was, and pinched, with fatigue deeply bruising hollow eye-sockets and red-rimmed eyes. There was something painfully moving in that London look, something we had to respect.

Ada had appeared in the hall to welcome a much needed reinforcement for her kitchen, but at the sight of this little woman's evident exhaustion her grim old face softened.

'You'll be wanting some coffee and a hot bath,' she said. 'Come along with me.'

'Thanks,' said Evelyn. 'But could you make it tea?'

As they disappeared behind the baize door we saw Ada put a sturdy arm about Evelyn's braced shoulders. They were two of a kind.

'Ada'll take care of her,' said Joy. 'And we must hurry over to the Manor House. It's our bath night, too!'

When we got back to dinner I was amazed to see Evelyn, spruce in her starched white overall, waiting at table with the girl from the village. It was she who cleared the table for dessert and she who placed the port in front of the Colonel with the experienced confidence of one whose early training has been impeccable. Evelyn, I thought, I hand it to you!

Afterwards I spoke to her alone in the Colonel's study.

'Did you lose much? Tell me what happened.'

It was everybody's story – the story of Evelyn's bomb. But she told it with North Country brevity. Her bomb had landed in the garden and blown out doors and windows, rendering the attic flat uninhabitable. She was at Gracie's Old Lady's at the time.

'Were you alone when you got home and found what had happened?'

'Yes,' said Evelyn, and suddenly the brutal impact of that moment hit her anew and she turned her face away from me.

'In a day or two, when you're rested, we'll make a plan,' I said. 'In the meantime do you think you'll be all right here?'

'Yes,' she said. 'And I'm very grateful to . . . everybody. I'll do my best to help wherever I think I can be most useful.'

'Well, the first thing is to get some sleep. It's nearly ten. Heavens, I must hurry, or I'll be be late for prayers!'

At that Evelyn laughed, and so did I.

'Yes,' I said. 'For the time being we've both lost our independence. But we'll get it back.'

That night I could not sleep. My maid's little face – the face of London – haunted me. As a melody or a perfume may wound and disturb with associations of half-forgotten love, so the London look had reawakened my new-old affinity for the city in her suffering. Alice and the 'electric women' would be trundling down the Mile End Road to the desolation of the docks, or Tower Bridge, or wherever else they might be needed.

'We can manage,' she'd said, when I'd rung her up to say I was leaving. 'After all, if we can't get someone else, we can still carry on one short.' I'd put down the receiver with a sense of guilt and shame.

Yet letters from my husband imploring, even commanding, me to keep away from London lay on the bedside-table. The palms of my hands tingled with remembered fear. But I *must* go back, I thought, there may be something I can salve from that buried box-room. They've probably dug it out by now. *In any case, I must go back!*

CHAPTER FOURTEEN

'...FROM DAY TO DAY...'

'YOU must learn to live like a soldier' my husband had written, at the beginning of the war, '... from day to day, even hour to hour ...' And that was how it had turned out to be. The morrow was always a question mark.

Within a week London had drawn me back. I had to go. I felt about going back as I had felt about hunting in Hong Kong and paper-chasing in Shanghai, and getting my first job on a London newspaper – a sort of gasping terror in mortal conflict with strong belief that one must not be dominated by one's fears, for I am a woman of many fears, and to let in one would be to open the gates to a host.

I returned to my Chelsea flat on an afternoon of wind and sun – a laughing wind that skipped through the ruins, heedless as a child, stirring up the grey dust and blowing the dry powdery smell of wreckage hither and thither. Great tenements, ancient churches, and lovely little streets and corners, with queer improbable houses and cottages, had perished in the wholesale destruction.

Through the paneless windows of my flat I could see that laughing wind tossing the white plumes of the power station into the sunny sky – plumes on the helmet of a sturdy old warrior standing firm over his fallen comrades.

I tried the water, the light, the gas. Nothing. I sat on my bed and picked up the telephone. Strange! It was working. I dialled Marion's office number.

'Joy-Joy, you shouldn't be back in London!'

'Mary Ann, can I come to you for a few days? I've things to settle up in London. They've dug out the box-room and I think I can find our trunks. They'll be crushed, but the clothes may be in existence still—'

'Of course, but we get it pretty lively round Ruislip.'

'One does most places round London, I imagine.'

'When will you come? Tonight?'

'If I may.'

So it was decided.

Alice was in, too, when I called her up.

'I could take my turn this week. Wednesday and Thursday. Or have you found someone else?'

'No, we haven't. It isn't so easy these days . . .'

I put the receiver down with a feeling of light-heartedness. It was good to be back where things were happening.

Marion's bungalow garden was untidy and the woods round Ruislip were turning gold. There was a fire in the hearth when I arrived soon after seven, and Marion had just got in.

She seemed slighter than ever, but as vital; a tiny dynamo setting the wheels of normal life in motion wherever she went. We ate our supper by the fireside, and presently, during the nine o'clock News, the radio faded, and, in its place, we heard the jungle sounds of the blitz – a doleful wailing, and then the pulsing mosquito; unearthly whistlings and crashes; the roaring of a mighty lion shaking the bungalow, followed by the monstrous beating of some gigantic disembodied heart and the barking of long faceless iron throats . . .

'The guns,' said Marion. 'We have the barrage now. That metronome beat is a naval pom-pom. Come out and see the show.'

We stood on the little shingle path and watched the stupendous fireworks over London – blinding lightning, the sudden glare of fire, bouquets of flame expanding and scattering their blossoms of death, and the lonely beauty of a flare sinking earthwards out of the night. And, interlacing these, the white searchlight ballet danced its formal measure in vast seeking sweeps across the torn backdrop of the sky.

'Bertie says the Northern Lights look like the barrage over Scapa Flow – like this then.'

It was fitful. When the thunder died down for a space so did the lightning.

I found that Marion had established a blitz-drill. The two bunks in her concrete garden hut were made up, and, whenever the *thrum-thrum* was overhead and *whoomphs* were near at hand, we slept there in the company of The Fritz. It was like sleeping in a tiny ship's cabin, and often the walls trembled as if waves beat against them.

In the menaced intimacy of the cabin we talked. The Fritz was coiled down in his basket, long, supple, lacquered black, with his sensitive patrician nose twitching as he dreamed.

'Tell me about when you were small,' I'd demand. And Marion would obligingly throw out fragments of a childhood utterly different from my own, though both of us were the daughters of doctors.

Compared with Dr. Packer, my father's professional life had not impinged greatly upon that of his home. It was true that Cookie was frequently seen to boil sinister shining instruments on the kitchen range.

'What's that, Cookie? What's it for?'

'I dunno, Miss Yoy. Dese is werry funny scissors, I mus' say! I don't much fancy de look of dem!' That with a knowing giggle. And, often enough, Daddy was called out in the middle of a bridge game, when some impatient reserve, always at hand, heaved a sigh of relief and sat down in his place opposite my mother to play his cards.

And, on those days when the maid was out, I was accustomed

to seeing my mother's baffled expression as she strove to elucidate the mysteries of messages taken by Cookie.

'*Who* did you say wanted the Doctor, Cookie?'

'Mrs. Syphon, Madam . . . Sypher – Simon . . . somet'ing like dat—' Cookie frowning and fiddling with her apron in prodigious efforts of memory, and Mother going through a mental list of patients beginning with S.

'Could it be Styles?'

'No . . . not exac'ly Styles . . .'

'Smythe perhaps?'

Dawn breaking on the dark horizon of Cookie's countenance.

'Dat's it, Madam! Smit'!'

The telephone was a constant reminder of his calling, a little black slave-driver day and night. But at least his consulting rooms were not in the house but in the town, in Adderley Street, and, when he took me with him on his rounds, we went by car along the sea and mountain roads of the peninsula, so it did not take all day.

My late father-in-law, however, had had the responsibility of a widespread country practice in Shropshire, the core of which was a spacious house he had caused to be built on a wooded hill above the village of Cressage. The house stood in fine grounds, wherein my mother-in-law, who had a keen social sense, had enjoyed giving garden parties and getting up tennis and croquet tournaments. Behind it were roomy stables for the Doctor's hard-worked horses, and there, from old Dick, the coachman, little Bertie picked up the rich leisurely Shropshire dialect and brought it into the house with the smell of horse manure and old leather – much to the disgust of his fastidious mother.

That mother of three girls and a boy, all much of an age, ordered her household on the lines laid down by the inexorable Mrs. Beeton, whose 'Book of Household Management' had a prominent place on her bookshelves. It was a large and cumbersome establishment, for the surgery and dispensary were on the premises, and the Doctor's assistant lived with the family. Then there was always a foreign governess to teach the children French and German, and quite often there was Ludwig, a young German medical student, who spent his vacations at Cressage, and with whose people on the Rhine Bertie spent several months at the age of twelve. For my mother-in-law was a pioneer in the human exchange system of travel now so much in vogue owing to currency restrictions. She, too, was financially restricted, since a country doctor is seldom a wealthy man, but she was also quite determined that her children should be good linguists with a European outlook on the world as opposed to an insular one. For this purpose she alternately imported French and German governesses into her remote country house and exported her children to France, Germany and Switzerland for large portions of their education.

The Doctor himself was an enthusiatic sportsman who believed in his fellow man. From him his children inherited a facility for games, and his son learned the ritual of shooting and fishing. In their holidays Bertie and Marion often accompanied him on his daily rounds in the gig, bowling swiftly over the country roads in the wake of his unprofitable practice. He was welcomed everywhere. Those who could afford his services paid for them, and those who could not received them free. His sort will soon be found no more in England.

Marion said: 'I think the best time Bertie and I ever had was one summer when we had whooping cough. We were turned out to grass like two animals and no one took any notice of us. It didn't matter how grubby we got or what we did, so long as we kept out of everybody's way, so we were seldom in trouble. Ordinarily we were often in hot water. Once Bertie borrowed Daddy's shot-gun to try some target practice; the cook had all her washing on the line that day, blowing in the breeze, and the temptation was too much for Bertie – a moving target – so he fairly riddled her pants . . .' Her cough broke into her laugh.

After the 1914–18 War the Doctor had fallen ill, and, for many years he was an invalid, needing two nurses. The family fortunes dwindled, the big house on the hill was sold, and every time the son came home from the sea to the cottage in which his parents now lived, he found some familiar piece of furniture missing. His mother, who 'never complained and never explained', waved away his enquiries with the diplomatic evasion of which she was always mistress; if he persisted she refused to answer.

'You know her,' said Marion. 'Never says more than she means to. Proud as the devil and never gives in.'

I smiled, remembering a certain recent occasion when my mother-in-law had exhibited quite a Nelson touch in disdaining surrender. Her eyes had been troubling her for some time and her son-in-law, Professor Capon of Liverpool University, with great difficulty persuaded her to go with him to a specialist. The specialist, warned that his patient might prove a trifle perverse, was nevertheless astonished at her lack of co-operation.

'Now, Mrs. Packer,' he said gently, seating the old lady in front of a scroll of hieroglyphics. 'What letters do you see in the top row?'

My mother-in-law, horrified and exasperated at the appearance of a blurred and dancing signal, which, in her view spelled out no less a word than Disaster, did not use the Nelson phrase, 'I'm damned if I see it!' but displayed, instead, the Nelson spirit.

'I shan't tell you,' she replied tartly.

She was, in fact, one of those frail little old ladies of England with iron in their veins. After this unfortunate *contretemps* her good eye ceased altogether to function, and her children grieved to know that now she was nearly sightless, for she loved to read the French and German classics which she still managed to obtain from the second-hand bookshops where her small figure, much afflicted with rheumatism, was well known.

'What does she do now?' I asked Marion. 'Without reading she must find the time endless.'

'She reads,' said Marion, from the lower bunk.

'But I thought her good eye was done for?'

'It is. But she has discovered that her bad eye was only a "lazy eye", and it's begun to work again.'

I laughed. 'Your mother never has had patience with a shirker. Even her own eye can't get away with it. What a woman!'

While I was enjoying the hospitality of the bungalow, Joy Borrett had made, and put into effect, her plan for being within reasonable distance of London so that she could see something of Jack and put Daphne to a day school. With these ends in view she had arranged to live with her Uncle and Aunt in Bedford, leaving small Kingsley with his dragon and his grandparents in Hereford.

These kind relations of hers now offered to take me in, too, until the Christmas holidays, and Evelyn would be a useful addition to the household.

'It'll give you time to collect yourself,' said Joy. 'And you can go up to London quite easily from Bedford if you must.'

The next few weeks linger contentedly in my memory.

Bedford was in the unfortunate position of being the obvious reception area for refugees from London and the Midlands, to say nothing of an infiltration from Dover. Thus the Billeting Officer was the local Bogey. For, if there is anything more unpleasant than being bombed out of your home, it is being swamped in it. It is lovely having guests, but it is also lovely seeing them go, and, in reception areas, where the guests were not even invited, that second, almost ecstatic pleasure was often too long deferred.

Joy's Uncle Noel and Aunt Mabel, who were both realists and extremely kind-hearted and conscientious, accepted the fact that for an indefinite period they must bid good-bye to the privacy of their home life, but the wave which swamped them was, at least, a family wave. And the high-hearted courage and cheerful efficiency with which Aunt Mabel rode it still leaves me wondering, for she was an indefatigable war-worker and organizer with never a spare moment.

As for Uncle Noel, many years older than his wife, now, in his seventies, finding himself the head of a swollen household of women – I can only assume that he must often have craved to be back in command of the senior house at Bedford School, from which he had retired some time since. But, like all those with the habit of authority, he was also a master of self-discipline, and his courtesy towards us all was unfailing. At the same time he commanded our respect.

'If Uncle Noel sends for you in his study, beware!' Joy warned me.

His study was his quarter deck, and, whether he ever sent for me among the defaulters or not – as my mother-in-law said to the specialist – *I shan't tell you!*

Like his Hereford brother, the Colonel, Uncle Noel had been a rowing-blue at Cambridge, as, in due course, were three of his four sons, so here too I found the walls decorated with the impedimenta of the river. And at the bottom of the long garden, behind the house, were hives where busy Bedford bees competed with their Herefordshire rivals in the manufacture of translucent honey. So, every now and again, we were privileged to behold Uncle Noel, arrayed in a veiled Trilby hat and gauntlets, extracting the sweetly dripping honeycombs in the teeth of an army of furious bees against which he seldom bothered to use a smoke screen.

'They don't sting me,' he said. Bees and boys. He could manage either.

On Sunday mornings we went to church in the Chapel of Bedford School only a few minutes' walk from the house. I enjoyed those services nearly as much as those on board a ship with the smell of the sea on the wind and the deep voices of sailors singing the hymns.

Uncle Noel and his party occupied a pew facing the choir, seats of honour, I fancy. The swagger of the surplice and the glamour of the gown! One followed the other. First the choir boys, starched and smarmed, their countenances shining with Sunday saintliness, so that I was put in mind of words in the baptismal service that had once deeply impressed me at the christening of my infant son. 'Grant that the Old Adam in this Child may be so buried that the new man may be raised up in him.' If soap alone could wash away that stubborn Old Adam, these boys were, for the nonce, New Men.

Following them came the Masters, dignified in their gowns. In the body of the Chapel sat the remainder of the boarders with a few parents or friends, beatified by shafts of sunlight coloured and filtered by the narrow stained glass windows. There was always a twittering and cooing from without, as if birds were determined to join their pæans of praise to those of the humans.

Then, strangely, as the service progressed, the little polished choirboys were emptied of their virtue, and there was fidgeting under the oak rail and wandering eyes. Unruly locks of hair sprang up on smooth round heads, and here and there a nose was furtively picked as that indelible Old Adam proclaimed his immemorial right to the transient New Man. Yet, when the organ notes called them to their feet, the were once more transformed. Heads tossed back, mouths opened wide and notes of purest gold quivered in the vaulted air. Sadness seized me then that the creaking gates of adolescence should ever close up such angel singing. The voice of the soloist, flute-high and clear, conjured up the memory of a single nightingale pouring forth its heartbreak song among the moonlit cypresses of Greece . . . and then another memory . . . a boy on a crowded platfrom at Victoria – *Listen well, my heart, you will never hear this young unbroken voice again!*

'. . . the grace of Our Lord, Jesus Christ, and the love of God, and the fellowship of the Holy Ghost, be with us all evermore. Amen.'

I used to go to London two days a week to continue my work with the canteen, and I stayed with Marion, or with Alice, or at Bax's house, which had by now become a hostel for orphans of the storm. During the next few months Bax was host to a perpetual bombed-out-house-party which varied as his friends lost and found flats.

For the rest of the week I took charge of the local Citizens' Advice Bureau, established by the National Council of Social Service in the headquarters of the Bedford W.V.S. It was my business to help people with their many and various war problems, from what rates they should pay on a partially blitzed house to finding relatives missing after an air raid. I was issued with pamphlets from the N.C.S.S. giving the latest war-laws, and, in cases of urgency, I was authorized to consult a local lawyer. It was human and interesting work, and one of its most difficult – and admirable – aspects was the reluctance people showed to accept 'charity'. If sent to the Assistance Board they almost invariably protested. 'I couldn't go there, Miss! I've never claimed public charity in my life and I couldn't do it now. I have my pride!' Their pride. One was always up against that powerful ingredient in the make-up of the common man and woman. It was all that was left to many of them, but its value was beyond price.

At the end of November I received a telephone call from London which caused me great joy and amazement.

My brother, Norman, now a Major in the South African Medical Corps, had been sent to England to study certain remarkable advances in plastic surgery – the tragic surgery of war – and he expected to be in England for three or four months. On the strength of this, I made up my mind to return to London and find another flat which he would be able to regard as a base. Or perhaps that was just my excuse for doing what I had been contemplating.

I discussed the matter with Evelyn, who said frankly:

'Well, Madam, I want to get back to London, too. But I feel that I must take on a man's job. Gracie says their porter is leaving, and she thinks I could do his job – the lift and messages and all that sort of thing. I'd like to take it on. But I don't want to let you down.'

'Don't worry,' I said. 'I'll find a service flat. Go after that job and get it.'

So the next time I was in town I went to see my old friend, Mrs Hooper.

I had first met the incomparable Mrs. Hooper in China ten years earlier, where, in the French Concession, I had often watched her play forbidden roulette with the wealthy Chinese. The house in which they played was carefully blacked-out, not against air-raids, but to mislead any officious policeman into thinking the place was deserted and empty. She was a woman so habituated to the fantastic that she was no longer capable of astonishment, and her gusto and zest for life was unsurpassed. The years had added somewhat to her weight and she had long since abandoned golf and tennis, but she still played an optimistic game of bridge and was always ready to stake her fortune on a poker game. However, she had now discovered a new gamble – the best yet – and, while Death hurled his loaded dice from the heavens, Mrs. Hooper snapped her fingers in his face. I am willing to swear that no human being in London, throughout the war, enjoyed the appalling thrill of the blitz as she did.

'I'm coming back to London,' I said, when her gentle little maid of infinite refinement showed me into her mistress's lounge, which was both extremely modern and extremely comfortable.

Mrs. Hooper rose to greet me, a figure immaculate and substantial, and she said in her full deep voice:

'Well, frankly, my dear, I don't know how you've stayed away so long. I wouldn't miss a moment of the blitz!'

'Then tell me where I can find a service flat. That's the problem of the moment.'

She gave the matter her consideration. After a while she said: 'There's a place in St. James' – Number Eleven, King Street – where a lot of China people used to go. If it's still in existence it might be just the thing for you. It's old-fashioned, but it has atmosphere. Shall we nip into a taxi and go along?'

Thus, presently, the heavy door of Number Eleven, King Street, was opened to us by a dark saturnine porter with a pronounced cast in his eye.

'Good morning, Frederick,' said Mrs. Hooper. 'I didn't expect to see you here after all these years!'

'Good morning, Madam', said the porter, with a smile made

remote by the eye that was not with us. 'I am very glad to see you, too. In these days one loses touch with people.'

I can only describe his voice as gentlemanly. Frederick had distinction. The moment I saw him I knew that my search for a service flat had ended where it had begun. The combination of Number Eleven with Frederick's squint was final. For eleven is my lucky number, and a squint is worth more to me than a whole bagful of black cats.

CHAPTER FIFTEEN

NUMBER ELEVEN

BUT what of the Grey Mistress while I was succumbing to a squint and a lucky number on a wintry November day in London?

She was steaming into the Mediterranean. At Gibraltar the men were going ashore with high hearts. There was sunshine by day, no black-outs at nights, and luxuries in the shops and bazaars to be bought for sweethearts and wives. The Captain purchased two leather 'dumpy cushions', three bottles of Chanel Number Five, and nine pairs of silk stockings for a total cost of twelve pounds, while his Coxswain had beaten down an Indian dealer from ten shillings to seven shillings and sixpence for a 'beautiful pink silk double bedspread', and, ever solicitous for the health of his young wife, who 'suffered from her head', he had laid in a stock of her favourite headache cure which could be had for half-a-crown in Gibraltar as opposed to three shillings and sixpence at home.

Vice-Admiral Sir Lancelot E. Holland had now hoisted his flag in the *Manchester*, and of him my husband wrote to me:

> 'He is such fun to talk to and so cultivated . . . has a mind as sharp as a razor and deep. So is not fussy. I have decided the fussy ones are those who doubt their capacity. L. E. Holland is arrogant and intelligent. A beautiful combination. I know so many who use arrogance to hide their lack of intelligence . . .'

At Gibraltar, however, the ship embarked more than silks, scents and headache cures. In fact, she took on the headache itself in the collective person of several hundred airmen and soldiers urgently needed in Egypt, where General Wavell was preparing his first great offensive. The ship was to steam in convoy through the Mediterranean in company with Admiral Somerville's Force H, escorting aircraft-carriers and fast merchantmen with fighter aircraft and ammunition on board – a precious and vital cargo.

Off Cape Spartivento the convoy sighted a superior force of Italian warships, and a sharp engagement ensued in which the Italians turned tail, with one of their number, hit by H.M.S. *Manchester*, blazing from stem to stern.

The Captain's private account of the action included several of those small human incidents which he never found beneath his notice.

'A great cheer went up when the silk battle ensign, presented by the City of Manchester, was broken at the masthead.

'Throughout the battle we had 660 airmen and soldiers on board. They were put under cover and behaved very well, and soon were helping transfer ammunition from X and Y turrets to A and B.

'Just before the action started Dog Shrapnel carried out a tour of inspection of the ship, starting with me on the bridge. He didn't mind the guns firing. 'Nothing after Dunkirk!' he said.

'Leslie, with British *sang-froid*, gave birth to yet another family in the boiler-room.'

In spite of its adventures the precious convoy got through to Alexandria with almost perfect naval punctuality. 'Two minutes late, pilot!' said the Captain to the Navigator, with mock severity.

Of the spirit of the Mediterranean Fleet, my husband wrote:

'There is a marvellous spirit here. So refreshing. They all swear by A.B.C.' (Admiral Sir Andrew Cunningham. Commander-in-Chief of the Mediterranean Fleet, who later succeeded Admiral Pound as First Sea Lord) 'and their morale is a hundred and fifty per cent. Thank God for it!'

By 13th December the *Manchester* was back in Scapa Flow, and the womenfolk at home were foolishly hoping for such peace-time joys as Christmas leave.

Number Eleven, King Street, in its heyday and fully staffed, would have been quite beyond our means, but London, between September 1940 and August 1941, was deserted by the many, and only the few remained. Expensive peace-time flats and suites could be had for a song.

My suite, on the second floor, comprised a double bedroom, sitting-room and bathroom. The rooms were lofty and panelled, the furniture was heavy and Edwardian, and there were large Chinese vases on the mantelpiece. The couch and easy chairs were brocaded in old rose, and the whole place breathed a personal atmosphere, a feeling of permanence and continuity.

Every evening at dusk, one or the other of the aged maids, Kate or Ella, crawled in to draw my heavy brocade curtains and make sure that the black-out was flawless, then they'd put a match to the fire, getting down on creaky rheumatic knees to do it. Presently Frederick, or his opposite number, Cyril, appeared to ask what time I wanted my supper. Cyril was as volatile as Frederick was sombre, a sort of Jemminy Cricket of a man with a prancing gait and a lively wit. Both were veterans of 1914–18, and before that Cyril had served in the Indian Army.

Soon after dark, with monotonous regularity, Wailing Winnie raised her voice and the heavens filled with the soft persistent sobbing of the enemy raiders. The the guns roared in Hyde Park and my curtains billowed inwards on the great draught of their breath.

Cyril, cavorting in with my supper tray on high, said, 'Leave the doors open, Madam; doors jam and you don't want to be trapped like a cockroach in the kitchen cupboard! I told cook you wanted your sole fried, but she's done it *a la Walewska* – she never hears a word – never even hears the guns – and swears she can't read my writing!'

Sometimes he told me about former occupants of Number Eleven.

'That luggage piled up on the first floor landing – that belongs to Miss Edna Best . . . Mrs Herbert Marshall . . . went off to America in a great hurry, she did. Used to be at the St.

James's Theatre. We've had a lot of stage people here, being right opposite the theatre.'

His favourite topic, however, was India, and he had been in his element when Mahatma Gandhi had arrived to stay at Number Eleven complete with retinue of disciples and goat.

'The goat was a bit tricky, we haven't really got accommodation for a goat, and I used to take it for walks sometimes. Quite a problem serving the meals, too, because they all sat on the ground, and I'm not as supple as I used to be!'

At nine o'clock Ella, bent and wizened, crept in with my hot-water bottle. So old was Ella that I felt she might disintegrate at a breath, then she'd confound me by picking up the heavy coal-scuttle and tipping slack on to the fire.

'Keep it alive, Madam. A fire's company.'

'Yes, thank you, Ella.'

The noises from without crashed and whistled. I was reluctant to let her go. She told me that she was Austrian, naturalized long ago, before the last war. 'I lived in Vienna as a girl . . . once I was betrothed to a violinist in a great orchestra . . . but he married somebody else and I came to England to forget about him.'

I sought the little sallow wrinkled face, now greyly bearded, for vestiges of bygone beauty, and looked away.

'Did you succeed in forgetting?'

She shook her head, smiling.

'Never. So now, in my old age, I still have a young man in my life . . .'

As she went out, I called after her.

'Leave the door open, please . . .'

'Yes, Madam. Don't feel lonely or nervous. We are all here. You have only to call or ring.'

Was she not afraid herself? I wondered. Had love of life worn so thin that danger of death was a matter of indifference? Or did she reassure me as part of an age-old habit of care for others? Ella was not of this screaming world in which she lived so precariously.

I had not been in residence long before a number of our friends took up their abode in King Street.

Mrs. Hooper's gorgeous daughter, Sheila, and her handsome husband, John, who was in the Fleet Air Arm and appointed to the Admiralty, were the first to arrive, and their suite was just along the landing from mine. Sheila was in the Military Transport Corps then, driving for General de Gaulle's Fighting French, and she used to tell John, with mischief in her husky voice, that one day she would elope with a Frenchman. John only laughed. 'People who threaten to commit suicide never do it!' He could match her for wildness any day in the year. Much later, when they agreed to part company, Sheila did indeed marry a Frenchman – an Army Officer of very particular gallantry.

Then Colin, who had been commuting from Hertford, decided to take a suite; and Philip Rhodes, who had given up his house in South Audley Street, blew in and out for a night or two whenever he was not rushing round the country on mysterious errands to do with prisoners escaped from Europe. Often in his company was a thin dark young woman with immense startled brown eyes like those of the fawn Bambi, when he had just lost his mother. She was South African from a wild and beautiful part of Natal, but she had made England her home and was working in a 'hush-hush' organization in the city. Then the Borretts appeared for a week-end occasionally; to say nothing of my brother Norman. Not that one ever *can* say nothing of Norman.

For Norman is our changeling. Ever since, at the age of three days old, he disdained his mother's milk, that 'quaint baby' has been unexpected in his behaviour. When my mother made the acquaintance of her mentor, Carnegie, she confidently presented a copy of 'How to Make Friends and Influence People' to her younger son. Norman gave his mind to the book and studied the method with that concentration of which he is capable to a marked degree. Here was the key to *savoir faire*; but the science of Tact and its application were not always the same thing, and Norman invariably applied the right treatment to the wrong people with disastrous results. 'You just have to take him as he is,' said mother, after that, and she was not displeased to find that Carnegie had not succeeded where she had failed. Some could take my brother's eccentricities and some could not. Those who could were rewarded by finding a generous and affectionate nature expanding in the warmth of their comprehension, and those who could not were spared Norman's endeavours to display tact which were as much touched with the Monkey's Paw as Joy Borrett's wishes.

Joy, who often wished on extravagant lines, had frequently

expressed a desire to see the abode of the First Lord of the Admiralty at Whitehall and one night this came to pass.

Jack and she went to a party at which Mr. A. V. Alexander was present. When it was over he offered them a lift home, 'But my driver can put me down first at Admiralty House,' he said. As Mr. Alexander bade them good night he slammed the door of his car, but some object prevented it from closing with its usual facility.

'Something's caught,' said the First Lord. 'The rug perhaps.'

But when he reopened the door he saw Captain Borrett hastily withdraw an unrecognizable finger. Much concerned, Mr Alexander insisted on administering first aid in his flat immediately, so Joy had her wish and saw the apartments of the First Lord at Admiralty House.

As soon as they got back to King Street she woke my brother Norman from a deep sleep that he might go and minister unto Jack. Norman, seeing her much distressed, thought to reassure her, so, as he examined the unpleasant mass of bloody pulp that had been Jack's middle finger, he said, 'My dear girl, I don't know what you are fussing about. This is a beautiful finger, quite the nicest jambed finger I've seen in years.' With which he bandaged it up again, while the solicitous wife muttered balefully, 'Beautiful! My poor Jack's finger *beautiful*! What heartless brutes doctors are!'

At first Frederick, who was of a cynical temperament, looked askance as well as askew upon my week-end visitor, but when photographs of Molly and Richard – Norman's wife and little son – adorned the flat from Friday to Monday, and disappeared with my brother for the rest of the week, he accepted the relationship as being above reproach.

Norman, who is dedicated, body and soul, to his profession of surgery, was intensely interested and enthralled with the great advances made in plastic work. The young martyrs of the Battle of Britain, with their burnt hands and feet and faces, were being remade at East Grinstead that they might live and fly again. Richard Hilary, the doomed young author of 'The Last Enemy', was one of the many 'Few' to suffer and win through, only to lose his life in the end. Norman had fearful and wonderful, and sometimes humorous, tales to tell when he came to town, even if he did usually tell them in the wrong company!

I always awaited his arrival on Fridays in trepidation, for often he lost himself. Travel in England was at that time like a trip through the Haunted Castle at a fun-fair. You were conveyed in pitch darkness through nameless stations to a problematical destination, so that any stray enemy parachutist who had boarded the train might be baffled as to his whereabouts. My brother, though no parachutist, was among the many innocents to be hoodwinked by these precautions, and on one occasion he sprang nimbly into the snowy night when the train stopped at what be believed to be East Grinstead, only to find himself rolling down the steep embankment of an unknown siding while the engine chuffed off with a mocking shriek, leaving him to nurse his bruises in the icy midst of nowhere.

Then, when he did arrive, he had an odd knack of unearthing curious down-and-out individuals and bringing them home with the trusting air of a dog who has just disinterred an old and fruity bone with the intention of enjoying it on his own hearth-rug.

'Darling,' I'd protest. 'Must you really bring old Stinkerwitz back with you when you find him decorating the Overseas Club. His gin consumption is phenomenal and my supplies are not.'

Norman would look mortified. 'I'm awfully sorry, Joytje. I'll get some more gin. And it really was a kindly act having poor Stinker to supper. He's so frightfully homesick.'

I sighed. Norman's kindly acts could be two-edged.

But with the presence of my brother my hunger for first-hand news of the house under the mountain was partially appeased.

'Is Piet happy?' I'd ask. 'Does Mum find him too much for her?'

'Your mother finds him a handful,' he'd admit, characteristically waiving his claim to our mother with the adjective 'your'. 'But it does her good to have something to worry about. Keeps her young. In any case, his inventiveness makes him very little trouble at home. When he's there he's in his workshop, and when he's not in the workshop or at school he's either on, in or under the water. He and Hans and Ronnie made a diving outfit out of an old petrol tin, some rubber tubing and a hand-pump. One of the three explores the bottom of Kalk Bay Harbour – about twenty feet down – while the other two pump. Of course, the pumpers get bored and forget their job, and the chap down below pulls the plug with no results . . . they nearly drowned Hans that way, so Gran objected. Then they built a speedboat and tried it out on Zeekoe Vlei till Ronnie broke his arm aqua-planing behind it, and the Yacht Club wrote to complain of noise, smell and general danger to life and limb. So, what with one thing and another, the dear old lady does get a bit hit up at times.'

I had to laugh. 'All Piet's fairy godmothers blessed him with the same thing – initiative. It's a bit overdone.'

It is curious how the quality of awareness in human beings lies dormant or quickens according to the impulse of events or experience.

I remember seeing a film called 'Queen Christina' with Garbo and Gilbert as the stars. It was a very long time ago, and the picture has faded from my mind, except for one scene.

The young Queen has spent a night with her lover. He has gone and she is alone. She wanders about the room they have occupied, stroking here a brocaded hanging, there a velvet cushion or the arm of a chair, exploring the texture of silk and the grain of wood. Presently she leans the lovely curve of her cheek against the post of the great canopied bed. She is a woman sentient and aware, with every faculty sharpened by that experience we know as love. It is as if she feels the sap flowing again in dead wood, glass sharp in silk and satin, metal threading brocade – as if she sees her servitors for the first time as human beings, each with his own private joys and woes. Today she is alive and aware as never before, the pulse of universal life throbbing in every particle of her being.

A night of Gilbert awakened Queen Christina as interpreted by Greta Garbo. Nights of Goering did as much for me.

During the long months of the Battle of London I, too, was conscious of curiously heightened perception. Moments of such incongruous beauty remain with me that even now they make me catch my breath. Immortality is the core of beauty, and here and there I saw glimpses of the indestructible in the midst of destruction. There was a wild cherry tree laden with blossom in the terrible wastes of West Ham; there was the dome of St. Paul's, dove-crowned, against the murky aftermath of the Great Fire Raid; there were the water-fowl on the Serpentine in the shadow of daily mounting wreckage dumps; and, even on the branch of a willow overhanging 'Duck Island', there were the initials of a boy carved on the eve of war – the initials of my son. People, too, came sharply into focus – Sheila, sword-thin in the khaki scabbard of her M.T.C. uniform – slouched exhausted by a fire in her flat, but with the mischief and the nonsense still bright in her heavy-lidded eyes, and her incorrigible mother, Mrs. Hooper, relating her incredible experiences as a 'Nippy' at the Soldiers' Club and relishing the near misses that always failed to pick off her flat. I sensed the tingling fear in the conscientious finger-tips of the girl who shampooed my hair, hurrying to be done and home before 'it' began; and I could feel the strain behind the smile on the face of the librarian who gave me my books. 'It makes one scratchy under the collar, sleeping under the kitchen table every night!' And of course, there was the tonic of an evening spent at Bax's with our host blandly oblivious of the fluctuating pandemonium without and within, for his flexible house continued to absorb and disgorge a steady procession of friends and acquaintances temporarily dislodged by the blitz. The little maid, Olive, pale but spry, never ceased to serve well-cooked dinners on, and not under, the elegantly appointed table, and Bax's only cause for apology was the reminiscent rumble of the food-lift in sympathy with the constant sounds of collapsing masonry that came to our ears from Paddington and the Edgware Road. We played some astonishingly bad bridge those evenings to the music of a radio-gramophone. Rachmaninoff and Wagner raised their melodious voices against those of Mars, and I was reminded of the 'Lacquer Lady' and that memorable description of the Burmese Palace murders when the King commanded that music play day and night to drown the sounds of slaughter.

I learned something of the mental and physical manifestations of fear in those days. I found my thoughts difficult to assemble when the sirens wailed, my palms grew clammy, my tummy hollow, and, though far from bored, monstrous yawns pressed up from the caverns within me. In buses and tubes I speculated upon the extent of personal fear my fellow-passengers suffered, and respected them for the turnip faces they put on it. At dusk it seemed to me that the traffic panted at the lights like a live thing running before the hounds of night, and I can recall the deep surge of relief relaxing every tense nerve of my body when the 'electric woman' stopped her little car in King Street in the violent bloom of approaching darkness. 'Well, there you are. See you tomorrow... No, we won't stay now. Better not be caught in it – the sirens are going.'

As the great doors of Number Eleven closed behind me I'd sigh and pause for a moment before going upstairs. See you to-morrow? Maybe. One never knew these days.

CHAPTER SIXTEEN

APRIL FOOL

AFTER all, that Christmas of 1940, there was no leave for the *Manchester*, Corney's young wife had to wait for her pink silk counterpane and her headache cure, and I had to content myself with a quiet Christmas dinner with my brother. We went to Quaglino's and drank the too familiar toast of 'Absent Friends' in champagne. His thoughts were with his wife and little son in South Africa, and mine were shared between the house under the mountain and a grey cruiser I knew not where.

In fact, she was on patrol among the ice-floes of Greenland.

Strange how peaceful that Christmas was! For forty-eight hours the Prince of Peace reigned in London and the voice of Wailing Winnie was still.

It was not until the middle of January that Bertie came on leave to Number Eleven – real leave, a whole month; for the ship was in dockyard hands at Newcastle-on-Tyne for a much-needed refit and would not be ready for sea again for several weeks. The nightly blitz still continued, but it had eased down, and we both enjoyed ourselves to the full.

One day Bertie said: 'When the *Manchester* goes back to sea in the spring she'll go out into the oceans – that's my guess – and there'll be few, if any, chances of my seeing you. So it would be a good idea for you to go back to South Africa if we can arrange it.'

My heart leapt like a porpoise. To go home! Yet, already in 1941, it had become extremely difficult to get a sea-passage without very good reasons, and air travel was even more impossible. Still, there might be a chance, and, for the matter of that, I knew that a convoy would be leaving soon, because Norman was standing by to sail, and so was Jack Borrett, who had been appointed in command of a cruiser in the South Atlantic.

So, with Colin's help, I applied for repatriation at South Africa House, and was told that I would hear further in due course. It might be weeks or months before I could hope to get a ship.

We finished our leave in London with a wild party at the Café de Paris. It was in the nature of a farewell to Norman and Jack as well as to Bertie, with whom I proposed to go to Newcastle for a short while before he sailed. Joy Borrett was spending Jack's last few days in England with him at Number Eleven; she had never taken partings easily, and her vivid imagination did not help her to face the prospect of her husband back at sea. So the atmosphere was one of ephemeral gaiety strung thin as a spider's web over the quivering leaves of anguish.

'Snake Hips' Johnson and his negro band of fifty strong played the tunes of the day with their war-time nostalgia of present love and laughter – tunes that sang of yesterday, but said no word about tomorrow or 'love you *forever*'. There was no tomorrow, no forever, for those who sang them; there was only yesterday and now, there were 'These Foolish Things' and 'That Lovely Week-end', and, of course, 'A Nightingale Sang in Berkeley Square'! Soon after midnight some cute little cabaret girls, dressed as jockeys, pranced in on wooden rocking-horses, and, when they tethered their beasts, they danced for us. And afterwards the men rode the wooden chargers in a race for a magnum of champagne. We became hilarious over tall Norman's efforts to adapt his long limbs to the squat shape of his toy steed.

On the way home that other nightly turn by Herman Goering was in full swing, and the little silver stars of God blinked blindly behind the dazzling Satanic constellations of death.

A week later 'Snake Hips' and his negro players were plastered all over the walls of the Café de Paris, for the bomb that swished through the ceiling landed in the very centre of the band, and, for many of the dancers that night, and the cute little cabaret girls with wooden horses, there was nothing any more – not even the song of that West End nightingale.

Early in March I went with Bertie to Newcastle in the Jaguar, and, on the way north, we stopped at Heswall in Cheshire to spend a few days with my mother-in-law, who had just recovered from pneumonia.

There is no doubt about it, my mother-in-law possessed many qualities in common with the women of ancient Greece. With an Athenian worship of culture and good manners she combined a Spartan outlook on physical or emotional weakness.

She looked small and pinched, but she firmly dismissed the matter of her illness and declared herself in the best of health. Her rheumatism made it extremely difficult for her to move, but she countered this handicap by starting early. When it was near luncheon she invariably asked me the time.

'Twelve minutes to one, Mother.'

'Then Bertie must go and wash his hands, as everybody here is very punctual for meals.'

With that she began to stow her crochet away in her big work-bag, and I helped her to her feet.

'Would you like to go to your room, Mum?'

'No, thank you, love. I'm quite ready.' And she would begin inexorably to make her painful journey to the door of the upstairs hotel lounge and across the landing and down the stairs. I would escort her, and Bertie would rejoin the convoy outside the dining-room at precisely the same moment as the head waitress hammered a large brass gong.

Mother was right about the other guests. Moved by hunger, punctuality, or the fear of finding everything 'off' if they were late, they trooped in to meals almost before the last echo had died away. Our progress was slow and stately, with Mother bowing to right and left in queenly fashion; sometimes she'd pause at a table to say, 'Bertie, you must have a word with Mrs. Pigeon; she was very kind to me while I was ill.' Such were the only references she ever made to her recent severe illness. We took her out for little drives to see cronies of her own generation – we assessed her age to be about eighty, for she would never reveal it to her children – and she returned from these jaunts tired but in good heart.

'Poor Cousin Janet,' she'd say. 'She's really grown very old – and so hard of hearing. What an affliction!' Or 'Old Mrs. Snooks appears to have lost all coherence of thought, but then she always was a muddle-headed creature.'

When she observed her contemporaries, deaf and woolly-witted, her voice gained in confidence and her eye kindled with a mischievous sense of superiority. My mother-in-law had her faculties under excellent control, and her dry sharp wit, often spiced with a dash of malice, was ever present in her conversation or in her brief characteristic letters to her son or to me, written in an angular foreign hand that never wavered. She was in many ways a very remarkable person, but, as a daughter-in-law, I was particularly struck by one aspect of her astonishing self-mastery. Never once had she been known to interfere in our married life, and never, whatever her private opinion, had she permitted herself to question any of the difficult and heartbreaking decisions it had been our lot to take as best we might. I believe that when her only grandson was sent to South Africa in 1940 she was profoundly shocked and upset, but she acknowledged my letter with a short note commending my common sense, though she added: 'I was surprised, of course, as surprised as if I had heard that the King and Queen were leaving the country . . .' That was the nearest she ever came to reproaching me for anything. And how well I understood her sentiment!

The other guests in the hotel treated her with deference, and one or two even ventured to show her a certain tentative affection, for she could be extremely gracious and charming when the mood took her. She was crocheting a little rug for me then, a Joseph's wrap of many colours, and they were beautifully blended in a pattern to enchant the eye, 'a garden pattern' she called it.

'We learned to think of music in terms of colour in my youth,' she said. 'Notes have colours, and colours are music. This should be a pretty song – a pastoral song.'

When the time came for her to bid her son good-bye, she did so in the upstairs lounge with the great windows looking out to sea. One or two people glanced up curiously from their books or papers as she rose painfully to her feet to embrace him.

'God bless you, my son,' she said in her soft voice, and she was smiling.

We left her standing there in her black dress, with the lavender shawl over her shoulders. and her fingers, swollen with rheumatism, still clasping her crochet. Would they meet again, these two, the son going back to the ocean and the war, and the old lady drawing near the end of the journey?

Snow lay deep in Newcastle when we arrived, but its glittering face was sullied by the Tyneside mobile smoke-machines belching forth oily smoke to hide the river and the dockyard from the indefatigable raiders.

I went on board with Bertie one day, but the ship was as ugly and helpless as a woman in the throes of a permanent wave, and the noise of the riveters was deafening.

I met Shrapnel, the Fighting French dog, again, but he was in disgrace, having recently been demoted from Able Dog, First Class, to Ordinary Dog. Shrapnel had, in fact, been court-martialled at Scapa Flow with all solemnity in the dinner hour in the presence of the ship's company. The charges were three.

> 'For that he, Shrapnel, Able Dog First Class, Official Number 752, belonging to His Majesty's Ship *Manchester*, then being a dog subject to the Navel Discipline Act, did, on the 8th day of January, 1941, fight with Leading Cat Leslie, Official Number 571, also of His Majesty's Ship *Manchester* on the Island of Flotta at Scapa Flow . . .
>
> '. . . did improperly leave His Majesty's Ship *Manchester*, thereby remaining absent without leave forty-eight hours.
>
> '. . . was guilty of an act to the prejudice of good order and naval discipline in returning on board the said ship with his coat in a filthy and neglected condition, thereby bringing discredit on His Majesty's canine uniform . . .'

When the findings of the court and Shrapnel's papers were submitted to the Admiral for confirmation Lancelot Holland saw fit to burst into verse, and the Captain, on reading the stanzas, informed his superior officer that his poem on the subject of Dog Shrapnel's misdoings must, with all respect, be described as 'doggerel'.

I also made the acquaintance of Spartivento, one of Leslie's kittens born during the battle of that name. He was an attractive little fellow with his mother's silky black coat and rather dashing personality, and he had been assigned by Coxswain Corney to the Captain's quarters as the Captain's personal kitten and mouse-catcher designate.

While the *Manchester* got ready for sea, terrible things were happening in Europe. Hitler attacked the Balkans, overran Yugoslavia and advanced into Greece from the north. It was clear that our brave ally was doomed.

One afternoon at the end of March I received great news. A letter from South Africa House informed me that a passage to Cape Town would be available some time after 15th April, and that I must stand by to sail any day after that date. I had reason to believe that after April no further sea-passages would be granted to private people, and I was exultant, for my intense desire to see my mother and my son had grown as the possibility materialized.

When Bertie returned to the hotel I showed him the letter. He read it slowly, then he plugged his pipe in silence and began to pace up and down our bedroom. Was he worrying about the Battle of the Atlantic? Yet he had long since agreed to my taking that chance.

I said uncertainly, 'Is anything wrong?'

'I don't know,' he answered. 'I really don't know what you'll think. You see, I've had a letter too.'

He handed me a small sheet of cream Admiralty note-paper.

> 'I have much pleasure in informing you that the First Lord has approved your appointment to *Excellent* in command, in charge of the Gunnery School, Portsmouth, to date 15th June, 1941.'

It was signed by the Naval Secretary to the First Sea Lord.

I said at last: 'A shore job in June ... but that's wonderful ... Portsmouth, Whaley ... It's a marvellous job, isn't it?'

'It's a very good one. We could take a house somewhere outside the port.'

'For how long would it be?'

'Eighteen months, or thereabouts.'

Eighteen months ... and the sea-routes closing steadily on civilians. By then it might be too late. Here, in my communication from South Africa House, might lie my last chance of getting home for who could tell how long ...

'Will you go to sea in the *Manchester* till June?'

'Yes.'

Presently he added, with a glance at the two open letters on the table, 'What will you do about this?'

The old conflict of husband against child churned me up as never before. I believed that my little schoolboy needed one of us as the baby and the child Piet had never done. For once I was unsure of the answer to his question.

'You must give me time,' I said. 'Perhaps I could go home and come back . . .'

'If you go, it will be for the duration. That's the understanding with South Africa House.'

'I must check up on it.'

He was right. When I returned to London I was told that if I sailed there could no question of returning. It would be 'for the duration'.

I wired Bertie. 'Have decided to stay but want Piet back. Do you agree?'

'Delighted,' he replied.

It was 1st April – April Fool's day.

CHAPTER SEVENTEEN

BLITZ AND 'BISMARCK'

As soon as I received Bertie's wire I wrote to Mother to ask her to make some arrangement to send Piet back to England. Less than three weeks later I wrote again, reversing the decision. This second letter was written from Marion's bungalow. It speaks for itself, and I think would be of more interest to the reader than a cool-headed description of an experience already dimmed by time.

C/o Marion,
Ruislip.
Saturday, 19th April, 1941.

'My darlingest Mummy,

'When you read this letter I want you to realize that I am "well and happy" and that all the horrors I am about to describe are over and done with. But I think, since they *have* happened and no bones broken (as far as I am concerned!), you would probably like to know everything and get the thrill of a first-hand account of the biggest raid on London of the war, and of our neighbourhood in particular.

'Incidentally, I am writing in pencil because my fountain-pen is no more and Marion appears to have no pens in her bungalow. Like Peter, she is not a letter-writer and never has the implements for writing at hand . . .

'*Later. 9.45 p.m. In Marion's shelter-cabin.*

'The enemy raiders are throbbing overhead, and we are snugly settled in Marion's shelter – she, I and the dog. Also, she has produced a fountain-pen. I tried to buy one today, but there isn't one to be had. Like most things, fountain-pens are "unobtainable".

'Well, to go back to Wednesday night's great "Reprisal Raid". The Alert sounded during the nine o'clock news, and it was obvious from the start that the raid was to be severe . . .

'Cyril, the comical little porter-butler-and-everything-else, was on duty, and part of his job was fire-watching, which means being on the roof to see that incendiary bombs are put out before they start fires. And, as we heard stuff whistling and whooshing down, Cyril would dart up on to the roof and then come back and tell us the news.

'Whooosh! Up goes Cyril to see. Comes back.

' "That was the Piccadilly Hotel! There's a gas-main blazing, a huge white light just near the Ritz!" Wheee! "That was Victoria! A blaze started there—" and so on.

'At midnight there was a lull and I determined to go to bed and get some sleep. I put my siren suit over my pyjamas and tucked up with a book. But it was no good. The blast from A.A. fire kept billowing the curtains in, and bombs seemed to be raining down. I got up and went to the first floor landing, where I found Miss Hillsom, the manageress, Miss Seager, her assistant, the two very old maids, Kate and Ella, and Miss Hutton, who was the only resident in at the time. She is very lame and moves with difficulty. The cook, who is seventy and crippled and stone deaf, was in her room along the landing, in bed.

'Presently John and Sheila, who had been out to dinner, came in with another naval officer called "Cocky". They had not been in two minutes before there was a long screaming noise and every window in the place blew in. John said, "I'm going out to see what's happened!" And Sheila yelled to me to stop him. I might as well have tried to stop an express train. As he and Cocky got out there was another whoosh!

and Sheila and I lay flat. One must. We were holding hands, and her hands were soaking wet, and she just moaned, "Oh, God, John – John is outside!"

'Then it landed. The building reeled. Cyril shouted, "Christie's is on fire!" Christie's shared a wall with Number Eleven. The place was an inferno in no time. Cookie, who had been blown out of bed into our midst, swooned, and I dosed her with whisky from my flat. The two old maids, cowering like squaws under their eiderdowns, were stunned.

' "Are you all right, Ella and Kate!" I asked.

' "Yes, thank you," they said very politely.

'Miss Hillsom's only thought was to dash upstairs and rescue her canary, which she did. Sheila was out of her mind with anxiety for John, but he and Cocky came and told us that the whole neighbourhood was ablaze. "You must get what you can from your flat now," said John. "In half an hour it will be too late."

'It was lighter than day on the stairs, flames leaping outside the empty window sockets, and the crackle and glare was terrific. We seized armfuls of clothes and rushed down and dumped them on the pavement, and all the time the raiders were drumming overhead and the bombs were dropping. We hurled whole drawers out of the windows, and a lot of my underwear was left hanging from the broken frames like Chinese banners!

'I put my jewels, my Chanel 5 and my diary into a zip bag and carried my tailor-mades over my arm. In the hall again we found the others sitting blankly. The crackling of the fire was deafening.

'John said, "Everybody must get out of here!"

' "They can't," said Miss Hillsom. "Cook and Miss Hutton are too lame to move."

'John said, his arms full of stuff: "It's madness to stay here. This place is a target – oh God!"

'A ghastly whistling, and Sheila said, "Joy-Joy, this is it. We three will go together." And we clung while it came. I thought, "Piet will come back and find no mother" and I knew, in that moment, that, if I got through, he must not be allowed to risk returning and perhaps finding neither of us. *There was time to think all that because they take ages coming down* – like the Polish pilot who baled out and told Bertie that he "slept a while on his parachute"! But it wasn't "our bomb", it was Christie's again. Well, that settled it. John and Cocky practically carried Cookie out of the building, and I said "Miss Hutton, will you let me help you?" She was very sweet and sensible, and she just said, "I'd be very grateful."

'So we got under way and made for a shelter a few hundred yards away. She must have suffered agony. The sky was a canopy of sparks floating down on us and there were billows of smoke behind the leaping flames. The heat was terrific and you couldn't look at Christie's. When everybody was in the shelter we dashed out again to get our cars that were in a garage in Duke Street just round the corner. And a brave taxi-man had turned up and was piling our stuff into his taxi. John and Cocky never stopped working, directing us all, never losing their heads and taking complete charge. At last a beautiful rosy dawn broke – pale pink clouds all mixed up with the flames, and then the All Clear sounded as the raiders made for home.

'We drove our salved belongings to Mrs. Hooper's flat in Bayswater, passing craters and wreckage everywhere. She had spent most of the night waiting for her last moment to come. She was horrified when she saw our condition. We were black as niggers and our eyes were too inflamed to see! Anyway, we scrubbed ourselves, and had coffee and sausages and went to bed. It was six a.m. At nine I was up, cabling you to keep Piet, and at nine-thirty was back in King Street to see if there was anything more to be rescued from the flat. Sheila's side of the building was burnt to a cinder . . . my flat was in existence in part, but flooded, and what was left in it had already been looted.

'Poor Cyril and Frederick (his opposite number) and Ella and Kate and old Cookie have lost everything. Norman will be interested to know that Cyril was a hero throughout, never even thinking of himself. In fact, he became so suicidal in his zeal that we had to restrain him from rushing into the fire to bring things like china jerries! The last I saw of him was going away in a taxi. In it he had a few belongings and an old hat box – his total salvage. He peered out and grinned and said, "Good-bye, Mrs. Packer. I'm off to Berlin to see 'Itler about this 'ere!" Pointing to King Street. At that I wept for the first and only time. Eleven King Street was Cyril and Frederick's home for thirty years. It was their whole life. Yet

Cyril, up to the very last, could have his little joke. Norman, who knows these folk, will feel as I do about them.

'In Berlin they are rejoicing and the flags are in the streets to celebrate the great Reprisal Raid. In London the dead are being dragged from under the wreckage. Thousands of them.

'Norman will be interested to know that the Overseas, just round the corner, was burnt out with terrible casualties.

'Well, it's over now. But that night I knew what Hitler meant to do to this island, and realized that all my sentiments about Piet must stand aside. He cannot come back to such things, and perhaps even worse.

'When I went to our Post Office to tell them to send letters on to the Bank, it wasn't there. Just an enormous crater. A man was digging in it. I said, "Where has the Post Office gone?" (meaning "Where is it operating from?") and he laughed and said, "Down the 'ole, Miss."

'The tragedy of my poor neighbourhood was dreadful – like the City. And *this* is civilization!

'Darling, this letter is not for Piet as I don't want him alarmed and upset about my safety. I will send him my own account of the story from a less dramatic angle. Anyway, I will be back in Bedford soon, very safe in every way!

'Am dead tired and must get some sleep.

'Ever your loving JOY.'

Thus, on Saturday, 19th April, I wrote about Wednesday, 16th, while Marion's little concrete cabin shuddered, for London was receiving further punishment on a grand scale.

Ever afterwards those two dates have been known to Londoners simply as 'The Wednesday' and 'The Saturday'.

A few days later I received an anxious letter from Bertie:

'I heard with horror on the wireless that London had had her worst raid of the war and a famous auctioneer's is burnt out! Can it be Christie's? Are you safe? . . .'

After the events recorded in the foregoing letter my kind friends in Bedford once again offered me sanctuary, and I remained with 'Uncle Noel' and 'Aunt Mabel' until Bertie left the *Manchester* some six weeks later.

De Parys Avenue, in its bright garment of bud and young leaf, was disfigured, and so was the long garden behind Uncle Noel's house. The lawn was like a schoolboy's hair, shaggy and unkempt, in constant need of cutting, and Joy and I mowed it of an evening and clipped the borders round the rose-beds with Aunt Mabel's big shears. For, while Jack was in the South Atlantic, Joy and her daughter divided their time between Bedford and Hereford.

When I think back of the Bedford interludes I can smell the summer scent of mown grass and roses, and the aromatic winter fragrance of the quince sticks Uncle Noel used to put on the fire. I can see Aunt Mabel making the freshly-ground coffee in the glass percolator after dinner, and then, when her husband retired to his study after the News, she might relax and allow the knitting to fall from her hands, and her fine steel-grey head to nod. Then, perhaps, she lost herself in a dreamland where her prisoner-son was restored to her.

Now, though the prisoner-son is safely home, Uncle Noel is no longer in the house in De Parys Avenue. But, in his study, lined with his books, and warmed by an old-fashioned stove, there dwells the great-hearted spirit of one who combined kindliness with command even in the twilight of his days.

That spring the tragedy of Greece was enacted and, much to our grief, the lovely land, where we had been so happy, was overrun by the Germans.

About this time, too, much to my husband's regret, Vice-Admiral Lancelot Holland left the *Manchester* to take command of the Battle Cruiser Squadron and presently hoisted his flag in H.M.S. *Hood.* So the Captain moved into the Admiral's quarters which he shared with Leslie's small black kitten, Spartivento. He wrote to me:

> 'Corney takes care of Sparti, who is to be your kitten when we are ashore. The little creature follows him all over the ship like a dog. When I commented on this, he said, perfectly seriously, "You have to master 'em early. That's the secret." Just as if he were a lion-tamer!
>
> 'You will be amused to hear that Ordinary Dog Shrapnel is in the news again, this time in the "Sporting and Dramatic". He has been invited to become a member of the Tail-Waggers' Club. He has personality, that dog – quite amazing.
>
> 'Last night the Padre gave one of his "Saturday Night at

Seven" series of interviews with members of the Ships' Company on the broadcaster. So far he has interviewed a jockey, a rat-catcher (known as a rodent operative!), a bagman, a publisher's reader and a Sadler's Wells ballet dancer – all temporary sailors!

'Am reading Stefan Zweig's account of *Scott in the Antarctic* in the original German. Sent me by Mother. It's inspiring, to say the least of it, and his last letter never fails to move me ...'

And then his little cat, the battle-born baby of that hardy 'rodent operative' Leslie, began to ail; and he noted the somewhat monotonous course of Sparti's distemper in the icy zones off the south coast of Greenland.

'20*th May*. Very cold all this week and snowstorms for two days. When will Spring come? Let alone Summer!

'Parachute troops have landed in Crete.

'Cat gave two miaows and was sick on my carpet.'

'21st *May*. Nothing to report.

'21.20. Cat piddled on my slippers.

'21.25. Cat gave two miaows and was sick on my carpet.'

Two days later there was no longer any question of 'nothing to report'. The *Manchester* and her accompanying cruisers were ordered to the north-east to cut off the *Bismarck* and the *Prince Eugen*, which had broken out of the Denmark Strait and were being remorselessly shadowed by the *Norfolk* and *Suffolk*, with rain and snow-storms reducing visibility to a minimum. Should the great battleship shake off her pursuers it was probable that she would double back, in which case the *Manchester* and the force with her were standing by to intercept her retreat.

On Empire Day, 24th May, a signal was handed to the Captain which caused him grave concern.

It said that the *Hood* had blown up at 06.15 that morning, and added:

'For Captain. This message has been twice received and very carefully deciphered.'

On the 26th May he wrote:

'Am still very sad because I hear there are only three survivors from *Hood*, so my kind clever cheerful Holland must be considered lost with his staff whom we all liked so well.

'This seems bathos. But things close at hand affect one, too. Little Sparti, my black kitten, born and bred and reared in *Manchester*, had got sicker and weaker and weaker, and yesterday afternoon he could only just walk. He lay in his box in my sea-cabin and could still give a feeble movement of his tail when I rubbed him under the ear.

'As I went on to the bridge to shift berth Corney, whom Sparti adored and followed like a dog, came up to me with a face as long as a sea-boot. "Cat's dead", he said, and went away.

'Sparti was wrapped in gay bunting, and, like a sailor should be, he was committed to the deep. The cold green waters of Hvaalfjord have him safe. He was such a cheerful little chap and I miss him very much.'

By 26th May the *Bismarck* was still being relentlessly shadowed.

'No further reports', noted the Captain of the *Manchester*, who was plotting the action with every signal that came in. 'It must be getting dark there. Destroyers should be able to shadow during the night. Pray God we get her down and avenge the *Hood*!'

On 27th May, at four a.m. he wrote: 'The situation is developing beautifully and classically', and at eleven a.m.:

'Have just broadcast to the Ship's Company: "*Bismarck* is being heavily engaged by *K.G.V.* and *Rodney*. *Dorsetshire* has been ordered to torpedo the *Bismarck* at close range." A cheer came up the hatches from between decks.

'This must be the end. Thank the Lord *Hood* is avenged and fifty per cent of Hitler's battle-fleet destroyed!'

But while the German battleship was meeting her doom in the grey Atlantic, far away in the sunny Mediterranean a little battle-worn anti-aircraft cruiser was assisting in the final evacuation from Crete. That 'green' ship's company, which had put to sea less than two years ago – many of them for the first time – had become a seasoned crew habituated to bitter and arduous service. Now, for days and nights they had been without rest, and both men and officers were desperately in need of sleep. So it was with infinite relief that the *Calcutta* put into Alexandria for forty-eight hours' respite. But she was immediately ordered out again on one more mission. There was no one else to send. The men might be dead on their feet, but they must go back to sea, back into battle.

One more mission.

Off the coast of Crete she was attacked by an enemy force of dive-bombers. The weary guns' crews were still at their posts when the blue Aegean closed over her, and the last that was seen of the *Lucky Calcutta* was a white cockatoo flying like a battle ensign from the masthead.

CHAPTER EIGHTEEN

'EXCELLENT'

MY husband left the *Manchester* where he had joined her – in Scapa Flow – on 5th June, 1941, and ten days later he took over command of H.M.S. *Excellent*, the Naval Gunnery School.

We rented a house just outside the little town of Fareham, five miles along the coast from Portsmouth, which was still receiving the attention of the *Luftwaffe*.

It was quite a small house with no particular character, but it had a lovely garden, and, when we moved in, the roses were in full bloom and the borders were a blue mist of larkspur and delphinium. To me, 'Fareham Croft' was a 'happy ship'. We had many interesting guests to stay with us while we were there, but their presence was less important to me than the absence of one I had come to know too well – that faceless Stranger whose name was Fear. For a whole year I forgot about the Stranger, and there was no Grey Mistress to lure my man into dangerous deeps. There was H.M.S. *Excellent*, of course, but a ship that is not a ship can never tear the heart out of a man like a 'steel box with the lid down'. Nor can a ship's company of some two thousand men, constantly changing in the course of gunnery training, exact the emotion called forth by a close community of several hundred who 'literally sink or swim together, pass through the same dangers and share their pleasures'.

Whaley, when first I knew it just after our marriage, was a small green oasis cut off from the wastes of North End, Portsmouth, by a creek spanned by a drawbridge. Its reputation in the Service was one of ferocious discipline and efficiency, and nobody, except the aged pensioners who tended the beautiful gardens, the aviary and the zoo, ever moved across the lawns and wide parade ground except at the double – though, on Sunday mornings, after church, the officers had been wont to relax and saunter with their families down to the pleasances and pits wherein dramatic birds and beasts were confined.

Now, in 1941, there were still the birds, but the more savage beasts had disappeared, and, in their place, was a tablet on a windy bluff marking a communal grave. It was inscribed:

'A.R.P.
SHOT ON 27th MAY 1940
In Memory of
Lionesses .. .. .. Lorna and Topsy
Polar Bears .. .. Nicholas and Barbara
Sun Bears .. .. .. Henry and Alice
These animals were put down 17th May
1940 in preparation for German Air Raids.
Their loss was keenly felt by the whole
Whale Island community.'

Their erstwhile quarters now housed rabbits for the pot, and after church we admired the pigs bred on the island for the same utilitarian purpose; then, as it drew near Christmas time, a flock of geese grazed on the football field, and there was one with four stripes on his sleeve who was known as 'the Captain's goose'. Like ghouls we watched the Captain's goose plump up. Turkeys were scarce that year, and one exotic officer had peacock for his Christmas dinner.

The German air raids, anticipated by the demise of the big animals, made their ugly gashes in the buildings and pitted the lawns, one of which was now sown with mangold-wurzels. The Captain, pointing this out to a party of American visitors, said to one very solemn and humourless Senator: 'This crop here will presently be converted into milk – enough to supply all our Messes.'

The Senator was impressed. 'What process do you use?' he asked.

'We feed it into one end of a cow and draw it off the other,' said the Captain. The Senator was not amused.

Coming, as I did, from the Battle of London, I was accustomed to the sight of ruination, yet, even so, the destruction in Portsmouth and Southsea tore my heart. Whole districts were razed to ground level, and already the purple fireweed and strange anonymous creepers had taken possession of the principal shopping streets, where once I had wheeled my son in his pram.

It was curiously light and airy, and one had the feeling that all this had gone, not yesterday, but in some long ago convulsion.

For all that – or because of it – the spirit of Nelson had never been stronger in the port. The *Victory* had come into her own again. The stalwart wooden ship in her dry dock dominated land and sea. She seemed enchanted – sacrosanct. Even when a high explosive bomb burst in the bottom of the dock under the bluff of her bows, blowing a great hole in her six-foot hull of British oak, the old *Victory* just gave a shrug and a wriggle and settled down once more to her century-old defiance of 'the battle and the breeze'.

When Admiralty House had been partly demolished in 1940 she had been freshly painted and recommissioned for the use of the Commander-in-Chief, Vice-Admiral Sir William James, who had decided to use Nelson's day cabin in the stern gallery as his office.

Admiral 'Bubbles' James is well known outside, as well as inside, the Navy, not only as a naval officer, but as a writer of distinction. He is the grandson of the painter, Sir John Millais, who once used the angelic-featured child as his model for the dreamy-eyed, curly-headed little bubble-blower, who adorned hoardings all over the world when the picture was commercialized to advertise a certain high-grade soap.

That same curly head, now nobly white, with a profile eagle-keen, was once more the subject for an artist's genius. The sculptor, Frank Dobson, was making a bust of Admiral James for the Navy, and, while engaged on the work, he was the guest of the Wardroom Mess on board H.M.S. *Excellent*, where he was also modelling the head of a sailor – the typical sailor, if there is such a man – young, lean and bony, with scanning-the-horizon eyes.

I often saw Frank Dobson on the island, a slight dishevelled figure in sandals, red-bearded and narrow-featured, shy as a fox, the meagre progenitor of those elephantine female nudes who for a while disposed their massive limbs upon the greensward of Battersea Park in an Open-air Exhibition of Sculpture.

He liked Whale Island. 'Nobody bothers me,' he said.

That is one of the qualities naval officers learn in their close communal life. To leave others in peace. Frank Dobson was grateful for it.

My household at 'Fareham Croft' hinged upon the remarkable personality of Able Seaman Foot, who was attached to the Captain's quarters at Whaley, but who came to help us in the house and garden.

This gaunt old sailor belonged to the school that believes that 'there is nothing the Navy cannot do'. During his Service career he had learned the art of barbering, and when in due course he left the Navy (many years before World War Two) he set up a one-man business in a provincial town in the south of England, where he had become a much loved and respected figure. Loyalty and honesty were inscribed all over his craggy countenance; you had only to see Foot to know that he was a man who understood the meaning of the word 'duty', and I often saw him scratch his old-fashioned head in puzzlement at the notions of the new young conscripts.

'Puts themselves first,' he said. And to him this seemed odd, since, to all right-thinking men, the Navy must surely come first.

When the war called him back into the Service a succession of substitutes took his place in the barber's shop, which his wife was determined to keep going in his absence. His clients, on the whole, bore bravely with the rude ministrations of his understudies, but there were days when there was an anxious look in the old sailor's eyes, and then we knew that 'the wife 'll 'ave to give the new man notice' and that the life of that one-man business was again in jeopardy.

Able Seaman Foot was not only a sailor, a gardener and a gentleman's hairdresser, but he was also a natural born cook, a fact which we discovered when our Wren cook went sick at a vital moment.

A King in exile had done us the honour of deciding to spend a week-end at 'Fareham Croft', incognito, and, a few days before the event, our cook was taken ill. Foot offered to deputize till a substitute could be found, and so excellent did his cooking prove that I asked him to help us out during the royal visit. He complied with great modesty but without turning a hair, and from then on he remained in supreme command of our kitchen.

We also had a young steward for training – a crooner with a guitar and a temperament – and from time to time we were given a hand by a lively girl called Ruby or a dreamer called Dora. Ruby was hoping to be released from the Wrens to marry an agricultural worker and set up house, while Dora believed that 'a girl's best friend is her bicycle' – a point of view I became less and less able to endorse as time went by. The steward's name was Ash, and Foot, with no malice and more acumen than he knew, invariably referred to the lad as 'Hash'.

Corney, now promoted to Petty Officer, came often and mowed the long lawns between the herbaceous borders. Foot watched the big man with admiration, and remarked that Petty Officer Corney didn't know his own strength. He was particularly impressed with this blind spot on the part of the Isle of Wight man when together they sawed up the limbs of a dead tree in the grounds. When Foot and 'Hash' lay panting with exhaustion Corney was just getting into his stride.

I had grave difficulties in the town over marketing, for the newcomer has no privileges. It is the old customer who very naturally gets the last sausage or that one small kidney, or the bottle of salad cream from under the counter, and, when I came back empty-handed and shame-faced, Foot would smile mournfully and shake his head.

'You'll get no change out of them merchants in the Outside World,' he'd say. In his estimation there was the Navy and there was the Outside World. He had experienced both. In the Navy people helped each other, in the Outside World it was each for himself. Yet, by virtue of some strange alchemy within himself, his own home-town was never included in that place of outer darkness to which he so constantly referred, and when he returned from week-end leave there was invariably a chicken or a rabbit concealed in his seaman's blue and white handkerchief, whence he conjured his prize with his modest yet triumphant smile and presented it to me with 'the wife's compliments'.

Where Foot dwelt there also goodwill prevailed.

We were in Portsmouth for eighteen months.

During that time Russia was attacked by Germany, and by the end of the summer of 1941 the German advance had swept deep into the heart of the Soviet. December brought the criminal attack on Pearl Harbour, America's entry into the war, and Japan's lightning occupation of key points in the Far East and the Pacific. Early in 1942 we suffered the loss of two magnificent warships, the *Repulse* and the *Prince of Wales*, and, for the first time, the voice of Churchill faltered as he told the House of this disaster. In the Desert our armies were thrown back, and in North Africa the French were unco-operative. Goebbels noted in his diary:

> *20th February*, 1942. Although England is fighting against tremendous obstacles, it cannot be said that morale is low. The English people are used to hard blows, and, to a certain extent, the way they take them compels admiration. In times of crisis the British Government profits by the pig-headedness of the national character . . .'

So, by and large, we were passing through an evil stage of a war that had brought us little in the way of success to offset the long recital of 'sad and heavy tidings'.

Yet, for me, that eighteen months at Portsmouth was a time of happiness, for, so great a factor is personal content, that it can survive a holocaust. It is the butterfly in the cannon's mouth.

It was a time of laughter, too, which amounted upon occasion to hilarity. The complete ban on private petrol had convinced me that I must, for the first time in my life, become acquainted with one of those steel monsters Dora regarded as 'a girl's best friend'. My husband viewed the decision with scepticism, but, on his firmly established principle of never damping an intelligent display of initiative, he agreed to lend me his co-operation. Thus he summoned his henchmen, Coxswain Corney and Ordinary Seaman White, his elderly cabin-hand, a bashful and inarticulate sailor by no means lacking in naive humour.

'Corney,' he said. 'Madam is going to learn to ride a bicycle, and, as it is always the Captain's Coxswain who teaches the Captain's wife to ride a bicycle, I suggest you make enquiries in the Isle of Wight and see if you can buy a second-hand machine.'

'Aye, aye, Sir,' said Corney, with his gleaming smile. 'And where will Madam learn, Sir?'

The Captain indicated the expanse of green lawn outside the window of his cabin. 'Out there. Then she won't hurt herself – much. I leave it all to you and White.'

Corney found a very tall antediluvian contrivance in the Isle of Wight, where the unobtainable can often be discovered, and this he purchased for two pounds by the judicious exercise of his experience of bargaining in the Indian shops of Gibraltar. Thereafter he and Ordinary Seaman White set me upon my antique nag, and, helpless with respectful mirth and panting with exertion, they pushed me round the football fields while the dazed faces of young officers peered out of windows, gleefully awaiting the inevitable climax when, deprived of seamanlike support, I rode with deadly accuracy, albeit at an angle of forty-five degrees, straight into the goal-post, the only object within hundreds of yards.

I also practised on the lawns at 'Fareham Croft', when Foot and 'Hash' took over from Corney and White, while Ruby or Dora demonstrated, with dash and abandon, the art of travelling on two wheels. When they mounted my island steed, however, they expressed themselves baffled. It was not of their generation.

'It's a camel, not a bike,' said Ruby candidly. 'You'll never do any fancy riding on this!'

Yet she was wrong.

One evening Humphrey Bradbourne, serving in H.M.S. *Collingwood*, the nearby training establishment, came to dinner with us, and, when he asked me how the cycling lessons were progressing, I boldly informed him that I could now ride alone and unaided. He demanded a demonstration. We went out into the moonlight, where I rode my vintage machine round the lawns for his benefit. So palsied were the wobblings of my wheels, so wild and uncanny the deviations of my course, that he was reduced thereby to a state verging on hysteria. In private life he had been a theatrical agent, and he now said, when his powers of speech were restored: 'I'd offer you a fortune for that turn! It's the funniest thing I've ever seen. You'd bring the house down!'

Nevertheless, came the proud day when, festooned with a bag of golf clubs, I rode five miles to Lee Golf Course, passing the gates of H.M.S. *Collingwood* with a disdainful smile of triumph. Beside me, similarly accoutred, rode the Captain of Whale Island, crouching over a bicycle that had belonged to his son at the age of ten. I don't know what Humphrey would have offered for the double turn!

CHAPTER NINETEEN

FILM STARS AND FRANKEE

THE blitzed King's Theatre at Southsea had now been redecorated and was reopened in great style in the spring of 1942 with three performances on three consecutive nights.

My trick-cyclist act was not on the programme, so the audience had to make do with Tommy Handley on the first night. What a ball of fire that 'little twirp' turned out to be! Pompey devoured him. On the second night Robert Montgomery graced the occasion with his presence, and at the third performance Noel Coward took part. We put up both Robert Montgomery and Noel Coward at 'Fareham Croft'.

The film star, now a Lieutenant-Commander in the United States Navy, was then Assistant Naval Attaché to the American Embassy in London, But, even before his country had entered the war, he had driven an American Red Cross ambulance in the Battle of France, while his wife had done war work in England. When she finally returned to America she had taken with her a number of English children, including those of the actor-playwright, Emlyn Williams. When I asked him if his wife was also a film star, he replied, 'God forbid!'

Robert Montgomery was as unassuming as he was attractive, and he had considerable dignity. His extraordinarily light grey eyes were those of an intellectual. He talked vividly of his experiences in France, and it was easily apparent that he was a person of character with a strain of idealism running through the cynical realism inseparable from his association with the silver screen.

The lively Ruby put out his white pyjamas with an unholy thrill such as her honest agricultural lover could never hope to wring from her, and my young friends in the neighbourhood haunted our doorstep with improbable messages in the hope of a twinkle from the star.

After the performance at the King's, Robert Montgomery appeared in person on the stage and made a short speech. We were amazed to find that he was extremely nervous beforehand, but he spoke with great sincerity and simplicity to a naval audience whose warm-hearted reception of himself had moved him deeply.

'I see your port, and how terribly it has suffered,' he said. 'And I see all of you here tonight, full of courage and joy of life . . . patching up your theatre and carrying on, keeping up your hearts and your spirits, and I can only tell you that I love you for it . . .'

Montgomery meant what he said. He himself had given up the treasure trove of Hollywood to enter the war long before his country was our ally. He had done it because he had imagination and humanity, and, as he spoke to that Pompey audience, they sensed those qualities in him, and they knew that it was the man, rather than the actor, who was with them that night.

They were not white, but purple, pyjamas Wren Ruby put out next night for Noel Coward. But, though his taste in night attire might be different from that of the film star – who had, incidentally, played Noel's part in the film of 'Private Lives' – he, too, was prey to an agony of nerves as we drove through the moon-bleached ruins of Southsea to the theatre.

'Anyone would be with a voice like mine,' he said. 'When I open my trap I never have the faintest idea what noise is coming out!'

But the songs – gay, cynical, brave and haunting – delighted an audience who had seen so many Coward plays tried out at the King's before going to the West End.

Then he recited Clemence Dane's inspiring poem, 'Trafalgar Day 1940' written when a bomb crashed on to the altar at St. Paul's, waking the spirit of the little sailor so dear to the heart of Portsmouth.

> '. . . waves of thunder and dust
> broke against Nelson's tomb.
> Even then, "they" were not afraid.
> They were proud of all they had done.

Nobody warned them they did not know, none said:
"It is dangerous to wake the dead."

'For the Nelson spirit slips easily out of a shroud
into the morning, down Ludgate Hill,
slenderly moves in the crowd
hither and thither at will,
slipping between the people going to work,
stiff from a shelter bed.
Then somebody says: "What flashed
like stars in a row, breast high?"
A girl says: "A man passed by
with a pinned up sleeve." '

The waves told the *Victory* that Nelson was awake – that he was everywhere and, as we listened, it seemed to us that he moved among us – 'our little man with the smile and the four-fold star!'

'Nelson is everywhere.
He stands in the wreck of the road.
He sweeps up the broken glass.
He fights with fire and despair.
He feels for, he fingers your heart
till it beats in your breast like a drum.
This is the Nelson touch.
Pass on the news–he's awake!
Nelson expects so much.
Nelson expects that this day
each man, for the Island's sake,
will do his duty . . .'

The words felt for and fingered our hearts – Noel got his audience that night with the Nelson touch.

Noel was, at that time, inflamed with the inspiration for his naval film, 'In Which We Serve', and, over that week-end which he spent with us, he talked about it with burning enthusiasm – almost exaltation. It was to be the life-story of a ship from birth to death – of a destroyer-leader like H.M.S. *Kelly*, which had been commanded by his close personal friend, Mountbatten.

'The ship . . . what she means to the men who sail in her—'
'And the women who don't,' I added.

He had been waiting for that. He made me tell him how a wife feels about her husband's Grey Mistress – the rival she cannot fight and comes to love. And, when I had done, he put his arms impulsively round me.

'Thank you,' he said. 'You've given me something tonight!' He wanted his story to be true, authentic down to the last detail, and now a woman – a Captain's wife – had contributed a sentiment he fully understood, one he could so well interpret through the sincere and lovely personality of Celia Johnston.

'What will you call your film?' we asked.

He answered without hesitation.

' "In Which We Serve" . . . the Fleet in which we serve . . .' And then, with the trained memory of the actor, he recited the prayer from which the words were taken – a prayer used every day in the Royal Navy, and one which embodies both the duties and the aspirations of those who serve in it.

Till the night he spoke them I had never realized the beauty and import of the words.

> 'O Eternal Lord God, who alone spreadest out the heavens, and rulest the raging of the sea; who has compassed the waters with bounds until day and night come to an end; Be pleased to receive into Thy Almighty and most gracious protection the persons of us Thy servants, and the Fleet in which we serve. Preserve us from the dangers of the sea, and from the violence of the enemy; that we may be a safeguard unto our most gracious Sovereign Lord, King George, and his Dominions, and a security for such as pass on the seas upon their lawful occasions; that the inhabitants of our Island may in peace and quietness serve Thee our God; and that we may return in safety to enjoy the blessings of the land, with the fruits of our labours, and with a thankful remembrance of Thy mercies, to praise and glorify Thy Holy Name; through Jesus Christ our Lord. Amen.'

After church on Whale Island on Sunday morning, Noel and Harold Skyrme, the Commander, drove down to the *Victory* to call on the Commander-in-Chief. They did not go by car, for Harold was a keen horseman who had revived an ancient custom allowing the Commander of the Island two horses for use in the course of his duties. Thus Noel and Harold saved petrol and drove through the port on a cold grey morning in the Commander's little trap behind a spanking pony, much to the gratification of the populace, who had got wind of the expedition and who turned out to cheer it.

Noel came down to Portsmouth again later in the year, bringing with him Ronald Neame, David Lean and Gladys Calthrop, the brilliant team who were working with him on this picture so close to his heart.

Gladys wore the neat khaki uniform of the M.T.C. which well matched her strong personality. She had a deep voice and whatever she said was worth saying, for she used words with feminine imagination but masculine economy. She was designing the sets for the home scenes, and her observation was intense, exploring down into the roots of character and psychology for every tiny detail that might be found in the home of a Mrs. Corney or a Mrs. Captain.

Noel and his team were taken to watch the guns' crews training in the North-East Battery, and into the Dome, where a pom-pom was mounted to shoot down shadow dive-bombers, and on to a dummy bridge to see a night action. He was promised the loan of guns' crews from H.M.S. *Excellent* for his battle shots, and he told us that the Army had granted him officers and men from the Coldstream Guards for the scenes depicting the return from Dunkirk.

As the film neared completion we went to Denham to see the final shots taken. Many of those Guardsmen had been through the reality of the scenes they played beside the model destroyer disembarking them in the long shed of the studio.

'Remember . . . you are *very* tired!' came the amplified voice of the producer. '*You are very tired!*'

We attended the *premiere* at the Gaumont and found ourselves part of a largely naval and highly critical audience. Along our row we saw the beautiful fine drawn profile of Lady Louis Mountbatten, sitting between her husband and the First Sea Lord, Admiral Sir Dudley Pound. When the Captain's wife receives the telegram saying that her husband is safe we heard a sob catch in her throat; she had known more than one such poignant moment. When the film was over someone asked Admiral Pound his opinion of it.

He said: 'It must be very good to make the First Sea Lord cry!'

It was indeed a very good film. I doubt if Noel will ever make a better. For he made that picture with all that was best in him, as a heart-felt tribute to the Service he loves and admires and to which he believes that England owes the lion's share of her greatness.

We now acquired a cat – a small skinny black and white kitten with a deep rumbling purr. 'Frankee-the-Yankee' was no ordinary kitten; he was the natural successor of little Sparti, who had found a watery grave.

The *Manchester* had met with a 'spot of trouble' after Bertie had left her, and she had sailed to the United States to be patched up, for, at that time, many of our damaged warships were refitting in American dockyards as part of Lease-Lend.

The ship's company of H.M.S. *Manchester* lost its heart wholesale to Philadelphia, including Able Dog Shrapnel and Leading Cat Leslie. Shrapnel, with Latin instability, had his head completely turned by the attention he received and applied to be seconded to the U.S. Navy. So the *Manchester* lost her Fighting French dog. Leslie, however, contented herself with participating in Lease-Lend in her own small way, and, on the way home, in mid-Atlantic, the cruiser's complement was enriched by the addition of a new American family of rodent operatives.

This family was nearly two months old when the ship put into Portsmouth before sailing for the Mediterranean.

Coxswain Corney went on board with the Captain of Whale Island to see old friends, and, among his former shipmates, he found Leslie with her latest infants. Corney well knew my weakness for kittens, so he persuaded someone – Leslie perhaps – to allow him to adopt one of the trans-Atlantic children. So that evening Bertie came home bearing a very small black kitten on his shoulder. It had a splash of white across half the tip of its nose, and this gave it an odd lop-sided, almost hare-lip appearance, while its whiskers were even then out of all proportion to its size.

We called the new arrival Franklin D., but he soon became known as 'Frankee-the-Yankee'. Frankee had peculiarities. When we set him down on the summer-sweet springy turf among the rose-beds and the bright herbaceous borders, he said 'Miaow' in a very small surprised voice and lifted up his paws in turn, shaking them as if they were wet or ticklish, and stepping very high and gingerly.

Bertie laughed. 'He's never walked on anything except a hard deck, and he just can't fathom this grass at all!'

He couldn't fathom flowers either, or shrubs, or trees, and he went round very cautiously and suspiciously exploring the new jungle in which he found himself. He never became a tree-climber or showed the slightest interest in birds, for sea-birds are too big for seafaring cats to bother about, but he was death on all rodents and insects. Never was there such an active hunter as Frankee, and he had a method. He was a veritable Red Queen out of 'Alice in Wonderland'. It was one bite and 'Off with their heads!' A family of voles in the garden was ruthlessly executed, and Frankee brought in the tiny decapitated corpses and laid them at Foot's feet in the kitchen. He was immensely independent and hunted his own meat ration. He preferred his milk out of a tin. He was, in fact, an interesting example of the inherited influence of environment – his mother's environment and his own early training, for Leslie was an indefatigable trainer of kittens. To Frankee 'Fareham Croft' was a sort of elaborate and stationary ship.

Meanwhile his mother sailed once again with her cruiser. Then one day Bertie brought me *The Times* and showed me an official Admiralty communiqué issued at 2.30 p.m. on 14th August, 1942:

> 'Naval operations have been taking place in the Western and Central Mediterranean during the past few days. . . . These operations have resulted in supplies and reinforcements reaching the fortress of Malta despite very heavy enemy concentrations designed to prevent their passage . . . packs of U-boats, large numbers of torpedo-carrying and dive-bombing aircraft and strong forces of E-boats operating in the central narrows.
>
> 'The enemy force never came within range of our ships and turned back on being attacked by aircraft. . . .
>
> 'The Board of Admiralty regrets to announce that the cruiser H.M.S. *Manchester*, Captain H. Drew, D.S.C., R.N., was damaged and subsequently sank. Many survivors have been picked up and it is probable that others have reached the Tunisian Coast, since the position in which the ship sank was close to the Coast. Next of kin will be informed as soon as possible . . .'

Among those who reached the Tunisian Coast was our friend, the Commander, 'Johnny' Hammersley Johnstone, who was taken prisoner by the Vichy French, and who remained in captivity under deplorable conditions until our invasion of North Africa in November. Then, in company with many others, he was repatriated and arrived in Portsmouth wearing a strange conglomeration of borrowed clothes and carrying only a little Red Cross bag of comforts and a pair of flannel pyjamas he had washed for himself on board. His Irish wife, Clare, who had been in a fever of anxiety about her 'Jonathon' for many weeks, came to meet him, and we put them up for a day or two.

When we had heard the story of the sinking of the *Manchester* in full detail, we asked Johnny what had become of Leslie the cat. And, while American Frankee purred on his lap, he told us.

When the ship was sinking a young sailor tried to rescue Leslie, but the little black cat, for the first and only time in her life, scratched and bit at a well-meaning shipmate. In that tragic hour some instinct beyond human comprehension bound her to the only home she knew, and she refused absolutely to be saved.

The last that was seen of her was a sinewy black tail, very erect, disappearing into the boiler-room where she had always taken refuge in time of danger and where she had given birth to her innumerable offspring. The young sailor, sick at heart, had to leave her to her fate.

CHAPTER TWENTY

'PACK AND FOLLOW' AND FAREWELLS

It was at 'Fareham Croft' that I continued writing the biography, 'Pack and Follow', which I had begun during the long noisy nights of the London blitz. It was eventually published in 1945 after many vicissitudes and during a period when there was an acute shortage of paper.

Why does one write an autobiography? Why am I writing 'Grey Mistress' now?

Partly because of the power of suggestion and partly because

I suffer from that chronic rash, the itch to write. The itch is a relentless fever, always there, under the skin of its victim, ready to flare up on the smallest encouragement, vulnerable to heat and cold and every chance contact. Life is the material upon which it feeds, flesh and blood is its nourishment. Sometimes it withdraws, the better to spring out again with redoubled vigour. It is never dead, only dormant.

The writing itch is my bane, and the conditions of my life have fostered it. How often have you heard someone say – perhaps with a sigh – 'I could write a book about my life'? They could, too – if they happened to be plagued with pen-fever. For every life is a tale worth the telling. Children, who are so wise in their innocence, know that truth is more fascinating than fiction. 'Tell about when you were little', they beg. And, when you have told, they say, wide-eyed and wondering, 'That's a *true* story, isn't it?' If you shake your head they feel cheated. Your gold was counterfeit. They want a *true* story. So do we all. If we go to a cinema to see the shadow-play of the life and times of some historical character we resent the twists put in or taken out by Hollywood or Denham. Deep down we know that Life is a better spinner of yarns than he who 'adapts it' to the screen.

So there it was. Nature had put the wanderlust in my heels, the itch to write between finger and thumb, the love of life and the love of a sailor in my heart – and a book had to come of it. I didn't realize it, though, till my friends kept saying, 'Why don't you write a book about all the places and people you know, and the things you've done? You should, you must!' That was where the power of suggestion came in. If a thing is said often enough it takes effect, hence propaganda and advertising. So I began to think about writing 'Pack and Follow', just as 'Grey Mistress' was conceived years later when so many kind readers wrote to me and said, 'Tell us more of this tale that is life; tell us about your war!'

At first glance the writing of an autobiography would appear easy.

There is your material in the attic of memory; select what you want, dust it, and set it out. Then it becomes a curiously prickly business, an impertinence dominated by the first person singular; so that the writer, in a fit of self-consciousness, strives to subdue that ebullient ego and lamentably suffocates it altogether. My husband said as much when I showed him my first tentative beginnings.

'No. It's no good like this. Be yourself. Express your own ideas and feelings about things, and then it may be worth doing.'

'You mean I must write subjectively – from inside out?'

He smiled. 'I mean exactly what I said.'

He was right. And, once I got started, what fun it was!

Memory danced through the fields of past experience, across the Seven Seas, over the golden spires of Eastern pavilions and among the singing silver southern stars. Such wealth was this! The Stranger and the War were remote when I entered my Kingdom of the Past. There was no need to write for effect, one had only to write for oneself. All this seems simple when one is happy. There was only one present shadow on that happiness – the old familiar ache for the house under the mountain. And that shadow was dispelled as my pencil flew over the pages of my big exercise book. 'Pack and Follow' took me home.

Only once did personal grief touch my life at that time.

Dinkie Bain-Marais had returned to England, and she and Colin had taken a pretty modern cottage in Hertford. We often went to them for week-ends, and, on one of these occasions, she met us on our arrival with the news that Colin was not well. He was suffering from an attack of 'muscular rheumatism', so was keeping in bed.

'But he's very depressed,' she said, with a troubled frown. 'More than he should be, somehow.'

Bertie went in to talk to him, and came to me afterwards with a grave face.

'I don't understand it. Colin gives me the impression that he thinks this is the end. . . . He's the last person to give in about anything. . . . I can't make it out.'

But Colin had seen the 'Angel at the river's brink' and he knew that already the 'darker draught' was being held to his lips. Within the month his widow was returning to her homeland with the ashes of one who had lived his life with simple courage and to the full.

That autumn we heard that my husband had been appointed in command of his old and beloved battleship, H.M.S. *Warspite*.

Twenty-six years earlier, as a young Sub-Lieutenant, he had

served in her in the greatest sea battle of all time, when two hundred and sixty warships of all sorts blazed at one another on 31st May, 1916, in the grey North Sea. That day he saw the terrible spectacle of three British battle-cruisers blow up in a sheet of flame, one after the other, while, in his own ship, the helm jambed and, out of control, she pirouetted crazily towards the German High Seas Fleet, a helpless target for their concentrated fire. Three gun turrets were put out of action and only the fifteen inch guns in A turret, under his command, were still firing. It seemed that nothing could save her. And then suddenly the enemy was seen to turn away as the Grand Fleet, under the command of Admiral Jellicoe, appeared on the horizon and put them to flight.

Jutland has since been claimed as a victory by both sides – the Germans because they darted out of the Heligoland Bight, inflicted severe losses on our Grand Fleet, and darted back; and we because we retained our mastery of the seas. The fact is that the German High Seas Fleet was penned in for the rest of the war, and only emerged again to surrender at Scapa Flow.

The wounded *Warspite* limped into Rosyth after Jutland with the gory glamour of one who has borne the brunt of the battle.

It was therefore with a strange feeling of fatalism that I heard that my husband had been appointed to this ship in which, as a young officer, he had been blooded.

'Of all ships the *Warspite*!' he said, thrilled and half incredulous. 'That I should get my old *Warspite*!'

In the dusk of the garden Frankee-the-Yankee walked delicately beneath a frosty mauve forest of Michaelmas daisies and sniffed at the bright faces of dahlias. The autumn smell of a bonfire, damped down for the night to betray no glow, was still in the air, and ground mists swirled ghostly on the grass. In the lanes the beech leaves were scattered guinea-gold, and the bracken was bleached blond in the woods. It was the season of nostalgia, of farewell to summer, of winds with the fore-taste of winter on their breath. It was the sad season.

He was to join the *Warspite* in the South Atlantic early in 1943, and he was to sail in the cruiser *Sussex*.

'What are we going to do about you?' he said. 'We must get you to South Africa somehow.'

There was no Colin to help me; and Sydney Waterson had been replaced by Deneys Reitz as High Commissioner, already a sick man, destined, like his friend Colin, to die in exile from the land he loved above all else in the world.

I went to see him at South Africa House. Deneys Reitz was old then, a grizzled sturdy Boer with light, intensely blue eyes constantly seeking the window of his great office. He had fought England remorselessly and to the bitter end in his time, and had suffered exile in Madagascar rather than take the oath of allegiance to the conqueror. Then Smuts, his old comrade and leader, had persuaded him to come back – to stop and start again. Now Deneys Reitz's son had lost an eye and a hand fighting for England.

'Like him up there!' he said, with a glance at the little Admiral, high and solitary on his column above the Square.

I asked him if there was any chance of getting a passage home. He shook his head. 'It's too late now. Only people in war jobs can get priorities. I'm sorry . . . I know how you feel.'

I left him with a heavy heart. He was standing at the window staring at the pigeons in Trafalgar Square, envying them their freedom. He loved birds. As Minister of Lands in South Africa, he had made the Union into a great bird sanctuary. Birds, animals, the veld, these were his life. Game and Bushmen ran free in the great Reserves of South Africa, while he, who had helped them to that freedom, was caged in a shining London office. Deneys Reitz came of a race of hunters and pioneers, and now, as I closed the door of his room, I knew that I had closed it upon a homesickness as devouring as my own. For the High Commissioner, the magnificent building in Trafalgar Square was the House of Exile, and, like Paul Kruger, the old President of the Boer Republic, he was fated to end his days far from home.

Wherever we turned we met the same reply. Sea transport for civilians was at an end. Two years ago I had had my chance. Now it was too late.

'You must get a war job that will take you to South Africa,' said Bertie grimly.

'Yes. But what?'

'God knows.'

We left 'Fareham Croft' in the New Year and said good-bye to Able Seaman Foot, who had gone back to the Captain's quarters at H.M.S. *Excellent*, and to Frankee-the-Yankee, who had found a home with the family of an old shipmate from the

Manchester. Ruby had married her agricultural worker. 'Hash' had gone to sea, and Dora and her bicycle had returned to the Mess at Whale Island.

We had a room in London on the eighth floor overlooking the Green Park, and Bertie was standing by to sail. Coxswain Corney was to sail with him, and his young wife was daily expecting her first baby. We hoped it would arrive in time for him to see it. The *Sussex* was in Scapa Flow and they were to join her there.

So the night came when we met Corney at the barrier of number thirteen platform on Euston Station. The big Isle of Wight man mustered his smile, but it did not come so easily. The baby was still on the way.

It was a foggy night and the long troop-train was packed to capacity. As it steamed out I heard the songs and the laughter of the lads leaning out of the windows in the brave high spirits of youth going to war. A voice called out 'Cheer up, Blondie!' and then the train was out of sight. I felt someone take my arm.

'Come on,' she said. 'They've gone. The train's gone.'

She was no better than she should be, but I shall never forget the way she marched me down the platform, her arm through mine. 'It's horrible to say good-bye,' she said; but cheerfully, as if she had said it too often to care any more. 'Here's a taxi. Will you be all right?'

'Thank you . . .'

'That's O.K. They'll be back before long. Don't you worry! Cheerio!'

The scent she used smelt of vanilla, and in the foggy night I did not see her face. But I know that she was kind.

In the Isle of Wight, a few hours later, young Mrs. Corney gave birth to a son – a fine boy, the living image of his dad.

CHAPTER TWENTY-ONE

SICKNESS OF MY ERA

IN the three months that followed I found it hard to count my blessings. Yet I had many. Friends and somewhere to live, and, when there was sun, it poured into my little room overlooking the park. There were always birds on my parapet, sparrows and pigeons waiting to share my breakfast; and, on bitter cold days, the gulls flew in from the river, whirling and crying among the naked trees.

I found it impossible to go on with 'Pack and Follow'. The first half was already in the hands of my agent, who hoped to find a publisher on the strength of the work as far as it had gone, but, for the moment, the heart had died in me, and with it the impulse to write. I was sick and out of condition like a pining animal, and my sickness was that of my generation and my era.

All over the world men and women were in exile, cut off by war from their loved ones, eating out their hearts for home.

Three years had passed since the spring day in 1940 when I said, as my little schoolboy clasped his arms round my neck for the last time, 'I'll be following you, Piet . . .'

Three years had stolen that little boy. What changes had they wrought? What had they done to my son? He was sixteen now. At the end of this year he would write his matriculation and leave school . . . oh, no, he would not fail the exam.! *He* was not going to stay on at school, he was going to get into the war just as soon as he could! In South Africa there was no need to wait for your age-group, you only needed seventeen years to your credit, and your parents' permission to join up. Before Christmas he would be in it. . . . At sea? In the air? In the Army?

Then, too, my mother had achieved her three-score-and-ten – that human signpost pointing the last lap of the earthly journey.

With Bertie's departure my intense longing to see these two

again had welled up from the depths of my being in a flood of anguish. The dyke, formed by his presence, had crumbled, and aching waves of nostalgia beat upon my heart and flowed into my throat and behind my eyes, till it seemed to me that I was a pitcher filled to the brim with tears. A touch, a jolt, and some were spilt.

When you are happy you can get away with things; when you don't care a fig whether you win or lose, you win. But when you cry within yourself '*I am poured out like water, and all my bones are out of joint*' you are no good to yourself, or to anybody else.

I knew that to be so, just as I knew that a human being with a grievance is the most boring of all crashing bores. So I groped for my drowned gaiety, and tried to wear that drenched and limp commodity like a cloak whenever I sought some particular war job I hoped might lead me home. I shed my pride when I pinned that garment of sodden gaiety round my throat outside the office of Mr. So-and-So or Captain Such-and-Such, who might be able to get a journalist out to Cape Town in publicity or propaganda.

For a natural-born journalist, I am a remarkably poor liar, and when Mr. So-and-So flung at me, 'You're South African, of course, so I suppose you've strong personal reasons for wanting to work there?' I answered frankly.

'Very strong reasons . . . but apart from that, don't you see that my being South African is a help! I know the country and the people – how they think and feel—'

But Mr. So-and-So had lost interest; and, as I left his office, that insecure bedraggled cloak of short-lived brightness slipped from my shoulders, and I knew that I must get away – quickly – before the shameful manifestation of my sickness got the better of me. For I do not weep prettily.

If you want a job, it's one thing. If you want to ride a job, it's another. My 'strong personal reasons' for wishing to work in South Africa told against me. Very well, then, I must extend my scope and prove my usefulness. Past experience of journalism wasn't good enough; I must have present experience to justify my claims, and it must be wider than mere writing. How to set about it?

Under the acute unhappiness of that time something within me – something stern and almost frightening – was strengthening hourly, and there were times when, as I did my face, I found myself saying aloud to that mirrored image which grew daily thinner and harder, 'I *will* get home! I'll do it somehow!' And then I'd turn away abruptly, for I was half afraid of this strange woman with the iron in her soul, who looked back at me with such cold determination in eyes that had once been warm and quick with life and fun.

It was important to get to work before the industrial machine sucked me into its maw, destroying what faint hopes I might cherish of making my way to Cape Town.

I began gently, with an article here and there for papers published in South Africa, but with a London agency. And presently I found that the Ministry of Information could use features with propaganda value. And here opportunity lent a hand, as she so often will for those who believe in her, seek her, and recognize her when they find her.

The Head of the South African Section, a brilliant and lively girl from Pretoria, said to me one day:

'Have you ever broadcast? Because the B.B.C. could use talks to South Africa and you could do them.'

'I could learn,' I said.

That was how I came to be given an introduction to John Grenfell Williams, the Director of the African Section of the B.B.C.

Grenfell Williams was not at all what you might imagine a B.B.C. official to be, for he was neither impersonal nor pedantic. He was, in fact, blessed with a charming 'fireside' manner, and a reassuring humorous smile. He wanted a series of talks on 'Aspects of Life in England' under war conditions, and he gave me a useful line on script-writing. 'Pretend you're talking to someone you know – quite naturally . . .'

Someone I knew? That was easy! Presently he put me into the hands of an attractive prematurely white-haired young woman, who introduced me to the little 'sock' that linked me with my country six thousand miles away.

She said, 'Don't be so polite! Politeness is *soo refeened* on the air . . . and you have to be careful with wistfulness. It becomes terribly *mournful* over the microphone! There, now, smile when you say that bit! People can *hear* a smile, it's warm and pleasant, and they find themselves smiling in sympathy as they listen.'

She made a record of my talk and played it back to me to illustrate her meaning.

'Yes,' she said, laughing. 'I knew you'd be surprised! Nobody ever recognizes their own voice, and women are always amazed at how high their tone is pitched. You need to drop it a bit when you talk on the air, and brace up the sentiments so you don't sound tired or dismal.'

When 'In Which We Serve' was about to make its debut in South Africa I told the inside story of Noel and the picture and the part played by the Navy and the Guards. 'Leslie the Sea-going Cat' made a broadcast on her own. I took Springboks, with the orange flash on their shoulders, round ruined London and showed them her wounds, where the fireweed flourished, and the shining reservoirs in basements excavated by German bombs. Not again did the City intend to be caught at low tide with an insufficient length of piping to bring the life-saving water from the river! And then we went back to a studio in Number Two Hundred Oxford Street, and, in an interview with me, the boys 'talked home' to their folks quite simply and spontaneously and with only the skeleton of a script.

Away, on the East Coast of Africa in the *Warspite*, the Captain wrote in his log:

> *Good Friday – St. George's Day – Shakespeare's birthday*. Heard Joy last night interviewing two S. African sailors – quite good, but not enough Joy!
>
> *Joy*. 'I hear sailors have a girl in every port.'
>
> *Sailor*. 'Well, I can't say. I haven't been to every port!'

So, in one way and another, I began to learn a little about radio technique.

I worked feverishly, to try to prove – by producing results – that I could be an asset in any organization dealing with propaganda, little dreaming how improbably far those seemingly futile efforts were one day to lead me.

Meanwhile the weeks slipped away and turned into months, and, in the park, the young leaves thrust up silvery velvet knots on the bare austerity of wintry branches. Soon Piet would be having his Easter holidays; already, whatever happened, it was too late for me to hope to share them with him. I used to watch those buds as if they were the sands in an hour-glass. If I'm still here when the trees are in leaf I'll die! I thought.

A friend helped me at this time – a man with a strong strain of mysticism in his nature – one who could draw power from the Infinite because he was blessed with faith.

He said: 'If you want something enough, it *has* to happen. Only believe that, and one day, when you least expect it, you will take up that telephone and hear that you are going home.'

Wanting is having – if the wanting is great enough. That was his creed. And one night I saw a curious, even terrifying, 'Monkey's Paw' example of its operation.

Jack Borrett had returned from the South Atlantic, and had been reappointed this time to a shore job in Algiers. He was standing by to fly there in a bomber. Joy was frantic at losing him so soon again.

'If only something could happen to stop him going—' she tempted fate. 'Something *must* stop him!'

But the last day came, and the last evening. It seemed there could be no eleventh hour reprieve. I had a few of our mutual friends in to drinks, including Philip Rhodes and his Bambi-girl, and the man who was something of a mystic.

Jack had been down to an Air Ministry establishment in the country for altitude tests, and was very amusing about it.

'They put you in a decompression chamber,' he said, 'to see if you can stand flying at an altitude of twenty thousand feet in a bomb-rack. If you explode they know you can't and another chap has to fill your job.'

'Well, they haven't tested you to destruction, old boy,' said Philip. 'You look ready for anything.'

Joy, white-faced, and cold to her finger-tips, disagreed.

'I think he looks awful. Bright red.'

'What time do you leave, Jacko?' someone asked.

'Six a.m.'

Joy looked as if she might faint.

Soon after midnight I was awakened by my telephone bell.

Joy said, 'Jack has collapsed. I've managed to get a doctor, who's with him now. Heaven knows what's happened! But one thing is sure – he can't go tomorrow.'

The altitude tests had strained Jack's heart and caused a haemorrhage in one ear, and he was gravely ill for many weeks, so that someone else had to go to Algiers. When he was well, he was sent to Northern Ireland in charge of an important naval base, and his wife and children went with him.

At almost the same time Philip Rhodes was appointed Naval Attaché in Dublin, and presently married his beautiful brown-eyed Bambi-girl.

Meanwhile Bertie had touched at Cape Town and spent a few hours in the house under the mountain. 'You would hardly know this fine young stripling as our little Piet . . .' he wrote in a letter giving me all the news I craved. He added that people liked my London broadcasts, and that, as a result of these, I might be 'asked for' to work in radio and writing in South Africa, in which case there was a chance of a passage through South Africa House. Hope, that hardy plant that had flowered and died so often of late, put forth its blossoms again.

Two days later the telephone rang.

'This is Dash – South Africa House. Can you come and see me immediately?'

My heart sprang into my throat and the room whirled. I could scarcely speak. Could it be that my friend's prophecy was really coming true!

'Mr. Dash . . . have you good news for me?'

'Come and see me,' he repeated tersely. But he had not denied it.

'I'll be with you in ten minutes.'

I put down the receiver and leaned against the wall. Tears of relief streamed down my face as I said aloud, 'Thank God, oh, thank God!'

Mr. Dash said, a quarter of an hour later: 'Can you leave London tomorrow?'

'Of course.'

'It's not much of a ship,' he said, 'and I advise you not to go.'

Poor man. It was his unhappy task to inform next of kin when casualties were known. Those in the last convoy had been heavy. Hitler's U-boat packs were taking terrible toll of Atlantic shipping.

'I'd go in a canoe.'

'Well, if you're so determined, sign this, and state your next of kin.'

I was told what train to catch and given luggage labels. They had numbers on them. No port of embarkation was mentioned, and the ship was nameless.

'You'll need to give notice at your hotel, but don't say anything to your friends – no farewell parties. Just disappear.'

In Liverpool I telephoned my sister-in-law, Dorothy, and she and her husband drove me to Heswall to see my mother-in-law. We did not tell her that I was leaving England and, as she bade me good-bye, she said: 'When Bertie comes on leave I'll see you both again. God bless you, love.'

I was glad of her blessing. I needed it. Moreover, I felt that we would never meet again.

Next morning, down at the Mersey Docks, I stood in a long queue, waiting to pass through the Customs and Security barriers. There was a thin grey mizzle, and I observed my fellow travellers with interest. Belgian Legionaries, a few sailors and airmen, a sprinkling of civilians and a surprising number of women, two of them with infants in their arms. Presently, deprived of ration books and gas-masks, we filed on board a small camouflaged cargo-boat.

By noon the sun had broken through, and we sailed in one of the biggest convoys ever to leave Liverpool. About a hundred ships of all sorts took up their positions in lines ahead, and in the middle lines – the precious heart of the convoy – were the great troopships bound for North Africa, carrying the men needed for the invasion of Sicily. Destroyers and corvettes raced up and down the lines and a Sunderland flying-boat circled overhead.

The creak of timber and throb of engines, the wheeling gulls, the smell of tar and rope, the damp salty air . . . these things were music in my ears and frankincense and myrrh in my nostrils. The iron that had entered my soul in the months of waiting, hoping and fearing, transforming a human being into a hard painful knot of concentrated will-power, melted away and left me soft and warm again, a woman of flesh and blood.

A girl in spectacles stood beside me at the rail. We lay out in the bay; there was no one to see us off. Behind her glasses her eyes gleamed with the spirit of adventure. This war promised her excitement, after all – travel, romance maybe . . . she was going to Egypt, in some Government job. Anything could happen in Egypt! She had never been to sea before, and it seemed to her rather brave and wonderful to make her first voyage in the Battle of the Atlantic.

'Are you nervous?' she asked.

'No,' I said. 'Are you?'

'I don't know . . . my family certainly is!'

'They needn't be. Nothing can go wrong with us now.'

'You seem very confident.' Then she peered at me with eager short-sighted eyes that were, at the same time, curiously penetrating. 'I believe you have a hunch about this trip,' she said, smiling at me. 'There's something about you . . . well, you just *look* as if nothing could go wrong! Where are you going to anyway?'

I smiled back into her face, whipped pink by the freshening breeze, with strands of fair hair, sun-bright, blowing across her thick-lensed glasses.

'I'm going home.'

CHAPTER TWENTY-TWO

CITY ON THE SEA

Two days before I had sailed a Government White Paper had been issued on Sea Transport and extracts were printed in the Press. So I had learned with interest that if I should find myself in an open boat in shark-infested waters I need not worry when a hungry man-eater rubbed himself against the boat, he would not be attempting to capsize it but would be innocently scratching his sea-lice like a dog with fleas using the underneath of a bed as a back-scraper. But if any member of our company should announce his intention of stepping into the local for a Lager he must be restrained, for in the case of delirious ship-wrecked mariners 'into the pub' generally meant 'out of the boat'.

Our first night at sea we were assembled in the lounge aft and the Captain gave us a brief talk.

Passengers must co-operate with the officers and crew. It was most important to observe black-out regulations. One selfish cigarette smoked on deck after nightfall might endanger the entire convoy. Ladies should wear slacks, if they had them, and, as in the blitz, a small emergency bag should be kept ready packed and always at hand. Life-belts must be carried always and everywhere. Water would be rationed, for there was no knowing how long we might be at sea before putting into port. Volunteers were needed to take a turn at submarine watch – two hours at a stretch. That was all, thank you.

Our ship, originally constructed to take a dozen passengers, was carrying a hundred and twenty-five, so we were closely packed, six to a normal two-berth cabin. My companions were the spectacled girl and her friend in the British Council bound for Egypt and romance, a medical missionary on her way to Central Africa, a distinguished lady with considerable experience of Abyssinia, and an adventurous Scottish woman doctor who were on their way to Addis Ababa to help the Emperor to organize the social and medical welfare of his country. The distinguished lady also had with her on board an Abyssinian aide-de-camp, who shared a cabin with two Jesuit priests and a man possessed of a devil. This devil travelled with us all the way to South Africa, for our crowded conditions compelled us to share him with his victim, who spoke to him shrilly at meals and often addressed him in loud dramatic tones in the lounge, crying, 'Don't shoot, you fool! I tell you I'm not a spy!'

While the Jesuits seemed powerless to exorcize the fiend from their cabin, he who was possessed had little difficulty in turning out the likeable Abyssinian. He complained to the Captain that the colour-bar could not be ignored, and presently the fortunate African found himself the only person on board with a cabin to himself. Even so, this charming and modest intellectual could hardly have enjoyed the voyage, during which his patroness was deeply and perpetually concerned about the kind of reception he might expect to receive in South African hotels. She often appealed to me for the reassurance I was unable to give her. Meanwhile the little black gentleman sat apart from the rest of us and contemplated his narrow hands with sorrowful eyes as if he longed to draw off the funereal gloves with which nature had provided him. He wore his skin like a garment of sackcloth and ashes, and shared with his erstwhile fiend-ridden cabin-mate the tragedy of a private daily martyrdom.

The greater part of our complement was composed of Belgian Legionaries *en route* for the Congo. At night they sang French soldier-songs in deep resonant voices or took the girls to see the phosphorus on the water. There was also a leather-faced French elephant hunter who varied the chase by stalking an attractive young missionary round the deck with what success I would not venture to suggest.

A Brains' Trust was organized, but the only question and answer I recall was 'Is there really a place where elephants go to die – the Graveyard of Ivory?'

Leatherface, the hunter, told us that African legend credited such a tale, but that common sense would indicate a more plausible theory. Elephants, in their periodical migrations in search of water or grazing – if one could apply such a term to the meals of mastodons – often had to traverse deep ravines and wide rivers, and it might well be that the older beasts, worn down by the centuries and knowing themselves unable to trek on, simply remained on the river's brink to die, while the young and lusty members of the herd travelled on to the promised land.

But, if the Graveyard of Elephants was a place of mystery the Graveyard of Seamen was – according to our young cabin steward – a place of pride. Tattooed on his forearm he wore a ship plunging bows-on into the deep, which was embellished with a scroll inscribed with the words, 'A Sailor's Grave!'

'Morbid, I call it,' said our stewardess, a pretty girl who had seen her last ship go down within ten minutes of being torpedoed and who did not relish a daily reminder of the experience. There was a sombre, almost a sulky courage about the Merchant Navy. Life at sea had little to offer them save danger and sacrifice. The thrill and glamour of the Royal Navy was not for them; they were the hunted, never the hunter, and they all knew that it was only a matter of time before they 'got theirs'. I doubt if it often occurred to them that they were England's life-line, and that without them she must perish.

I took strange pleasure in my solitary hours of submarine watch up in the Oerlikon gun-turret open to the weather and the sky. Especially when they fell in the early morning and only those with duties to perform were about. Then the cold glory of the sunrise on the shifting shoreless ocean filled me with a sense of the infinite, and, while my eyes sought the feathering of the water or the thin rod of a periscope my thoughts were with those who have 'seen the works of the Lord, and His wonders in the deep'.

Owing to our comparative unimportance we were placed on the perilous outer wall of our city on the sea, flanking the heart – the precious troopships. Often a destroyer, with 'a lean and hungry look', ranged up and down our lines, tigerish and menacing, a better friend than foe. And sometimes the vast silence was broken by the blasts of a siren, heralding a grotesque unwieldy dance as ships swung out of line and a hundred white wakes waltzed hither and thither breaking formation to confuse the aim of enemy submarines. Or maybe it was only a practice manoeuvre. We never knew.

Because I was happy my desire to work returned, and I finished 'Pack and Follow'. It was quite like the old days of being a news reporter on the *Daily Express*, for I had to work anywhere regardless of interruptions, such as friendly fellow passengers breathing down my neck as I typed – 'You don't mind if I watch you at work? I'm dying to know what it's all about . . . do read me some of it . . .' – requests which made me feel even hotter than did the tropics, for I have never got over the peculiar inhibition which makes writing appear one of the more reprehensible forms of self-indulgence. The most private spot I could find in our very communal ship was a little landing at the head of the companion leading to the boat deck, and there, on a solid little table, I set up my typewriter. It was immediately outside the Gentlemen's, and my work was punctuated by the sound of slamming doors and rushing water and enlivened by the indignant glances of embarrassed individuals. I didn't care. And presently they grew accustomed to me, as if I had been one of those withered hags who eke out a sunless existence in the white-tiled bowels of the earth.

One evening at sunset we came to the first of our unmarked crossroads, and the greater part of our convoy, with the escorting destroyers, steamed away in the direction of the Mediterranean. The boys on board the great troopships leaned over the rail and waved and cheered, and we waved back, wishing them Godspeed and good luck.

A few days later another line left us heading for South America. Our city on the sea had dwindled to the size of a village in the desert. The last lap of the journey we travelled alone. In time our little ship was destined to meet the fate of the *Manchester* and the *Calcutta* – but not yet. My greatest personal scare that voyage was when I found the mysterious spoor of some beast in our water basin.

'A mouse!' I said.

The Scottish doctor peered down from her upper bunk, her grey plaits tightly braided round her small intellectual head.

'Too big for a mouse,' she said simply.

The lady with a mission to Abyssinia gasped and turned pale.

'Rats!'

'Without a doubt,' diagnosed the Scottish doctor.

I reported the matter to the Chief Steward.

'Can't get rid of the brutes,' he said frankly. 'The ship was fumigated in Liverpool, and we took all the cats off beforehand. The silly idiots went straight back on board and were all gassed. The rats had more sense.'

Like Leslie, ship's cats seem to be cursed with a suicidal form of fidelity – while everybody knows about contemptible rats . . .

I recalled my friend Mrs. Hooper's story of Sheila's ugly nurse whose nose was bitten off by the same ship's rat who had gnawed off a morsel of Mrs. Hooper's own big toe, and I slept fitfully till a small report announced that our rat, on his way to the water-hole, had been caught in the apple-baited trap the Steward had set for him. A few days later, after nearly six weeks at sea, we called at Walvis Bay in South-West Africa, where we collected two indefatigable rodent operatives, a leggy young cat and her grandmother who was far gone in pregnancy. We were on the last lap of our journey.

Meanwhile I was obsessed by some extravagant notion that Bertie and his *Warspite* might be somewhere near. I even dared to hope that once again the laws of probability would be turned topsy-turvy by an indulgent fate and that I might find him in Cape Town to welcome me. But the fates had already been over-generous and now they adjusted the scales. The *Warspite*, originally destined for the Far East, had received new orders and had sailed instead for home and Scapa Flow. Thus one night, South of the Equator, she had actually been within hailing distance of our little ship as we went our way and she hers. My husband had guessed that I might possibly be in the outward bound convoy, but when I went on morning watch the ocean was empty to the horizon and I could not know our paths had crossed that night.

'Darling,' said my mother, taking me in her arms when at last I was safely back in the gabled house under the mountain. 'Bertie has been here. You've missed him by a fortnight.'

She combined a new air of frailty with her habitual astonishing alacrity. Beside her stood a tall lad, sunburnt and muscular with defiant eyes quick to humour, and an arrogant way of carrying his head. He looked down at me – *down!* – and smiled, and his expression was suddenly so shining that my heart turned over. He said in his deep unfamiliar voice:

'This is the greatest thing, Mom – your being here . . .'

I buried my face against his broad shoulder to hide a sick longing for the boy who had reached up to clasp his arms about my neck, the boy who'd whistled out of the corner of his mouth and designed aeroplanes, the boy whose heavy tears had fallen into the scrambled eggs that last night. . . . I looked up at the strange young man who called me Mom – and I believe that in that moment we were both afraid.

PART TWO

CHAPTER TWENTY-THREE

HOME

APART from certain superficial changes 'Tees Lodge' was as I had always known it. It would take a more personal catastrophe than a world war to shake the structure that had grown up over a period of fifty years on the firm foundation of accumulated habit.

Since my father's death, five years earlier, my mother's bereaved affections had sought more and more solace in her immediate family circle. Though she never offered advice uninvited, she liked to follow all our activities. Her children and grandchildren could always be sure of her ear and her full attention. Their problems were hers. 'One has to take an interest' was the way she put it.

As we sat on the stoep in the autumn sunshine, we caught up on the lost years with a word here and a suggestion there. I heard about friends and relations 'Up North', the boys who had been taken prisoner at Tobruk, and the wives left behind. It seemed to me that the only full and satisfying life was that of the teenagers, still at school, like my fifteen-year-old niece, Yasmin, and her younger brother, David. For them the war was still out of focus, and peace not too far off.

'David's no trouble,' said my mother. 'But Cecil finds Yasmin very temperamental and intense. The child's a born artist. You should see her sketches . . . they're so alive.' She found me a few of her grand-daughter's drawings of Piet's old dog, Gyp, now in the twilight of his days. I had to laugh.

'They certainly are! Even poor old Gyppy looks quite full of beans here!'

'She wants to study art in Italy after the war . . .' Mother shook her head, troubled at the notion of her blonde granddaughter's impact on fiery Italians.

'As for David,' she added. 'The dear boy wants to learn the ukulele! It'll be the saxophone next. In my time we danced to the 'Blue Danube", but these days you young people jig and jazz to the most ear-splitting caterwauling—'

We were all 'young' in my mother's eyes, no matter what our ages. I was lumped in with the grandchildren as 'you young people', and so were my sisters-in-law; my brothers were still 'the boys'; and the domestics – Cookie in her sixties and Teena, who was ageless as the Sphinx – were 'the girls' because they were Coloured and dependent upon their employer, who felt a strong sense of responsibility towards them.

'I don't think you need worry much about David and his ukulele,' I said. 'He sounds a real little tough according to Fred. Rugger, boxing, sailing, deep-sea fishing – so why not a ukulele round a camp-fire, by way of a change?'

She laughed and agreed.

'Then Richard—' she continued. 'Will you believe it, Molly writes that that six-year-old child has announced his intention of studying the stars when he grows up, and perhaps being a parson "as a hobby"!'

Norman had been posted to a base hospital in Durban, and his wife and little son were with him there.

But it was Piet, of course, who was best situated for exploiting his grandmother's gentle 'interest' in his pursuits, and I soon discovered that he had persuaded her to finance various ship-building enterprises in the workshop round the corner of the stoep by the oak tree. Ship-building seemed to her a right and proper holiday occupation for the son of a Naval Captain, and a model *Manchester* of no mean proportions had come into being.

'He worked on it last holidays, and on the week-ends,' explained mother. 'And, of course, Hans and Ronnie helped him.'

Hans and Ronnie were class-mates of Piet's and his closest friends. The three were inseparable. Ronnie was the most lovable. He had gaiety, good nature, good looks, and a remarkable facility for making allowances for the rest of the world. Hans, on the contrary, was reserved and held strong and immovable views on many subjects; and, since it was impossible for him to argue with easy-going Ronnie, he and Piet would become involved in prolonged discussions as wrangling and inconclusive as any peace conference. When the dispute concerned the engine of the *Manchester*, or the *Warspite* now under construction, Ronnie invariably had to give the casting vote.

Piet's models had to work. Everything, in his opinion, should have driving power. Thus his workshop, when he was home, constantly reverberated with hideous metallic noises and the horrid rushing roar of a large blow-lamp over which he frequently singed his forelock, much to my alarm. The rest of the household was accustomed to this peril and ignored it.

'Miss Yoy mustn't worry,' shrilled Teena, comfortingly. 'When Master Peter's head is on fire he yus' dips it in de tub.'

The rainwater tub had stood round the corner of the side stoep ever since I could remember. It was only partially emptied when water was drawn off for the garden, and curious creatures, like X-ray versions of worms and spiders, had their insubstantial being within its depths. No doubt they found their days enlivened by the periodical advent of a scorched shaggy human head plunged suddenly into their midst.

'The trouble,' said my mother, 'is that none of the domestics get on with my work when Piet is here – except, of course, Cook. He's like his great-grandfather, Lang Piet, who could always keep other people busy with jobs for him. Arend neglects the car, and the gardener forgets the flowers while they give him a hand with this or that. As for Teena – it's Teen here and Teen there, and no matter what he asks her to do she does it for him . . . spoils him outrageously . . .'

I smiled. 'You don't of course—'

'Well,' she admitted, 'perhaps in some ways . . .'

The school where Piet was a boarder gave Sunday leave after chapel to all the boys who lived near enough to go home. So Sundays usually found the three friends occupied in the workshop. And at the end of the day they produced a list of urgent requests for Gran. Could she *possibly* get them this, that and the other during the week, ready for next week-end?

Shop assistants in South Africa adopt a personal attitude towards their customers, and some of the incongruous requests put to them by the dignified old lady with the snowy hair aroused their interest.

'Copper piping, Mrs. Petersen! But we haven't been able to get that since the war.'

'Well, perhaps you could help me . . .' The confidential tone, the gentle appealing manner, the yarn about the young grandson were invariably sure fire. In the end the salesman bethought himself of a man who might have a little – not much, mind you, and not for sale, but still it might be worth while to go and see him . . .

On the following Sunday the lads would be awestruck and deeply impressed, for they had realized full well that they had demanded the impossible. And Peter would be filled with pride in his magnificent grandmother.

'How did you do it, Gran? Gee, you can get away with anything!'

She hastened to tell him and thus improve the shining moment.

'All a matter of Carnegie, my dear – just a little tact.'

Carnegie, the exponent of tact, had long been recognized by all of us as my mother's mentor. She attempted to instil his doctrines into her entire family with admirable persistence, though Norman and I often disappointed her. Her dependants she also inoculated with her gentle notions, not always with unqualified success.

When Arend and our gardener – his deaf son, David – had one of their periodical misunderstandings, my mother urged her factotem to be more tactful with the lad.

'Why not reason with the boy when he's troublesome,' she'd suggest.

Arend, who had fifteen children at home, was not convinced. He twiddled his cap in his hands as he stood outside the French window, and at last he said with sad and respectful logic:

'It's werry difficult to reason wit' a deaf person, Madam.'

My mother sighed, and dropped the subject.

But if Arend was impervious to tact, his regard for truth – one of the few qualities his mistress placed even higher – could at times be disconcerting.

Just before my arrival the house had been painted outside and in, so that it should look its best and brightest to welcome me, for those at home had never doubted but that I would soon come safely back to them. Arend had done the job aided by an enormous Coloured man of quiet and courteous demeanour. This man had come to the door in search of work, and mother, who prides herself upon her ability to 'sum people up', had reached a favourable conclusion about the stranger. When the task had been satisfactorily completed she told Arend to make a note of the man's name and address as he appeared to be a useful odd-jobber.

'Oh, yes, Madam,' he agreed. 'And he's a werry *good* man, too.'

'Why, in particular, do you say that?'

'Well, I ask him if he is married, and he say to me: "Arend, I was married, but I am married no more. I kill my wife wit' a chopper." I t'ink he was a werry good man to speak de trut' like dat.'

My mother, nonplussed, had to stifle her mirth.

Our little Cookie's daughter, Chrissie, was now married, and her place in our home had been taken by one of her cousins, an enchanting little brown girl of fifteen with the shyest smile I have ever seen and an Oriental slant to her brilliant squirrel eyes. Josephine still had the child's habit of breaking into an unselfconscious run on the slightest provocation, and, when summoned by one of her aunts with the shrill cry, 'Yosephine', she flitted off to answer the call with one slender little paw holding on to her frilly cap with its velvet bows.

'I can't think why the child doesn't fix it properly with a couple of hairpins,' deplored my mother. 'It always seems about to fly off her curls.'

Josephine was, in all things, the antithesis of the elephant. She was dainty as thistledown and remembered nothing. In conversation with my mother she hung her head with its insecure decoration and glanced up timidly through long lashes, murmuring a soft, 'Yes, Madam,' 'No, Madam,' or 'Auntie tol' me to do it that way—'; and, as 'Auntie' might have referred to either Cookie or Teena, there was often some confusion for my mother to sort out with her customary patience.

The war had receded. It now seemed an evil dragon which puffed and blew somewhere across the oceans and way beyond the blue horizonal mountains. We all had personal interests at stake, the Coloured as well as the white, for the Cape Coloured Corps – known locally as 'de Cape Corpse' – had absorbed a number of young male relatives of the various 'Tees Lodge' domestics. Yet it often appeared to me in those first weeks at home that the house under the mountain was the magic circle – the plot of ground known as 'home' in a children's game. Outside it you were vulnerable and the game could rage furiously – the terrible brutal game of war – but once you touched down within the green-painted iron railings and the high bougainvillea covered walls, you were 'home', untouchable and safe.

CHAPTER TWENTY-FOUR

ENTER AND EXIT NORMAN

OUR normal social circle at the Cape had been bereft by the war of the male element. Only the older men and the boys remained, and a few who could not be spared, but their meagre numbers were swelled from time to time by the transitory influx of Service men in warships or troopships, who were always the objects of what someone lightly called 'all-embracing' hospitality.

Hospitality, one of South Africa's most generous and characteristic contributions to the war effort, was organized in part by my efficient friend, Miss Lucy Bean, a quiet, humorous and determined woman with a persuasive personality. All over the Union private homes were opened wide to receive men going to the war or coming from it. Through Lucy's agency they could choose the sort of leave they needed and wanted – a gay coast resort or a lonely farm, fishing, swimming, shooting, golf, sightseeing or just resting among the hills and vineyards. Money for war charities was raised by fairs and fetes and those other social rackets that combine extortion and entertainment.

All my friends were in war jobs. My attractive sister-in-law, Fred's wife, Cecil, was driving for the Navy and working in a Seaman's Canteen; Dinkie Bain-Marais was in charge of a little shop in which were sold the by-products of the wool industry, sheepskin slippers, toys, rugs and novelties made by rehabilitated ex-servicemen. Her helpers were voluntary and her profits went to war funds. She soon conscripted me as one of her saleswomen. Her daughter, Shirley, was a nurse in the hospital for blinded soldiers, sailors and airmen, and it seemed a pity to me that the lovely face and figure should appear no more to those she served than a dream picture conjured out of the night.

I soon found plenty of work to do at the South African

Broadcasting Company writing topical scripts and taking part in plays and sketches. Some of the features I wrote were to stimulate recruiting, for there was no compulsory call-up in South Africa; others were to stress the fact that 'careless talk costs lives', and all had the promotion of the war effort at their core.

My book, 'Pack and Follow', was finished and had been despatched to England by sea. Several months elapsed before I was able to ascertain that it had become food for illiterate fish. 'All parcels sent to the United Kingdom between 10th June and 20th June must be regarded as lost' the *Cape Times* informed its readers one morning in Mail Intelligence.

'That's really too bad!' lamented my mother, who 'took an interest' in my literary activities.

'I'm not so sure,' I said thoughtfully. 'It could do with a lot of re-writing. I'll get busy.'

So it was not till late in August that Part 2, revised and retyped, set off on its journey once more, this time expensively by air.

That winter my brother, Norman, and his wife, Molly, with their little boy, Richard, came to stay with us. Norman had been stationed at the Military Hospital in Durban in charge of the Plastic Unit, and was now, at his own request, to go north to a base hospital in Cairo. But first he was entitled to a fortnight's embarkation leave, so the family had packed up their temporary abode in Durban and returned to the Cape.

Their arrival at 'Tees Lodge' was characteristic of Norman, who seems more subject to the minor irritations of life than many of us.

When I met them at the station after their long exhausting journey, I found Molly on crutches, Richard pale and fretful, and Norman harassed and much concerned about the well-being of one, Sandy, who was travelling in the dog-box.

As Norman strode down the platform in the direction of the guard's van he explained that Molly had tripped over some luggage when she got out at a wayside station to buy a newspaper, and had cut her shin almost to the bone.

When I had commiserated with this misfortune, I said, 'You didn't mention in your letter to Mum that you were bringing a dog. She'll have a fit. You know how she is about animals. She only puts up with Gyp because he's been at "Tees Lodge" for centuries.'

'Oh, dear,' said Norman. 'I thought poor dear old Gyp had gone to a better world . . . I worked out his age and it didn't seem possible he could still be around.'

'Well, he is. He's pretty moth-eaten, poor old boy, but nobody dares say so in Piet's presence.'

Norman said, in a crestfallen voice, 'Sandy's such a sweet animal I thought if your Mother saw him she'd be bound to love him, but it didn't seem Carnegie to mention him in advance.'

'It won't be Carnegie to bring him home either,' I said frankly. 'And Mum never loves any dog until he's become an established habit.'

Sandy was an Irish terrier with all the charm of his race. Apart from an endearing appearance, his love of children was his outstanding virtue, and he allowed Richard to make free with his anatomy as the child thought fit. For Richard's pleasure, he would masquerade in a hat or permit himself to be ridden round the garden. But where other dogs were concerned the Irish in Sandy took its belligerent form, and where the terrier was there also would presently be a fight.

Thus we had no sooner entered our gate than Sandy displayed a sixth sense which warned him that in this domain he might find himself challenged, although the aged warrior, Gyppy, had been hastily spirited away to the back garden till it should appear judicious for the animals to meet.

Mother, the warmth of her greeting tempered by the inclusion of Sandy, said: 'I hope you don't propose to keep him here. Gyp would never tolerate it.'

Molly said, 'No, Mum, he's going to Dorothy tomorrow.' Dorothy was her sister.

Norman beamed his approval at his wife, and whispered to me, 'That's Carnegie. Molly's just thought of Dorothy.'

Half an hour later, as we were about to go in to supper, we heard a sinister hubbub from the direction of the side stoep. Gyp, who despite his years, had a sixth sense as infallible as Sandy's own, had escaped from the back garden and come round the side of the house to investigate the cause of an unaccountable uneasiness which made his hackles rise and his nose twitch.

Sandy, observing the old dog hobbling blindly past the locked workshop in the wintry dusk of approaching night, uttered a low growl and made defiant soil-scraping motions with brisk back legs that flung dust and grit into the face of his reluctant host. He then swiftly put Gyp's private oak tree to the use for which nature had intended it. Gyp followed suit with less abandon and a twinge of rheumatism, baring his teeth and snarling the while. Sandy, who had contained himself for endless hours in the dog-box, capped the gesture with one of youthful dash and arrogant contempt. After these preliminaries the battle was on.

Norman deftly saved the situation by rushing out and picking up both dogs by their tails and dipping their gory heads in the ever-useful tub. He then put three stitches in Gyp's cheek and shut Sandy in the woodshed. Yet no one congratulated him.

We had just finished a somewhat chilly meal in every sense of the word when Teena, who had been bathing six-year-old Richard, hurried into the study.

'Miss Molly,' she said, with an air of urgency. 'I t'ink I ought to tell Miss Molly dat Master Richard is covered with flea-bites an' we must do somet'ing about dem.' Her voice soared to incredible heights as was her wont when she was disturbed.

A significant look passed between my brother and his wife.

'Norman,' said Molly, from the couch where she lay with her bandaged leg up, 'I think you'd better go and see Richard for yourself.'

Norman went to his son's room and came back presently. He said in some exasperation, 'You'll have to go, Molly. I'm a surgeon not a nannie. It's women's business to know the difference between chicken-pox and flea-bites.'

'Chicken-pox!' exclaimed my mother.

Molly gave her a disarming smile. 'There was an epidemic in Durban, Mum.'

As we went in a body to inspect the boy I wondered what other relevant information Carnegie and Norman between them had seen fit to withhold from our mother.

Little Richard's petal white skin was covered with a rash of tiny pink spots. 'Mum . . .' murmured Molly. 'I'm afraid it isn't fleas.'

So poor Norman spent his leave in purdah and departed a fortnight later wondering anew at the perversity of fate.

Soon afterwards I received a cable from my agent that 'Pack

and Follow' had been accepted for publication by Messrs. Eyre and Spottiswoode.

'You are an author, darling!' exclaimed my mother, and embraced me warmly.

Next day we knew that I was an author with chicken-pox.

CHAPTER TWENTY-FIVE

THE 'OLD LADY' LIFTS HER SKIRT

FOR me the tempo of life had eased down, for Bertie it was speeding up. The *Warspite* had given brief leave in Scapa Flow and had then made her way to the Mediterranean. Like the boys in the troopships with our convoy, she was destined to play her part in great events.

On 2nd July Admiral of the Fleet Sir Andrew Cunningham sent a message to those under his command, in which he told them what it was necessary for them to know about the plans for Operation Husky – the invasion of Sicily ... 'the most momentous enterprise of the war – striking for the first time at the enemy in his own land.' He also made clear their responsibility.

> 'Our object is clear and our primary duty is to place this vast expedition ashore in the minimum time and subsequently maintain our military and air forces as they drive relentlessly forward into enemy territory. In the light of this duty great risks must be, and are to be, accepted. The safety of our own ships and all distracting considerations are to be relegated to second place, or disregarded as the accomplishment of our main duty may require. On every commanding officer and rating rests the individual personal duty of ensuring that no flinching in determination or failure of effort on his own part will hamper this great enterprise.'

Ships and men must give of their best and more.

The 'Old Lady' rose to the challenge as only she could do.

There came a day on 17th July when she was ordered to

bombard Catania from 18.30 to 19.00 and not a second after. She received the signal in Malta at 12.15.

'We raised steam like mad and were clear of the harbour by 13.15,' wrote the Captain afterwards. 'If we averaged our maximum 22½ knots we could not get to Catania until 19.00. Too late. We must do more. Off we went, and presently we were doing 8 revs more than our maximum . . . suddenly our steering gear stuck and we went round in a savage circle. Quickly got auxiliary steering gear connected – but we lost ten precious minutes. If all went well we could still open fire at 18.45 for fifteen minutes.

'At 18.43 we were passing through the Open Fire Position at 16 knots and opened fire. A great mass of smoke and dust rose up out of the town right on the spot . . .'

It was after this bombardment that Admiral Cunningham sent his famous signal. 'There is no question that when the Old Lady lifts her skirt she can run. Operation well carried out.'

This 'lifts her skirt' message caught the popular fancy and the Press and radio played it up. So, in 'Tees Lodge', we read and heard about the Catania bombardment, and suddenly the war was close again, and pride and fear whirled round in my chest like the two tigers in 'Little Black Sambo', who chased each other round a tree at such speed that they melted into a little stripey pool in the shade.

But, in my case, the tiger, Fear, was devoured by the tiger, Pride, on 10th September when, after the first invasion of the mainland of Italy, the Italian Fleet surrendered and was led triumphantly into Malta by the 'Old Lady' herself.

In some curious way this thrilling climax to the Sicilian campaign was a blind alley beyond which my imagination did not go. It was as if I had read a story in which everything turns out for the best and the heroine lives happily ever after. My heroine, the Grey Mistress, under the command of one who loved her well and who had shared her dark hour at Jutland, had taken the honours in the first great victory of our terrible struggle which had brought the naval might of our Mediterranean enemy to anchor 'safe under the guns of Malta'.

I could see again the remembered battlements of Valetta, pale gold in the summer light, dghaisas swaying on the sparkling cobalt of the water, warships at anchor, and high above the Grand Harbour a crowd on the Barracca waiting to welcome a fleet. Only now Malta was the George Cross Island and Valetta of the Knights of St. John of Jerusalem lay in ruins. Warships in the shining creeks would be battle-grimed and maimed, and those who watched a defeated foe approach their shores would be haggard and lean, a people who had suffered starvation for many months till the Navy had brought them deliverance at a heavy cost of ships and men. Between these Maltese people and the Navy was a bond of life and death. The Italian ships would be fine and almost new, little damaged in battle, while their escorts would be war-scarred and seasoned. Proud, at the head of the line, I could see the 'Old Lady', H.M.S. *Warspite*, who could give of more than her best when more than her best was needed.

For the moment the towering sandstone fortifications of the Grand Harbour, where long ago I had stood so often to watch ships sail and ships come home, were the cliffs against which my imagination broke and recoiled.

The S.A.B.C. invited me to give a broadcast about the George Cross Island, and this I did one evening on the National Programme after the News.

My chicken-pox had taken its departure. Altogether I was very happy.

When I am happy I want to write. Thoughts skim through my mind, swift and bright as kingfishers – too elusive for capture sometimes, but with a winged vibration quick with life. And when it is also spring in the Cape Peninsula, and the daisies are fleecy on the grass and downy mimosa loads the air with fragrance and trees and shrubs burst into blossom overnight, then my pen is eager to rush into a new venture.

Piet understood this intangible creative restlessness.

'I know how you feel,' he said. 'It's the way I get when there's an idea for a new engine at the back of my mind and I can't get hold of it. I lie awake in the night thinking about it, and it's always there, floating about in my head, and then suddenly one day it shoots forward with a bang and I can start work on it.'

'That's exactly it,' I agreed. 'I don't know what I'm at yet. No concrete idea has shot forward with a bang.'

If anyone asks Piet's advice, really wanting it, he gives his full attention to the problem under consideration. He did so now.

Presently he said: 'Why don't you start on Lang Piet? You've always wanted to. And there you have a real first-rate story.'

Lang Piet (Tall Piet) Marais, my late grandfather, had been the Big White Chief of our tribe, a patriarchal figure with unquestioned authority. His oft-quoted sayings and spectacular doings formed the unconscious basis of much of his descendants' way of thought and behaviour. Young Piet had always been fascinated by tales of this almost legendary character, with whom he appeared to feel a sympathy even more powerful than that of ordinary kinship.

Lang Piet's life had been one of adventure and enterprise in that exciting age when the hinterland of South Africa first began to give the promise of untold wealth. He had been born in 1838, the historic year of the Great Trek, on a Stellenbosch wine farm. At the age of seventeen he had left home and trekked north to the border town of Graaff-Rienet, and then, on, in the dusty wheel ruts of the covered wagons, to the new young Boer Republic which was being painfully established across the Vaal. There he founded a family and made a fluctuating fortune.

His problems were those of the country to which he belonged. Born of Dutch and Huguenot parentage he married a Roman Catholic girl of Irish and English descent. He was forever pulled two ways and he developed perhaps too much tolerance in matters of race and religion. He was, like so many South Africans, clannish to a fault, inclined, with his sons and daughters, to be arrogant and overbearing, though with Sarah, his wife, he was ever mild and tender. Sarah was the core of his being – his life and his luck, and for many years her gentle hands held back the avalanche of personal tragedy that so dramatically overwhelmed him in the evening of his days.

'I don't think I can do it, Piet,' I said. 'I don't know the period, and I'd make terrible mistakes.'

'You can learn the background. You know what's more important – the man and the country.'

'My knowledge of the man is a childish memory, and hearsay—'

'You can't have everything. Why not write and ask Uncle Wilfred what he thinks?'

Uncle Wilfred was the only surviving son of Lang Piet. He was a man about thirteen years younger than my mother, his sister Ellen, to whom he was extremely devoted. He lived on a farm in the High Veld some seventy miles from Johannesburg. I took Piet's advice and wrote to him.

His reply was evasive.

'Come and talk it over,' he suggested. 'Bring Ellen. Mike and I will give you both a hearty welcome.' ('Mike' was Edyth, his wife.)

'Shall we go and talk it over?' I asked my mother. She said, in something of a flutter:

'I really don't know if I could face the train journey at my age! Two nights of it ... and you know my claustrophobia—'

I knew her claustrophobia. We all endured it with her in one way or another when the icy blasts of winter roamed unchecked round the house because she couldn't bear the windows shut. When her friends came to bridge with her, and snow lay on the mountains, they wrapped themselves up in all their warmest garments and nerved themselves for the draughts that would whistle round their heads because of 'poor old Ellen's claustrophobia.'

'I mean,' said mother humbly, 'it would be awkward if they put a third person into the compartment with us – the windows ...'

'Darling,' I said. 'We'll be two to one. If they put somebody in with us she'll just have to stick the howling gales – and it's not as if it's winter – it's spring! Anyway, I'll explain everything to the guard, and if you'll just do your best to look very old and decrepit, he'll surely see reason. Leave everything to me, and I'll look after you.'

But my mother was more accustomed to looking after people than to being looked after, and found herself quite unable to sustain the doddering role I would have imposed upon her. So we had not been many hours on the Johannesburg mail before she had taken complete control of both of us. She brought her old friend Carnegie into play to obtain good seats in the diner and a compartment to ourselves, where she was able to open windows to her heart's content. Her qualms dissipated, she abandoned herself to the long-forgotten enjoyment of a visit to 'Strehla'.

The last lap of our journey we did by car through the veld in the full glory of spring. The grain-lands were brilliant green and warm amber; shining willow-fringed dams, avenues of blue gums and firs and tall windmills indicated the presence of an occasional homestead. The wind sang in the corn, the birds wore their gaudy courting plumage and clouds of scarlet and yellow finches twittered in the rushes bordering the spruits; while widow-birds, with their long black and white kite-tails heavy and dripping with dew, rose clumsily from the morning crops. Here and there we saw a golden auriol poised on a wire fence, small and perfect against the sky. Or flocks of guinea-fowl scuttled through the long grass in swift speckled blue-mauve ripple. And then at last there was 'Strehla' on the horizon, a stone, single-storeyed, red-roofed house surrounded by trees.

'There . . .' said my mother with infinite satisfaction. 'That's the new homestead Wilfred built himself, and the house just near it is Kathleen and Towzer's.'

A few minutes later the promised hearty welcome was ours.

CHAPTER TWENTY-SIX

'STREHLA'

THIS new homestead was not the same as the one in which I had spent so many happy girlhood holidays. For my uncle was gradually disposing of the responsibility of his many acres and he had already sold the big house and the greater part of the property, retaining only this one small farm for himself. Soon he intended to give up this last interest too and retire to live at the Cape, where he had already bought a house overlooking the sea. Of recent years his health had been indifferent, and his devoted Edyth had suffered great anxiety on his behalf so far from medical aid.

'I can't take it,' she confided to mother and me, when rapturous greetings had been exchanged and Uncle Wilfred had sauntered down to the orchard, leaving 'the girls to unpack and pow-pow'. 'When he gets one of his attacks I feel quite desperate alone here, with only the servants, and no one except

Kathleen and Towzer near at hand. No doctor within fifty miles!'

Kathleen, Edyth's sister, lived on the adjoining farm with her husband, Towzer, and we had not been half an hour at 'Strehla' before she came over to join us in a cup of tea, bringing one of her delicious home-made cakes with her. She had changed very little since I had first met her when my friend, Marjorie, and I had stayed at the big house over the rise, and she had told us – then freckled flappers of fifteen – that if we anointed our faces with sour cream nightly we would acquire beautiful complexions.

'Is it really sour cream that's kept the lines at bay?' I asked her now.

She laughed, and her enormous brown velvet eyes sparkled. 'If they *had* been kept at bay – which they haven't – it would be the high-veld air and the quiet life we farmers lead.'

'And a placid nature,' put in Edyth, who was as mercurial as her sister was tranquil.

'You must come and see Peefoe,' she added to us. 'We've still got him. And the youngster who carried in your bags is his son, Jermyn.'

Peefoe was a cheerful African who had come into my uncle's employ twenty-five years ago at the age of fifteen and who, trained by Edyth, had long since developed into a first-class cook. At regular intervals he returned to his distant kraal, but he always came back to 'Strehla'. And, as he grew older and married, each time he went 'on leave' his tribe was the richer by a head of cattle or a few goats, and, in the fullness of time, by the arrival of another glossy-skinned piccaninny.

Peefoe was kneading bread in the sunny kitchen when we went in with Edyth. A glass dish of pink-gold paw-paw, shaped into small rounds, stood on the deal table in a bowl of ice; biltong – dried buck meat – hung on a hook looking like an old piece of shoe-leather; and a basin of rich milk waited to be skimmed. Outside the window a bush-shrike uttered the staccato cry of *bok-bok-makierie*, from which he takes his Afrikaans name.

Peefoe wiped his hands on his striped apron and bowed low. He spoke in the deep rumbling voice of the Transvaal native, and he had all the courtesy of his leisurely people.

'Welcome to "Strehla", Missus – welcome, Miss Joy. How is young Bass Peter?' Peefoe knew 'the Old Missus' well and was glad to see her. And young 'Bass Peter', as a little boy, had also been a guest on the farm.

Peefoe's son, a slim lad in spotless white uniform, stood politely in the background, an almost cynical expression upon his inky countenance.

'Missus is surprised to see Jermyn, my son?' smiled the father.

'He was a piccaninny when last I heard of him,' said the 'Ole Missus', expressing the astonishment expected of her. 'And he was doing very well at school.'

'Trust Ellen to say the right thing,' murmured Edyth to me.

Peefoe's smile broadened till it almost included his ears. 'Yes, Missus. He passed his exams top of his class.'

'Jermyn, my son', belonged to the new era. He had education, and with it that air of indefinable superiority towards his elders which could at times be galling. Our own Cape Coloured of the older generation had the same difficulty in maintaining full parental control in the face of a decided handicap – their own ignorance and the accomplishments of their offspring. I had often heard Teena lament her illiteracy. 'Dese young people don't know how lucky dey is, Miss Yoy. If I could live my life again, and have what I wanted, I would choose education.' The young Cape Coloured learned to read and write in two languages, Afrikaans and English, while, in the elementary school-houses dotted about the veld, the modern African children went one better and studied their more primitive lessons in English, Afrikaans and Sesuto or whatever their tribal language happened to be.

When the amiabilities had been suitably exchanged we left the bright kitchen and sauntered down through the flower-garden to the pear-orchard in search of my uncle. Both he and Edyth were feeling emotional about 'Strehla' at that time. In spite of the advantages of the new home they had bought at Kalk Bay, they had misgivings about moving. Wilfred's roots were deep in Transvaal soil, and they both knew that transplanting him would be a bad wrench. We found him standing on the upper boundary of the orchard, hatless, with the light wind stirring his thick iron-grey hair, his eyes upon the wheatfields and bean crops and the wide cultivated lands undulating to the horizon, where an avenue of blue-gums marked the approach to the original 'Strehla' homestead.

'To think, Ellen,' he said, 'that when I first came to this place with George forty years ago it was nothing but grassland as far as the eye could see . . .'

George had been Wilfred's favourite brother. Together they had begun the great task of making this land productive. Then George, whose wife disliked farm life and whose children were of school age, had drawn out, and Wilfred, with Edyth's help, had gone on alone. Building, planting, irrigating. His life, his fortune and his heart had been put into 'Strehla'. He had scattered shining dams upon his land, and planted breaks of trees on barren windy slopes and, though he allowed no shooting on his property, the wild creatures of the veld had retreated before the cultivator's harrow. New farm-houses had come into being at his will to house his tenant farmers; and gradually, if he thought they loved the land and served it well, he had helped them towards the ownership of the farms they worked. He was a scientific agriculturist, a man of means and influence, their adviser and their friend. Now, in the autumn of his years, the unpretentious homesteads were established all about, the land was prosperous, and his task was done.

Soon he would abandon these beloved acres – yet George, who had left with such reluctance long ago, had recently returned.

George had said, in his will, that his ashes must be scattered over 'Strehla', and so his sons had chartered an aeroplane and, swooping low over the farm, had consigned the remains of their father to the bright Transvaal air.

'He landed on these zinneas,' said Wilfred, with an affectionate smile, showing us the upright gaily-coloured blooms that were the joy of Edyth's heart. 'Here is George, Ellen, literally still with us.'

Ellen stared at George, incredulous and a trifle shocked. 'Darling old George,' she murmured, somewhat at a loss, dragging her grey surprised eyes away from the strange heavy ash still lingering in the zinnia leaves. 'He was always so full of fun.'

George's father, Lang Piet, was also with us – though less literally – in the weeks that followed; and so was Sarah, the strong gentle girl he had married and brought to this raw land then so harsh to women not necessarily of pioneer temperament.

He joined us most often in the evenings when we sat in the

lounge that was all windows and looked out upon the land he had bought blind for two hundred pounds half a century ago to help a stranger out of a fix, and which he had given his sons, George and Wilfred, never even having seen it. Or his fastidious ghost entertained us at dinner when Jermyn's white-gloved hand poured the wine of Lang Piet's own Stellenbosch valley into our glasses, and the candles lent their soft glow to the polished table and the gleaming silver and glass.

'Well, Mike,' my uncle would say to his wife. 'Even Lang Piet couldn't have found any fault with this young turkey. Peefoe's roasted it to a turn. What do you say, Ellen?'

The romance and variety of Lang Piet's life was a constant source of interest and amusement to us, and, as memory awoke in his son and daughter, Edyth and I listened enthralled, or rocked with laughter, for Lang Piet had lived in an age when a joke was something you could see and feel as well as hear – not a mere 'shaggy dog' story, or some fatuous allusion. Jokes then were so meaty you could really get your teeth into them, and they sounded good to us retold by my tall uncle with his quiet infectious chuckle.

We drove over to Pretoria one day to see where Lang Piet and Sarah had lived when the administrative capital of the present Union of South Africa was still only the young heart of the new Boer Republic springing up in the game-infested grasslands, long even before the leadership of Oom Paul Kruger and the discovery of the fatal gold that was to take his country from him.

Now the lovely little town lay in its hollow in the hills, veiled in a parma violet mist, for the jacarandas were in full bloom, a canopy of cool delicate leafless mauve over every avenue and garden and a carpet of mauve underfoot. It was so quiet in the residential districts, away from the shopping centre, that you could hear the soft fall of petals on the red earth as a breeze shivered the branches, and outside my Aunt Blanca's house, which was our headquarters for the day, a dazzling green woodpecker drummed on a silvery trunk.

Aunt Blanca, Uncle Belfield's widow, had been a reigning beauty in her day and was still the queen of her class. She was an ardent republican, and so, as is very often the case in South Africa, we agreed to differ on politics and forget them for the day. And this was easy as we had a long way to catch up on family gossip. We drove round the town, through streets that bore the name of my grandfather and some of his sons, for that was how Pretoria grew up – round its residents. On the heights, crowned by the Union Buildings and Government House, were the official homes of the Cabinet Ministers – among them our friends Sydney and Betty Waterson – and the fine mansion of the Premier.

But, down in the old town, we saw the ramshackle single-storeyed house with its zinc roof in which Paul Kruger had dwelt through the stormy period heralding the birth of the golden age in South Africa and the death of a pastoral nation. In the stable behind it stands the massive stink-wood trek-wagon of the old President with its six-foot wheels. Tattered banners and forgotten proclamations adorn the walls of the deserted rooms; and, on the stoep, where once the burgers took coffee with their leader, 'Oom Paul' (Uncle Paul), even such stalwart ghosts have long since been exorcized by the red dust of mechanized traffic. Opposite is the Dopper Church, where the President himself used to preach to his people the narrow doctrines of a Calvinistic faith applied to the daily lives of men and women whose law was the word of God – freely interpreted to suit the occasion – and whose story was that of *Exodus*.

Near the Market Place we found the Nigel property where my grandfather had built a house after striking gold. The house is now a hotel. Wilfred's recollections of living there were hazy, and concerned mainly with an adjacent ginger-beer factory which had afforded him and his brothers much entertainment and pleasure in one way and another. But then he had been very small at the time. Ellen's were not much more informative. Her childhood memories have a habit of veering back towards the convents in which she greatly enjoyed her education. Perhaps because the various convents she attended were havens of refuge in a turbulent early existence, for the Marais children were constantly uprooted and thrust into wagons and coaches and trundled round the wilds in search of some new dwelling-place to suit the capricious fancy of their restless progenitor. And, wherever Sarah trekked in the wake of Lang Piet, her Roman Catholic daughters were given their schooling at the nearest convent, while her Protestant sons were educated as their father thought fit. No Papists for him! Thus my mother's insecure childhood was strongly influenced by 'the good nuns' whom she loved deeply and who evidently returned her devotion; so, whenever I asked her about her little girl life, her eyes grew bright with affection as one or another of the 'good nuns' stood out from the scene in high relief.

But, as Wilfred could never focus 'Ellen's nuns', their shared reminiscences usually centred about Great Aunt Foley, who had lived with the family and who appears to have spent her time admonishing and dosing the children, who ran to her voluminous petticoats with all their joys and sorrows. It sometimes occurred to me that my Great-Great-Aunt-Foley must have had a good deal in common with Ellen.

Before going back to 'Strehla' my mother was the guest of honour at a tea-party to which Aunt Blanca had summoned all the available relatives. So 'Aunt Ellen' was enabled to inspect and approve a number of new arrivals – young husbands and wives and several great-nephews and nieces – which she did with her customary graciousness. That was the best part of the day for her. In life's card game this was the hand in play, and it promised well. The past to her is a hand played and forgotten, save for an occasional grand slam. Unfortunate calls were best obliterated from memory's marker. Anyway, in her view, life is living and looking forward. To look back is to grow old. Time enough for that twenty years hence!

We returned to 'Strehla' in the dusk, when the secret life of the veld stirs and is sometimes caught between the headlamps – a hare or a buck trapped in a corridor of light. Down by the rocky outcrop near the dam the little meerkats came out to pray, their tiny paws raised to the heavens.

As we got out of the car Uncle Wilfred looked up at the clouds massing across the moon, and sniffed the cool fresh night air.

'Tomorrow we'll have rain,' he said. 'It's lucky we got that wheat cut yesterday!'

Edyth said: 'It's lucky we went to Pretoria today. If the rains come in earnest the spruits will be flooded and the roads might be impassable.'

'Dear old Mike,' laughed my uncle, and put his arm round her shoulder. 'Always the woman's point of view!'

Lightning flashed livid along the sky-line, and a peal of thunder reverberated far off.

Next day the rain pelted down in steady sheets. The leaves of the fruit trees and zinneas were washed clean and sparkling, and Uncle George was swept into eternity.

During our visit Uncle Wilfred had been reading my carbon copy of 'Pack and Follow'. I knew that if he liked it he would do his utmost to help me with 'Lang Piet', if not the project was off.

So it was with some trepidation that I saw him come into breakfast one morning with my manuscript under his arm. He was smiling broadly, however, and his first words were reassuring.

'I enjoyed this stuff,' he said. 'Not the Chinese part. I don't like the Far East – never have. I can't get interested in those Johnnies with their back-to-front outlook on life. But, I must say, you understand your own country better than I gave you credit for.' He patted my shoulder and put the manuscript down on the table beside me. 'I think you should have a go at Lang Piet,' he added.

That was all I wanted to hear.

After that I began to assemble my notes, writing every morning for two to three hours.

Ellen and Wilfred were always content to be together, and often, when I was scribbling in the window-room that looked out over the veld, I saw them go off in the car across country to the mealie-fields, while Edyth, with a song on her lips, gathered flowers in her garden to beautify the house. She sang frequently in her sweet soprano, for hers was a gay and loving nature and she was glad of our companionship. Her day was crowded with little household tasks, and she was always busy and cheerful.

I smiled to myself as I paused, pen in hand, to stare out at the wide landscape over which my uncle's car travelled so confidently, for I could picture Ellen 'taking an interest' in her beloved Wilfred's beloved crops, and his gentleness with her ignorance. My mother had no knowledge of the land and of growing things; she liked her plants to have their heads above the earth with their eyes wide open, for she is not like our English Marion who goes down on hands and knees to her flowers and tells them to grow in their own language.

At eleven Wilfred would bring his sister back and we would have tea, and maybe Kathleen and Towzer, or one of the neighbouring farmers, would look in for a chat, and the talk would be of seasonal matters, perhaps in Afrikaans. No one concerned themselves much with the war. In the spring the immediate problems of the soil were of paramount importance. Talk of the war could be left to the radio.

In the evenings, after dinner, we generally played a rubber or two of bridge – mother and I against the other two. My uncle, who had been in the open air most of the day, yawned mightily over his cards, and Edyth, who was keen as a terrier to get to grips with the hand, would remonstrate briskly. 'Call, Wilfred! Don't just sit there *gaaping*!' A yawn in Afrikaans is a *gaap*, but how much more expressive is the word when spoken than when written! For the Afrikaans G is a gutteral revved up in the roof of the mouth, and the long weary sound '*ghrraar*' initiated by a deep indrawn breath, is exactly that produced by a whole-hearted yawn of abysmal boredom. So expressive a tongue is Afrikaans that many bi-lingual inhabitants of the country are apt to forget their cultural obligations towards it by adding ordinary English terminations to some of the more picturesque verbs.

Wilfred only chuckled when Edyth chided him. 'Old Mike's out for blood as usual! All right, my girl, here goes . . .'

My mother, enthroned in a high-backed chair, and looking rather fantastic in dark glasses and an eye-shade – for she was having trouble with her eyes at that time – called and played her cards with an air of aloof detachment consistent with her undisputed position of an authority in our midst. I too often had my mind elsewhere and gave myself away with the inexcusable query, 'What are trumps?'

We seldom missed the nine o'clock News, because I had to know how that distant war was progressing and Uncle Wilfred was interested in the nearer home reactions of the share market.

Thus it was that one evening I was shaken out of my 'Strehla'-born tranquillity by hearing of a naval bombardment at Salerno, where our troops were fighting against bitter opposition.

'For two days the battleships, *Warspite* and *Valiant*, steamed to within a mile of Salerno beach to send salvo after salvo of fifteen inch shells into German positions round the Allied bridgehead. The whole bombardment – the greatest support action in history – was planned in fifteen minutes.

While it was in progress waves of German bombers attacked the ships – but the Navy carried on and turned the scale of battle . . .'

Edyth looked across at me, and put her hand quickly over mine. Unconsciously she used her old name for me, the one which belonged to my girlhood.

'It must be all right, Childie; if the ship had been damaged they surely wouldn't have given her name.'

'They turned the scale of battle—' repeated my mother.

I said, 'But it's so little to hear! It tells nothing – nothing.'

Even then, I did not guess how much there was to tell.

We caught the night train from Johannesburg. But first we spent the day with my childhood friend, Marjorie Gilfillan. We had shared our schooldays, Transvaal holidays at 'Strehla', earnest endeavours to acquire beauty by means of sour cream, and all the many hopes and dreams of adolescence.

'You haven't changed – not an atom!' I said, hugging her. 'And you the mother of three great schoolboys!'

Marriage – mine to an English naval officer, and hers to a South African law student – had swept our lives far apart. While I had pitched my tent here and there, Majorie had put down strong healthy roots. She and her husband, Noel, had started from scratch, two youngsters just through University. Now they had three sons and several acres of land on a fertile ridge outside Johannesburg, looking down upon the city of sky-scrapers and white mine-dumps, right across the veld to the blue hills. Noel worked daily in the family firm of solicitors in Johannesburg and the farm was Marjorie's concern. Only now Noel was away 'up north' with the Army.

'It's glorious having your own land,' said Marjorie. 'But it makes a slave of you. There's always some new thing to be done.' She looked radiant in her slavery.

It had been the empty land first, then the house and garden, then vegetables and poultry, and now a dairy herd.

'And bees – I mean to keep bees later on . . . and, when we can afford it, we'll have a tennis court and a swimming pool.' She was full of plans and growing interests.

She gave us an excellent dinner, and everything we ate was a product of 'Littlefillan Farm'. Even the bread was made at home by the Zulu cook.

'And this cream is Joy's,' said Marjorie, laughing. 'She's our best cow, named for you.'

'And I expect you've got Lizzie Arden for your special sour cream!'

That night, as the train bore us south, away from the wealth of Johannesburg and its sordid shanty outskirts, and away from the endless white dunes thrown up like ant-heaps by the swarming black activity underground, it seemed to me that Marjorie had given more to life than I had even dreamed of, and, as a reward, she had tangible profits to show for her investment – sons and a home for her sons.

'It must be wonderful to own land,' I said to my mother. 'To build and improve and get results. I sometimes wonder if I'll ever have more than six foot of earth for my own – or a ledge on a zinnea leaf!'

Mother said: 'Poor darling old George. . . . Joy, will you open the window? About half-way – and we can put up the shutter, if you like.'

Outside, the moon silvered the grasslands. The sound of our wheels was a lonely beat. We were infinitesimal in the empty magnitude of the night.

CHAPTER TWENTY-SEVEN

'YOU HAVE TO RUN RISKS'

OCTOBER, the most glorious month in the Cape Peninsula, was at the zenith of her fresh and fragrant beauty when I heard that my husband had been appointed as Commodore Administration to Admiral Sir Andrew Cunningham, Commander-in-Chief of the Mediterranean Fleet, whose headquarters were in Algiers.

Why had he abandoned his *Warspite*?

It was a long while before that question was answered for me and I could hear the full story of the 'Old Lady's' last exploit in Mediterranean waters, and all that followed. Though, in the House of Commons, on 21st September, Mr. Churchill gave his account of the progress of the Italian Campaign, and one of his statements was more than a little significant.

'From day three to day seven the issue hung in the balance and the possibility of a large-scale disaster could not be excluded. You have to run risks. There are no certainties in war. There is a precipice on either side of you – a precipice of caution and a precipice of over-daring . . . the battle swayed to and fro, and the German's hope of driving us into the sea after a bloody battle on the beaches must at times have risen high . . . The British Battle Squadron, some of our finest battleships, joined the inshore Squadron in heavy bombardment, running a great risk within close range and narrow waters from the enemy's aircraft, U-boats and the glider-bombs which inflicted damage on some of our ships. They came straight in and stood up to it at close range, equalized and restored the artillery battle. . . . It was right to risk capital ships in this manner in view of the improvement of naval balances.'

On 16th September the 'Old Lady', having completed the main part of her task – 'running a great risk within close range and narrow waters' – was threading her way through the shipping in the direction of North Salerno for her final bombardment when she was attacked by the new glider-bombs to which Mr. Churchill had referred.

My husband kept an account of subsequent events, as they happened, to use as a basis for the full official report he realized it would presently be necessary for him to make. The chances were that he would lose his ship. In any case, the projectiles with which she had been hit had not hitherto been used against our Navy.

That preliminary and personal account of the 'Old Lady's' ordeal is before me now. Though written under tremendous strain, the sharp, but flowing writing, with its customary indifference to such details as dotted i's, shows no trace of the writer's fatigue and deep anxiety for his ship.

Extracts from it tell their own tale.

16/9/43. 'Dead overhead we suddenly sighted three new oibjects – probably wireless-controlled bombs. It was clear they were going to hit us. It took two seconds. There was nothing to be done and I watched carefully.

'The first to arrive missed us by a few feet. A fraction of a second later one hit us just abaft the funnel. The third near-missed the starboard side.

'I was not thrown off my feet, but for the fraction of a second I had a kind of black-out like when you take a hard toss at football or off a horse. But I could see and think perfectly clearly all the time. Black smoke and dirt from the funnels and the hell of a noise. I thought the whole mast was coming down as it rocked and bent and whipped. For a moment I thought we were probably sunk and was quite prepared for the ship to break in two.

'No one lost their heads or shouted or anything on the bridge. They were all first-class and the A.A. guns which had opened fire kept firing. That was good.

'Then there was calm after the storm. I found the ship would steer, the engines were going ahead. A fire was reported in the hangar. "Put it out," I said. Then to Guns. "If we can steam and shoot we'll carry out our final bombardment."

'I set course up the channel. Then reports began to come in, all very calm and accurate. The P.M.O. reported some six killed and twenty wounded. The Chief reported some 4,000 to 5,000 tons of water had come in. Water was dribbling into all sorts of places . . .

'I kept going at six knots. Then the ship would not steer. We were in the swept channel and we steered round in a circle. I stopped engines. We were heading straight into the mines. A minesweeper sent us violent signals to get out of it. I couldn't, for the helm was hard over, and finally the starboard engine-room died out too.

'So there we were once again, going round in circles with our way carrying us and quite helpless.'

Long afterwards my husband told me of the strange familiarity of that day – so like that other one nearly thirty years earlier, when this same ship had waltzed helpless towards the enemy at Jutland. His first battle.

Now, once again, Captain, officers and men joined in the great endeavour to bring their wounded ship safely back to port. Her harrowing seventy-two hour journey from the coast of Italy to the doubtful sanctuary of Malta is one of the many epics of the war. Friendly Allied ships and tugs helped her on her way, sympathetic signals encouraged and heartened her and those on board served her day and night without respite.

Yet, at 2 a.m. next morning, the great ship had only succeeded in getting fifteen miles from Salerno. She was three feet deeper in the water, listing heavily, and 'the moon full bright'.

17th September. 'With the dawn the situation had worsened and there was much fatigue, for no one had had much stand-off during the last few days, and since the hit everyone was on their feet, either at the guns, hauling in wires, bailing, pumping or shoring up. Men were beginning to sit down and rest and drop off to sleep as they sat. But they were all marvellously cheerful, willing and fatalistic. I said a few words to the sailors over the broadcaster. Ours was a common hazard of war, we had done what we set out to do and had been hit. We had scared hell out of the German army and braced up our own soldiers, and we might even have turned the scale. I admired their good humour and hard work, and between us we would get the Old Lady back to Malta.

'As I write Stromboli is abeam. The flooding has been checked and we are still afloat. I am still without sleep, but keyed up, living on sandwiches and lemonade as the galleys are 'out'. And now on to the bridge to get through the Messina Narrows ...'

18th September. 'We had the hell of a night. . . . When we struck the tide-rips and whirlpools the ship became unmanageable. From midnight until five a.m. we were completely out of control and going through the Straits broadside on with all tows parted except one. However, just as the tide turned off Reggio to take us back up the Straits again, I got a tug on alongside each side aft and straightened her up sufficiently for the tugs forward to go ahead and get some way on the ship. Since getting through Messina all has gone well, and now, at nine p.m., we are off Cape Passaro and should reach Malta tomorrow morning.

'Got two hours' sleep this afternoon and am completely refreshed. John May, the P.C.O., was very good and thoughtful and had my sea-cabin picketed, giving instructions that no one was to be allowed to disturb me "Unless his journey was really necessary."

'Very busy making arrangements and reports so that immediate action can be taken as soon as we arrive.

'The sailors are splendid, as they always are when things go wrong, and I see them standing naked on the upper deck washing each other from buckets of salt water dipped over the side.

'Baling out compartments with buckets in this heat is hard work; about two hundred men are at it all the time.

'Everyone on board likes being asked where they were when the bomb hit us. I have asked everyone of my staff, and there is not one who would not have been in the exact spot if five minutes before (or one minute or two minutes) they had not done something else. A peculiar characteristic of train accidents, shipwrecks and bombings ashore is this type of human reflection. Peculiar because it gets you nowhere, and much better just to thank God or the Devil that you weren't there and forget about it.'

So, at last, on Sunday morning, 19th September, with her dead committed to the deep, with her weary sailors lined up on deck, and with her band playing, the 'Old Lady' entered the Grand Harbour which she had last entered so proudly in the hour of victory.

19th September. 'All the ships' companies turned out to see us go past and I got many signals. There is no doubt there was great anxiety that we should not get back. Well, we have. So for the second time in twenty-seven years I have limped into port in the *Warspite* heavily damaged.'

For a long time after that the 'Old Lady' was out of the game, and when, at length, she was healed of her wounds, those who had brought her safely home were no longer with her.

CHAPTER TWENTY-EIGHT

'HERE'S THE PLACE FOR YOUR SIGNATURE'

THE publicity received by the *Warspite* over the bombardment of Catania, the surrender of the Italian Fleet, and finally Salerno, had acted as a violent stimulant to my son's already over-bellicose inclinations.

Piet's tremendous determination to 'get into the war' at the earliest possible moment had increased with the years. It dominated his whole existence. The house under the mountain had become a hatching ground of warriors. Piet and his friends talked of nothing but 'joining up'. What in? Air, sea or tanks? Nothing else interested them. Ronnie was all for the Air Force, Piet was mad keen on the Fleet Air Arm, but many Bishops' boys had gone into the Tank Corps as that was undoubtedly the quickest way of getting into the actual fighting. And, as they talked, the flame of their enthusiasm burned in their eyes – but most of all, it seemed to me, in Piet's. In his green eyes it glowed fierce as the harsh flames of the blow-lamp that scorched his hair in the workshop.

The relationship between us was not always easy at that time. Savage little scenes flared up between us without warning. Often I took my troubles to Nannie, who had known us both since our respective infancies. She was keeping house for an old gentleman in Claremont, and, while he read or wrote in his study, she and I sat in the sunny back porch with the garden fragrance all round us, and, as her busy fingers knitted for 'our boy', she advised me how best to treat him.

'You've been three years separated, darling. You can't expect to have the same authority you had over the little boy . . . and you know you're both Tartars!' She chuckled, recalling the battles of will she had had with both of us in her time. 'You're too much alike, you two – but you are twenty-one years older. Just remember that, and try tact.'

I sighed. 'That awful Carnegie of Mum's—'

Nannie always did me good. She had many deep and agonizing worries of her own, but she seldom mentioned them. For years she had looked forward to 'just one more trip overseas' to the land of her birth. She still had relations in her native Dresden and longed to see them. But, for the second time, her homeland was at war with the country of her adoption, and the Nazis were earning their fabulous wage of universal hatred. To Nannie, brought up in sentimental, music-loving Saxony, the words Nazi and German were never synonymous – but she knew full well that they were one and the same to the rest of the world; and her heart was often heavy. When we were together the fetters of the present were loosened, and we laughed as we relived the happy carefree days we had shared with 'our child' in his babyhood. 'You mark my words', she had said, as he had bounded up and down in her arms at six months old and grabbed joyously at her grey hair. 'This boy has a will of iron!' We'd been amused at our merry infant being credited with so stern a quality, but she had known what she was talking about.

'He's in such a mad hurry to join up,' I complained now. 'He won't even wait for the matric results – though I'll try to make him.'

Nannie sighed. 'Here the boys can go at seventeen if they have their parents' permission. He'll never forgive you if you stop him. He's like a young lion on a chain.'

'I'll fight for every day I reasonably and fairly can. Even one day – a few hours – might make the difference—'

She ignored the break in my voice, and said practically:

'It's no good thinking like that. What's fate is fate.' She did not look at me, and her fingers quickened their pace as she turned the heel of a navy blue sock. Presently she got up briskly.

'Now I'm going to make us a nice cupper tea.' Her vitality was catching and her intention irresistible. If Nannie meant to cheer anyone up, that person was cheered whether they liked it or not.

So I'd return to 'Tees Lodge' after seeing her, feeling brighter and easier, and for a while all would go smoothly. Till Piet flung out one of his ultimatums.

'The day the Christmas hols. begin I'm going to join up.'

'You must wait for the matric results. If you fail it may mean another six months at school.'

'I won't fail.'

'You can't be sure.'

He looked down at me, with his head high and arrogant and his short upper lip shortened further by the thrust of his mouth.

'Ring up my housemaster if you think there's any reasonable doubt.'

'It's only a matter of a few weeks to wait for the results. Enjoy your holidays like a sensible mortal – you've earned them – and then you can go with my blessing.'

'A few weeks is too long to wait.'

Suddenly his face softened. 'Try to understand, Mom . . . we all feel . . . well, as if there's no time to waste – a sense of . . . of . . .'

I snapped bitterly. 'A sense of impending peace! I assure you, you needn't worry!'

He said stubbornly: 'I've waited four years already.'

'Four years – and you just seventeen! In England you'd have another year before you could be called up–'

His whole being tensed. 'And whose fault is it that I'm not in England!'

Here was the core of the resentment that had eaten into his spirit. He had been 'sent to safety' against his will, and now he was going to get out of that unwanted safety at the first opportunity.

On Sunday he came home with his friends and they gathered in his room – the room that had been his nursery and mine – for a strange ritual.

Piet had devised a Heath Robinson contrivance by means of which they could test the strength of their lungs by blowing liquid from a low level to a high one. They discovered that some such lung-test was used for the Air Force and Fleet Air Arm, and they were going to beat whatever standard was required. Going past the room I could see them through the French windows – one of them seated on the floor, blowing down a long rubber tube with fearful concentration as the water level rose in a glass bottle, while the others watched and encouraged him to greater efforts.

'They've thought of everything,' I said bitterly to Teena, who was putting some of Piet's washing to dry on the grass bank.

Her wide affectionate smile shone on her face as she answered loyally. 'Miss Yoy worries too much. Dey're only young an' full of life.'

'Full of hot air,' I said crossly.

'When Master Peter makes up his mind,' said Teena, her voice soaring with conviction, 'even Miss Yoy can't move him.'

In November a further boost was applied to their enthusiasm.

Dinkie Bain-Marais's son, young Colin, came on leave from the South African Air Force. He was a bomber pilot – a tall golden youth with his father's powerful physique and magnificent head. His wide-set hazel eyes and his curved eager mouth were always full of laughter. Dinkie was aglow with happiness that leave, and, when young Colin came into the dark little shop where we worked, a light seemed to blaze up for a moment, so strong was the life and youth within him.

One sunny Sunday morning he and his sister, Shirley, came to see us at 'Tees Lodge'. Young Colin wanted to bid us good-bye before going north.

The effect on Piet and Ronnie of this heroic personality in the khaki uniform of a lieutenant – for the S.A.A.F. takes army ranks – was dynamic. They too must fly, they too must be on the wing and off into the thick of it.

Have you heard a migration of birds pass overhead?

I have once. On the west coast of England. It was towards sunset when the air was chill with autumn and the leaves lay golden in the lanes. The birds – myriads of them – darkened the shot-silk evening sky till it seemed sprayed with an indigo pattern of shifting varying density. The whirr of their many wings was a shivery sound, not of this world, as they passed out to sea over the darkening Channel, and I found myself deeply moved by their flight.

Now, as I bad Colin good-bye and good luck, and saw the expression on my son's face, the memory of that hushed chill moment on the grassy English downs came back to me. They'd flown away – those little birds – driven by some primeval instinct, knowing neither whither they went nor why. A thousand dangers would beset the sunbright air they sought, and weariness lie heavy on their wings. They would drop in alien fields and far-off seas; or here and there one might rest while in the rigging of a passing ship – ragged, exhausted, hungry and afraid; but only the strong and the fortunate would survive.

Thus it would be with our sons.

So young Colin flew north, and, in the shop in St. George's Street, Dinkie went on selling sheepskin toys and slippers to English service men who wanted 'a little something for the wife and family at home'.

Piet and his class-mates wrote their matriculation, and the holidays came.

It was hot next day, breathless and glaring as Cape Town can be in December, with the mountain mauve glass, the sky a clear piercing blue, and the city burning white.

Piet and Ronnie had one of their interminable telephone talks in the gibberish that passed for conversation among their crowd, and presently Piet went out, whistling through the corner of his mouth, his shabby old dog at his heels.

The Noon Gun sounded as he came back. The drawing-room clock struck twelve and mother I glanced at our watches. Deaf David appeared at the French windows to ask, as he did daily, if 'Madam had any letters for de post', and Josephine came in with the sherry tray.

My mother said, her gaze on Piet coming up the flagged path between the lawns,

'Here he is! What now?'

He was radiant as he joined us. Beads of perspiration stood on the smooth upper lip that, as yet, scarcely needed the attentions of a razor – and there was that look in his eyes . . .

'There's this, Mom,' he said, drawing a crumpled slip of paper from his pocket. 'It's the permission to be signed before they'll take me. Here, Mom . . . here's the place for your signature.'

CHAPTER TWENTY-NINE

THEATRICAL EFFECTS

So now we had a young sailor about the house, and it was 'Teen, will you wash my suit? And, look – the trousers have to be pressed this way – seven creases for the seven seas . . .' He was in whites, and there was plenty of washing and ironing for the faithful indefatigable Teena. He was very particular about his silk bow and the 'SOUTH AFRICA' on his sleeve. It was on a tab with gold lettering for his best jumper. Ronnie, who was in Air Force uniform, mocked at Piet's sailor suit. 'I wouldn't be seen dead in that rig!'

Piet laughed. 'I hope I won't either!'

Piet had joined the South African Naval Forces with the intention of seconding to the British Navy and thence to the Fleet Air Arm. The Fleet Air Arm accepted the Air Force standard of colour vision, and he was confident that he would 'make the grade'. The training bases for the S.A.N.F. recruits were in the Peninsula, so he was often with us. It was too hot for the workshop now, and, in any case, he had lost interest in shipbuilding for the moment, so his spare time was spent joining in the normal summer pursuits of the youth of the Cape – swimming, sailing, dancing and falling in love.

He went often to the seaside home of a slender coltish sixteen-year-old with soft brown hair, eyes like a swift Scottish burn and tomboy habits. Her name was Glendyr, which means 'by the water', and she was a good friend and playmate. But 'too young', of course. Seventeen seldom takes sixteen seriously. Seventeen hankers after the glamour and experience of twenty-one. So our sailor adjusted the balance by dancing at Kelvin Grove on Saturday nights with a merry silver-gold wisp of a hospital nurse, a firefly girl with glinting emerald eyes.

'He's growing up very fast,' observed his grandmother. 'It's the girls instead of the workshop these days!'

Nannie, who was making him a navy blue pullover, said, as she fitted him for it: 'So I hear your Afrikaans has been improving lately?' Afrikaans was the home-tongue of the firefly girl. Piet looked self-conscious, and Nannie roared with laughter and clapped him heartily on the back. 'You're only young once, my boy. Make the most of it!'

That summer Noel Coward toured South Africa to raise funds for Ouma's Fund, and everybody rushed, at enormous expense, to hear this versatile entertainer, who was also the most successful playwright-composer-actor of the contemporary English theatre.

South Africans in their own country are, unfortunately, theatre-starved. For their appreciation of acting and plays they depend upon the efforts of those two brilliant and delightful actress-producers, Marda Vanne and Gwen Ffrangçon-Davies, who are doing all in their power to promote and encourage the theatre in South Africa, and on a few sporadic semi-professional semi-amateur companies. There are, too, certain University Dramatic Societies which produce plays in Afrikaans as well as English. And this is a good thing, for the language which is spoken in sixty per cent of South African homes should have its cultural representation.

Noel, with his actor's facility for languages, had taken the trouble to learn a certain amount of Afrikaans before coming to the Union. But in spite of this evidence of good will, his arrival had the effect of inflaming the ever-latent antagonism of the extreme Afrikaner Press. Mainly, probably, because he had come at the express personal invitation of the Oubaas, Jan Smuts, whom he had met on his Middle East tour, or perhaps because he was received in the towns with such frantic enthusiasm and was, at Government expense, given special trains and honours hitherto only conceded to royalty.

His programmes, with their scintillating variety of sophistication, sentiment and partiotic feeling, were violently criticized while audiences were cheerfully paying ten guineas a seat – towards Ouma's Fund – to see and hear him. Whatever he said or did became the subject of a letter, an article or a question in Parliament. Noel, amazed, bewildered, and not a little furious, found himself a political issue. For all that, the tour was an enormous success and the money raised exceeded all expectations. But not without a considerable expenditure of nervous energy on his part.

I was very happy to see Noel again, not only for his own sake, but also because I knew that he had been on board the *Warspite* and had seen Bertie, and, at his request, had given a special performance for the sailors on deck and had also arranged for the ship to receive a copy of his film 'In Which We Serve'. Even though his news of my husband was out of date by several months, it was at least first-hand!

One evening, during his brief stay in the Peninsula, my cousin, Cicely, and her husband, Cameron MacClure of the S.A.B.C., gave a small informal dinner for Noel in their enchanting little Spanish house on the eastern flank of Table Mountain.

It was a 'turn-about' evening, for our old mountain suddenly decided to stage its own special local drama for the benefit of the visiting dramatist.

Mid-summer, the dry season at the Cape, is the season of

fires. They flare up on the mountain, in the forests and in the bush, and do great damage – particularly in the young plantations on the slopes of Table Mountain. That is why every Cape Town telephone directory has a Peninsula chart with fire-fighting points ringed and marked, and anyone observing so much as a tongue of flame on the mountain-side is in honour bound to report it over the telephone without delay. But only too often the tell-tale smoke goes unnoticed till nightfall reveals a long glowing serpent devouring the precious trees and threatening the higher residential areas.

On this particular evening I drove Noel out to the MacClure home from the Mount Nelson Hotel in Cape Town where he was staying. As we rounded the de Waal Drive into the Groot Schuur Estate, where the wildebeeste and buck graze tamely on the shoulder of Evil's Peak and the lions roar in their great cages when rain is in the air, he broke off what he was saying to exclaim: 'Look at that!'

In the violet dusk we saw a band of leaping flame fringing almost the entire length of a deep ravine.

'It's Skeleton Gorge!' I said. 'It's spreading from the summit down to Kirstenbosch. It's quite near Mac and Cicely's place!'

Cicely, whose admiration for Noel knew no bounds, was excited when we arrived, both by the presence of her hero, and by the spectacular technicolour performance for which fate had given us seats in the stalls.

'Just look at the mountain!' she said, in her deep husky voice. 'A special show for Noel.'

We followed her slender supple figure on to the terrace behind the house, where we had cocktails under a pergola of trailing vine. As the darkness deepened we could see the Lilliputian forms of the beaters silhouetted vigorously against the line of fire that seemed to be advancing inexorably upon the MacClures' back garden. Noel was enraptured at the cinematic effect, but in a fever of anxiety about our district which seemed seriously threatened. He wanted to 'do something about it'. But we assured him that the army of beaters would gain very little by our presence, and he relaxed.

Mac, who had read the six o'clock news over the wireless in the course of his day's work, laughed and said: 'Leave it to the Navy! The boys from Pollsmoor Camp have been called out and are up there now. I expect Piet's among them, Joy.'

After dinner we had coffee on the terrace, and were relieved to see that the downward dance of the flames seemed to have been arrested.

Presently Noel played and sang for us – trying out fragments of melody that would one day go into some new Coward operetta. Mac, who had successfully written and produced several radio operettas, was enthralled. Time slipped away, and with it the waspish little exasperations that had so sorely tried the temper and temperament of the artist among us.

It was after midnight when we drove back to Cape Town, and, so hot and beautiful was the night, that Cicely and Mac decided to accompany us. Noel and Cicely came with me, while Mac drove three other guests in his car. Suddenly, on the Kirstenbosch Road, Cicely cried out:

'Stop! There's a new fire beginning!'

Sparks, blowing down from the main conflagration, had fired a patch of shrub low on the road and within range of a few darkened houses near at hand.

We stopped the cars, roused the sleeping residents, and then, regardless of our evening clothes, we broke off branches from the trees and set to work to beat out the flames.

Noel was in his element. As a spectator, his interest in the mountain drama had quickly evaporated, but now, as an actor, he played an enthusiastic lead. He rolled up his trouser legs, flung off his dinner jacket, and laid about him with a will. We tucked up our skirts and followed suit. By the time the owners of the houses joined us, slacks pulled hastily over their night attire, the potential fire was well under control.

Above us a glade of delicate young silver trees was luminous and ethereal in the starlight. Safe. But, in the beam of the headlamps, I caught sight of Noel casting an anguished look at his best evening shoes. Ruined.

CHAPTER THIRTY

A PLOT AND A PARTING

In April the hot violence of the south-easter dies and a chilly sparkle refreshes the air; brief showers fall while the sun still shines and the children say 'It's a monkey's wedding!' In the Avenue the busy squirrels hoard against approaching winter and gusts of wind from nowhere scatter the tawny oak leaves. On the Atlantic seaboard the icy waves toss their white manes angrily, and even the mild Indian Ocean grows cold and rough.

That was when Molly decided to take Richard to Hermanus to 'pick up' after the summer heat, and I went with them.

Hermanus is a thatched fishing village some seventy miles from Cape Town. It stands on flowering cliffs and surveys a varied and beautiful coastline where rocky promontories alternate with silver beaches washed by long rollers. Blue mountains enfold it, and down their gorges flow peaty streams swelling into dark coppery lagoons that empty themselves into the sea.

In spring the arums grow wild in the fields, and the mountains are agleam with shining satin proteas. In autumn the heath flowers again, the parched summer grass is revitalized, and the tang of the sea is sharp and clean in the keen air.

There are holiday hotels along this coast, good fishing spots, good – but dangerous – sea-bathing, and a pleasant little golf course shared with gentle cows, who gaze plaintively at the tempting greens so ingeniously fenced off from them. The local residents had joined generously in the hospitality scheme, and so had the hotels, and there are many English service men who will remember Hermanus with grateful pleasure.

A little further along the coast is my surgeon brother Fred's house, always a cheerful port of call when the family is in occupation. Week-end parties at 'Blue Roof' included grown-ups, children, dogs, cats, budgerigars, a domestic staff, and everybody's friends of any age and sex. The boys slept on stretchers on the stoep, wrapped up in zebra or lion-skin karosses, and the girls and adults made dormitories of the rooms. My sister-in-law, Cecil, full of sleepy charm, catered for all and sundry without appearing to give the matter a thought, and her guests always did exactly as they liked.

Molly and I went over to 'Blue Roof' after dinner on the Saturday of our arrival. We found a house-party in full swing. The youngsters were playing a noisy game of rummy; Fred and an R.N.V.R. Naval Officer were deep in a chess contest; and Cecil was one of a bridge four. A drowsy green love-bird perched on her shoulder, the Warsaw Concerto wept its heart out from an overworked gramophone, and the scent of moonlit meadows and the sea at high tide came in through the open window while the first fire of the cold season crackled in the grate. A very young harlequin Great Dane was spread under the long table where the boys and girls played, nudging her slender puppy body every now and again with excitable feet. Marmaduke, the sleek black cat, strolled here and there, rubbing his arched back against the legs of whoever he suspected might be allergic to cats. On a table Yasmin's sketch-book lay open and forgotten beside David's ukulele. Both were always to hand lest a sudden mood pluck at the restless fingers of their owners.

Cecil stood up as we came in, slight-hipped in her grey tailored slacks, sunburnt throat showing above her open-necked shirt.

'We've just finished the rubber. You two come in, and I'll play gin-rummy with Patricia . . .'

We took our places and cut for partners. I drew a young soldier on embarkation leave. Molly was paired with a naval Commander. It was as well that the young soldier was neither a good player nor a critical one, for just at that moment the gramophone discarded the Warsaw Concerto with an irritable click and the strains of Rachmaninoff carried me back to Hamilton Terrace and those long ago nights when God's heaven pulsed with the death that rides the clouds, raining terror upon the shuddering earth.

'Your call,' said Molly gently.

'I'm sorry,' I said. 'Pass.'

I looked at my sister-in-law and smiled. Molly was concentrating as only she could do, her clear blue eyes seeing nothing but the cards and the moves ahead, oblivious of the sights and sounds and general turmoil around her – and I wondered if even her remarkable self-control could have survived the holocaust when music alone held the voice of hell at bay. A child shrieked, a dog yelped, Yasmin pulled Rosemary's hair, and David began to play his ukulele regardless of Rachmaninoff's competition. 'Four no trumps,' said Molly, and looked expectantly at her partner. Yes, she would have been just the girl for our blitz bridge.

As we were leaving, Fred said: 'You must join us tomorrow for a *braaivleis*. We're taking chops and sasarties over to East Cliff and we'll grill them on the rocks. The boys'll fish and the girls'll do as they please – just as they always do anyway, bless them!'

He stood smiling beside Molly's car, stooping to talk to us through the window – a great big man with a great big heart in which dwelt a deep love of seeing others happy. His delicate surgeon's hands rested lightly on the open frame of the window, the hands of the healer, steady and confident.

'Could Richard come along?' asked Molly, her profile clear-cut and happy in the moonlight.

'Of course, bring the sportsman! He'll enjoy it, and there's always enough for all comers.'

Which was just as well, because Piet arrived that night soon after we had left, having hitched a ride from Cape Town, gaily confident that he would find a camp-bed and a kaross on Uncle Fred's stoep. As indeed he did.

So next day we cooked our *braaivleis* (grilled meat) over wood fires and made tea in billy-cans on the rocks. After lunch the men and some of the girls fished, and the rest of us went for a walk along the cliffs. Richard trod on a baby grass snake, which fortunately failed to bite him, and found a tortoise, which he insisted on taking home. He was much distressed when he observed a sea-bird vanish into a line of foam.

'It's drownded!' he cried. 'The sea-gull is drownded!'

Molly reassured him. 'It's only diving for fish, darling. See, there it is again – and probably a fish in its tummy.'

Richard was relieved. His humanitarian impulse stopped short of the pitiable fish.

Yasmin ran on ahead of us, fair hair whipped back from her flushed face, the harlequin Great Dane puppy bounding along beside her. They put up a pair of dassies – queer cliff creatures, half rabbit, half guinea-pig, and in some obscure fashion related to the elephant. But then everybody in South Africa is related to everybody else, however improbable, so the dassie is no exception. The air of East Cliff was so strong and salt that each breath was a tonic.

'I'd love a plot of land here,' I said. 'It'd be heaven to have a bungalow here.'

Richard said seriously. 'Yes, that would be nice. Then I could come and stay with you very often.'

And Yasmin, who had run back to us with her dog, said in her quick, almost gasping way: 'Oh, y-yes, Auntie Joy! And I'll design you a house.' Words tripped over one another in their eagerness to catch up with her flying thoughts. 'And, look, that's the Agent's cottage there – the th-thatched one on the cliff—'

'But it's Sunday,' objected her friend, Rosemary. 'What's the good of an Agent on a Sunday?'

'He's been to church this morning – I'm sure he has. And anyway, everything's different at Hermanus!' persisted Yasmin.

Later in the afternoon I strolled down to the rocks where the men stood with the dangerous wash of the waves over their bare ankles. They were absorbed, with the remote expression of fishermen at peace with the world upon their sunburnt faces. Only David, always alert and lively, was busy turning an octopus inside out. 'Wonderful bait,' he murmured. 'Nothing like octopus!' Piet was hauling in a catch – a Red Roman.

Presently I drew his attention.

'Up there is an Agent's cottage – he sells land. Let's go and see if he has any plots for sale.'

Piet, who is seldom surprised at my suggestions, however inconsequent or unexpected, gave the matter a moment's thought. Then he handed his rod to David. 'You take this over, will you?'

The boy looked up at his sailor cousin, his freckled face beaming, the skin pealing off his nose and his sun-bleached hair wild in the wind.

'Sure, man! That's my favourite rod!'

'It would be a good investment,' I said to Piet, as we made our way towards the cottage. My excitement mounted as my impulse grew into an intention.

The Agent was a retired Major, and he expressed neither

astonishment nor annoyance at being molested on a Sunday afternoon. Business hours were variable in his case.

'Where did you think of buying?' he asked, giving us chairs on his glassed-in stoep, high above the bay.

The most extraordinary thrill prickled all over me. In all our years of marriage we had never possessed anywhere of our own, never lived in any house, or camped on any ground we could call ours.

I said: 'On the foreshore – with a view.'

'Dear, oh, dear!' The Major frowned and shook his head. 'Foreshore's practically all gone. Now there are some lovely plots over at Mossel River, near your brother's place – at the foot of the mountain.'

'It's different air,' I said. 'The cliff air—'

'Yes,' he agreed. 'The cliff air is terrific. But—'

Piet broke in. 'You said *practically* gone, Major. That means there might be something.'

The Major went into his study and came back with a chart of the coast. He pointed to a square on East Cliff, and Piet and I glanced at each other scarcely daring to breathe.

'The best fishing site in Hermanus,' said the Major. 'It belongs to a man who might sell. He's just bought a bigger plot on the mountain-side. I don't say he will – but it is possible he might consider it—'

'Let's go and see it,' said Piet.

'Now?'

'If it wouldn't be inconvenient for you.'

The Major said it would be quite convenient and drove us out towards the New Harbour in his car.

'Here we are,' he said.

A wire fence encircled a square of land overgrown with shrubs and wild flowers. Tall orange lilies and frail tinkling grasses nodded in the evening breeze. Behind us curved the mountains, gold-dusted with autumn plants, and, at our feet, the cliff, terraced by the hand of nature, stepped down, ledge by ledge, to the turbulent sea. Ever and anon a roller crashed upon a tongue of rock and sent a rainbow tower of spray fifty feet into the clear bright air.

Piet and I climbed down to the water's edge, while the Major waited for us.

I said: 'It's the loveliest place I've ever known. I want it terribly.'

The tall young sailor at my side put his arm about my shoulders. The wind flipped his square collar up against his head and made a little flutter in the wide hems of his bell-bottom trousers. His eyes were thoughtful.

'It's glorious,' he said gravely. 'But it's going to be rather dangerous for my children when they come to stay with you.'

I caught my breath on a laugh.

'Darling, that's taking too long a view!'

Next day, when Fred's family and all their guests and animals and goods and chattels had been conveyed back to town, and Piet had hitched a dawn drive back in a market gardener's van, I bought the plot on the cliff.

When I knew that it was really mine, I went back to it alone to savour the strange new joy of this possession.

I stood among the grasses and lilies in the morning sunshine and looked across the water to the glittering white line of the dunes and the far curve of Cape Agulhas. Sea, sky and mountains belonged to me. The plume of foam flung itself into the air and fell away with a peal of thunder.

Would we ever build here? Would the children of a lad going to the war ever really scramble about these sun-warmed ledges?

Unfortunately not, but, for the first time, I had experienced the thrill of owning land – a plot with a view.

Piet's draft was to embark at Durban, and the troop train left Monument Station at seven on a winter's morning. Troops were to assemble at six. 'I'll take you down in the car,' I said, for he spent his last night at home.

Teena woke me with a cup of tea soon after five.

'Madam is awake,' she said. 'Madam wants to see Master Peter before he goes.'

'Is Cookie making some breakfast?'

'Yes, Miss Yoy.'

He'd be splashing in his cold bath now. Summer and winter Piet, like his father, woke himself up with the rude shock of a cold bath.

When he was ready he went into his grandmother's room to bid her farewell.

She was sitting up in bed, neat and immaculate with her silver hair brushed and shining. The tall lad bent down and put his arms about her and held her to him for a long moment, and in that embrace was all his unspoken gratitude for the years of loving care and tender understanding she had given him. To her this young grandson, born seventeen years ago in this same room, was more like a child of her own – her Benjamin.

'Well, darling,' she said, holding both his strong hands in hers. 'Happy?'

'Very happy, Gran.'

'This is the end of a chapter, Piet.'

His chin lifted in the gesture we knew so well, and there was that look in his eyes as he answered her – that bright heart-catching look that is beyond description.

'No, Gran. It is the beginning.'

Down at Monument Station, where the wind smelt of sea and rain, I stopped the car.

'Shall I come to the platform?'

'No, Mom. Go back home now. And thank you for bringing me down in the car.'

He got out, hauling his bag and hammock out of the back seat. Then he took off his cap and thrust his face in at the window, and I felt his rain-wet cheek against mine, and it seemed to me that all our past misunderstandings had been resolved.

'Totsiens, Mom.'

'Totsiens – so long, Piet – and good luck!'

There was mizzle on the windscreen and the street-lights cast their wavering glow on wet asphalt. It was the grey empty hour before dawn.

He strode away with his long swinging step, his heavy kitbag slung easily over his shoulder, his head high, and the seven creases of the seven seas very sharp in his navy blue trousers. I watched him out of sight. He did not look back. I had not expected that he would.

CHAPTER THIRTY-ONE

ESCAPE INTO THE PAST

ON the afternoon of young Piet's departure I went to see Charles and Maisie te Water. I had decided to visit the little Karroo town of Graaff-Reinet in search of atmosphere for 'Lang Piet', and I knew that it was the traditional home of the te Water family.

When he had left 'Nectar', the Stellenbosch wine farm that was his birthplace, my grandfather had trekked north-east to Graaff-Reinet, then the last outpost of the Cape Colony and the springboard for the new crop of scattered republics the emigrant Boers were founding across the Vaal and the Orange rivers and in Natal.

Charles had recently undergone a severe operation, and he and Maisie were living quietly in their Peninsula home on the mountainside. They saw only their intimate friends and relations. Charles, temporarily out of the diplomatic and political life into which he was to be so startlingly recalled in 1948 to fill the post of Ambassador Extraordinary and Malan's personal representative in world affairs, was then devoting himself to welfare work, town-planning and the study of those domestic problems which would inevitably flare up in South Africa as a result of the war. His remarkable library on all matters about Africa and her problems and development was not for show only. It was one which he knew as a student knows his text-books.

It was in this library that I found my cousin and her husband. The day was cold and rainy, and Maisie's dachshunds were spread sleekly in front of the fire, while the love-birds in their cage by the window brooded sleepily in the melancholy winter light. His recent illness had hollowed and shadowed Charles's face, emphasizing the curiously elusive fly-away appearance which characterizes his whole personality. His blue penetrating eyes warmed as he greeted me.

'So you want to go to Graaff-Reinet?'

'Yes. And I was hoping you'd give me a line on it.'

Maisie chuckled. 'He'll give you a line on it, my dear. Charles thinks the world of that little dorp in the middle of nowhere!'

Charles talks brilliantly of places and people near to his heart, and I listened enthralled to his picture of the little Dutch town that had come into being in the time of the Dutch East India Company to fill the civilized needs of the frontier Boers, cattle-men of the interior who supplied 'Jan Kompanie' with fresh meat and hides for the Colony and for passing ships. These 'trek-Boers' grazed their herds over hundreds of miles of open veld. Their farm-houses were rough abodes, very different from the stately gabled homesteads standing among the vineyards and fruit orchards of the Cape. Their womenfolk bought the necessities of life from itinerant pedlars, and their children gleaned a sketchy education from nomad tutors who spent a few months at one farm and then went on to the next in a sort of educational circuit. They depended for their contact with civilization on the Nagmaal (Communion), when the farmer piled his family into his trek-wagon and travelled to the nearest town for this religious gathering of a God-fearing and isolated people. At the Nagmaal young couples were married, children of all ages were christened, and women, long-starved of the companionship of their own sex, were able to exchange gossip, recipes, and news of the latest fashions being worn at the far away Cape.

The trek-Boers lived not only in isolation but in constant danger. The marauding Kaffirs, themselves nomad herdsmen, ranged across the borders of Kaffir-land and stole cattle, which they drove away into the thorn-veld. So the Boers became accustomed to taking the law into their own hands and riding out in commando to retrieve their beasts and punish the thieves. Often they returned to find their homes and crops burned and their families slaughtered. This bitter way of life engendered a hard independence of character and a contemptuous dislike of the distant Cape Government which hampered their actions and never gave them adequate defence. Whether it was the Government of 'Jan Kompanie' or of Great Britain made no difference to their attitude. Neither, they found, had any real conception of the frontier-man's problems.

'Yes,' said Charles. 'It was a storm-centre in the days of Lang Piet and before, but nowadays it's been left behind by the tide of progress – stranded – and it's the most peaceful spot in the world. It'll take you right out of yourself and your anxieties into another sphere. You must go to the old te Water house when you are there – I'll write to my aunt, Mrs. Keegan.'

Maisie said: 'Mrs. Keegan may remember Grandpa.'

I smiled. 'Hardly. He was there about 1853 – nearly a century ago.'

She said, golden eyes dancing: 'That's nothing. Everybody in Graaff-Reinet is over a hundred and in full possession of their faculties. It's something in the air. They mightn't know there's a war on now, but they'll tell you all about the last Kaffir war, whenever that may have been.'

I left Cape Town one afternoon and reached Graaff-Reinet on the following evening. The train followed the coast and then turned inland over wild mountains and on to the plateau of the ostriches. Then civilization fell back and the blue escarpments of the Karroo spread themselves endlessly under the sky. A milky moon washed a sugar-loaf mountain with a neat little town beneath it, and the guard, coming down the corridor, thrust his head into the compartment.

'Here we are, lady. That's Spandau Kop, and there's Graaff-Reinet at its foot.'

He took my suitcase from the rack and collected the S.A.R. towels and pillows. I said 'thank you' and gave him a tip, and wondered why in the world I had followed the crazy impulse that had brought me here to the edge of beyond.

My week in Graaff-Reinet was a clean break with the present, and my pleasure in the experience was greatly enhanced by the companionship of Una Gill.

Una, as her name would suggest, is like nobody else. She is the daughter of the late B. K. Long – a distinguished author and politician and one time foreign editor of the London *Times* – and the widow of the artist-sculptor, Colin Gill. She is a student and a writer, a tall aesthetic young woman with the features of a mediaeval saint and a most unsaintly sense of humour. She was in Graaff-Reinet on a historical paper-chase, and she pursued her trail with indefatigable patience and industry.

Una had received a grant from the Leverhulme Trust to track down all the documents she could find about early British settlement in South Africa. The scent had led this gentle but persistent personality into homes and farm-houses all over the Union, but the Eastern Province was her richest field, for it was here, along the border of the old Cape Colony, that the first British settlement scheme had come into being in the year 1820. Old diaries, private letters, journals and business records were all part of the mosaic of the past, and somehow Una was able to divine their existence in the most extraordinary fashion. She had only to hear a likely name to worm her way straight into the owner's attic, and presently she would emerge with some fascinating historical fragment he was not even aware of possessing.

She and I explored Graaff-Reinet together. The little town had scarcely changed in the past hundred years. It lies in a horseshoe bend of the Sunday's River, neat as a draught-board, with single-storeyed zinc-roofed houses and here and there a lovely Flemish gable. Water-furrows flank the wide earth roads in the Dutch fashion. The narrow stoeps of the houses command a view of the street, and figs, loquats and other fruits flourish in the long, walled back gardens. We stayed at the Drostdy Hotel in simple comfort, and every day, after lunch, we took our coffee and wrote up our notes on the sunny stoep, and marvelled at the abiding peace of our oasis in the Karroo. The hotel had been the old Drostdy (magistrate's residence) before the advent of British rule had ousted the Dutch landdrosts in favour of magistrates dispensing the law in the English language.

Every morning Una took an overall and a coloured handkerchief to tie round her head and directed her eager steps toward the old Murray Manse, which had once housed the Reverend Andrew Murray, who was, for forty-five years, the Predikant of Graaff-Reinet. There, in the attic behind the central gable with its winged hour-glass to remind the heedless that even here time flies, Una wrestled with a formidable mass of old letters and documents, and returned to the Drostdy round lunch-time with a sort of dusty glow about her.

'Tell me,' I said, 'how a Scottish parson came to be the Predikant of a community that must have been very largely Dutch.'

'It may seem odd,' she agreed. 'But it's very easily explained. After the Napoleonic wars, when the British took over the Cape, it was difficult to get Predikants from Holland, and, since the Calvinistic Church of Scotland and the Dutch Reformed

Church had much in common, a Scottish minister was always welcomed by the Afrikaners. Moreover, the official language of the Colony had been changed to English, and, as the preacher in those days was also usually the teacher, it was an advantage to have him instruct the children in the new language that was still foreign to them. Sermons were generally preached alternately in Dutch and English, and, so far had the Boers grown away from their Netherlands roots, that they might well have found the Reverend Murray's Dutch easier to understand than the Nederlands of a Hollander!'

Una's researches had given her a remarkable insight into the feeling that prevailed between Dutch and English in the early nineteenth century.

'The individuals understood and respected each other,' she said. 'There were plenty of grievances against the Government of the Colony, and plenty of reasons for them, but the English settlers were just as bitter about it as the Boers. And in the Great Trek of 1838 there were many English who went north with the Boers – far more than is generally supposed.'

Graaff-Reinet was the real starting point of the Great Trek. It was to this little town that the Boers from all over the unhappy and discontented Colony had come with their wagons and their livestock, here that they had gathered and received the blessing of the Reverend Murray before going forth into the unknown hinterland. Of course, they quarrelled and split, and different 'trekkies' went different ways and many suffered tragic and terrible fates. For only two things ever really brought the independent Boers together as one man – a massacre of their fellow trekkers by the Bantu, or the threat of the long pursuing arm of Imperial rule.

One afternoon Una and I were driven up to the Valley of Desolation by a kind acquaintance. Up we wound, some two thousand feet beyond Spandau Kop, then we left the car and scrambled along a narrow tortuous footpath to the lip of the ravine from which that lonely place takes its name.

Here the mountain seemed to have been cleft in twain by some colossal bygone quake. Volcanic boulders strewed the dry deep chasm fringed with livid thorn-bushes and prickly-pears. A troop of baboons with narrow frowning faces and rainbow rumps bounded away at our approach, fathers and uncles scooping up stray infants as they fled, mothers burdened by babies clinging under their bellies or straddling their backs. The baboons have reason to fear humans, for many of them are taken from this district for scientific purposes.

Millenniums ago all this had been under the sea, and even now the land seemed to flow, ocean-like, to the far horizon, where it swelled and towered and broke in wave upon wave of violet mountain ranges, growing ever higher till at last the white crested ramparts of the mighty Sneeuwbergen arrested the tumbled tide in forbidding grandeur against the sky. The pinkish land, velvety under its nap of low scrub, was patterned with the shape of the heavens and the speed of the wind, for great purple cloud shadows passed across its immense face alternately with patches of primrose sunshine, while here and there ladders of golden light laced the ethereal blue of African space.

Within the shining loop of the Sunday's River, set about with emerald squares of lucerne, lay the little town with its fruit trees and flowers and its long emotional history. Eagles wheeled above us, hawks hovered and struck, and the air was vibrant with wings and fluted bird-calls and churrings. Now and again a hare or a dassie sprang up, or a small bush buck, and lower down we could see the red native cattle, with tough rubbery tongues, grazing the rough grass and prickly-pears.

It must have been a strange and moving experience to stand here a century ago when the wagons and herds of the Voortrekkers set the dust swirling upon the pastel plain. I could imagine the grim determination in the minds of the men that day, the prayers in the hearts of the women and the excitement tingling in the scampering heels of children running alongside the long leisurely teams of oxen. I could almost hear the crack of the whip. 'Hey, you, Rooinek! Get a move on you lazy brute!' The lazy ox, the bad one of the team, was always 'Red-Neck' or 'Lobster-Back', the name for an English soldier.

And when they had gone on into the wilderness – those who 'went before' – what of those who were left behind?

There'd have been boys in Graaff-Reinet that day kicking disconsolate feet in the powdery dust scored by the tracks of a thousand great wheels; there'd have been men half ashamed because they had preferred their grievances to the risks their comrades ran, and the women thankful that they, at least, would not be called upon to bear their babies in primitive anguish beneath the canvas tent of a trek-wagon.

Had Lang Piet been there that day, instead of in his cradle in far away 'Nectar', would he have stayed behind? I thought not. For the way of youth is the way of the brave and the foolhardy. I had seen the eyes of my own young Piet when he had said good-bye to safety to go and play a man's part in a war-torn world, and I could guess how the eyes of the Boers and British looked that day when they turned their faces towards the unknown hinterland.

Those were the days when Graaff-Reinet was a starting point in a lad's life, the gateway to adventure. Now the sleepy town dozed in its isolation, divested of its youth by the tide of war and progress. Life, that had once surged so fiercely round the little Dutch Kerk and the market place, where the hunters of the interior had brought ivory and skins for sale, and tales of terrible black warriors, had gradually ebbed away, till only dreams remained, fragments of a robust pioneering history.

It was Mrs. Urquart, to whom I was introduced by the friendly helpful young lady in charge of the public library, who gave me my best glimpse of the Graaff-Reinet district as it must have been in my grandfather's time.

She was a slender white-haired widow, immaculate in appearance, active and vivacious in manner. She lived in an old Dutch house set in a beautiful rambling walled garden running down to the river's bank in the lee of Spandau Kop.

'I'll tell you what might interest you,' she said. 'I have all the back numbers of the Graaff-Reinet *Herald* – right back to 1852.'

She cleared a magnificent stinkwood table for me and together we laid upon it the heavy files of the district newspaper that had been evolved from the original *Chronicle of the Desert* first published in 1851.

Here was the spirit of the frontier.

I said: 'My grandfather worked for a few months in a general store called Meintjies and Dixon. He was a transport rider, too.'

She laughed and riffled the huge yellowed pages.

'Look at these advertisements of Meintjies and Dixon! They didn't miss much.'

A full-page spread informed us that in the year 1854 Messrs. Meintjies and Dixon expected from England:

> 'Parisian stays, Egyptian lace, bonnet trimmings, velvet bracelets, bleached sheeting and worked muslin sleeves . . . fancy doeskin shooting coats, printed moleskin trousers, fancy worsted cravats and white punjums of various qualities . . .'

It would seem that the ladies and gentlemen of the border kept up with the latest fashions. But the needs of their daily life were also adequately considered. The same consignment from England was to bring them:

> 'Brass stirrups, sailors' palms, sportsmen's knives, tinned iron spoons, fancy Dutch tinder boxes, Epsom salts, Holloway's ointment,' and, to round off this diverse list, 'tinned iron neck chamber buckets.'

And, that the mind should be served as well as the body, they offered:

> 'Choice new volumes of Homer, Shakespeare, Milton, Leigh Hunt, Dickens, Mrs. Edgeworth, Miss Martineau and Mme. Guizet. Also new music by D'Albert and Lindhal, etc. . . .'

Shopkeeping in a frontier province must have been quite an adventure in those days, for the merchandise had to come overland from the coast by transport wagon, and the convoys were frequently attacked by the Kaffir raiding parties. So young Piet was as often on trek with the wagons as in the store, and it was on one of these journeys that he met and fell in love with Sarah Belfield in Grahamstown.

It was only after he had gone on into the new Boer Republic that the frontier was made safe for the white settler by a strange perverse miracle of fate.

In the new year of 1857 a young Xosa girl prophesied that if her people would burn all their crops and kill all their cattle, the sun would stand still in the heavens, divine herds and crops would cover the land, and the Xosa ancestors would rise from the grave and drive the white men into the sea. Her hypnotic powers must have equalled those of Adolf Hitler, for the tribes believed her so implicitly that they did her dreadful bidding.

In 'Frontier Intelligence' the *Herald* letters gave constant news of this growing disaster, which even the most ardent and influential missionaries were unable to check.

'*31st January*, 1857. The Kaffirs are quite desititute and have killed their last herd of cattle, and, having divested themselves of every goat, they are now killing their cats! ... The Prophet's last is this – "The English and the Fingoes are *dead* though walking about"!'

It was the end of a sorely troubled era. The day came when the ancestors should have risen from the dead to lead the starving warriors to miraculous victory. But they remained in the long sleep, and the hungry despairing Kaffirs flooded across the border, not with battle-cries and in full war-paint, but as emaciated disillusioned supplicants for food. Gradually the survivors of this tribal suicide became farm servants to their erstwhile enemies, and never again were they a serious menace to the settlers in the Colony.

Meanwhile, in the north-east, the Boers and the great warrior races of the Bantu had come into the inevitable conflict of the pioneer and the aborigine. With blood and tears they were writing their page of history.

Una and I did as Charles had suggested and went to call on his aunt, Mrs. Keegan, who lived in the old te Water house which had been in the family for many generations.

It had the usual verandah and striped zinc roof, and great lofty rooms, and at the back was a lovely unkempt garden where lilies and roses bloomed beside fig trees and vines still heavy with huge magenta clusters of Barberossa grapes.

Mrs. Keegan was very tall and thin, with her wax-pale skin stretched taut over fine narrow bones. She had, beneath a stately manner, a sprightliness which delighted us. In fact, it scarcely surprised us when, a few days later, we saw this spry old lady driving her vintage car rapidly down the main street, scattering aimless pedestrians with prolonged and masterful blasts of her horn.

The te Water house was rich in family history, from the lacquer and gold Empire furniture and crystal chandeliers, brought from Holland early in the nineteenth century, to the framed samples stitched by the nimble fingers of those crinolined ladies whose pictures adorned the walls in charming conversation pieces. In this home was the atmosphere of timelessness we had observed in other houses where we had received the hospitality so characteristic of South Africa. Though Mrs. Keegan, and her brother, Mr. Willie te Water, who was staying with her, were both well advanced in years, they were touched by the magic of this Karroo town, which seemed able to halt the onslaught of old age beyond a certain point. At the prescribed three score and ten time withheld its ravages, and even those fortunate enough to chalk up a century remained at heart young septuagenarians.

When the Coloured maid showed us into the drawing-room someone was playing the grand piano at the far end. Heavy old-gold damask curtains were draped at the French windows and Venetian glass girondeaux caught prisms of light on the ornate mantelpiece. The player's touch was delicate and lingering, and we felt that our presence had broken into a reverie.

Mr. Willie rose to greet us and shut down the lid on the yellowed keys.

'Please go on,' we begged. But he only laughed and flexed the fragile fingers of his thin cold hands.

'My circulation isn't what it was,' he explained in a light husky voice, 'and I find my fingers disobedient and unmanageable.'

Mr. Willie, who was several years his sister's senior, appeared to be all spirit shining through the pale flesh that was as a vellum shade for the lamp within. Then Mrs. Keegan came in and we had tea and crisp home-made scones and cookies and water-melon and fig konfyt, and afterwards we looked at old photograph albums and talked about the days gone by.

Mr. Willie said: 'I remember your grandfather very well. Lang Piet Marais was in this house on the most exciting occasion of my life.'

It was not, of course, the seventeen-year-old Lang Piet Mr. Willie remembered, but a blond giant in the prime of manhood.

'It was in 1875, and the President of the new Transvaal Republic – President Burgers – was on his way to Europe in connection with gold discoveries in his territory. With him, in his entourage, was your grandfather. They came to Graaff-Reinet before sailing, and they spent a night in this house. I was a little chap of about ten. I remember it so well – the preparations for a wonderful dinner – and my mother's fine gown – and how thrilled I was when, after dinner, my father came to my room and made me get up and dress because the President had insisted that I should be brought in to play the piano for him . . .'

Mrs. Keegan said: 'My brother was an exceptionally good pianist in his day.'

Mr. Willie smiled and shrugged, but his eyes sought the cold slight hands that lay along the arm of his chair – the fingers stiffened with rheumatism.

'When I had finished playing the President sprang to his feet and said to my father: "I'll take the boy with me to Europe. He must have his chance to learn from the best master!" I remember that my mother turned very red and then very white and cried out, "No, oh no, Mr. President!" . . . But the tall man with the fair beard picked me up and swung me on to his shoulder, and said "*Alle wereld!* What a chance, my bootie!" That was your grandfather.'

'Did you go to Europe with them?'

Mr. Willie said: 'Big decisions are often quickly taken. . . . Yes, they took me with them the next day. I was homesick and your grandfather was very kind to me on that voyage. It was many years before I came back. . . . When next I saw Lang Piet Marais he had settled at the Cape – in that big house at Mowbray – Wheatfield – that was the name. I went there sometimes . . .' Mr. Willie's eyes narrowed as he brought the past into focus. 'Your grandfather had fine horses and fine daughters. There was the girl who sang – the one with the lovely eyes—'

'That was Ellen,' I said softly. 'My mother.'

The short South African twilight had begun to darken the room. In the shadows Mr. Willie's face was ghostly, and only his alabaster hands gleamed palely against the black lacquer chair arms. The long room was a museum. The figures of our hostess and her brother belonged there with the golden goddesses painted on the Empire chairs, and the crystal tear-drops of chandelier and girondeaux, with the great family albums and the grand piano on which a little boy had played to the President of a new republic and changed the course of his life.

The young Coloured maid came in to draw the curtains, and Una and I took our leave.

CHAPTER THIRTY-TWO

SEVENTEEN

I LEFT Una still knee-deep in the cobwebby past of the Murray Manse, and went my way to Grahamstown reluctantly. The journey was long, tedious and roundabout, and I missed Una's amusing and informative company.

Grahamstown, probably the best educational centre in the Union, is the worst served by rail. I had to spend a night at Port Elizabeth, a little white seaport with chiming bells and a creepy-crawly snake-park. I saw no elephants in the surrounding Addo Bush and was disappointed, as the S.A.R. attendant had assured me that the creatures were not locomotive-shy, and I had hoped for a glimpse of the herd which inhabits that area.

Grahamstown is a cultural gem in a lonely setting of endless thornbush. The town straggles under the forbidding majesty of Rhodes' University on the hill, and is, as yet, innocent of buses and trams, since there is nowhere not within easy walking distance of everywhere else.

Accommodation was difficult to get, for there was an R.A.F. training base not far distant in the semi-desert, and the camp-followers were thick as flies in the hotels and lodgings.

I'm back in the present, I thought, as I unpacked my suitcase in an ugly little room with a linoleum floor. And, with that thought, came another. It's no good trying to escape into the past because the present is painful. And there followed one of those inner conversations one has with oneself when there is no one else with whom to thrash a thing out.

Escapist me. ' "Pack and Follow" was escapism. Why not go ahead and write "Lang Piet"?'

Myself. 'Bertie was with you when you really got into the swing of "Pack and Follow". Your mind was at rest.'

Escapist me. 'It's at rest now – it has to be. After all, he's ashore . . .'

Myself. 'Exactly. But he *isn't* with you.'

Escapist me. 'Of course not. How could he be?'

Myself. 'There might be a way of getting to him.'

Escapist me. 'If there were, I'd find it. You know very well that wives aren't allowed with their husbands in a theatre of war. Not even the Commander-in-Chief can have his wife where he is.'

Myself. 'You haven't given your mind to this. There are women in theatres of war – not necessarily wives.'

Escapist me. 'I had Piet to think of.'

Myself. 'He's gone now – beyond your help.'

Escapist me. 'Stop pestering me with restless ideas! Leave me in peace!'

Myself. 'This isn't peace. It's war.'

Escapist me. 'You know this line of thought leads nowhere – only to heartbreaking hankerings and certain disappointment . . .'

Myself. 'It's nearly two years since you saw your husband off at Euston that horrible night. Two years . . .'

Escapist me. 'Let me accept it. Other women have to accept the inevitable.'

Myself. 'By all means accept the inevitable. Only a fool doesn't. *But are you positive this is inevitable*?'

I shut my suitcase with a bang and went downstairs. The hotel proprietor was in the reception office. In South Africa a hotel proprietor is usually his own manager.

I said, 'I want to get tomorrow's train to Cape Town.'

He looked surprised. 'But you've only just arrived. In a day or two we hope to give you a better room . . .'

'It's not the room. It's an emergency. I've had to change my plans.'

He shrugged his shoulders. 'You'll need to go to the station to get your sleeper from Port Elizabeth. We can't do it from the hotel at such short notice. In fact, I very much doubt—'

'It'll be all right,' I said.

It was.

But before I left next day, I found my way to the Convent where Sarah Belfield had been educated.

The sun shone on quiet dusty roads and single-storeyed colonial houses. Golden-shower tumbled over the high Convent walls. A white-habited nun received me in a large bare room occupied by statues of the Virgin and her Child and the Holy Saints. She had the fresh glowing complexion so often seen in convents, where cosmetics do not penetrate, and a warm Irish voice.

I told her my mission.

'Certainly, I shall show you round the Convent. And I'm sure we'll find your grandmother's name in our records. Then, you must be a Catholic, too—'

'No, I'm Protestant.'

Her pretty pink face fell in undisguised dismay.

'But your dear mother was surely Catholic?'

'Yes. But my father was not. They were married in the Church of England.'

She was deeply distressed. And presently she excused herself and hurried away to fetch a tiny bottle which had evidently once held lavender water.

'This is Holy Water,' she said. 'Give it to your poor mother – God bless her – and tell her that we will pray for her.'

So sweet and sincere were her words, that I began to understand why my mother's childhood had been so greatly influenced by these good women whose main concern was with the soul and the hereafter, and in whose hearts there dwelt such innocent faith and love for all mankind.

There was a little gold cross on a bracelet I was wearing. It had my initials on it – J.P. – but in truth they were the initials of my father, Julius Petersen. I showed it to her.

'This belonged to my father. It was given him by the Roman Catholic nuns of the Nazareth Home in Cape Town. He was their doctor. He seldom went to church, but he was always kind and merry, and everybody loved him. I think there are many roads to heaven, Sister.'

When she had given me tea, she took me round the classrooms and dormitories and into a little chapel where Our Lady stood in a bower of roses and gladioli, lit by scores of candles. In one of the classrooms there was a small wooden desk on which the ten-year-old Sarah had scratched her name some ninety years ago, and from somewhere the good nun even unearthed a thin grubby exercise book with 'Sarah Belfield' written on the fly-leaf in a neat child's hand.

We strolled out into the garden and through a haphazard orchard to the river, where Sister left me to sit and ponder by a little shrine of Our Lord upon the Cross. I thought that a Convent seemed an extraordinarily friendly place, far less impersonal than the average school. Sarah must have been a happy little girl in this agreeable setting. And, later on, she must have found Grahamstown gay after its own fashion. For, in her day, the little town was garrisoned by the red-coats, who were as popular with the girls as they were unpopular with the farmers. And there were constant excitements when runners brought news that the Kaffirs were massing for war, and women and children were brought in from the surrounding farms and the air was thick with rumour and menace.

Life in the mid-nineteenth century was never dull along this troubled border. There was always something happening – even if it was only the arrival of a convoy of merchandise from the coast in charge of a tall young horseman with a letter of introduction, who fell in love with a grey-eyed girl at first sight.

The story of British settlement along the border has always paled into insignificance when set against the spectacular exodus of the Voortrekkers with its strong biblical flavour, but it is a tale every bit as dogged and determined in its own way.

It seemed to me, as I sat in the Convent garden under the figure on the Cross, that here in this lonely frontier province the spirit that had won through some thirty years of strife and agony and bitter disillusionment was exactly the same as that which I had seen displayed in England under the blitz. It was the unimaginative and stolid fortitude of the 'little man' in the face of shocking perils entirely alien to his training or way of life.

The frontier Boer was born to an understanding of the veld and all that grew, or failed to grow, thereon, including the savage. He was the child of his environment, armed by heredity and his upbringing against the dangers of his existence. The average British settler was as fitted to the life of the border as was Daniel to take up his permanent abode in the lions' den. He was induced to emigrate to this 'paradise' by the fair promises of a Colonial Administration unscrupulously set upon strengthening its frontier with a 'human wall' against a fierce and cunning aborigine to whom, in its 'sales talk', it never even referred. The coming of the Machine Age, and the rigours of the Napoleonic Wars, had resulted in widespread poverty and unemployment at home, so it was comparatively easy to persuade men – especially young men – that they would be well advised to seek their fortunes abroad.

One of Una's most interesting discoveries was the journal of a certain Jeremiah Goldswain, who was one of the first party of settlers to come to the Cape Colony in 1820. The manuscript, ill-written and ill-spelt, is a plain and, in parts, unconsciously moving tale of a simple life always at grips with adversity. When she had shown me the original I had been forcibly struck by the spirit of obstinacy and enterprise shown by the young Jeremiah, who flouted the exhortations of his father, the tears and entreaties of his mother, and the lamentations of all his relations with the arrogant ruthlessness of his seventeen years.

Seventeen must spread its wings, in peace or in war. It must break new ground, even if it breaks its foolish head in the process. Seventeen is the same the world over and throughout the centuries, whether it happens to be a tall lad riding away from a Stellenbosch fruit-farm in search of a fortune; or a sailor, with the creases of the seven seas in his bell-bottom trousers, bidding farewell to the house under the mountain; or English Jeremiah Goldswain turning his steps towards the Greyhound Inn in the year 1819 to hear the honeyed words of the agent of the new South African Settlement Scheme, who assured his listeners that it would be their own faults if they did not go to the Cape of Good Hope and make 'a little fortune in a verey short time'.

When Jeremiah told his mother of his intention to take up this golden offer, she wept.

> 'When my mother could speak she said that I was a verey unduteyful Child and I being her onley Child she said: a Jerey you will brake my hart if you are deturmnid to go and leve me for ever, for if you do go I shall never see you again: at this time I felt that my hart was hard and semed to care for nothing.'

Young Jeremiah carried out his 'deturmation to go' in spite of the fact that all his friends and relations gathered in his home to stop him, and

> '... one and all begun to weep and declare that the first thing they should hear wold be that I was killed by the wild beast. ... I told them that if they did not leve off weeping and talking so much that I wold leve them that night and that they should never see or hear from me for ever: this quited them a little.'

This lad of character left his home in Great Marlowe on 26th December at eleven a.m.—

'—just as the bells were ringing for Church. They town ware thronged with spectaters to see us start from the Greyhound Inn and menney of them brought us on our way as far as Bissum in Barkshiear, a vilage about one mile from Marlow. At this place my Father and Mother left me, and it was a verey hard struggle for me wen I recved my Mother's Last blessing and she reminding me that I was her onley Child and fealing her emotions wen she imbraced me for they last time . . .'

And, indeed, that was the last time that English mother saw her 'onley Child'.

Jeremiah Goldswain arrived in Port Elizabeth on 27th May after a hazardous voyage of five months. He and his companions trekked by ox-wagon to a spot on the Bushman's River, some thirty miles from Grahamstown, where he lived under constant threat of violence, for farms were burnt and families murdered by the thieving Kaffirs as a matter of course. In 1822 he married a settler's daughter, and they built a home of watling and daub and thatched it with long grass from the lakes. They grew wheat and barley and kept a few cows and some poultry, and they reared a family. But not without the bitter tribulations of the pioneer.

When Goldswain rode away to one of the innumerable Kaffir wars, his wife behaved in the same fashion as did thousands of her sort in World War Two. She treated prowling enemies much as the women of the blitz treated bombs – with off-hand indifference to a very real, but accustomed, menace. And her husband was proud of her as every soldier is proud of his woman who 'can take it'. One night, when she was left in the house with her five children and a neighbour's wife—

'—Mrs. Goldswain saw they Kaffers rownd the House . . . a little Dog that barked at them they beat it or kicked it so that Mrs. Goldswain thought that they had killed him. Wile they Kaffers was trieing to open the kitchen door Mrs. Goldi wished to scream out to friten them away for she was afraid that they wold set the House on fier and then they wold be burnt to death: but Mrs. Goldswain wold not alow her to do it for if they did set the House on fier they cold git the Children down steares – all of them could go into the kitchen and be safe: as the kitchen was a flat rufe maid with Stone and lime and had no communication with the timber belonging to the other part of the House, and they could be quit safe all tho they mite be a little ill-convenced by the smoke. Every Night after this my Wife tuck her Gun upstares with her determine that if the Kaffer did com that she wold trie and shoot the first that entered into the House . . .'

When an officer of the border-patrol tried to induce this stalwart woman to 'evacuate' to the nearest garrison town she refused to abandon her home. She told the Captain quite simply that—

'—she cold not do it: he stormed and swore that she should go but she got the day. The Captain mounted his horse and informed her that if they Kaffers came and killed all of them it wold not be his falte . . . so away he and the padrole rode, they men looking back and laughing at the bravery of my wife.'

So they lived, like hundreds of others of those first English families, through active wars and uneasy peace, growing to hate the Government which consistently misled, and never protected, its settlers.

Goldswain got on well with the Boers, and was in sympathy with their grievances, which only echoed his own. In short, he adapted himself to his circumstances with the stoical acceptance of his kind. It never entered his head that he was courageous, though he was sure that he was much misused. He grumbled and carried on. And, in the end, he won through, like the great majority of others whose descendants flourish on the land and in the towns today.

No wonder Una Gill loved her work. She was delving deep into the human stories of the past, and her industry and imagination have since received the recognition they deserve. For she now has her own room at Rhodes' University with her records and her archives all to hand. She has been given the title of 'Field Worker in Historical Research', and, through her, Grahamstown has become the Mecca of a curious pilgrimage. From far and wide the descendants of the first English settlers come to see this tall slight woman so that they may give her a letter or a chronicle that will set one more trivial piece in the jigsaw of the past.

'If there is a scrap of eighteen-twenty toilet paper still in existence it will come to me,' says Una, laughing.

It was a brave story – that of the past – but in Grahamstown I knew that the call of the present was ringing ever more urgently in my ears. I must get back into the history of my own era – back into the war.

CHAPTER THIRTY-THREE

FIRST STEP

WHEN I got back home a fat batch of letters was waiting for me. I learned that my husband had now been appointed Chief of Staff to Admiral Sir John Cunningham, who had succeeded Sir Andrew Cunningham as Commander-in-Chief of the Allied Naval Forces in the Mediterranean. His headquarters had been moved forward from North Africa into Italy.

While he was still in Algiers Bertie had seen Piet, whose convoy had touched at Alexandria, where some South African troops had entrained for the Middle East while others had cooled their heels for a fortnight awaiting transport to the United Kingdom. Piet was among the latter, but he had managed to use the mark-time period profitably by hitching a destroyer and bomber ride to Algiers, where he had spent four days with his father. The young Able Seaman had been much embarrassed at having to acknowledge a Commodore as his parent, while that shame-making parent had been extremely proud of his sailor son. Piet had slept on a mattress on the floor of his father's tiny room, and Bertie wrote to tell me that 'my room was like the Widow Twankey's kitchen while Piet was here – with his smalls hanging out to dry everywhere. He was most particular about his appearance and spent a good deal of his time washing and ironing . . .'

'Listen to this, Mum!' Every now and again I read her extracts from my husband's letters or from Piet's hasty scrawl, and we laughed and marvelled together over the fact that they had met.

'They're both very determined,' she said. 'Piet had quite made up his mind when he left here that if his convoy went East Coast he was going to see his father somehow.'

Outside, the rain lashed the rows of carnations in their green-painted petrol-tins, and the mountain was hidden in mist. Fir-cones glowed in the grate, and their resinous fragrance mounted with that of the logs. Mother's special fire-screen kept the heat off her chair while I crouched on a cushion on the hearthrug, loving the warmth. The heavy curtains stirred with the wind, so that she was sure that the windows were open – just a little.

'Bertie says: "I wish I could get you here, Joy-Joy – but this is a theatre of war . . ." '

My mother made no comment, but as I folded my letters and put them back into their envelopes I knew that she was waiting for me to say what had been in my mind ever since I had left Grahamstown.

'Darling—' I said, staring at the burning 'donnaballs', as if seeking in their midst the legendary salamander. 'Darling Mummie, I have to move on . . .'

'But you've just said wives aren't allowed in Italy.'

'I know. But I can't stay here any more. I've got to get back into the war – somewhere, somehow—'

She said, with a half-sigh, eyes on her hands spread across the open page of her book,

'You're no better than your son. Couldn't you just be peaceful a little longer?'

Reflections of the firelight made prisms of her diamond rings. I knelt at her side and buried my face in her lap and felt the coldness of those ageing hands against my cheek.

'Sorry, darling—'

Presently, when I looked up, I saw that she had put away her dread of loneliness and her fears for those she loved.

'With Piet gone,' she said, 'there's nothing to hold you.'

There was no bitterness in the words, no hint of reproach. She summoned her defences. She must 'take an interest' and forget about herself.

'Have you any definite plans?'

'Well . . . it struck me that perhaps I could get to Egypt . . .

oh, I know one can't just *go* – it'd be necessary to get a job in Cairo first—'

'Why Egypt?'

'It's a move in the right direction. If I could get to Cairo anything might happen.'

She said: 'It's a long way from Cairo to Italy.'

'But it would be nearer the war – nearer where things are happening. Italy's out of the question, of course. I don't even hope for Italy. I've accepted that.'

'Have you?' said my mother. And her grey eyes looked straight into my heart and knew that I hoped for the impossible and accepted nothing.

Anyone who could get to Cairo could easily find work there. But that was not the order of events. No job in Cairo ready-made, no visa – no visa, no transport.

However, it was my good luck that personnel for Allied War Organizations in the Middle East had been largely recruited from South Africa during the period when the Mediterranean was closed and transport from England as little as it was lengthy. The administrative office dealing with such appointments still existed, and the virtual head of it knew me well and now gave me her unstinted and valuable aid. My experience of journalism and radio and the fact that I had worked for the Ministry of Information and B.B.C. in London, and for the S.A.B.C. and Bureau of Information in South Africa, pulled their weight too, and one day my kind friend told me that the Middle East Branch of M.O.I. could use my services in their editorial section.

'Here's their offer of a job – and salary quoted,' she said, smiling. 'Now it's up to you.'

A passage was arranged for me in a troopship leaving Durban at the end of August. The last few days flew by and my exhilaration was intensified by the first hint of spring in the air. A new adventure was afoot! Where would it lead?

The Durban mail train left at three in the afternoon, and in the morning I went down to the shop in St. George's Street to say good-bye to Dinkie Bain-Marais. The sun never snared that little shop, and it was cold when I stepped across the threshold. Dinkie was serving a bothersome woman who couldn't make up her mind whether she wanted flowers or springboks on the slippers she was buying. And I was so filled with my own happy excitement that I scarcely noticed the blank look in her eyes and the dazed sleep-walker way she moved and spoke. It was Molly who slipped out of the tiny stock-room and drew me to one side. It was Molly who told me.

The bothersome woman looked at her watch.

'Nearly eleven o'clock! Look, dearie, I'll go and have a cup of tea and think it over. You keep these two pairs for me and I'll be back in half an hour—'

Yes, she'd be back.

But Dinkie's Golden Boy, who had brought his own radiance into the gloom, was missing somewhere over Italy. Young Colin would never come back.

Durban blazed with cannas and flame-of-the-forest, the sky was purest blue and the city sun-drenched white. Great Zulus, barbaric in fur and feathers, loped along, harnessed to high leisurely rickshaws. Durban was not like China, where the human beast died between the shafts with ruined lungs; here the rickshaw-runner existed for the benefit of the tourists – a touch of African splendour. Along the beach strolled the bright-robed Indians, more prosperous than ever they could have been in their own mother country.

Durban is a very 'English' city in her outlook. Lush and semi-tropical upon her hills, she was kind, friendly and warm-hearted, anxious to do all in her power for the service men.

We sailed towards evening. Our small trooper carried a regiment of Cape Coloured and a battalion of the South African Engineer Corps. There were a few women and children on board being repatriated to the Middle East.

The 'Lady in White' stood on the quay with her megaphone to her lips and sang us out. No troopship or warship left Durban during those years without her songs and her blessings. The boys leaned over the rail and called, 'Give us "Sarie Marais"!' And, as she led them, their deep voices took up the refrain of the marching song of the Boer War that had become known now wherever the orange flash might be.

'O—bring my trug na die ou Transvaal,
Daar waar my Sarie woon,
Laar onder in die mielies by die groen doring–boom,
Daar woon my Sarie Marais . . ."'

The words faded on the freshening wind, and the substantial figure of the Lady in White dwindled and was lost. She had sung thus when the *Warspite* had sailed for home and crossed with my outward bound convoy; and again when my son had said farewell to South Africa and his boyhood. Now it was my turn.

It was stifling hot passing through the tropics up the East Coast of Africa, and at night the Captain allowed the women and children to sleep on the boat-deck under the stars. The white troops were herded close along the passenger decks and the Coloured boys, orderly and well-behaved, were billeted in the well-deck.

After dark there was always a sing-song somewhere – either the white troops sang their Afrikaans lietjies, or the Coloured boys crooned their nostalgic coon-songs in the Taal. By day there was the perpetual monotonous ritual chant of Tombola – 'Housie-housie' – which is part of every trooper's life – 'By-himself, number-one . . . all-the-sixes, clickety-click . . . legs-eleven . . .'

It surprised me to hear how much more Afrikaans was spoken than English, as if to prove that it was not 'England's war' this time, but the war of all mankind. Yet there were many English South Africans among the officers – some of them men from the Eastern Province who had left courageous wives in charge of lonely citrus farms on the fringe of elephant country.

Then, early one morning, some three weeks later, we felt the dusty desert wind and the glaring port of Suez lay upon our beam. Carrion crows, the scavengers of Egypt's cities, wheeled in the clear brittle air, khaki camels and khaki jeeps travelled along the khaki desert tracks each at their own pace, and our troops, ready to disembark, crowded along the rail. Some had been to the Middle East already, and were returning from leave; and in their eyes woke the remembered hatred of flies and sand; others were merely interested. All were glad to be on their way.

A steward found me taking a last look round my cabin to be sure everything was packed.

'A Naval Officer to see you, Madam.'

My heart gave a bound.

But the Captain in whites was a stranger to me.

'I've brought a note from your husband,' he said, as he introduced himself. He was the Naval Officer in Charge at Suez, and he was very kind and helpful. Bertie had written asking him to 'look after me'.

He took me ashore to lunch in his cool Egyptian house with palms in the dusty garden. He said, 'There's a naval van going to Cairo this afternoon. It could take your luggage.'

'Could it take me, too?'

He looked dubious. 'It wouldn't be very comfortable.'

'I don't mind. The boat-train doesn't go till late this afternoon. I'd like to get along straight away.'

'Well, it's up to you.'

So a young Jewish sailor from Haifa drove me to Cairo in his van. He talked about books and music and his childhood home in Austria. Another Jewish sailor sat in the back of the van guarding the luggage.

'He must,' explained the driver. 'This van doesn't close, and, in towns, when you slow down for traffic, the wogs just nip something out and you arrive at your destination with half your stuff gone.'

The Egyptians are great magicians, and the vanishing trick is their speciality.

We were in Cairo by six o'clock. And, thanks once again to the help of the Navy, I found accommodation booked for me at the Savoy Continental.

There were more letters from Bertie.

As Naval Chief of Staff in Italy he held out no hope of getting to Cairo on leave or for any other purpose. But he was thrilled that at least we were much nearer one another.

I was physically exhausted that night, but mentally on my toes. I unpacked a few things, had a hot bath and a good dinner, and then went to bed early. Tomorrow was going to be the first move in a far-reaching plan of campaign, and I must be rested and refreshed, ready to observe the lie of the land and its possibilities.

Through the slatted shutters came the multitude of sounds that are the voice of Cairo – the rumble of trams, the urgent pipping and honking of motor horns, drifts of tinny music from the café opposite, and always talk and chatter and argument – a hubbub forever on the verge of a fight.

Sleep put dark hands over my ears and relaxed the weariness of my limbs. Sleep kissed my eyes and promised me the world tomorrow.

CHAPTER THIRTY-FOUR

CITY OF INTRIGUE

MOST jobs to do with news and journalism are peculiar. They seldom have any shape, any limitations or any certainty. Those who hold them have to be constantly on the alert, alive to every opportunity, a jump ahead of every event, ready to catch it on the wing and turn it to account. It is an attitude of mind which comes easily to me, and from the moment of my arrival in Cairo I was aware of that forgotten sixth news-sense stirring, sniffing the air and pawing the earth.

My first duty was to report to the British Embassy. The Ambassador, Lord Killearn, and his wife and family were on leave in South Africa, but Terence Shone, the Chargé d'Affaires in his Chief's absence, was an old acquaintance of ours from the days when Bertie had been Naval Attaché to Greece, Turkey and Yugoslavia, and Terence had been First Secretary to the Legation in Belgrade.

He was tall, dark and distinguished, going a trifle grey, with the rarefied charm peculiar to the Foreign Office of the Old School, when a British diplomat represented the best his country had to offer of education, elegance, training in international affairs and that worldly experience which is born in a man and seldom acquired. Such old-fashioned traditional qualities may be discounted by the new ruling classes of our land as being unnecessary and unimportant, but, where strength is present with distinction, it is still invaluable in foreign relations wherein the prestige of British envoys once stood paramount.

Terence arranged for me to be issued with all the needful papers and permits, told me who to get in touch with at the Ministry of Information, Middle East – known as MIME – and took me back with him to a small luncheon party in his beautiful house set in a garden shaded by the trees of the desert, pale and delicate, with butterfly flowers hovering in the fragile foliage. Acting Rear-Admiral Barry Stevens, the Naval Commander-in-Chief's representative in Cairo, was also there, immaculate in whites, and with a monocle in his observant rather challenging eye.

Both Terence and Barry were most kind and helpful, and I soon realized that Cairo had a glamorous as well as a busy side to it. I gathered that my appointment at MIME was regarded as temporary and that I might soon be appointed to work in the Publicity Section of the Embassy.

Cairo, that September of 1944, was like a great Allied junction. Almost everybody there seemed to be *en route* for somewhere else. Within a few days I discovered, to my delight, that many of my friends of the happy days of pre-war Greece were in Cairo, waiting for the Allied liberation of that well-loved country to give them the signal to return to play their part in its rehabilitation. And presently Princess Katherine of Greece and her Lady-in-Waiting arrived from South Africa, where they had been living in a charming little house in the Cape Peninsula.

Allied Forces Headquarters, with all its side-lines, occupied the finest requisitioned buildings in Cairo, and its huge personnel was billeted all over that lovely city on the Nile. In the neighbourhood were military bases and hospitals, and, though I had hoped to see my brother Norman at the South African Military Hospital, he had already returned to South Africa. Out in the desert were the tragic camps for refugees and displaced persons waiting for they knew not what, but all hoping that some day life would begin again for them and theirs.

Prices were astronomical, so Government subsidized hostels housed Allied women staff, who were charged in proportion to their salaries, which were much higher than any they would be likely to receive at home. There was dancing somewhere every night and the atmosphere of the city was feverish and artificial – a 'boom-feeling', with all the hectic excitement of a boom at its peak, and a foreknowledge of the slump to follow. On the fringe of this 'boom' lay the hunger and want of the poor of Egypt, but it was only on the bi-weekly meatless days that anybody gave the local poverty and hardship a thought.

After a few days I moved into a Women's Hostel.

Some of my friends were inclined to raise their eyebrows.

'You may have to share a bedroom, and how will you like being subject to rules?'

I laughed. 'That's all right. I'm here to work.'

'Quite an original viewpoint.'

It seemed to me that my best way to court my old flame, Opportunity, was to live in the working women's atmosphere, where rumours of all the possible jobs in the various organizations were bound to circulate. There was a constant interchange of personnel from the different war units, though the authorities did their best to limit it.

The Head of the Embassy Publicity Section was a grey-haired Fleet Street man with a game leg, a humorous and powerful personality, and a very shrewd knowledge of human beings. He told me that he hoped to have a vacancy for me before long.

I said, 'Please be quite candid. Would it be unfair for me to look round on my own in the meantime? Unfair to you or MIME?'

His expression was quizzical, his eyes searching and direct.

'What are you after?'

'A job in Italy – if there is a chance of one.'

'Italy is a theatre of war.'

'That's one reason for wanting to go there.'

He said: 'I think I know of another reason. ... No, it wouldn't be unfair. Not at present. But, if and when, we take you on here, you won't be able to transfer. Till then you are free. I'll let you know when our vacancy occurs, and, on your side, if you enter into any negotiations I shall expect you to tell me. But Italy is very much an outside chance – if it's a chance at all.'

That was how we left it.

The hostel was near Gezireh Sports Club in a residential quarter of the great dusty city. Here beautiful gardens skirted the Nile and a sense of peace prevailed. It was a new modern building, cool and spacious, and I was fortunate in being allocated a small bedroom to myself. It led on to a little balcony, shared by two other rooms, and overlooked a quiet leafy avenue of pepper trees and acacias. Sometimes, when the King and Queen took an airing, their carriage passed that way with outriders and cavalry escort. The clatter of hoofs always called me on to the balcony in hopes of seeing that bright cavalcade, the scarlet and gold uniforms of the riders and the mettlesome glory of the snow-white Arab chargers.

'Gee, they're swell!' said the American stenographer from UNRRA, who was in the room next to mine. It was the siesta hour, and she had been washing her dark hair. It fell about her face with rainbow gleams as she leaned forward eagerly. 'Say,' she added thoughtfully, 'don't you think all horses are divided into Arabs and Jews? Arabs, with the lovely little sharp square noses and sensitive silk-lined nostrils, and Jews with the long curved noses and rather melancholy expressions?'

She was one of the lucky girls. Everybody envied UNRRA staff, who were paid on a dollar scale that seemed to most of us fabulous.

It was still very hot by day, and we worked summer hours.

Every morning, at seven o'clock, the official transport assembled outside the hostel. Breakfasts were hastily eaten and, with jerseys over our thin cotton dresses, we rattled off to our various places of employment.

I loved that morning drive in the back of the extraordinary old tumbril marked MIME. The air, sharp and dewy, still belonged to the birds, and it seemed to me very strange and lucky that anyone should pay me to be in Egypt at such a glorious time of the year. Tall-sailed felluccas drifted dreamily downriver on the morning breeze that set palm fronds trembling and shivered the leaves; little Arab boys turned somersaults and catherine-wheels on the pavements for the joy of life and a copper coin; and trams clanged furiously along, festooned with swarming clusters of humanity which disintegrated and reassembled at short intervals as individuals dropped off like ripe fruit, or popped on and attached themselves precariously to the human outriggers swaying wildly at the street-car's extremities. I was constantly lost in admiration for the agility of the Arab when he saw fit to abandon his Oriental repose. One moment he might be squatting in the sun with flies clinging to his eyelids, and the next he would be travelling with mad impetuosity in all directions. Like Dora of H.M.S. *Excellent*, he evidently regarded his bicycle as his 'best friend', and it mystified me to see the ease and dash with which these men in voluminous nightgowns sprang on and off their iron brutes regardless of that fearful central bar specially designed to imperil female attire. It was his way either to loiter deliberately or to stride along with the usual pendulum movement of the arm exaggerated into an ecstatic swing shoulder high with every step.

At one o'clock we trundled back to the hostel for lunch and did not return to the office till five. So it was possible to rest and go to Gezireh for a game of tennis or a swim during the midday break. All transport made a regular detour through Gezireh grounds to pick up Allied staff who had been enjoying the hospitality and recreation offered by this very generous club. At seven the day's work was done and the night life of Cairo, city of intrigue, stirred and twitched a wolfish nose.

There was always some amusement afoot. Dinner, perhaps, outdoors on a balcony above the moonlit waters of the Nile, or dancing at Shepheard's with fairy lights among the tall palm trees, or an open-air cabaret in the shadow of the Pyramids, or maybe just a meal and a cinema in the town. It would have been easy to linger on in this 'Whispering Glade' of ten thousand good intentions, dead and gone; but I was armed with an amulet against the seduction of Cairo. And this amulet was my secret determination to get right back into the war – and, if possible, into my husband's sector of it.

In 1943 the bitter struggle to get to South Africa had poured steel into my veins, and some of that stern alloy still remained to temper the lazy warmth of flesh and blood. Once again a goal was before me, and every word, sign and contact that might help me another step on the way was mentally pigeon-holed for use against the day when Opportunity should cross my path. In the meanwhile there was no dearth of work or play.

The Head of the Personnel Branch of MIME had a German name and a habit of pacing frantically up and down his office, hands clasped behind his back, head lowered with out-thrust jaw. His name, translated freely, meant 'For the love of Allah!' and his attitude to his staff was frequently to match. The Egyptian summer had taken its toll of the health of women unaccustomed to the climate, and the secretariat and typing pool were constantly depleted by sickness. On the executive and administrative side people applied for transfers whenever there was a chance of bettering their salaries, while others, such as myself, were suddenly thrust into the organization as temporary stopgaps. And there was always the problem of leave and billeting. Thus Mr. Love-of-Allah was faced with a perpetual human ebb and flow which must have caused him a chronic headache.

It was he who kindly arranged my accommodation at the hostel, ceasing his pacing for a few moments to put through the necessary telephone call, and he who presently turned me over to the Chief of the News Division.

The News Chief was a young Major with a pronounceable Polish name and the bland personality of one who had risen above the fretful urgency of a job immediately concerned with world events. He had a countenance as serene, unlined and unshadowed as a stretch of springy turf in full sunshine, and a voice as mellow as a summer's day. He explained MIME's set-up to me and showed me an impressive list of publications in English, French and Arabic which it circulated throughout the Middle East. Many topical features were written and translated in Cairo, where a certain proportion of the material was printed.

The Major had seen my radio scripts and cuttings, and he decided that I would be most useful in the Feature Section. So he summoned the Features Editor, a pallid young gentleman with a pair of cold blue eyes set flat on the surface of his face, and so oddly expressionless that they seemed anchored in the shallows of the mind rather than in the deeps of the spirit.

'Between you,' said the bland Major, 'it should be possible to think up some new ideas for feature stuff linked with news.'

The young gentleman silently motioned me to follow him into the dim dusty room from which he directed the stream of material to his many magazines and papers. He went to the shuttered French windows, through which roared the ear-splitting medley of sound that characterized a busy street in Cairo and closed them carefully.

'Unless you close the windows it is impossible to hear the human voice,' he remarked. 'Now we can talk. Will you sit down? No, I don't recommend a cane chair, they are infested with bed-bugs. Try the wooden kitchen chair, it's less comfortable but also less itchy.'

He sat at his desk and gazed pensively at the blotter, where a number of spidery little people performed curious antics. He took up his pen and added a minute top-hat to a toothpick man.

'You've been in the Far East, I believe?'

'Yes. Several years in China. And I've travelled in that area roughly from Java to Japan.'

'You know Malaya?'

'I've stayed there. Up country, as well as in the ports.'

'French Indo-China and Thailand?'

'I've been overland from Bangkok to Saigon—'

'Burma?'

'I've flown over it and spent a night in Rangoon – but I certainly don't know anything about it.'

He said, after a few more questions: 'At all events, you are familiar with the background.'

'To a certain extent.'

He looked up from his doodling.

'We want some articles on the Far Eastern War – not technical, but on human lines – you know the sort of thing . . . the effect of the war – of the Japanese Occupation in particular – on the lives of the people out there. Some economic facts and figures, of course, but not just the dry stuff. How do you feel about it?'

'Have you a reference library where I can get the facts and figures?'

'Yes, on the top floor.'

'Well, if you like, I'll go and browse around in there for a while and study the background material available. Then I'll give it a think and put up a few suggestions.'

'Do that,' he said. 'And remember most of our readers are Moslems.' He stood up and indicated various areas on a wall-map of the Middle East. 'Stuff is translated into Arabic and French for this section . . . Hebrew here . . . and in Italy, of course, we syndicate a good deal of English stuff to the Forces' papers – *Union Jack* and *Eighth Army News*—'

He added a few directives, points to be stressed or avoided, and sent for a messenger to take me to the library.

'Judith will help you,' he said. 'She's the librarian. An Egyptian girl. Talks too much and too fast. But knows her job.'

A few days later, my husband, who happened to be spending a week-end at the Commander-in-Chief's villa in Naples, went down to breakfast where the usual newspapers were on the table – the American *Stars and Stripes*, and the British *Eighth Army News* and *Union Jack*.

The Commander-in-Chief looked up from his coffee.

'You didn't tell me your wife was writing for *Union Jack*,' he remarked.

'I have no reason to think she is,' said Bertie.

'Well, I have,' said the Commander-in-Chief drily. 'Here you are. An article on the Chinese Tommy – what he is paid, what he wears, what he eats, how he marches and fights and thinks and feels, and how he spends his leave . . . signed Joy Packer . . .'

'Hell's delight!' said Bertie. 'Where would she get her information?'

'Wherever she gets it, she's not likely to find anyone here to contradict it,' said the Commander-in-Chief, not without a trace of envy, and immediately contradicted several assertions in no uncertain terms.

My source of information was Judith – Egyptian Judith, who was to play the part of Coincidence at a vital moment in my life.

CHAPTER THIRTY-FIVE

NO RED CARNATION

JUDITH had many qualities as a librarian, but one she lacked. She neither imposed, nor practised, the rule of silence. And I soon found that anyone coming to collect reference material from her invariably settled down for a chat and a cup of thick powdery Turkish coffee brought by the floor-messenger, a handsome beige man in a red fez, who appeared in answer to her shrill cry 'Abdullah!' and vanished again for an unconscionable time till she flounced to the door and yelled once more, like a steam engine approaching a tunnel, '*Abdullah!—*' followed by a flood of Arabic, which I am sure was not always ladylike.

She was a Spanish Egyptian with a quick temper, a quick intelligence and a tongue that was apt to run ahead of both. She had a strong nose, a full scornful mouth and a pair of magnificent almond eyes. Two plaits of blue-black hair were coiled about her head like ropes around a neat parcel packed with ideas and inspirations. Her desk was by the window, high above the city with its domes and minarets, its palms and clanging trams, and against the clear cobalt sky there was always the wheeling pattern of crows.

Next to her desk was that of the lazy little Greek girl who

was supposed to be her assistant. Marika was an indolent near-blonde, with sling-heeled sandals and very thin silk blouses. When she walked across the room to get a file of cuttings from a shelf, or to shriek for the wretched Abdullah, her loose heels clacked noisily on the bare boarded floor and her little sharp breasts bounced provocatively with every step. Her lips were scarlet and pouting and she was filled with discontent. But once I saw her happy.

Through the open window came the sound of a demonstration, and Judith leaned far out and yelled to us.

'It's Greek students! They've mobbed the trams, they are riding all over them – on the roofs and everywhere – they are waving flags and going mad! It's the liberation of Greece! The British are in Athens!'

Then Marika rushed to the window and would have fallen out if Judith had not grabbed her flimsy blouse. And presently, when the swarming trams had gone their way with their tumultuous burden, she flopped down at her desk and buried her face in her arms. 'I am so happy – so happy . . .' she sobbed.

I went back to my files telling me about the Japanese occupation of Burma, about their subtle schemes for the 're-education' of conquered children, about the Resistance Movement in the Philippines and the enslavement of the populace wherever the Rising Sun showed its face; but a new idea was playing will-o'-the-wisp in the back of my mind. What about UNRRA into Greece? I knew and loved Greece, and, since there seemed no likelihood of getting directly into Italy, why not explore the possibilities of UNRRA to Greece, for later, perhaps, it might be – in fact, would be – operating in Italy . . .

That afternoon at Gezireh I discussed this new notion with some of my friends from Athens. They were all tremendously thrilled with the news of the liberation, which must surely herald their own return in the near future. One of them happened to be in close touch with the American Director of the Aid to Greece Section, and he gave me an introduction to this active personality, who had known and worked with my husband in Athens during the period just before the war.

UNRRA's afternoon hours began and ended earlier than MIME's, so when the UNRRA bus trundled through Gezireh an hour in advance of MIME's I piled into it and was conveyed to the headquarters of the United Nations Refugee and Rehabilitation Association.

The Director of the Greek Section was about to fly to Athens next day, but he found time to see me and to pass me on to Mr. Jason, the tall aesthetic-looking American-Greek in charge of Publicity.

Mr. Jason had the personal charm and apparent indifference to detail which characterized his Mediterranean countrymen, but he also had a practical American training. It seemed that he needed someone to edit a monthly magazine to be produced in Athens, representing 'UNRRA to the World'. This editor would also be responsible for hand-outs and assistance to foreign journalists and any other publicity matter about UNRRA in Greece and the Greek islands.

Negotiations with Mr. Jason went well, and within a few days the prospect of an appointment, with a salary which I privately regarded as princely, seemed more than favourable. In fact, all that was required was confirmation from New York. So, as I had promised, I went to see the Head of the Embassy Publicity Section to tell him what had happened.

He said: 'Greece . . .' and looked thoughtful. Then he added, 'Well, when it's clinched let me know.'

Back in the library at MIME Judith said: 'You have a pleased sort of glow about you. What's happened?'

I said, 'I'm rather excited. There seems a pretty good chance of my getting to Greece with UNRRA.'

'Oh!' cried Marika, her soft lazy voice suddenly urgent. 'Take me with you! I have relations in Athens. I long to go to Greece – I have never seen the Parthenon – or my relations! You must give me an introduction to the man – *please* . . .'

I laughed, and promised to tell Mr. Jason that I knew of a Greek-speaking clerk with French and English, and Marika relaxed. She would go and see him the very next day. Judith screamed for Abdullah and demanded coffee for three.

'So that's what you wanted, is it?' she asked.

'Not exactly. But it's the next best thing.'

'What did you really want?'

'To go to Italy. My husband is at Caserta . . . I haven't seen him for two years . . .' To my horror, my eyes suddenly filled with unexpected tears, and I turned away quickly and went to the window, staring out at swimming domes and minarets, amber and rose in the evening light.

Abdullah came in and set down the coffee tray.

I said, 'Tell me how *you* are getting on, Judith?'

Judith, like everyone else in Cairo, was restless to move on. She had received a scholarship to London University, but could not get her visa and transport to England. She was twenty-two and obsessed with a horror of her student years slipping past before she could use them to full advantage.

She gave her scornful shrug. 'Goodness knows when my visa will come through . . . don't let's think about it.' She looked up as one of the French translators came in, and she began to laugh and flirt with him, switching to her harsh rapid fluent French. He sat down in the cane chair opposite her desk, and I smiled to myself. He wouldn't be there long. Every wicker chair in Cairo – even those at the best hotels – harboured a voracious community of bugs. The creatures lurked in the seats, arms and legs, and grew fat on a deliciously varied human diet. They never left their secure little world to travel away with their donors, they were far too intelligent for that. They merely popped out for a nibble and popped back again till the next victim should present him or herself.

After a while the Frenchman got up scratching his bare elbows – for everybody worked in their shirt-sleeves – and, muttering something about '*ces sacrés poux*', followed the clacking sloppy heels and undulating hips of Marika over to the shelf where his files were kept.

Judith said, as if our earlier conversation had never been interrupted, 'I have a friend working in Italy – a girl friend.'

'Then she must be attached to one of the fighting services, because no civilian women are allowed there yet – not even UNRRA.'

She shook her head vigorously.

'No. She's not in one of the uniformed services. She is a civilian in P.W.B.'

'I've never heard of P.W.B.'

'It's hush-hush – something to do with propaganda. I don't know what the initials stand for myself, but I do know that P.W.B. can use people with radio and journalistic experience. In fact, I should have thought you'd be right up their street. My friend told me before she left that they were crying out for writers—'

'*Judith!*'

The air vibrated about me. Opportunity does not meet you under the clock wearing a red carnation in his button-hole so that you may know him when you see him. He is an unknown name, an unheard voice, an unseen form slipping through the crowds, but to those who seek him his presence is unmistakable. Quick! Catch his coat-sleeve before he has time to escape! He is slippery as a fish, evanescent as a chance shaft of sunlight on a cloudy day. Grasp him and hold him – *Quick!*

'Judith, who gave your friend her job? Who do I get in touch with? Tell me a name – someone who knows about P.W.B.!'

'There's a man called Ex. He used to work here at MIME. He's the one, or I think he is.'

'Where do I find him?'

She took up her telephone and called A.F.H.Q. exchange.

'This is MIME. I want Mr. Ex's number – in P.W.B. . . . it's urgent.' Her enormous black eyes sparkled as she held her hand over the mouthpiece. 'Shall I get him if I can?'

'Yes,' I said. Don't take time to think and consider when the phantom figure seems near, just plunge and hope – that is the only way!

I heard her say, 'Mr. Ex . . . this is Judith in the library at MIME. Here's someone wants to speak to you. Mrs. Packer – she's working here—'

The receiver was in my hand and a crisp incisive voice was saying, 'Yes, what is it? *Who*?'

There are times when all the unknown resources in one's being muster themselves, sharp and bright, to meet a sudden emergency. Instinct and flair take over and fight a preliminary battle for common sense to follow up later. Now I remembered two things. Keep it brief when you're talking to a busy man, and, out of my radio experience, came the remembered lesson that a smile 'comes over warm'. When I put down the telephone I sank into a chair with my knees shaking.

'Well?' said Judith.

'He'll see me the day after tomorrow at three thirty.'

'Good.'

'What's he like? Give me a line.'

Her lip curled. 'You won't get any change out of him. He's brilliant, but he's ice.'

'Married or single?'

'Married.' Her eyes became reflective, melted a little. 'He adores his wife. She's sweet, as a matter of fact. She works at A.F.H.Q. – I don't quite know what she does . . . Here – you look as if you could do with a cigarette—'

She pushed an open packet of thin gold-tipped Egyptian cigarettes towards me, dry, light and scented.

'Thanks,' I said. 'And not just for the cigarette. Anything could happen now.'

Judith laughed. 'I agree. And if you stay in that chair much longer it will. Bugs don't waste time either.'

Fate's favourite game is Cat-and-Mouse, and that night I was stricken with 'Gyppy tummy'. The form of this affliction then prevailing in Cairo was virulent. It pole-axed the sufferer. It caused retching, running, cold sweats and deathly swoons. The Egyptian floor-servant who found me collapsed outside the ladies loo called the matron, and together they got me to my room. The matron summoned the doctor, who had a special mixture he invariably prescribed for 'Gyppy tummy', and this he now gave me with the warning that I would need to spend a few days in bed. 'Of course, it may be jaundice,' he added with a benevolent smile. 'There's plenty of that about – rather a violent brand.'

I was pulverized, physically and mentally.

By noon next day the doctor had decided against jaundice, but emphasized the necessity for complete rest. Matron ordered me a special diet, and I discovered that the rules of the hostel required its inmates to do exactly as they were told in the event of illness.

So, on the following afternoon, I had to get up furtively and sneak, unobserved, out of the building to keep my appointment with Mr. Ex. Before doing so I took a double dose of the doctor's opiate, for, although my symptoms had ameliorated, I was by no means 'safe'.

There was a taxi-rank some five minutes' walk from the hostel, and today it happened to be empty. No taxis there and none in sight. I waited in the hot sun with one anxious eye on my watch. Ten past three! To be late would never do. Just then a jeep appeared, driven by a small shrivelled American negro. I hailed it wildly, and the little negro put on the brakes and drew into the kerb. He wore the khaki uniform of a transport driver.

'Please,' I said breathlessly. 'Are you going to A.F.H.Q.?'

'Near enough, lady.'

'Can you give me a lift, or isn't it allowed to take civilians?'

'That's Okay, lady. Climb in.'

So I took my first ride in a jeep and arrived at Allied Forces Headquarters at exactly three-thirty. Sentries, barbed wire and check-points made sure that only authorized persons entered these imposing premises, but at last, after all formalities were completed, I was ushered into Mr. Ex's study by a cheerful girl secretary.

Mr. Ex rose and offered me a chair. I put my brief-case of cuttings and scripts on his desk.

'I'm sorry I'm late. There was no taxi, and I had to hitch a ride in a jeep with an Ethiopian driver.'

He smiled – a brief, brilliant smile turned on and extinguished, leaving his face cold and almost hostile.

'That's all right. Taxis can be difficult in Cairo.'

It was very hot, and Mr. Ex was in his shirt-sleeves, but they were immaculate blue shirt-sleeves and lent him no air of informality. They merely served to emphasize the light wiriness of his frame and the preciseness of his movements. He had keen red-brown eyes. Ruthless, I thought, intolerant of muddle or prevarication. I'd better put my cards on the table and condense what I had to say.

'Well, what can I do for you?' said Mr. Ex.

I said, 'I know nothing about P.W.B. – not even what that stands for. But I've heard that it needs journalists with a knowledge of radio work. If that is so, I may be useful to you. If not, I won't waste your time.'

'It is,' he said. 'But we've shifted most of our staff to Italy.'

'I've heard that, too. I want to go to Italy.'

Mr Ex's eyes flashed like bronze javelins in the sun. They struck. 'Why?'

Judith had said, 'He adores his wife.' I told him the truth.

'My husband is at Caserta. I haven't seen him for two years.'

His smile took a cynical twist, but was not unkind. 'What is he doing there?'

'He is Chief-of-Staff to the Naval Commander-in-Chief.'

'Can't he get you there?'

'No – unfortunately.'

'So you think *we* will.'

I laughed then, and so did he. 'Not unless it's worth your while. I'm here to persuade you – convince you, in fact – that I *am* worth sending to Italy. Some of the proof is in this brief-case.'

'Go ahead,' said Mr. Ex, and leant back in his chair.

I told him all that it was essential for him to know, including my negotiations with UNRRA, my link with the Embassy Publicity Section, and that I was already working for MIME and doing freelance broadcasts for Egyptian State Broadcasting.

'I'm doing a talk for them tonight after the news,' I added.

'What on?'

'The human angle on the Chinese soldier.'

'What do you know about that?'

'I know Chinamen – and one can learn facts.'

He grinned. 'Facts on Chinamen won't help you in Italy. Can you speak Italian?'

'Not yet.'

The answer seemed to amuse him.

'You realize that, if we took you on, there'd be no guarantee where you'd be working. It certainly would not be Caserta.'

'That's all to the good. Service wives are not allowed to be with their husbands – there's some sort of rule about it.'

'And you hope to get past it?'

'In a manner of speaking – yes.'

'You're candid, at all events.'

'Mr. Ex,' I said earnestly, 'everybody in the world who goes after a job has some personal reason for doing so. The only material consideration is whether they can fill the bill.'

He pushed a form towards me across his desk, his red-brown eyes twinkling. 'You'll need to fill this bill to start with. It will take you some time and some thought. My secretary will help you, if you like.'

'Thanks. I'd be glad.'

'By the way, will MIME release you?'

'Yes, that's understood. Any time I wish.'

His narrow nervous hand touched my brief-case.

'Can you leave this stuff? I'd like to have a look at it.'

'Of course.' As I rose to go, I added, 'One thing more. Will it take long for you to give me a decision?'

'Is there any hurry?'

'I can't keep UNRRA on a string.'

He said drily, 'It would surprise me very much if any women were allowed to go into Greece for quite a long time.'

Here was an undercurrent – something I did not understand. I recalled the Director of Embassy Publicity saying 'Greece ...' in a thoughtful way.

I said, 'They have other units – the Balkans ...'

He said, 'I will have to make my report and send it to Italy. The final decision rests with them there. I can write tomorrow and ask them to reply by signal. Say, in a week's time ... yes, probably a week today I could give you an answer.'

Back at the hostel I telephoned Mr. Jason at UNRRA.

He sounded grieved. Everything, he said, was held up indefinitely. Later, perhaps ...

I went back to bed. My tummy was indignant, so was the matron, who had been in to see me and found me gone. The world was lost in waves and waves of nausea.

Next day the papers informed me that there was chaos in Greece. Civil war.

CHAPTER THIRTY-SIX

'VILLA EMMA'

A WEEK passed.

I was back in the library trying to write an article on the Japanese Occupation of Indo-China.

'Judith – I must telephone Mr. Ex. I can't wait. He said he might know by today.'

She got the number and handed over the receiver. She was smiling and holding her thumbs, tense with interest.

'Mr. Ex? Joy Packer here. No chance of a signal, of course?'

'Yes. It came half an hour ago.'

I felt rather sick and it was difficult to breathe.

'What did it say?'

'If you are prepared to sign a paper promising to work anywhere in Italy, we can take you on.'

The room was a whirling tower, whirling like the crows in the hot Egyptian sky. My bones were light as a bird's, I had wings and might fly out of the window, over the waving plumes of the palm trees and the gilded domes, over the thin exclamation marks of minarets. How keep my feet on the earth?

I heard my own voice, cool as rain falling through bright sunshine.

'What is the salary?'

He told me. It was more than I had dared to hope.

'Split—' he said, 'a proportion to be paid to you in Italy as living allowance, the rest into your bank here or in London.'

'When do I go?'

He laughed then. 'Come and see me this evening. Five o'clock.'

I went to ask Mr. Love-of-Allah about my release from MIME. He was patient and friendly after his own restless harassed fashion. I left him pacing up and down, up and down, like a caged puma in a parma-violet shirt.

There are high lights of anticipation and excitement in life worth much struggle, suffering and suspense. This was such a one.

When I went back to Mr. Ex's office he greeted me with amused cynicism.

He said. 'I've been in touch with MIME. They'll let you go.'

I smiled. 'I expect that counts against me?'

'Not necessarily.' He handed me a slip of paper. 'Sign here. *You* guarantee to work wherever we send you in Italy. And *we* guarantee nothing. If we find you are no good we see that you are repatriated as far as Cairo.'

He turned me over to his secretary for further formalities. She gave me a series of new permits and passes.

'Do I wear a uniform?' I asked her.

She shook her head. 'The Americans do. We don't. Though it may be necessary to do something about it later. We are an Anglo-American set-up, but we are each responsible for the rules that govern our own personnel.'

Presently she took me back into Mr. Ex's office, where I was introduced to a Colonel who, in time of peace, was an engineer with great experience of the Balkans.

'The Colonel is in charge of our Balkan unit,' said Mr. Ex. His eyes twinkled. 'I think we might switch her over to your outfit, Colonel. Mrs. Packer has been in Yugoslavia—'

The Colonel chuckled. 'That's probably where she'll finish up.

But my group will be cooling its heels for quite a time, I fancy.'

I said: 'Please tell me – what is P.W.B.?'

They looked at each other and laughed. Mr. Ex said: 'You might get a good many peculiar answers to that question! But the initials stand for Psychological Warfare Branch. P.W.B. is officially the Psychological Warfare Branch of Allied Forces Headquarters in Italy.'

I was deeply impressed, almost overwhelmed.

'What are its activities?'

'The name is legion,' said the Colonel.

'You'll learn all in good time,' said Mr. Ex. 'And remember one thing. We never talk about Psychological Warfare. We refer only to P.W.B.'

'When do I go to Italy?'

'You stand by from now on. It may be the day after tomorrow, or in a fortnight's time. It depends when we can get you a place in an aeroplane. You telephone my secretary in this office every evening at six o'clock from wherever you may be, and you say, "Do I leave tomorrow?" She says yes or no. If it's yes, we send transport and your travel orders to your hostel at midnight, and you will be conveyed to a military aerodrome in the Desert and you will probably fly at dawn. You are allowed twenty-five pounds of luggage. All right?'

'Wonderful – when it's "Yes"!'

'And now we'll go to Shepheard's for a drink,' said the Colonel, who was a practical man.

It was 'no' for three evenings. And then, miraculously, it was 'YES'.

Dawn mists rose like steam from the Desert's dusty face and evaporated in the cool bright upper air. The Dakota warmed through her engines, and we strapped ourselves into the aluminium basins that served as seats.

The passengers sat in two rows facing one another; the bolts on the portholes rammed into their shoulder-blades, and their discomfort was intense. These transport planes were used mainly for dropping paratroops, who must have been thankful when zero hour released them from their positions of torment.

I was too happy to care about the hard slippery metal seat or the agonizing bolt, or my uniformed fellow-passengers – all men. In a few hours we would be in Naples. Barry Stevens had given me a telephone number which would find my husband. Sitting, facing inwards, we could not see the sun rise in the clear Mediterranean sky, or get a view of the battered coastline of Malta where we came down to refuel. Nor, later, could I see the curve of Salerno Bay where the 'Old Lady' had delivered and received such severe punishment, or the cone of Vesuvius flying its white pennant above ruined Naples. Yet none of these limitations mattered, for, apart from an appalling spell of pea-green air-sickness, which I liked to think was a hang-over from my go of 'Gyppy tummy', I was so unbelievably thrilled that I felt air-borne all on my own. The magic of the blue and gold world outside our silver cylinder was not something external, but something deep in my own light uplifted being. For the most poignant joy is that which is preceded by pain and apprehension – like the agony and triumph of child-birth.

The young American pilot-officer pushed his head through the partition dividing the control-cabin from the fuselage. 'Strap your belts. We're landing!'

I felt the augmented roar and vibration of our engines as we banked and circled, and the harsh rush of the wheels on the runway at Capodichino airport, and then, in the amber light of late afternoon, I stepped on to the brown earth of Italy.

The American sergeant who checked our papers in the transport office said:

'P.W.B. Then you'll be wanting transport to P.W.B. headquarters in Naples.'

'Where is Caserta?' I asked.

'The other way. About twenty minutes in a jeep.'

'Is a jeep going there?'

'There's always a jeep going to Caserta.'

'Can I hitch a ride?'

'Sure, if the driver's got room.'

'Could you find out?'

'Sure, I could.'

Sure, the driver had room. Had I time to telephone? Sure, I had, if I made it snappy.

I gave the Freedom number of the Naval Headquarters, and spoke to Tim Sherwin, my husband's secretary.

'Joy! . . . But we didn't expect you to arrive till tomorrow. Commodore Stevens sent the Chief-of-Staff a signal.'

'I know. But someone dropped out and they put me in at the last moment.'

'The Chief-of-Staff is out of his room. I'll go and find him.'

'No, Tim, don't! Just tell him I'm hitching a passage in a jeep right away.'

'Then come to Archway Eight. Corney will meet you there.'

'I can't believe it!'

The green plain of Naples swept up to the hills, and a magnificent avenue of sycamores marched up to the vast square Palace of Caserta.

'Here's the Naval Block,' said the young American driver, and reined in his jeep on its haunches at the entrance to Archway Eight in the huge circular courtyard. He threw out my suit-case and brief-case on to the paved steps, revved up his engine with an aggressive roar, and was gone before I could thank him.

Corney stepped forward and took my bags. He seemed no more surprised to see me than if we'd met in Portsmouth High Street. His sunburn was deeper, his smile as wide and white as ever.

'We knew you'd make it somehow, Madam.'

'Two years is a long time, Corney ... How's your wife, and the boy – and your mother?'

'The wife's fine, Madam, and she says the boy's thriving – growing bigger by the hour. My mother's been very ill again, the doctors gave her up – but she fooled them all right. They can't catch her, her constitution beats them every time.'

He drew a snapshot from his pocket.

'Here's the boy, Madam. The wife says he's very old-fashioned in his ways ...'

'But he's the living image of you – and what a sturdy lad!'

I gave back the snapshot and followed the tall broad-shouldered figure up the wide staircase and along a stone corridor, arrowed: 'To OFFICES of the COMMANDER-IN-CHIEF MEDITERRANEAN ROYAL NAVY.'

'Here we are, Madam.'

Corney tapped on a door, marked 'SECRETARY to CHIEF-OF-STAFF' and we went in. Tim Sherwin sprang to his feet and Corney put down my suit-case and disappeared. On Tim's desk were photographs of the baby boy he had never seen and his fair-haired wife, Kathie.

'This is a great effort!' he said. 'Very exciting.'

Although he was smiling his face wore the drawn tense look which unconsciously prepared me to find changes in my own husband. The years of peril were stamping marks never to be erased.

'You'll find the Chief-of-Staff free,' he said. And opened a communicating door between his office and the next.

I was dimly aware of a tall screen dividing a big map-lined conference room from a huge desk with an elaborate system of telephones and switchboards. Behind it was an open window, framing the wide plain of Naples and the shining ribbon of the Volturno. A familiar figure came towards me, arms outstretched, and then I heard Tim Sherwin softly close the door.

The week that followed was magical.

I learned that I was to work in Rome, and, since the P.W.B. courier was booked for the next few days, I would have to 'stand by' in Naples, where I could either find my own accommodation or stay in a P.W.B. billet.

'My own accommodation' was something straight out of a dream.

The Naval Commander-in-Chief, Admiral Sir John Cunningham, was blessed with a quick wit, a prodigious command of language, both good and bad, a dry sardonic turn of humour, and the hardest head and softest heart in the world. I am sure that he deeply disapproved of his Chief-of-Staff's wife dropping out of the clouds into Italy, and that he was greatly relieved to know that she would not be working in Naples or Caserta. Rome, five hours away by road, was near enough in all conscience. But, whatever his private opinion may have been, his attitude towards the intruder was one of the utmost kindness and generosity. During the brief hiatus between my landing at Capodicine and travelling to Rome to take up my job with P.W.B., my husband and I were both his guests at 'Villa Emma'.

Naval life is all parting and meetings. There is heaven and hell in it for the wives of sailors, and I had known my share of both. We had said good-bye in Chatham and met again in Hong Kong; we had parted in Japan and found eath other once more in Malaya; I had seen a warship sail from Plymouth and been greeted months later under the battlements of Valetta. And all these had been high moments in our lives. But they had not possessed the strange miracle quality of this week in Naples. They had been moments anticipated and planned in time of peace, when such plans could reasonably come to pass. They had seldom been dependent upon great endeavour and the elements of luck and coincidence, nor had they been preceded by months and even years of anguish and suspense. They had lacked the total unexpectedness of this extraordinary gift of the gods – to say nothing of the peculiar glamour of the place.

Even now, when I turn life's prism in the light of memory, the long rose-red villa in the Bay of Naples, where Nelson is said to have fallen in love with Emma Hamilton, is caught in a radiance as bright as the first gold of morning on the white summit of Vesuvius.

This villa, some distance from grievously wounded Naples, seemed oblivious of the tragedy of war. It hugged the rocky sea-wall and gazed across the sparkling water to the islands of the bay and the curving coastline backed by the volcano and the distant mountains beyond. It trailed a wild garden behind it, with pergolas of vines and groves of oranges, and at its feet lay a little boat-house and bathing place approached by way of grottoes and rock-gardens.

The place, requisitioned for the use of the Commander-in-Chief, had been sumptuously modernized by its wealthy Italian owner, and it is doubtful whether the British Ambassador and his beautiful wife ever lived in the present house. Be that as it may, the spell of the Divine Lady, who graduated from cook's daughter and kept woman to Ambassadress and boon companion to a Queen, lingers in those romantic surroundings. It was easy to imagine Emma standing on the terrace above the bay seeking the white sails of 'the little Admiral's' flagship. Theirs was a story to appeal to any woman, for, despite the sordid angle of the faithless woman and the complacent husband on one side and the wronged and patient wife on the other, it was a story of gallantry and true love – one that began in Naples and only ended in Portsmouth when Nelson, 'brave as a lion and gentle as a lamb', came home in the *Victory* for the last time.

The Wren officers loved being invited to 'Villa Emma'. Its associations enthralled them. My husband said: 'I believe they think of Emma Hamilton as a sort of super Wren who rather overdid her duty to the Navy.'

I met a number of Wrens in that first week, and what admirable girls they were! And how deeply appreciated!

In England a Wren was just a good smart girl doing her war job; in Italy she was an adventurous rarity and a fine fair-skinned contrast to the local 'signorina'. The Wrens were a perpetual source of interest and enchantment to naval officers, who, at home, might well have taken them for granted. They were an inexhaustible topic of conversation, and strong men spoke of 'our Wrens' with protective chivalry and a glow of sentiment. Even the Commander-in-Chief was genuinely touched when he inspected Wrens' quarters at Caserta, and observed that 'nearly all these poor children have cuddly toys beside their pillows'. In his masculine eyes the 'cuddly toy' was not so much a perennial fashion among young women, as the pathetic symbol of homesick youth.

The 'poor children' themselves were having the time of their lives, and to most of them the Italian adventure was idyllic – 'something out of this world', including sunshine, picnics, week-end leave to sight-see in Rome, and romances almost as beautiful – if less sad and sophisticated – than that of the Divine Emma. For good measure they had their full share of hard work and responsibility.

They were tender-hearted girls and they were deeply sorry for the havoc and devastation of Italy and the misery of the Italians, but they agreed philosophically that if you backed the wrong horse you must be prepared to take the consequences.

During the next few glorious days, with the tang of autumn in the air, I was left to my own devices. The Commander-in-Chief, accompanied by my husband and the Flag Lieutenant, left immediately after breakfast for Caserta, roaring up the long Italian roads with a miniature white ensign flying from the radiator cap and two suicidal motor-cycle outriders clearing the way, and they only returned late in the evening just in time for a bath and dinner. I read and rested and wrote long ecstatic letters home. Whatever might lie ahead, these few days held nothing but pleasure, contentment and gratitude.

On the night of our arrival the Commander-in-Chief gave a dinner party. The guests of honour were Admiral Kent Hewitt, in Command of the American Naval Forces in the Mediterranean, and British General Sir Henry Maitland Wilson, who had relieved General Eisenhower as Supreme Allied Commander in the Italian theatre.

'What are they like?' I asked my husband, while we were dressing. Fortunately my twenty-five pounds of luggage had included an evening dress.

'You'll like Kent Hewitt,' he said. 'We all do. He's done magnificently in the Mediterranean war. He's a fine strong job, kind and loyal, with a Napoleonic profile.'

He told me that 'Jumbo' Wilson had been in the 'toughest jobs' in the Mediterranean, including the first entry into, and evacuation from, Greece. 'Very solid and imperturbable,' he added, 'with little twinkly eyes.'

The feminine element in the party was supplied by a charming Wren Officer, called Arabella, with smiling eyes and gentle manners; an American Welfare Officer with cloudy blonde hair, a wicked line in perfume and the fascinating name of Miss Tootle; and Lady Ranfurly.

Hermione Ranfurly, General Maitland Wilson's Personal Aide, occupied a position which was an interesting feature of World War Two.

The Americans had discovered that the female Flag-Lieutenant or Aide-de-Camp was just as efficient and a great deal more decorative than her male counterpart. Thus it became customary for women to be appointed as Personal Aides to high-ranking officers. The idea was quickly popularized, and attractive P.A.'s blossomed forth in the most unlikely places. Junior Officers, and even civilians, unofficially promoted their favourite stenographers to the coveted status of P.A., which carried many privileges not accorded to humdrum secretaries.

There was, however, nothing bogus about Lady Ranfurly. She was the shining example of the perfect Personal Aide, a sparkling and soignée young woman with sleek dark hair smoothly dressed. Her tailored white evening gown clung to her excellent figure. She talked well and listened even better, and she combined gaiety and badinage with an air of discreet deference to any very senior officers.

'Now *who*' – said my husband – 'would rather have a rabbit-faced young man with a moustache as his Aide?'

Admiral Cunningham, however, had resisted the latest innovation in war fashions, and his Flag-Lieutenant was tall dark

Gerald Pawle, an international squash player, journalist and script-writer for the B.B.C.

Gerald told me that the King had recently visited the Italian theatre, and that the remarkable contrivance in our bedroom – almost like a large lion's cage made of mosquito-netting – had been specially designed and constructed in order that His Majesty should not be plagued by the mosquitoes which haunted the villa in summer.

Admiral Hewitt had also given preference to a naval officer as his Flag-Lieutenant – a very lively and well-connected young man-of-the-world with a social instinct to match his considerable courage. I was struck, that evening, by the good-will and excellent understanding which evidently existed between the British and American Admirals and their Staffs.

Dinner was a cheerful meal, and nobody even mentioned the war. Admiral Cunningham indulged his hobby of starting half-a-dozen arguments and manipulating their direction with the skill of a small boy operating the points of his model railway and switching his little tin trains on to whatever lines he fancied.

After dinner we put on wraps and went on to the wide terrace above the sea for coffee and liqueurs. There was moonlight on the water and a faint red glow in the sky over Vesuvius. The night was fragrant with flower scents, and somewhere a Neapolitan fisherman was singing in his boat.

'Well,' said the Commander-in-Chief, his humorous expression alight with kindliness. 'What do you think of Italy?'

'I don't know,' I answered. 'I'll tell you that when I've seen something of it. "Villa Emma" isn't Italy, it's Eden. No wonder Nelson lost his head, his heart and his sense of proportion here!'

Beyond the Garden of Eden lies the Wilderness, and I knew full well that my time in Paradise was short. It was of no consequence. For a spell I could afford to eat of the lotus. The words of the Persian poet, Omar Khayyám, came to my mind:

> 'Unborn tomorrow and dead yesterday
> Why fret about them if today be sweet!'

CHAPTER THIRTY-SEVEN

WILDERNESS

I WENT through the gates of Paradise into the wilderness beyond, sitting in the back seat of the P.W.B. courier-car, squeezed between a swarthy Italio-American Army Captain and Mr. Philip Hodge, the representative of a New York publishing firm. The comfortable seat beside the G.I. driver in front was occupied by his sprawling gum-chewing G.I. friend. American G.I. Joe is the equivalent of British Tommy Atkins. He is better paid and better equipped, but by no means better disciplined or better mannered. Quite the reverse.

The courier-car was an American command-car – a not very glorified jeep, rough, rattling and recklessly driven.

Mine was a Cinderella exit.

The golden autumn of 'Villa Emma' had lost itself overnight in the ragged windy cold of approaching winter. The day of departure dawned grey over a sea flecked with angry white. The Commander-in-Chief's glittering luxurious car, with its white ensign and the dashing outriders, put me down at the dirty draughty entrance of the P.W.B. building in Naples. My husband said:

'Good-bye, Joy-Joy. Keep your tail up.'

The Commander-in-Chief gave me his kind humorous smile and waved away my efforts to thank him for his hospitality. Then, with the terrifying roar of motor-cycles and the taut shuddering of the white ensign, they were gone.

That five-hour drive to Rome was stark realism. The ruins of war were no new sight to me. But the massacre of these Italian coast towns was something right outside my previous experience. They had been bombed from the air, shelled from land and sea, and fought through in long bitter hide-and-seek battles that had left scarcely a wall standing. And there had, of course, been the deliberate demolition of every power plant, bridge and rail-head that might be of use to the advancing Allies. The Germans had applied a ruthless policy of 'scorched earth' to their erstwhile Allies, and had taken with them everything they could loot, including young Italian males to work for them in forced labour camps.

Now we saw pallid men and women crawl out of holes in the ground to buy their meagre food supplies from barrows and cook their meals over charcoal burners in the ruins. When we had cause to slow down in the towns shivering, shoeless children ran after us and called out thinly for 'Caramele – cigarette!' and our Army Captain threw them a few sweets or some gum as one throws crumbs to sparrows. If there was time, he spoke to them in their own language – the tongue of his forebears.

I was soon to learn that P.W.B. was largely staffed by Americans of Italian descent, who still spoke their mother tongue albeit with a transatlantic accent. They were part of the proof that the United States is closer to Europe in kin and interest than she knows. All over liberated Europe they were coming back – the American-born Yugoslavs, Hungarians, Czechs, Greeks, Norwegians and Italians, who seemed best fitted to help in the rehabilitation of the country from which their roots had sprung. The United States is so much more European than our own island – but she forgets it in time of peace.

It was a curious thing, however, that in general the Italians had little respect for these prodigal sons of Italy and America who had returned with new ways of pronouncing the beautiful Italian words and new habits of patronage. They were inclined to feel that the scum that had blown off the face of the land and settled far afield had been blown back by the winds of war. It was an odd, unaccountable and unjustifiable resentment which was no doubt rooted in envy.

Every bridge along the way hung broken-backed over river and ravine, and we crossed on the iron mathematical span of the Bailey bridge. Along the roadside we saw the burnt-out wreckage of tanks, guns, aeroplanes and trucks, and yet, distressing as these sights might be, they struck me less than the works of nature which had survived the holocaust – the robust green and copper-gold of orange groves and the frail beauty of poplars tossing autumnal auburn tresses in the biting wind.

The mine-torn road was occupied solely by military traffic and the long crawling truck convoys that caused our hasty driver to swear the oaths of Brooklyn under his breath. Little houses stood shoulder-high in the flooded Pontine Marshes, drained, irrigated and cultivated in the 'good days of Fascism' and now swamped once more by war. Army signs informed us that we were in a malarial zone. When the driver had occasion to stop, none of us dared take advantage of the opportunity to venture into the fields because more large notices stressed the disagreeable fact that mines had only been cleared within three feet of the verge.

'Farming is going to be a dangerous occupation for many years to come,' observed Mr. Hodge, and yawned. He yawned frequently.

As we approached Rome the driver began to stand on the accelerator like one possessed.

'What's his panic?' I wanted to know.

Mr. Hodge had fallen asleep. When I knew him better I realized that Phil Hodge always slept in vehicles, even when his life was at stake. The Italo-American grinned.

'If we don't make P.W.B. within twenty minutes the G.I. Mess will be closed and the driver and his buddy will have to make shift with sandwiches. It won't be their fault if they have to do that!' He glanced at his watch '*We'll* be all right,' he added with satisfaction. '*Our* Mess closes a half-an-hour later than theirs.'

That was one of the many rather absurd things about P.W.B. The conditions of the road between Naples and Rome made it touch and go whether the courier could leave one point after breakfast and still reach the other before lunch. The accomplishment of this feat was, in his eyes, of primary importance, and, in order to carry it out, the safety of his cargo and all distracting considerations such as road blocks and other vehicles were 'relegated to second place or disregarded', with the result that P.W.B. transport and personnel were treated as expendable and piled into the ditch with the utmost abandon.

We roared through the great gates of the Eternal City and past famous monuments to the past that had gone unscathed in the present conflict, and soon we drew up with an evil jarring of brakes at a huge stone edifice in the camber of the tree-bordered Via Veneto, where P.W.B. had replaced the S.S. Headquarters which had previously dislodged the Confederazione Fascista Agricoltori.

The courier hurled out our gear and bounded up the wide stone stairs like a maniac.

'He'll just about make it,' said the Italo-American, and followed him more leisurely.

I looked rather helplessly at Mr. Hodge, who himself seemed hesitant about the next step.

'Have you any idea what we do now?'

He pushed back his wide-brimmed felt hat on his thick grizzled hair, yawned, and scratched his head.

'I know that I report to our personnel office. But I couldn't say where the British one is . . .'

'Never mind,' I said. 'I'll find it.'

It crossed my mind that life could be overfull of the new-girl-at-school feeling, especially for those of us who live, 'like soldiers, from day to day'. School, university, marriage, new places, new faces, new jobs – always the same thing, a finding of one's feet, sometimes easily, sometimes painfully. Well, here it was again.

The British Personnel Office was on the third floor. Everybody had gone to lunch except a peevish-looking red-haired secretary. She took my travel orders and asked me which section I was to work for.

'I'm going to see Mr. Rainer this afternoon,' I said. 'I expect he'll decide.'

John Rainer, a brilliant Fleet Street man, was the head of the Rome branch.

'You can't,' she said crossly. 'He's in hospital. He came back from Florence yesterday and the courier had a smash. He's been badly hurt.'

'I'm not at all surprised,' I said, recalling our own hairs-breadth escapes. 'Who do I see then?'

'His American deputy,' she said.

P.W.B. was like that – an integrated unit. It worked on alternates – American, British, American, British – from the top down. It was part of Lease-Lend, and the British personnel were, as might be expected, the 'poor relations'.

'Where do I find a billet?' I asked.

'You'll have to go to the P.W.B. Mess – the Botticelli Hotel – till you can find somewhere better, if you can't stand it. And you'd better hurry along now or you'll miss your lunch.' (The 'Botticelli' is not the right name, but it will suffice.)

'Is it far?'

'No. Just up some steps alongside this building, and there you are.'

'I'll need a porter.'

'Ask for one at the reception downstairs here. There's usually some scruffy creature about who'll take your bags.'

'Thanks for your help.'

'That's all right,' she said, and fed a sheet of foolscap into her typewriter with a frown. 'P.W.B.'s a shocking place to work in,' she added. 'Everybody's so unorthodox.'

The porter, who was indeed 'scruffy', deposited my suit-cases in the small dingy entrance of the Botticelli Hotel, and, suitably rewarded, took himself off.

'What room, Signora?' asked a dignified hall-porter, who had a pale green cynical face and a dark green frock-coat.

'I don't know. I've just arrived. What rooms have you?'

His smile was ironic, his English impeccable. '*Il sergenti* allocates the rooms. His office is there.'

The American sergeant in charge of the Mess was sitting in his minute over-furnished office making out accounts. A G.I. sprawled at his side, his feet on the desk. Both chewed gum companionably. *Il sergenti* was small, wiry and dark, with the quick jewel-black eyes of a lizard, and a long Italian name abbreviated to 'Cookie'. Back home in the States his mother kept a grocery store and there was a young wife with a Hollywood face. Her photograph smiled at him across his desk – it was a soft smile framed in a fall of light blonde. Cookie was, in common with the rest of a war-weary world, extremely 'browned off'. Two things were uppermost in his mind – the fact that his mother needed him in the store at home, and the fact that he needed the girl with the Hollywood face here.

I stood and waited. Neither the sergeant nor the stooge paid any attention. At last, in his own good time, Cookie's lizard eyes flickered upwards.

'Checking in?'

'Yes, please.'

'Name?'

I gave it.

'How long staying?'

'I've no idea. Some time, I suppose. I'm to work here.'

He flipped over the pages of a register and marked my name on an index card.

'Number Seventy-Six.'

During this brief exchange the stooge had remained impassive, army boots undisturbed on the desk, but his frank casual stare reminded me that I must appear very travel-worn and untidy.

'Number Seventy-Six,' repeated the suave porter, and handed me over to the care of an unappetizing page-boy. 'It's on the third floor, and the elevator doesn't work. We have very little electricity in Rome.'

Number Seventy-Six was at the end of a passage. The page knocked, and, receiving no response, butted the door with his behind. As the catch did not work it opened obediently and revealed a dark little lobby which might have accommodated a couple of coffins fairly reasonably. On one side of this lobby was a narrow bedroom, and on the other a bathroom and a lavatory, which surprisingly and mysteriously flushed itself as we entered. A poltergeist must have taken up his abode there for the loo worked only when it felt inclined and never when necessity demanded.

The bedroom had an air of Bohemian squalor. It contained two beds cheek by jowl, a small wardrobe and a large chest of drawers. The floor was covered with linoleum, and a shabby easy chair was piled with a queer assortment of odds and ends – a portable wireless, a paint-box, some sketch books, a pile of old *Times Literary Supplements*, a torch, a few little articles of newly washed laundry, a work-bag overflowing with stockings in the last stages of holes and ladders, and a brown Teddy-bear. On the chest of drawers, which also served as a dressing table, was a half finished bottle of Silver Fizz gin, and one of repellent green synthetic fruit juice with a sticky mark round its base, a box of Pond's face powder, an open lipstick, a brush, comb, and shoe brush and chamois. On the commode next the bed nearest the one small window was a shaky reading lamp, a book on modern French art and a miniature of a woman with a charming foreign-looking face. The small square window faced across the dark chasm of the street into the opposite windows of the third floor back of the main P.W.B. building from which I had just come.

When I investigated the interior of the wardrobe I found a few little rags of dresses that might have fitted a thin child of twelve and a pile of old copies of *Life*, the *New Yorker* and the *Saturday Evening Post*.

The page gaped at me. He was waiting for a cigarette, the chief tip-currency in a land where money had ceased to have any value. I opened my bag and gave him two.

'But this room is occupied,' I said. '*Occupato.*'

The boy grunted, shrugged his shoulders and departed.

When I had washed and tidied myself I went down the stone staircase spiralling round the non-functioning lift, and, after a quick lunch in a dirty and deserted dining-room, attended by unshaven Italian waiters, I returned to the office of *Il sergenti.*

Cookie and his companion ignored my presence.

I said: 'I'm sorry, but there's been some mistake. Number seventy-six is occupied already.'

They received this information in astounded silence, staring first at me and then at each other.

'Wha' do you know about that?' vouchsafed the stooge at length, with a low whistle.

Cookie's expression was that of an outraged lizard.

'Did you expect a room to yourself?' he enquired, with icy indigation.

'Of course. Why not?'

'Why not?' echoed the stooge, and uttered a mirthless hoot of laughter.

Il sergenti leaned forward with his elbows on the desk and studied me with cold interest. He was a man of few words, and those few effective.

'Listen,' he said. 'Do you know something? *Colonels* are doubling up.'

And with this, to me, surprising statement, he removed the chewing-gum from his back teeth, clamped it under the desk, accepted the *camel* proffered by the stooge, and applied himself once more to his accounts.

As far as Cookie was concerned, I had ceased to exist.

CHAPTER THIRTY-EIGHT

INITIATION

THE American deputy to the recently damaged British director told me to report to Captain Carrick R.A., head of the Publications Section.

'We have some plans for you,' he said. 'Carrick will explain. First floor, end of the passage.'

The building was huge, stone and bitterly cold, for winter had already struck at Nothern Italy and her breath was in the wind that came sweeping down to scatter the leaves in the Via Veneto.

I found part of the first floor flooded, and shivering Italian typists paddling bare-foot through two inches of icy water. No one seemed surprised, but then no one was ever surprised at anything in P.W.B. The flood had, however, been stemmed at the entrance to Publications Section.

I knocked on a door marked 'CAPTAIN CARRICK', and a rather pretty girl with a pale unhealthy complexion and swollen hands opened it. This was Gabriella, the Italian typist. She was clad, like all the locally employed girls in P.W.B., in a shabby little dress, not warm enough for the time of year, and her legs were encased in bright green hand-knitted woollen ski-socks that left her knees bare and blue with cold. She was forever chafing her chapped hands and blowing on them. On her feet she wore wooden clogs. The locally employed staff earned a mere pittance, but they could get their midday meal in the P.W.B. Italian Mess, and this doubtful privilege, in a city where starvation had laid hands on many homes, meant more to them than money, which, with inflation at its zenith, had little value in any case.

'*Il Capitano via*,' she said, in the pigeon-Italian that had come to be the conversational medium in Italy under the Allied Occupation. '*Ritorno subito.*'

The office was a long slit running from a wide window into comparative darkness. By the window was a large desk, tidy and impersonal, and at the other darker end of the room was a typist's table.

Gabriella put a chair for me, and seated herself at her type-writer. She cast me an engaging smile and began to clean her nails with a toothpick. But, at the sound of a brisk step in the stone passage outside, she hastily put away her toothpick and rolled a sheet of paper into the Olivetti.

'*E il Capitano*,' she said.

I heard a fragment of tune tunelessly whistled, and the door opened smartly.

Kenneth Carrick, who was to be my immediate boss for nearly a year, was a war-time soldier in the Royal Artillery. He had been on coastal defence while England was in danger of invasion, then he had applied to be sent abroad. In normal life he was a permanent political agent for the Conservative Party. He was always very trim in his personal appearance and his habitual politeness masked a certain ruthlessness, for he was a born fighter and improviser. He was receptive to new ideas and believed in decentralization, which was just as well, as I learned a fortnight after joining the section when he was spilt into a ditch by the P.W.B. Rome-Naples courier. His head was cut open and he was concussed. It was quite a time before his crisp brown hair, sprinkled with grey, covered the ugly gash and he was able to do a full day's work without giddiness or headache. In many ways Captain Carrick was a lonely man, for he had none of the vices of the menagerie at the Botticelli. He neither smoked nor drank, and was, by disposition, reserved and fastidious.

He had a nervous habit of screwing up his hazel eyes, and he did so now as he asked me to take a seat and settled himself behind that extremely non-committal desk. As he spoke he tapped his blotter with a pencil, twisting it between ever restless fingers so that it performed a small unceasing handspring.

'You'll be working in the Copy Department,' he said. 'Writing pamphlets mostly. I'll explain about that later.'

In the meantime he told me briefly and lucidly what it was necessary for me to know about P.W.B. and the Italian situation in general.

At last the secret was out – or part of it, at all events.

P.W.B., I was told, had its own presses, newspapers and publications and its own radio and films. It virtually controlled the intake and output of information in the Italian theatre. It had other operational activities which came within my experience later on, and certain aspects that remained a mystery to me. I shall only touch on those angles of the organization which affected me personally, as I should be no more capable of explaining the full ramifications of psychological warfare than would an ordinary seaman be able to give a detailed exposition of the whole vast system of Admiralty.

Nor can I do more than sketch the immensely confused situation inside Italy at the time. An Italian Coalition Government existed and operated under the auspices of the Allied Commission in Rome, which was responsible for Italian rehabitation. It was also subject to the control of A.F.H.Q. at Caserto, where the Supreme Commander was concerned, first and foremost, with winning the war, and nothing that happened inside Italy must interfere with this objective.

P.W.B. worked closely with the Allied Commission and received its directives from A.F.H.Q. It was responsible for telling the Italians what was being done for them and what they could do for themselves.

Italy had fought and lost a war; she had signed an armistice which had brought no peace; her ally had occupied her land and turned it into a battlefield, and, as he was driven back, he had looted and destroyed. Now old and young shivered in the ruins, and hooliganism flourished, for, when a man is destitute, he must steal to live. Internally she suffered the extra anguish of a complex civil war. The King had abdicated in favour of his son, Prince Umberto, who was now the official Head of the State and sponsored by the Allies. But a large section of his own people were against him, feeling that the taint of Fascism had already too deeply touched the House of Savoia. In the north, Fascist divisions were fighting with the Germans, while other regiments had joined forces with the Allies. All over the country the Partisans – fruit of a courageous underground Anti-Fascist Organization – were meting out rough justice to Fascists, wherever they could find them, while aiding the Allies in a grim guerilla war of sabotage and vengeance. The Communists were, of course, making capital out of the general misery and confusion. By and large, Italy was very sick, and so shut in with her own sickness that she was oblivious of everything outside it.

'Our business is to help the Italians to help themselves,' said Captain Carrick. 'We must show them how to co-operate with the Allies in the rehabilitation of their country. And we want to get them thinking on democratic lines. Now I'll get Carol to take you round our Information Centres to give you a practical idea of what we are doing.'

He turned to the typist, Gabriella. 'Ask Signora Carol to come here, *per favore*.'

Gabriella disappeared through the door marked 'COPY DEPARTMENT' and presently a pretty dark woman came in.

'Of course I'll take Joy round,' she said, in answer to the

Captain's request. She added, with her attractive smile, 'We all call each other by our first names. It's simpler.'

Her accent was American. As she spoke she drew a pair of fur gloves over her small hands, already swollen with chilblains.

'Come with me,' she said. 'We'll get a car from the transport office.'

P.W.B. Information Centres were dispersed throughout the various parts of the city. They were small shops selling British and American publications translated into Italian. War maps and news photographs in the windows illustrated the progress of the war, and there were various displays of aspects of life in a democracy.

The cold, hungry, over-civilized Italians were starved of more than food. They wanted information about other lands, and to emerge from their spiritual isolation. They knew where Fascism had got them. What was this other formula – Democracy?

'But what really is democracy?' I asked Carol. 'Do any of us really know.'

She indicated the Four Freedoms framed on the wall.

'Roosevelt does. There you have it. Freedom from fear, freedom from want, freedom of thought and freedom of worship. It's a foreign conception to a totalitarian state.'

Until that moment I had taken democracy for granted. Now, for the first time, I began to think about it. So, when presently Churchill defined it, I typed his words on the red ribbon of my typewriter.

> 'The foundation of Democracy is the humble ordinary man who keeps his wife and family, fights for his country in need, and votes for the man he wishes elected to Parliament. But he must do all this without fear of intimidation or victimization.'

Carol picked up a book very plainly produced by the Ministry of Information. 'A curious best-seller, you might think,' she said. 'But a best-seller just the same – *Il Piano Beveridge.*'

'The Beveridge Plan – a best-seller!'

She nodded. 'It's an encouraging sign. It means that these people who have been shouted down and forbidden to have any ideas of their own for twenty years are beginning to think for themselves again – to show curiosity. They want to know how you, in England, care for your community from birth to death.'

I said presently: 'If the Italians are really so poor, how can they buy this stuff? You say they can't even afford the price of bread—'

'These prices are purely nominal,' she explained 'With inflation at the point it is, what difference can a few lire make one way or the other? When they've read this stuff they can light their fires with it – if they have any fuel!'

'Can't we afford to give it away?'

She laughed. 'Oh, come now! You know nobody wants something they can get for nothing. They feel there's a catch in it.'

Carol was our 'ear to the ground'. She mingled with the crowds and found out what publications were most popular and why. She was an American of Italian parentage, and, with her friendly charm and Latin appearance, she was well suited to her work. She had recently strengthened her ties with Italy by marrying the leader of one of the six official Government parties.

We had tea at the Y.W.C.A. and Carol told me more about our work and our fellow workers, and afterwards she walked with me through the Villa Borghesi Park to the great old gateway at the head of the Via Veneto, where she left me to return to her own apartment.

Rome was very lovely that November day. The trees, in the glory of their autumn foliage, were softened by the bloom of dusk. Children scampered on the wide lawns, and the troops on leave sauntered about the leaf-carpeted paths and presently found their way to the clubs and rest-camps dotted about the Park, for Rome, that year, was one enormous leave-base. The bootblacks under the massive walls had packed up their impedimenta and departed, and so had the vendors of those trinkets men bought to send home.

In the Via Veneto brassy-haired girls clattered along on their wooden platform shoes seeking the glances of American soldiers, their ears alert for the password every G.I. and Tommy knew, '*Buona sera, signorina!*' They preferred Americans. Americans had more candy, cigarettes and lire than anyone else.

This was the hour of the 'signorinas'. After dark, even before the curfew chased them from the streets, they were afraid. There was much to fear in Rome after nightfall. And not least of its perils was a gang of ruffians headed by a boy of sixteen.

His followers were children, some no more than ten years old, but they were all experienced murderers, bandits, pimps and black-marketeers. They held up supply vans, stole weapons and ammunition and used them without compunction; they attacked and stripped civilians and left them naked and unconscious in the darkened streets. Sometimes, for spite or perverted lust, they caught and tormented girls who went with Allied troops. It was easy to see who had fallen into their hands, for the heads of their victims were shorn – the black or brazen heads that had tossed so provokingly only a few hours earlier.

It was many months before the police nets drew in these juvenile criminals who terrorized a city and lived like ghouls in caves and ruins.

The Botticelli Mess, where we ate our daily cabbage soup, fried spam and canned fruit, was like a murky third-class station buffet. There were slapdash Italian waiters, wine-stains on soiled table-cloths, and usually a few drunks and 'bomb-happies' spoiling for a fight. The lounge was little better. There was a minimum of electrcity that icy winter, so there was never heating or sufficient light to penetrate the fog of smoke. At first these things dismayed me. Afterwards I took them and everything else for granted.

On the evening of my arrival I ate an early supper and went straight up to bed.

Number Seventy-Six, in the sickly glow of one dim bulb, was no more inviting than it had appeared at midday. The bath was dirty and the water cold. I unpacked a few things into two vacant drawers and made it clear to a slovenly-looking maid that I needed more blankets on my bed. She made it equally clear that there were none. '*Mi dispiace . . . e la guerra.*'

I spread my coat on the bed furthest from the window, pulled a jersey over my nightgown and golf socks on to my frozen feet, and turned out the glimmer of light.

There were jeep noises from the street, and strains of music from the lounge downstairs. Someone was playing the piano and playing it well. I recognized the dances from 'Prince Igor', but I did not know that the stirring emotional passages were called forth by the nicotine-stained fingers and sick heart of a young Welsh lieutenant who had not been home for three and a half years, and whose wife had said, 'Three years is my limit – after three years I reckon to tread over the traces . . .' He was of no consequence. Nobody cared about his troubles; they all had plenty of their own. He was just a symptom of our nostalgic era, and of the Botticelli, where men sought oblivion in *vino rosso* that they might not fear the future.

Soon I fell asleep.

Somewhere near midnight I was disturbed by the cautious opening of the door. The moon was high and its white radiance poured through the uncurtained window.

There was a figure in the doorway, slight and unreal. I saw a small pale face surmounted by a high cloud of dark hair, and a voice, clear and sweet as a well-bred child's, said: 'I'm sorry, I didn't mean to wake you.'

My room-mate had come in, Suzanne.

I said sleepily: 'It must be annoying for you to find someone here. There didn't seem much choice.'

'That's all right. I expected it sooner or later,' she said.

She did not turn on the light, and I was aware of her quick neat movements as she undressed and crept into bed.

'Good night,' she said. 'Sleep well.'

In the silence that followed I heard her strike a match. A band of moonlight fell across the foot of her bed, and the dark river of her loosened hair flowed across her pillow. Her eyes, in the light of her cigarette, were open – long luminous cat's eyes, brooding and remote.

I woke next morning to hear a sonorous cry from the street below – '*Bottiglie! Bottiglie!*' (heaven knew, there were always empty bottles to be collected from the Botticelli!) and, as if called by a familiar alarm clock, my companion stirred, stretched her thin arms, mewed appealingly once or twice, and then, with one cat-spring, was out of bed and closing our open window before slinking into the bathroom with a shiver and moan for a hasty lick and promise. Ten minutes later she had piled up that mass of hair, dabbed lipstick and powder on to a face as delicate and exotic as an Aubrey Beardsley drawing, and bounded downstairs to nibble her spam and waffles with famished distaste before disappearing into the pandemonium of Basic News.

That cat-spring of Suzanne's was the beginning of our day in the months to come just as the red glow of her cigarette was always the end of it.

CHAPTER THIRTY-NINE

RIDICULOUS

My life in Rome that winter see-sawed between the ridiculous and the sublime. The Botticelli represented the ridiculous and was the Marx Brothers' background from which I emerged occasionally into the white light of the sublime – such as going to opera and hearing 'Tosca' magnificently performed in the city to which that beautiful dramatic production most intimately belongs.

My work became more absorbing as time progressed, and I enjoyed it because it was in touch with world events on one side and with the immediate needs of the Italian people on the other; and, even more perhaps, because it brought me into close personal contact with all sorts and conditions of human beings. The elaborate network of P.W.B. embraced many strange elements. There were the British and American civilian staff, and there were the military personnel, not a few of whom had been in the lines and sent back to P.W.B. to recover from the state we knew as 'bomb-happy'. There was also a motley collection of journalists, artists, film and radio experts, and a varied nucleus of Central European refugees employed in radio monitoring and other sections of which we knew very little. P.W.B. World Radio Monitoring Report, Basic News Summaries, and other reports marked, Confidential, Secret and Most Secret, were read daily by my husband at Caserta, who, like most of their readers, gave little thought to the organization behind them.

My own work was in the Copy Department of Publications Section – Inspiration Corner, we called it – where everybody was busy writing pamphlets, booklets or posters on whatever subject they were told.

Inspiration Corner was even less easy to write in than the library at MIME in Cairo, and I was often thankful that my early training had taught me to work in the hubbub of a newspaper office. Nobody payed the slightest attention to the *SILENZIO* notice on the wall, and there was a continual flow of vistors and not a single bug to chase them away.

The permanent occupants of the room were Carol, who, when she was not out or on tour with her 'ear to the ground', was writing her reaction reports with her numbed swollen fingers. How cold it was – till the day it snowed (for the first time in seven years) when one of our 'bomb-happy' soldier messengers began smashing up our office chairs and burning them in the empty grate. Then there was Bruno Zevi, an excitable aggressive American of Italian parentage, who was writing a pamphlet on town planning with particular reference to the London Plan; and slim intellectual Marjorie Fergusson, who was the boss's American Deputy, and who was writing about Discussion Groups. Carol, Marjorie and Bruno were a discussion group in themselves. Every morning, they read the various official Italian newspapers, and presently, as Bruno came upon some paragraph which he took to be a manifestation of Fascist sentiment, we would hear a furious bellow of rage and a mighty thumping on his desk. Then his torrent of impassioned Italian would bring Carol and Marjorie to their feet and the debate would be launched. Bruno was always vehement, Carol tolerant, and Marjorie detached and objective, seeking in all things some lesson whereby we might profit in our work.

All three had belonged to a powerful Anti-Fascist Society in America, and, now that the moment had come, they were ardently bent upon the projection of Democracy. When they become involved in one of their discussions others invariably drifted in, lured by the shrill trumpeting of Bruno. Perhaps it might be the artist sculptor, Spadini, who designed certain special displays in our Information Centre, or the brilliant anti-Fascist journalist, Orlando – nephew of that great Prime Minister, who in 1918 had been one of the Big Four with President Wilson, Lloyd George and Clemenceau. Orlando came down to our room from the floor above like a giant sloth swinging down from its tree. He spoke as he wrote, with cold intensity, but his voice was curiously hoarse and muffled. Sometimes it was the Hungarian Jew in charge of the Film Section who came in, with his resigned mournful face and unfailing kindliness, in sharp contrast to the American-Armenian Art Director with whom he frequently worked on poster advertisements for his films. The American-Armenian – small, swarthy and bitter – hated everybody in our Department, yet he could never resist the sound and fury of Inspiration Corner. Between them they created more uproar than a Cape south-easter. But presently, a thin sound would insinuate itself into the tumult, weaving through the chinks in the windy speech, and wherever it touched, a stillness fell *Il Capitano*, whistling his little warning tune, had strolled into the room, glancing up at the *SILENZIO* sign, and strolled out again. That was Ken Carrick's way of dealing with a somewhat tumultuous staff, where silence and a look counted for more than words.

'Well,' Orlando would say, heaving himself to his feet. 'I'd better be going. *Arrivederci.*'

'*Anche io,*' Spadini would murmur. And they would melt away, followed by the Hungarian and the Armenian.

The other British denizen of the Copy Department was Lieutenant George Bowman, a lively young man who was too short-sighted for active service. He was a schoolmaster by profession with a special knowledge of languages, and an un-English gift of 'going foreign'. Whether he was in France, Spain, Germany or Italy he changed his psychology as automatically as a chameleon takes the colour of the bough on which it finds itself. George always had 'bags and bags of ideas' and it was his habit to pace vigorously up and down the office, dragging inspirations out of his head with handfuls of childishly soft fair hair.

George was writing a pamphlet on democratic education and editing certain medical and scientific magazines. The output of our Department was, of course, all translated into Italian by P.W.B. translators.

Outside our room was our publications library where Italian Dr. Milano and American Phil Hodge shared the services of a dazzling typist called Mimi, whose mottled knees above her red ski-socks were as perpetually frozen as her tiny hands. The cold struck up to the marrow of our bones from the stone floors and the building resounded to our coughing, sneezing and snuffling. George had a chronic cold, and Bruno, who suffered from chest trouble, came to work with a thermo-pad under his coat. This he plugged into the power plug beside his desk, and when the electricity failed – as it usually did – he swore in temperamental Italian, unplugged himself and stamped up and down the room, growling ferociously as he crossed and recrossed the hair-tearing George.

About tea-time every day George Bowman was invariably seized with a particular restlessness. 'He'd take off his army glasses, revealing the raw mark the sharp heavy steel bridge had left on his nose, wipe them, put them on again, groan a bit over the Education Bill which was the subject of his pamphlet, and prowl to and fro with a threatening eye on the telephone. When it did ring it was usually for Bruno, but sometimes, round four o'clock, it was for George, who'd bound towards the instrument and shout a fierce interrogative 'Yes?' into the mouthpiece. Then he'd relax and his wide good-natured mouth would break into a broad smile.

'Marj . . . tea? Yes, rather. I could do with bags and bags of tea. Pop in on your way down.'

Five minutes later we'd hear the staccato tap of high heels on the stone floor, and a neat chubby little girl with a mane of silky brown hair would be smiling up at George as he flung on his overcoat and looked round wildly and short-sightedly for his cap. Marj Poole's eyes were very clear amber and her teeth protruded slightly, which gave her smile a certain schoolgirl guilelessness. Her figure, however, was naughty-nineties and she was justly proud of her trim feet and ankles.

'How is the book getting on, George?'

Her words were clipped, with a suspicion of a lisp, and she had the Italian way of enunciating double consonants separately. She was the daughter of an Italian mother and an English father, who had died during her infancy. So her mother had brought Marj back to Genoa, where the girl had lived till the age of fifteen, when she had returned to England to school. Like so many of her generation she had graduated straight from the schoolroom into a full-time war-job. She was now doing work connected with the Partisans. We did not know what it was, but we knew that it was vital and extremely responsible.

'Come along, Georgie,' she'd say, presently. 'I'm hungry.' George would throw her a bemused glance, say 'Half a second—', scrabble all his papers helter-skelter into a drawer and make for the door at her high narrow heels.

'Where shall we go? Y.W.C.A. or Eden?'

'Oh, Eden,' she'd say over her shoulder, and lead him away to their paradise of cakes and tea.

'Are they engaged?' I asked Bruno the first time I saw them go off together.

He snorted. 'Heavens no! George is terrified of matrimony.'

Carol said nothing. She just smiled and bowed her dark head lower over her reaction report.

In the evenings I went back to the crazy hurly-burly of the Botticelli and the cold little room I shared with Suzanne.

Sometimes I sat for a while in the ill-lit lounge, and, if he wasn't otherwise occupied, Figaro brought his sketch-book and his crayons and sat beside me, and we'd build my dream cottage by the sea. Figaro was an architect, and he came from the deep American South and spoke in a soft slow southern voice. He said he liked to 'keep his hand in' by designing houses, just for 'the fun of it'.

'Tell me about the site,' he said. 'A cottage has to match its surroundings.

I told him about the blue sea and the blue mountains and the lilies and heather that clothed the cliffs at Hermanus, and about the thatched fishing village where the air is nectar of the gods.

'You'll want it thatched then,' he said, with his pipe between his teeth, adding its quota to the mist of Chesterfields, Camels and Gold Flake. 'This sort of thing, perhaps . . .'

So my dream home grew in the twilight of the Botticelli lounge to the sad surging music of the Welsh Lieutenant with the bitten nails and the bitter smile. And, as he sketched this or that, Figaro said, 'You see, this is how we have it at home – my wife knows just what she wants in her kitchen, and then my boy – he's the same age as yours or maybe a bit younger – has very definite ideas about his bed-study . . .'

Marj Poole liked to stroll over with George.

'Lovely to have a little home like that – don't you think so, George?'

George shied nervously, seized off his glasses and polished them.

'You'll have to go to South Africa, then. There'll be plenty of people in England wanting little houses after the war.'

'He'll be one of them,' smiled Figaro, as they drifted away.

'Not if he knows it,' I said.

'What man ever knows it till he's putting a wedding ring on a woman's finger?' said Figaro. 'And then it's too late.'

Over his shoulder I could see Suzanne perched on a high chair in the tiny bar, surrounded by the 'little men' who beset her path – ('Oh, Joy – there was a little man I promised to meet tonight, and I can't think where, and I forget his name!') – and for whom she cared as little as the Cat Who Walked By Himself cared about the human cave-dwellers in his jungle. 'Brushes them off,' Figaro said, 'just brushes them off.'

But there was a lean Irish journalist not so easily brushed off. He had a sense of fantasy and flamboyant humour that made her laugh when he was sober, but when he'd drawn his NAAFI spirit ration he was dangerous. Those nights we heard him mount the spiral staircase unsteadily to the room above ours, which he shared with a dour Lowland Scot.

Suzanne would say, with a tightening of her lips: 'There'll be the devil to pay tonight.'

We'd lie very still in the dark and listen, and presently the bangs and crashes would begin. Next morning Pat and Mac both came down to breakfast with swollen eyes, broken lips and bruises, and Mac would say: 'Well, who in hell can stand being waked out of a sound sleep and asked if he wants to buy a battleship!'

Suzanne had the independence of a cat without its selfishness. She walked by herself as much as it was humanly possible to do in the communal conditions under which we lived – not physically, but spiritually – and 'all places were alike' to her. She was a Bohemian to the marrow of her bones, a carefree collector of human oddities and rich in the quality of pity. Whatever she had she shared and never did she ask a favour for herself. That winter she adopted Stella.

CHAPTER FORTY

NUMBER SEVENTY-SIX

STELLA was a translator in Basic News. She was seventeen, with a round childish face which in repose was curiously forlorn. Stella seemed to come from nowhere and belong to no one. She spoke perfect Italian and French and a soft foreign-sounding brand of American. She came into the 'locally employed' category, and, as such, did not live at the Botticelli, although she had been specially privileged to mess there.

I made her acquaintance one stormy night when I went up to our room and found an army stretcher jammed between Suzanne's bed and the window.

Two faces turned on their pillows to greet me as I came in. Sue's dark tresses streamed over her shoulders and her long eyes harboured an apology. Stella was giggling mellifluously under a mixed collection of coats and waterproofs – mine, Sue's and her own threadbare winter coat which she had long since outgrown, for she was a big girl. She was nursing the teddy-bear.

'This is Stella,' introduced Sue. 'We were playing ping-pong downstairs after dinner when it came on to rain cats and dogs. It was too wet for her to go home, and, in any case, the man who was supposed to take her back was drunk, so I borrowed a stretcher and here she is.'

'I hope you don't mind,' cooed Stella. 'It's such fun being here . . . and isn't he *sweet* – this bear! Oh, I do wish I had a bear to cuddle every night – or a baby. How lovely it must be to have a little baby to snuggle in your arms.'

When I knew her better I realized that if Stella could have three wishes, they would be for an American passport, an American husband and an American baby. One could only hope that she would receive these blessings in the conventional order.

'We've been telling stories,' said Sue. 'True ones. Stella told about running away from home because she was miserable there, and hiding in the mountains, where she took refuge in a convent, and there were battles all round, and the Allies came, and Stella got a job with P.W.B., and she lives in a wretched little room in the house of an awful old woman who hates her – but she won't go home. She'd sooner die.'

Stella said, 'And Sue told about being a little girl and living in Malaya where her father was a planter up country. He had a huge snake as a pet, and one morning it plopped down out of the rafters on to the middle of the breakfast table!'

I was not surprised. Extraordinary facts about Sue's colourful past slipped out from time to time in the course of our casual conversations. Like so many children with parents in the Far East she had known no real home. She had been brought up in Paris by her French mother's Nanna. At the outbreak of war her parents had been in England on leave. She was eighteen, and she refused to return to Malaya with them. Instead she joined the A.T.S., and was presently seconded to P.W.B. because French was her second language and she knew some Italian.

Suzanne picked up the little miniature on her bedside table. 'This is my mother. I think she has a lovely face. She escaped to Australia when Singapore fell. My father was taken prisoner. She heard from him once – just a card saying he was all right. That was a year ago. Since then we've had no news.'

Stella said, 'So now it's your turn to tell a true story – something about South Africa. Sue says you are South African.'

'All right,' I agreed. 'When I'm in bed and the lights are out.'

Before turning out the lights Suzanne opened the window as we always did, no matter how bitter the cold. To do so, she had to stand on Stella's stomach, which produced a sort of earthquake among the coats and a rhapsody of musical giggles. Then there was darkness and the glow of Sue's last cigarette, and I was telling them a tale about camping in the bushveld with my brother Norman. They hugged themselves, and Stella gasped, 'Oh, you could make a cat laugh! Isn't this wonderful, just like being in a dormitory at the convent again – but with nobody to come in and say, "No talking, girls"!'

Suddenly I remembered how it had touched the Commander-in-Chief to discover that Wrens kept 'cuddly toys' on their beds – how it had made him feel that their schooldays were only yesterday, just a few paces back in the journey that had brought them so far from home. Yet the Wrens were little caged birds, well cared for and living under conditions both orderly and sanitary. Here, indeed, were orphans of the storm. Suzanne, whose eyes could be hard and cynical – 'Parties!' I'd heard her say. 'A few years ago parties meant frilly dresses, silk sashes, crackers and jellies. Now they mean *drunks*!' – and seventeen-year-old Stella, sleeping in her shabby underwear because her escort had been too fuddled to see her safely back to her wretched lodging in the dark loneliness of a city given over to vice and violence. I recalled the lost look on her childish face as she sat by herself in the mess, crumbling her bread on to a wine-stained table-cloth, wondering perhaps what would become of her if she failed to hold down her precarious job. She had no security other than her trust in God and the friendship of Suzanne, no talisman against evil save the little gold cross she wore on a chain round her neck.

'Are you both Catholics?' I asked.

'Yes,' they chorused. And Suzanne added, 'My mother's family are devout Catholics – but really I think I must be a Pagan.'

'I'm a convert,' said Stella with pride in this display of wisdom on her part, and paying unconscious tribute to those good nuns who had given her sanctuary and nursed her through a severe illness. 'Are you a Catholic, Joy?'

'Not exactly – though I suppose you might say I was a Catholic once removed. My grandmother was – but then my grandfather's family was very ardently Huguenot.'

They giggled and fell silent.

Overhead we heard Irish Pat take off his boots. He had two pairs of boots – his 'soft' ones and his 'hard' ones. These were the 'soft boots', so we merely heard two loud bangs. When he took off his 'hard boots' the plaster showered from the ceiling on to our faces.

Upstairs a good deal seemed to be going on.

After a while I said: 'I think he's playing croquet.'

'Or hockey,' suggested Sue, a notion which was greeted hilariously by Stella.

'There's that girl again – the ghost,' said Sue indignantly, as someone opened the outer door into our lobby and used the loo we regarded as our personal property. The ghost slammed the outer door as she returned to her room, and the loo flushed itself cynically five minutes later.

'Eleven o'clock,' said Sue, staring at her luminous watch.

Upstairs there seemed to be a skittle alley with ace performers scoring bulls.

'He's asked Mac if he wants to buy a battleship,' said Suzanne. She yawned her kitten yawn, mewed a little and turned over and went to sleep.

'You don't mind her, do you?' Suzanne asked, a few days later, when Stella's pitiful possessions began to percolate into our small available space.

'Not if you can persuade her not to use my comb, powder puff and lipstick quite so freely.' It had become accepted between the three of us that Stella was Sue's responsibility.

'But, Joy,' protested Sue. 'You must tick her off when she

does that. She's a huge puppy, quite untrained, and it's up to us to train her.'

That evening I found on our dressing table a cardboard box labelled 'STELLA', containing powder puff, lipstick and a comb. Sue had been shopping. I was not a little ashamed.

Next day I got back from the office to find still further signs of infiltration. An iron hospital cot had been placed in our crypt of a lobby, an open suit-case lay beside it and unfamiliar clothes were hanging on the bathroom pegs. To reach the loo it was necessary to step over the foot of the cot, just as in our bedroom the only access to the window was over Stella's stretcher. Unless the bedroom door was open the crypt was unlighted and unventilated.

'Who can they have put there?' I asked Sue, really horrified.

'An American girl. She's nice. I knew her in Algiers.'

'But they can't! It isn't sanitary, and the poltergeist will keep her awake all night.'

Thoroughly incensed, I went down to the office, and for once found Cookie unaccompanied by his stooge.

'Look', I began. 'You honestly can't allow any girl to sleep in that black hole of Calcutta outside Number Seventy-Six. It isn't hygienic. She gets no light or air and—'

'Take it easy,' said Cookie, his lizard eyes on the defensive. 'It's only for two days. I wouldn't put anyone there for longer than that. But until we take Bologna and people move on there won't be a spare bed in the place.'

'She won't get any sleep either,' I added. 'Her bed is practically in the loo which flushes automatically whenever it feels inclined.'

'You're lucky,' retorted the Sergeant drily. 'Most people come in here to complain that their loos don't flush at all.'

The wretched American girl, who was as good-natured and philosophical as any human being I have ever met, enjoyed the hospitality of our crypt for five whole nights, and after that it became a sort of transit camp for temporary guests. When there was no one else in occupation Stella slept there. She cared nothing for the dark, the airlessness, or the poltergeist, providing only that she could belong in Number Seventy-Six. And Cookie, who could give as well as take, closed a beady black eye to her officially prohibited appropriation of one of his precious beds.

CHAPTER FORTY-ONE

SUBLIME

If P.W.B. had its secrets, I had mine too.

Bertie was my secret.

My friends and fellow-workers knew that I had a husband in the Navy – 'somebody at Caserta' – but the fact that he was Chief-of-Staff to Admiral Cunningham was one I had been at pains to conceal. However, early in the New Year of 1945, his promotion to Rear-Admiral and confirmation in his present appointment was noted in *Union Jack*, and the cat was out of the bag.

That evening Sue said: 'This Admiral Packer mentioned in *Union Jack* isn't by any chance your husband?'

He had telephoned the good news to me earlier in the day, and there seemed nothing for it but to confess the truth.

'Well . . .' said Sue, on a low whistling breath. 'To think I've been sharing a room with an admiral's wife!'

'You haven't,' I said, and felt abashed. But only for a moment, because I knew that all people were alike to Sue and that she reduced them to their basic value just as surely as she did the news.

A few days later my Admiral came to Rome for a long week-end's leave and I soared from the ridiculous to the Grand Hotel, taking my evening dress with me. For a few days I meant to wallow in the glamorous side of Rome, which I had glimpsed from time to time when the British Naval Representative on the Allied Commission had swept me out of the Botticelli to a Sunday lunch on the Golf Club Terrace, where Roman society still gathered as it had done in the days of peace, or to dinner in the Grand Hotel, which possessed the agreeable distinction of a Mess for V.I.P.'s. There was soft music at the Grand instead of an unholy clatter, and there was the added interest of certain proud pathetic survivals from the past. In the magnificent lounges and adjoining Black Market restaurant there were always groups of very old and aristocratic members of pre-Fascist Roman society. On the withered parchment of these aged faces was inscribed a tale of disillusion and of disdain for the present, very passing, show. Their earthly time and worldly fortunes were running out together. Soon there would be nothing left. The wide lands from which they had derived vast incomes lay ravaged by war, their many palaces and villas were ruined or requisitioned, they had little now save their poodles, their pride and their memories.

Bertie said, as we unpacked our suit-cases in a luxurious suite with private bath but no hot water:

'Henry and Alice Hopkinson are here. He's in some diplomatic capacity at the Allied Commission.'

This was exciting news, and we immediately telephoned the Allied Commission. We found that they were living in part of a historic palace near the Colosseum, and we dined with them that night.

We had not seen either of them since the blitz when I had helped Alice out with her mobile canteen team. As a diplomat, Henry was entitled to have his wife in Rome, for, from time immemorial diplomats have enjoyed privileges not accorded to lesser beings. But it was Henry's intention to abandon his extremely promising career in the Foreign Office in favour of politics. Alice was as forthright as ever.

'I envy you,' she said to me. 'You're lucky to be here in a job. I'm determined to get one, too. I don't want to be paid, but I do want to work for the war. People here think it's crazy.'

It did not take her long to find the work she was looking for – a job requiring integrity, intelligence and discretion, but her action in preferring work and responsibility to idleness was not in the feminine Roman tradition.

We all spent the following cold brilliant day at the Golf Club – a Saturday. Henry played polo, and Alice and I made up a four at golf with my husband and the Naval Representative in Rome.

My caddie was a very small, sprightly boy wearing a German forage cap and German top-boots which reached his skinny thighs. When I drove my ball into a miniature lake he waded in after it, returned it to me triumphantly, smiled gaily, and stood on his head to empty the water out of his boots.

That night we dined with American General Brown, the Military Governor of Rome, in a private room at the Ambassadors' Restaurant, where there was a cabaret afterwards. The guests of honour were the British Ambassador, Sir Noel Charles, and Lady Charles, and Congress-Woman Claire Booth Luce, the playwright, and wife of Henry Luce, the publisher of *Time, Life* and *Fortune.*

I was keenly interested to meet the author of that successful satire, 'The Women', with its glittering dialogue and merciless portrayal of the American woman of fashion.

The night was icy, and the ante-room in which we had our cocktails was heated only by a small and smelly oil-stove. The guests gathered round it making conversation and noble efforts not to shiver. The Ambassador had agonizing neuritis in his arm and showed it as little as the Spartan boy with the fox gnawing at his vitals. Lady Charles had platinum hair and a lovely figure, and wore clinging black satin which showed both to their fullest advantage. The last to arrive by a wide margin was the playwright, who demonstrated her flawless sense of the theatre in making her entrance.

Her dress was midnight blue, and a tulle Madonna scarf, sprinkled with tiny constellations, sparkled on her blonde hair. She paused effectively in the doorway, allowing a picture of surprising beauty to imprint itself upon the imagination. Then she stepped gracefully forward and, holding out her slim hands to the warmth of the little oil-stove round which we stood, she spoke her opening line in a low studied voice.

'The heart of the room is beating right here.'

It was a winning stroke. There was no come back. The General performed the introductions.

Claire Booth Luce was making an exhaustive tour of the liberated areas of Europe with a party of Congress Men, and during dinner she excused herself to broadcast her impressions to the United States. She displayed no nervousness. To eat her ice-cream or 'talk home' was all one to her. In fact, she did both.

Her poise throughout the evening was infallible, except for one small moment of unconscious humour when the ladies found themselves alone after dinner where the gentlemen would seem unlikely to join them. Owing to a slight confusion with doors the lovely leading lady found herself returning into the 'wings' whence she had come.

'Exit this way,' said the Ambassadress, with her enchanting smile. 'Unless you propose to give us an encore.'

Lady Charles, I learned later, could match the spirited dialogue of 'The Women' when she felt inclined.

I was aware, that evening, of many hairline distinctions between wit and humour. No one could deny Claire Booth Luce a penetrating and exquisite mastery of wit.

Rome had much to offer troops on leave; and those who did not come exhausted from the lines, showed a strong appreciation of music and art of a quality hitherto unknown to most of them.

My husband and I went to an Art Exhibition in the Palazzo Venezia, organized under the auspices of A.M.G. It was not just an Exhibition of peculiar merit. It was unique in the world. An enormous number of Italy's foremost art treasures had been brought from all over the country at the outbreak of war to be stored in the Vatican City, which was rightly regarded as being sacrosanct. This magnificent collection was now on view in the historic setting of the Palazzo Venezia. So we saw not only the most superb examples of Italian Renaissance Art and many masterpieces of other lands, but we saw them in the great halls and armouries of the Popes, which Mussolini had turned into his own vast offices and conference rooms. We stood for a while on the balcony from which the Dictator had declaimed and thundered at the crowds in the Piazza, and we watched the conquering troops strolling in the sunshine out of the winter wind. In the Palace opposite, our host of the night before administered the military government of the city.

'If Musso could have seen into the future when he talked to his people,' I said, 'he wouldn't have enjoyed the picture. I wonder what the end'll be – for him – for Hitler . . .'

My husband said, 'Before the year is out we'll know.'

'Well,' said Phil Hodge, when I returned to the Botticelli like Cinderella to her chimney corner. 'Back to earth.'

I laughed. 'That's the first week-end I've ever spent with an Admiral.'

He gave his half yawn and his half smile, and ran his fingers through his crisp iron-grey hair.

'*Et enfin c'est la même chose*,' he said. '*Camerieri, due verre del vino rosso!*'

One rainy night in February I went with Figaro and Phil Hodge to the studio at Radio Rome, where they were performing the 'Pearl Fishers'. Bizet's music, with its sense of alternating storm, torment and deep peace enthralled me, but afterwards, while we waited in the wind-blown rain for our P.W.B. car, which was, as usual, lost, I began to shiver violently while my hands and face were burning hot. Next morning I awoke feeling really ill.

Sue said, 'Where does it hurt?'

'My face. I've got toothache all over the left side of my face – especially up here near my eye.'

'Perhaps it's your eye-tooth,' suggested Sue with a worried frown. 'If you aren't better at lunch-time I'll take you to hospital.'

'To hospital!' I was appalled.

'We always go to hospital when we're ill,' she said. 'Doctors won't come and see you. You have to bundle up and go to hospital.'

My temperature soared, and I flinched when Sue brought me cabbage soup from the Mess at lunch-time.

'The waiters won't serve anything in the rooms,' she said. 'That's another reason for going to hospital. One can't miss one's food.'

She packed my night-things and, while I protested feebly, piled me into a P.W.B. car and spirited me off to a military hospital somewhere on the outskirts of the city. Suzanne always knew where to go and what to do in an emergency. The amazing competence of that little Bohemian never failed to astonish me.

'I'll come and see you tomorrow,' she said, as she left me in a three-bed ward with a physio-therapist, a threatened appendix, and an English girl who had shared our crypt and who was suffering, like me, from an acute sinus infection.

After ten days' incarceration I decided that I was well and wished to return to work. The medical officer in charge thought otherwise. I consulted Sue.

She said: 'They can't *force* you to stay, because you are a civilian and not subject to military discipline.'

So I signed a paper to the effect that I went at my own risk, and departed under Suzanne's wing and a cloud of disapproval.

'Now you report to Captain Bordon,' she said.

Captain Bordon, in charge of British personnel, was a thin dark man who was having trouble with his teeth. His red-haired worried-looking secretary said, 'You ought not to leave hospital under these conditions. It's most unorthodox. Why is everybody in P.W.B. always so unorthodox?'

The Captain said: 'You'd better take a few days sick-leave, if Carrick can spare you.'

Ken Carrick was agreeable. 'Take a week off. There's not much doing now, but soon there'll be plenty.' He whistled his little tuneless tune and offered no further information. The silences of Captain Carrick were his most exasperating feature.

I rang up my husband at Caserta.

He said: 'This is wonderful! I'm alone here at the villa. Pat and Jasper are both away with the C.-in-C. and won't be back for at least eight days. There's a naval car coming down from Rome tomorrow bringing two of the staff off leave. I'll arrange for you to get a passage.'

That evening the Hungarian in charge of Film Section publicity had dinner at my table in the Mess.

'You should come to the P.W.B. documentary of the opening of the Ardeatine Caves,' he said. 'We're showing it tonight.' His long mournful face was sadder than ever.

'I'd like to,' I said.

I knew the appalling story of the Ardeatine Caves very well – as we all did.

Our billet had previously been occupied by the German S.S. Police, who were bitterly hated in Rome. And, early one morning, as a detachment of thirty guards were marching down our street to their headquarters, they were blown to pieces by a bomb concealed in a little hand dust-cart. As a reprisal three hundred Italians – men, women and boys – were rounded up, herded into some deep caves outside Rome and shot. The entrance to the caves was then dynamited. The remains had recently been excavated by the Allies and given Christian burial amid tragic scenes.

That film, made for record purposes, gave me a grim idea of what occupation by a ruthless ally-enemy can mean to a city. Certain industrial districts in Rome had been bombed, but physically her wounds were the lightest scratches as compared with the deep scars of London. It was morally she had suffered. We, in England, had been lucky.

Next day, in company with a naval officer and two Wrens, I drove once more along the war-torn road to the south.

This time we did not follow the coast but went by Monte Cassino, where the shell of the ruined monastery looked down from the sad grey hills. In caves at its feet dwelt those survivors of a town now razed to the ground. But road-gangs were at work and new walls were rising out of the waste.

Four months had passed since I had travelled the road to Naples, and I found that my experience with P.W.B. made me seek new features. I looked for the signs of regeneration and welcomed them – fields where the Sappers and Partisans had raised the mines and the white oxen ploughed again; Italian labourers rebuilding the graceful stone bridges alongside the Bailey span or working along the railway so that trains should run once more; fishermen putting out to sea from patched-up harbours; and here and there the strong dry smell of kilns manufacturing bricks for the reconstruction of homes.

As we went further south we saw young leaves on the vines and the first sprays of blossom fluttering frail pennants of spring.

That week alone with my husband at Villa Masoni was, for me, an interval of profound refreshment.

The tall dilapidated villa outside the village of San Lucia, three miles from Caserta, was loved by the sun, which spilt over verandahs and balconies into the big rather bare rooms. Round it lapped the hills, quiet save for the tinkle of goat-bells, and beneath it was spread the tapestry carpet of the Volturno, where the shining horseshoe bends of the river held shimmering grey-green olive groves and the bridal beauty of fruit orchards in early flower.

In the villa garden there was always bird-song, and girl-song, too, for two cheerful black-eyed maidens did much of the work and washing of this small well-appointed Mess. I often heard them laughing as they hung the laundry out to dry in the shrubbery, and talking their pidgin-English, pidgin-Italian to 'Poppa' White, that honest Able Seaman who had once helped teach his Captain's wife to ride a bicycle.

Maltese stewards looked after us, and had even decked out the villa with flowers stuck firmly into vases, man-fashion, just as they were. Instead of rubbery pancakes, I had eggs for breakfast laid by the chickens in the garden, and there was a white Angora rabbit who was the household pet and who lay in my lap like a cat.

In the evenings we went for walks in the budding hills, where the charcoal burners had their smoking mounds, and all day I lay and read and rested, happy in the privacy I had missed more than I knew.

Back in Rome, Ken Carrick said: 'We're leaving for Florence next week. Only a few of us are going on. George and my secretary, you and me, and I'm taking our Italian artist, Roberto. I've organized a three-tonner for ourselves and our luggage and office equipment. And we're giving Marj Poole a lift. Some of her section is moving on, too.'

That was how I came to know that P.W.B. was 'folding up' in Rome and being taken over in part by civilian organizations. Marjorie Fergusson and Bruno were to remain, and so was Carol. Phil Hodge, whose business was with Italian publishers, would keep his headquarters in Rome.

Those of us who went forward with P.W.B. were to be attached to General Mark Clark's Fifteenth Army Group Headquarters in Florence.

'It's a military area,' said the Boss. 'So you'll need a uniform when we're travelling. I don't know what sort of work you'll be doing. We'll see when we get there.'

So I wore the battle-dress of a soldier, with P.W.B. flashes, and, on a sunny morning, we all piled into the back of a three-tonner outside the Botticelli. A crowd collected to see us go.

Sue said: 'We'll meet again somewhere else – one always does in P.W.B.'

Stella put her childish face forward to be kissed and pressed a bunch of daffodils into my arms. 'You'll see,' she said. 'I'll be in Florence soon. I have a feeling.'

Roberto, the willowy Italian artist – a youth of nineteen with a lock of romantic black hair – wept as he bade his girl farewell. George looked wildly round for his cap and exchanged a few final pleasantries with the Welsh lieutenant as he bustled Marj Poole into the truck. And Ken Carrick, looking more immaculate than ever, said good-bye to no one.

So we passed through the city gates on the long road to the north – the road that led away from Rome, and further still from Caserta, and eight hours later, coated from head to foot in fine grey dust, we arrived in Florence at the P.W.B. hotel. We were stiff and exhausted and there was no hot water to wash off the dust. But our dinner was excellent, for we were now on

British Military rations – than which there are no better. I was given a room with Marj, and the beds were comfortable.

'This mattress!' I murmured, as I sank into it. 'Bliss!'

'Should be,' said Marj, with a giggle. 'I'm told they only took the red light down a week ago!'

CHAPTER FORTY-TWO

FLORENTINE SPRING

AT first my life in Florence seemed idle and delightful. The month of March came in like ice-cream and hot golden syrup – cold crisp air and bright yellow sunlight. There were daffodils and lilac on the flower barrows in streets that curved like narrow canyons between the tall mediaeval houses with their wrought iron balconies and gothic windows; and the Arno flowed, jade green and swift, between her ruined banks, beneath a Bailey bridge where once the lovely Ponte Trinità had spanned her foaming shallows. Children, with ash-pale faces and toothpick rickety legs, frisked upon her sands like lambs in spring. On the Lungarno, where Dante first saw la bella Beatrice – the lovely inspiration of his poet's soul – Allied troops strolled with the shabby dark-eyed 'signorinas'. And in the beautiful square palace of the powerful Medicis, patrons of art and culture, a war organization had its headquarters. The Cathedral squares and gardens were disfigured by huge black military signposts telling the troops the way to clubs, recreation rooms and canteens. Round all the roads to the north the historic houses lay in heaps of rubble.

The Florentines grieved for their city with bitterness and despair, yet somehow the city itself rose above its gashes and cares and its waves of warriors, hostile or friendly, as Nelson's Column soars above the droppings of the pigeons at its base.

I experienced an agreeable sense of peace in those first days in Florence, for the manageress of our Mess was not an American Sergeant but a well-bred Italian woman with a fluent knowledge of English, and presently she allocated me an attic to myself. I think the real reason for this blessed privilege was Giovanna.

Giovanna was her niece, a pink-faced university student, with enormous blue eyes and two thick ropes of flaxen hair which she coiled in the nape of her neck or left swinging over her shoulders like a schoolgirl. She wanted English conversation lessons, and I wanted Italian, and the manageress suggested that we come to a friendly agreement. This we were both eager to do, but there was a difficulty.

'The only time I can fit it in is in the lunch hour,' I explained. 'And the only place we could be undisturbed is in my bedroom . . . now, if I had a bedroom to myself, it would all be so simple . . .'

Strangely enough, all was soon made 'simple', and, when I had eaten an early meal in the Mess, I would go to my room to wait for Giovanna, who pounded up the five flights of stairs (there was, of course, no power for the elevator) and arrived flushed and breathless at my door. Giovanna always did everything with all her heart and two steps at a time. Then we'd sit at my little table in the window and read aloud and discuss what we had read. One day we worked in English and the next in Italian. The sun lay warm and glowing on the red-tiled rooftops those early afternoons, and plumes of young leaf nodded here and there among the higgledy-piggledy chimney-pots, while doves wheeled round domes and spires and the tall square tower of the Medici Palace.

How different was Giovanna from the cold little woman who had given me my first elementary Italian lessons in Rome! How different from the parrot teachers of the Berlitz School here in Florence, where I went for an hour at eight o'clock every morning. She was so young and intense, so ablaze with the great beautiful burning thoughts of idealistic youth, that she became frustrated to the pitch of desperation when she could not explain them in her stumbling English. And then, suddenly, she would toss back her fair plaits with a gesture of impatience and break into Italian, crying out louder and louder what she had to say as if to compel my understanding with her very vehemence. When I, in my turn, could not make myself understood, I was apt to stare out of the window as if to draw inspiration from the bright air, and she would watch me, holding her breath and waiting for me to find the word that would unlock the gate of meaning.

On my way back to the office in the afternoon I often saw her, standing beside her bicycle outside the hotel, muttering to herself, 'Through, thought, thorough, cough, rough, bough . . .' Then she'd mount and swoop away towards the Duomo, passing me with her pigtails swinging and her young pink face filled with concentration as her lips continued to move through the rocky shoals of English pronunciation.

Our office was in a narrow street near the Piazza del Duomo, and to reach it one went past the main P.W.B. headquarters which was, for all the world, like any newspaper building. There were many strange and mysterious editorial sections, there was the constant thunder of the presses, and there were always army vehicles outside waiting to take away great bales of literature.

P.W.B. in Florence was not concerned with the nice little posters and pamphlets we had written so diligently in Rome. P.W.B. in Florence was operational, in support of General Mark Clark and his Fifteenth Army Group. The material that was carried away in army trucks – often by South Africans with the orange flash on their uniforms – was in German or Italian. It would be shot out of the mouths of cannons or dropped out of the bellies of aircraft. There were leaflets telling the German soldier the truth about his homeland and his chances of winning the war, and there was *Front Post*, the amazing tabloid newspaper that gave him news, good and bad, long before he received it from his own news-sheets. On the leaflets and on *Front Post* there were surrender instructions and coupons. For both, the slogan was 'the truth and nothing but the truth'. That was the strength of Allied propaganda. It stuck to the truth. Even in the bad days it had done that, and now that the tide had turned that fact was remembered. The truth had become a bitter weapon with which to attack the morale of the lonely German troops in the mountains of Northern Italy. Their own command was not going to tell them of the shattered home front shrinking hourly as the Allies closed in like Nemesis upon the last fortresses of Germany. *Front Post*, with its illustrations, and its brief unslanted communiqués, was their news link with home. When it was delivered short of their lines they risked death by running out to pick it up.

The Italian leaflets were Marj Poole's concern. They kept the Partisans informed of what was happening and of what was planned. I think the Partisans, hiding in their frontier fastnesses, must often have cursed those fluttering leaflets dropped from the air. Their needs were many and material, and material was still short.

We often saw the Partisans in Florence – rangy Robin Hood fellows with shabby clothes and bandoliers and pointed green felt hats. They did not move like clumsy disciplined khaki-clad troops in big army boots. They moved warily, wherever they might be, for they were conditioned to stealth and danger. They were the masters of sabotage, the dreaded shadowy death, and if they were caught they were tortured and their families, too, were made to suffer death or torture.

Marj Poole's office adjoined ours, and these young men appeared and disappeared mysteriously – always singly. But sometimes one came into our room to see Emmanuela. He was dark and handsome, with a cold watchfulness in his eyes that was foreign to the youth and ragged gallantry of his bearing and the gaiety of his smile. When he talked to her Emmanuela raised her blonde head and her pale dead young face, and a spark of forgotten life shone suddenly in her green eyes. Her soft deliberate voice became almost animated as they spoke in quick colloquial Italian, and smoked her American cigarettes. She always had American cigarettes.

'*Arrivederci*,' he'd say, reluctantly, at last.

'*Ciao*,' she'd answer, and the brief light in her face would be extinguished as she turned back to the news photographs strewn over her desk.

Emmanuela and her photographs, George Bowman and I shared a narrow office partitioned off from the Art Department, where the melancholy Roberto produced lay-outs and effective headings for the feature panels in our Information Centres. Roberto was always ailing. If he hadn't a toothache, it was a stomach-ache, and he sighed perpetually after the girl he had left behind in Rome.

Every day vast quantities of news and feature photographs were serviced to our office from Rome, and it was Emmanuela's job to translate all the captions into Italian.

Her father had been the Italian Consul to an American city in his daughter's childhood, so she had learned to speak her soft attractive American at an early age. Later she had been to Florence University where she had taken her degree. When I met her she was twenty-four years old, with a face cast in a childish and lovely mould, pale ash-gold hair and a figure that might well have been enticing had it not been for the lethargy that seemed to hold her in a deadly thrall. This air of listlessness clung about her like a miasma. It rendered her colourless and empty – a lamp without a light. It caused her to move as if she walked under the sea, subject to invisible pressure. Only when the young Partisan came and leaned over her desk to talk his fiery Italian and flash his white teeth did the light flare up for an instant.

'He was a friend of my boy's,' she told me. 'He belonged to that other life.'

The 'other life', to which she seldom referred, was that in which she had met and married 'my boy'. They had been nineteen then, and 'so happy we were crazy . . . even when we hadn't a sou we found things to be happy about – just being alive and together! We were in love with love and each other and our country, too. We believed in Fascism – and, I promise you, it was good in the beginning . . .'

It was bold of her to be so frank. She never hesitated to admit that she had been ardently Fascist – and there were few who did that once the Allies came into occupation. But then Emmanuela had ceased to care what she said. She was deep in her disillusion.

'Fascism seemed so wonderful – for a while it was – and then it dragged us into this war at the heels of Germany. It destroyed my country – and my life—'

Her boy had gone to Africa to fight.

'One thing I'm glad of,' she said, with her face softening. 'He knew about our baby before he went away. He was so happy about that – we both were . . .'

Three days before the birth of their baby she heard that her young husband had been killed. Her baby – her little son, 'he was so perfect! They let me see him before they took him from me' – was born dead. Emmanuela lived, but there was no longer any life in her.

All that was long ago. Three years ago. Now, because she spoke good American, and was intelligent in her own remote disinterested way, and efficient too, she held a job in P.W.B.

'I joined P.W.B. in Rome,' she said. 'My mother lives there, and I was with her when my boy was killed and my baby died.'

'It was bad luck on you being sent to Florence.'

She stood up and went on to the little balcony outside our office. She looked down on to the narrow street, partly in shadow between the tall buildings, while the sun fell across her white lifeless skin and the pale hair she wore tied back with a ribbon round her head like an illustration of 'Alice in Wonderland'. A flower-seller passed under the window with a barrow of spring flowers – mimosa, almond blossom, purple iris and lilac.

She said: 'It wasn't bad luck. It was my intention. I meant to get to Florence. And when Milan is liberated I shall get to Milan. Milano is my city, it is my home. And I will get there.'

Her face had set and hardened, and I felt a sense of relief that she had within her a purpose – something to live for and work for. Home-coming. Always there was this – this home-looking – in the hearts of human beings.

I said: 'You're surprisingly honest. You are telling me that you are riding the job.'

Her expressionless green eyes summed me up calmly.

'With someone else I might not be so frank. But what about you? Are *you* in Italy by chance? Or are you, too, riding a job?' She smiled. 'Somehow, I think you understand.'

'I understand.'

'And if I am riding the job, as you put it, what does it matter so long as I do it reasonably well and give satisfaction?'

'What indeed, Emmanuela?'

'I am paid a song for my work. We all are, we locally employed Italians. I don't care. Money has no value here nowadays. Food has. I get something to eat in the P.W.B. Italian Mess. And transport has. I shall make myself indispensable so that I am needed in Milan. When the time comes, P.W.B. will be glad to take me there.'

I said: 'If I can help you when the times comes, I will. In the meantime, do you want a hand with your pictures? You can show me how you classify them and I'll file them for you.'

'You're very kind. I'd be glad – if you aren't too busy.'

I laughed. 'There's no job for a copy-writer here.'

I was not particularly busy at first, though the shape of my future work was gradually taking its own form as I began to plan displays and features for our Information Centres, and the regular presentation of news in pictures to be changed daily in our showcases in Florence, and bi-weekly throughout the surrounding districts.

Between us, Emmanuela and I altered the dull captions of the photographs we received and made connected stories of desultory material. We dramatized the stuff with which we dealt, and together we strolled round the city and watched the ever-increasing crowds round our windows. They were the gauge of our success or failure.

One day Emmanuela said: 'I'm getting interested in our work. I used to just do it. Now it's different.'

I knew it was different. Instead of the listless obedient 'By all means' with which she had hitherto greeted my suggestions and helped to carry them out, she now began to produce her own ideas. 'Let us do a thing,' she would say. I was always glad when she said that. It was a show of initiative, the rising of the sap.

There were always people strolling in and out of our office.

Sometimes it was the young South African soldier wanting news photographs for the Army Information Room. He spoke with a strong Afrikaans accent and told me he belonged to the Orange Free State.

'Are you enjoying Italy?' I asked him.

'Yes, in a way,' he said. 'But not Florence.'

'Not Florence! But it's such a lovely city!'

He said: 'Man, it suffocates me! Look at that street down there – shut in so that you can hardly see the sky. If I could just get one look at the veld!'

He was not an articulate young man, and he had come a long way from home.

'I'll be glad when we get cracking at Jerry again,' he said. 'Thanks for these. Totsiens.'

Other times Gladys Hutton came in from the section about which we did not enquire. She was very English in her appearance, with her simple black dress and her small pale face telling its tale of rare beauty. But there were touches of Italian frivolity about her too – an exquisite Naples cameo brooch and the halo of fine black tulle over her snowy hair. Often she brought me a vase of spring flowers gathered from some friend's garden and set it on my desk. She spoke Italian like her own language, and loved and understood the sunny gracious people of a land that was surely dedicated to the gods of love and fertility rather than the grim god of war now in possession. She had lived in Naples till the war had destroyed her home, then she had made her way to Florence, where she had seen the long terrible battle for the city fought out with one side of the river in German hands and the other held by the Allies.

The Fascists had never bothered to intern her. What harm could she do – this delicate little old lady who was as dry and sweet as potpourri – who loved Italy and had spent much of her life there, whose interests were in art and culture and who augmented a modest income by translating highbrow Italian literature and poetry into her perfect English? What harm indeed? None. But Gladys was of the breed of those I had learned to know in England during the blitz. Fragile as spun glass, she rang as true, and did not hesitate to risk the slender thread of her life that others might be saved. How she accomplished that is her story and not mine, and perhaps one day it will be written. In the meantime, she showed me much of the beauty of her beloved Florence and something of its cultural influence and romantic character. For every Italian city has its own personality and way of thought and its own pride dating back to the not far distant past when Italy was divided into the city states usually at war with one another.

One day, when she came in, she saw a series of photographs lying on my desk. She took them up and glanced at them.

'Do you like them?' I asked. 'They belong to a set about the reopening of Florence University. We want to do a feature about the regeneration of education in Italy.'

Pleasure flooded her small fine-featured face.

'What a good idea! Have you ever read the speech the Rector of the University made that day? I have a copy of the English translation.'

She brought it in to me presently. 'If you read this you'll understand the spirit of Florence.'

That oration of Professor Calamandrei was one of moving beauty. It was a cry from the very soul of Culture.

> 'You know that in Italy, and especially in Tuscany, every hamlet and hill, every turn of the road, has its character like a living person. There is not so much as a bell-tower of a parish church that is not connected in our hearts with the name of a poet or a painter or with the memory of some historic event as important to us as the joys and sorrows of

our own family. This is not a question of literature, but of life. . . . These places are flesh of our flesh, and we can be as anxious about the fate of a picture or a statue as of a dear friend or relative . . .'

One day Gladys took me to the historic Palazzo Corsini to tea with her friend, Donna Lucrezia Corsini. We passed through the great courtyards, through terraces of statues, up wide marble flights of stairs and through vast echoing banquetting halls until we came to the small curtained doorway which marked the diminished living quarters of the family.

Our hostess, though no longer young, was one of the most fascinating women I have ever met – small and slight with a husky humorous voice, grey wavy hair, an expressive mouth and a pair of flirting dark eyes that held, in their luminous depths, the elixir of eternal youth.

Tea and sugar were scarce, but, had there been none, it would have been unimportant, for there was the wit and enchantment of Donna 'Rezia' and the retiring dreamy charm of her musician daughter, Anna. They both spoke flawless English and made light of the many difficulties under which they lived. But there was often sadness, and even bitterness, behind the mask of mockery which Donna 'Rezia' wore when she spoke of the misfortunes of her country and herself.

'See,' she said, drawing me to the window over the Lungarno. 'When the Nazis decided to evacuate Florence and retire north they made up their minds to destroy all the roads and bridges. You have never seen the bridges over our river. They were very beautiful – part of our history – especially the Ponte Trinità. . . . The German Consul here was a good man. He did what he could to help us all. Well, one day he came to Anna and me and told us to leave our home until these things had been done. It was even possible, he explained, that part of our Palazzo Corsini might be ruined. So we packed up a few oddments and went to the house of a relative . . .' She paused, and there was deep sorrow in her voice as she continued.

'When we stood here – as you and I do now – and looked down for the last time at the Ponte Trinità . . . it was like saying good-bye to a dear and innocent friend upon the eve of execution . . . ah—' She shrugged her shoulders and turned away from the window with its view of jeeps noisily crossing the iron Bailey bridge. 'Have another cup of weak tea, my dear, and be thankful your green little England was never overrun by friend or foe.'

It was typical of the flexibility of P.W.B. that my job in Florence was, at first, undefined. Jobs in this curious organization grew and dwindled as the need for them came and went.

It was the same with George Bowman. Much of the important work he had been doing in Rome, such as editing scientific journals, had been turned over to Philip Hodge or Dr. Milano. As copy-writers we were, in this highly operational zone, useless. But the Boss soon made it clear to us that we must extend our field in new directions.

So, as preparations for the Spring Offensive intensified, the activity in our department followed suit, and presently we found ourselves up to our ears in the production of a portable exhibition of photographs showing the progress of the war from Alamein to Bologna. As Bologna was still in enemy hands the last part would naturally have to be added when the time came. The plan was that the liberation of Bologna would be closely followed up by George with his exhibition and the authority to open P.W.B. Information Centres. Stocks for these must also be prepared in advance. Thus, before long, the Boss had to find us another artist to assist Roberto, and another translator to help Emmanuela.

The artist was a petulant young man, and the translator was a languid Italian replica of Hedy Lamarr. Hedy typed her captions with one finger and at arm's length, lying back in her chair in an attitude of amiable exhaustion. She came from Trieste, and hoped to return there one day on the accommodating shoulders of P.W.B., but there was, in this natural wish, none of the inflexible single-minded purpose of Emmanuela. Hedy lacked the efficiency which would make her indispensable, but she had as assets her gentle indolent smile, her appealing beauty, and her knowledge of the written English word. The spoken word often baffled her, and she would look up at hasty George, whose 'bags of ideas' were apt to take their verbal form at full speed, with a shadowy alluring little frown so fetching that it robbed him of further speech in any tempo. If Marj Poole happened to come in and observe his difficulty and its cause she would translate for him firmly and brusquely, glancing the while at Hedy's deplorably typed captions. Then she'd shrug her plump shoulders and tap out of the room with a brisk click of her high heels.

George's exhibition was not merely a visual record of the Allied advance up Italy. It had many other aspects. Those that interested me most were the features showing the rehabilitation of liberated Italy. These also interested Emmanuela, who loved her country almost as much as she loved her city, Milan.

I often found her pouring over reconstruction features with her dead young face intent; and her eyes, when she raised them, were like those of someone waking from a long sleep.

'See,' she said. 'These children are being cared for by our nuns, but the convent is stocked with American supplies. These children were living in the ruins. They were stealing to live. It should never happen that circumstances make thieves of little children – *force* them into robbery to keep them from starvation!'

She began to be angry. That was good. And it was good when she 'stole' one of our photographs to pin it up on the plywood partition behind her desk. It was a close-up of a baby about to receive its bottle. Its mouth was expectantly pursed and out-thrust like the hungry beak of a baby bird. Then she took another for her gallery, not a baby this time, but four little horses with wind-blown manes on a snowy prairie.

'They're the prettiest part of the American Scene series,' she said. 'I adore them. Let's do a thing, Joy, let's have an interior feature for the Centres – one of outposts of America.'

'Outposts and how they are reached by civilization – the place of the aeroplane in the life of a great continent . . .'

In Emmanuela I was watching the rehabilitation of the mind and the heart.

The American P.W.B. photographer used to roam in and out of our office and discuss his pictures with us.

I said: 'There's so much American aid to Italy in your stuff. Couldn't you do us a few more British features?'

He shifted his chewing-gum from one cheek to the other.

'What British is there?'

'Well, there's the work that's been done at Naples and Livorno – harbour reconstruction and salvage. The German demolition of the harbours was a miracle of thoroughness, and the Navy's got them going again and is employing thousands of Italians in the process. They'll be ship-building again in Naples and Leghorn before you can look round.'

'Sounds like it might make a story.' His tone was dubious.

'Look,' I said. 'If I can get the Boss's permission we could fly down to Naples and then Livorno and I could do the copy while you get the pictures. I can fix the naval permission, I feel sure.'

'Sure,' he said. 'Suits me. If you got it laid on we could finish the job in four days.'

Ken Carrick screwed up his eyes as he looked at me.

'Naples? . . . Mmn. It'd make a good feature, and we've very little harbour stuff and no British. I'll let you know in a day or two. Transport's the problem. It'd have to be by air, and the courier's packed, as you know.'

But next afternoon chance played into my hands.

It was early April. The sun filtered into the office and gilded a vase of yellow roses on my desk and Emmanuela's ash-fair hair bent over the feature we were working out together.

'Mrs. Packer here?'

The voice was slow and pleasant, an American voice.

I looked up and saw a tall figure in the doorway, wearing battledress and the shoulder tabs of an American Brigadier General.

I stood up. 'I'm Mrs. Packer.'

'Your husband sends you his love,' said the stranger.

He had a lazy, rather saturnine smile and observant blue eyes in a weather-beaten face. He had iron-grey hair, pointed faun's ears, strong features and the look of one accustomed to having his own way.

'I thought you might like to come out to dinner tonight,' he said. 'My name's McChrystal.'

CHAPTER FORTY-THREE

FRITZEL

'MY name's McChrystal.' It was a name we all had reason to know.

Brigadier-General Arthur McChrystal was the Chief of Information and Censorship in the Italian theatre, and, as such, P.W.B. was one of his 'children'.

As I discovered when I knew him better, 'Art' McChrystal was the least conventional of men. He exerted his considerable authority with the minimum of fuss. At Caserta he did not ride round in a sleek army car, but in a jeep. And, although he had been a professional soldier for seventeen years, he had the born journalist's dislike of yesterday's news. 'Stale news stinks like bad fish,' he said. He was always out to help the war correspondents and to keep 'this goddam censorship' down to a minimum.

His career had held the variety that suited him to his job. He had been brought up in Salt Lake City, and declared, with a lively twinkle in his eye, that he was a 'good old-fashioned Mormon' and that twenty-three grandmothers had seen him off to the last war. Between then and now he had served in China, where he had learned to speak Chinese, and had later added spice to his army career at home by promoting prize fights, coaching baseball and football teams, and editing a sports magazine. When he retired from the army in 1937 he became a publicity man, and 1939 found him in charge of Amusements and Concessions – or, as he preferred to put it, 'sex and sin' – at the San Francisco World Fair. The war called him back into service, and, after being in action in North Africa with Eisenhower's Forces, he was promoted to Brigadier-General and made Head of Information and Censorship at A.F.H.Q., Caserta.

That spring afternoon, when he dropped out of the clouds into Florence, he had business with our branch of P.W.B. among other things, and, having met my husband at a luncheon with the Commander-in-Chief the day before, he had heard of my existence and offered to look me up. With him were two American war correspondents, and two army nurses made up our party of six for dinner at the Excelsior. Afterwards we went to a cabaret in a smoky vaulted cellar somewhere near the Lungarno.

After a time General McChrystal said: 'Your husband's dining with me in the Generals' Mess at Caserta the night after tomorrow. I reckon you should be there to look after his diet. Did anybody tell you that he'd been having a stomach-ache?'

'Nobody told me,' I said, 'and I'd love to supervise his diet. But Caserta is a very long way from Florence.'

'Not in my plane. We happen to have a spare place. Seems a pity to waste it.'

'When do you leave?'

'Eleven tomorrow. I could pick you up at the P.W.B. Mess.'

I said: 'Would you have room for a photographer as well?'

He offered me a Chesterfield, and I saw his lazy smile and one raised eyebrow behind a haze of smoke.

'Isn't that taking your personal publicity a little too far?'

I laughed, and explained the situation.

'There's a story we want to get at Naples – a P.W.B. reconstruction story.'

'Yeah – there are some mighty good stories round Naples,' said the General, who was in a flippant frame of mind. 'I know some.'

'About the photographer . . .' I murmured.

'My second name is Boy Scout,' said the General. 'So, if you insist on your private photographer, we'll have to pile him in with the mail. Shall we dance this one?'

The Generals' Mess at Caserta was no ordinary prosaic Army Mess, nor was it some requisitioned hotel. It was a camp on the summit of a forested hill above Caserta Palace, and it looked over the fields and vineyards to the sea. There, amid glades bursting into the glory of young leaf and threaded with the song of the nightingale, were American army huts of astonishing warmth and comfort. The Mess itself had the air of a log cabin, and at one end of the lounge a wood fire burned in a huge open hearth.

Art McChrystal said: 'Well, Admiral, I hope your wife got her story at Naples today. I brought her down here for the good of P.W.B.'

Bertie laughed.

'She got her story, and she's off to Leghorn tomorrow with her tame photographer to get the sequel. They're going in the naval courier-plane.'

'She should hang around here,' said Art. 'You never know when you won't get a wonderful story at Caserta. Have you heard the one about the Brazilian division—'

The Mess was not crowded. A few officers stood about smoking, exchanging desultory remarks and drinking sherry or gin. They looked much younger than their high rank would suggest, and very lean and fit.

With his back to the fire was a slight fair man with a thin face and a rather sleepy expression. A little dachshund, obviously very well bred, lay at his feet with its sharp nose against the fireguard and its eyes mournful and reflective.

'General Airey has just come back off leave today,' said Art, when he had introduced us. 'He's brought Fritzel with him as a souvenir.'

Major-General Airey was Intelligence Officer to Field-Marshal Alexander, who had succeeded 'Jumbo' Wilson as Supreme Commander. He had a manner so quiet and unassuming that it gave the impression of being deliberately self-effacing.

'Fritzel isn't used to communal life, yet,' he said. 'The little chap's still rather homesick.'

'There's someone I'd like you to meet,' Bertie murmured to me, presently. 'General Lemnitzer. He's American and the very greatest help to us. Lem has a way with all foreigners and he gets on famously with our people. He's over there talking to Thornton Wilder and Major Thruelson. Thruelson was the editor of the *Saturday Evening Post*, I think, and he's written a very lively book about the air-war in the Med.'

Thruelson of the *Saturday Evening Post* was dark, with a face which, in repose, was almost as sad as that of the little dachshund, but, when he talked, he was amusing, extremely well-informed and never at a loss.

'If only your English writer, Forester, would forget about Hornblower and stick to modern stuff like "The Ship" he'd really be in the big money,' he moaned. 'We lap him up, but our readers can't take Hornblower.'

My husband smiled. 'But we love Hornblower – not only in the Navy either. That period of history is interesting to us – especially today when we're up against it again.'

Thornton Wilder volunteered nothing. He was silent and rather taciturn that evening, a slim compact man with a strong sense of the futility of all things.

Lyman Lemnitzer, Deputy Chief-of-Staff to the Supreme Commander was tall, olive-skinned and dark-haired, with a gift for putting people at their ease. Studious by temperament, he did not lack gaiety and humour, and presently he began to tell me small amusing incidents about staff meetings and my husband. They made me laugh, for they were deftly drawn sketches of different people coloured by insight.

'That guy of yours brings everything back to essentials,' he said of Bertie. 'I wish you could hear him pull 'em back when they start getting away from the point. He's got a sense of proportion.'

'You've hit him off just right,' I said, and felt a stab of surprise that this American shoould have summed up my English husband so ably in half-a-dozen meetings and half as many sentences.

After dinner we had coffee at the fireside, and the little dachshund jumped up on to the low leather couch and curled up beside me with his chin in my lap and his sad eyes on my face. He was shivering a little.

'What do you want to tell me?' I asked, stroking the sleek head. 'I know a dachsie called Fritz who always joins in conversations. Doesn't he, Bertie – Marion's Fritz.'

'Our Fritzel knows that dogs should be seen and not heard,' said his master with a faint smile.

'Where does he come from?' I asked.

General Airey's quiet eyes were indifferent, almost remote, as he looked at the little animal. There was neither affection nor any particular interest in his expression.

'It's a Swiss breed,' he said. It was almost as if he had not spoken, and I did not notice then that he had not answered my question directly. He was as impersonal as Lemnitzer was definite, as elusive as the other was substantial. He stood by the fire and watched the play, and Lemnitzer took the stage. Fair and dark, objective and subjective, English and American, these two men formed a curious contrast and complement to one another.

Lemnitzer sat on the arm of the couch.

'Well, Fritzel—' he said. 'Shaking down?'

The little souvenir dog answered nothing. Just raised his melting eyes and sighed.

It was 4th April.

I could not know that I was holding in my lap the 'cover plan' for the two officers who had that afternoon returned from one of the most exciting and portentous missions of the war.

Airey and Lemnitzer had been to Switzerland, secretly and disguised, to establish contact with General Wolff, Chief of the Waffen S.S. in Northern Italy, who recognized that further resistance was useless. Germany was, in his opinion, beaten, and the sooner an example of surrender was set, the sooner the futile bloodshed would cease. In letting it be known that he was anxious to meet with Allied envoys he was acting without the knowledge of Hitler and Himmler, who were determined to continue the struggle in the hope of a rift between Russia and the Democracies, which would allow Germany to side with one or the other and still emerge victorious. One hint of what was happening would have cost Wolff his life and the two Allied officers the success of their mission.

While they were staying in Switzerland, Lemnitzer and Airey were ostensibly two American dog fanciers on leave. The purchase of Fritzel, buying his dog-biscuits and taking him out for walks, enabled them to wander about the town and the surrounding countryside and, in one way and another, the little animal was their 'cover'.

'The whole thing,' said Lem afterwards, 'was like living through chapters from Phillips Oppenheim!'

But weeks had still to pass before those chapters were concluded, much less published.

I was only away from Florence four days in all, but on my return I found that many things had happened.

The first person to greet me as I stepped out of the P.W.B. courier from Leghorn was Stella. In a glance I knew that Stella had changed since those Roman days when a 'lost puppy' of a girl had sought sanctuary in Number Seventy-Six.

Even then she had possessed all the dainty gestures of a pretty woman and they had seemed incongruous in the shabby untidy child. Now she appeared taller and thinner and better groomed, and when she put her face out to be kissed, first on one cheek and then on the other, it was as if she had grown into the unconscious coquetry she so often displayed. Her light brown hair and eyes were shining and her skin glowed.

She hugged me and said, with her melodious trill of a giggle: 'I told you I had a feeling about being in Florence soon – and here I am! I've brought you some letters from P.W.B. in Rome – your English and South African mail – oh, and an American letter too. It's in your room.'

'Come along up, and let's talk while I get clean,' I said.

We tramped up the five flights that Giovanna always took in her great bounding breathless leaps, and, as we opened my door, I saw a vase of flowers on my table by the window. It was so like Stella to put it there. She had so many of the charming

Italian graces. When I had thanked her, I said: 'But where's your stretcher?'

We both laughed as she admitted that she *had* been sleeping in my room. 'I told them downstairs that you wouldn't mind. And I arrived the very day you left. But now I've got another room all to myself – teeny-weeny, and beside the loo—'

'You won't mind that after our poltergeist in Seventy-Six!'

'Oh, Joy, I'm so happy,' she burst out, and did a little dance step in the American brogues of which she was so proud. 'So happy, so happy . . .' Stella could make more dove-noises than any human being I have ever met, and now she crooned her joyous refrain. 'Do you really like the flowers? I got them for you because I was so happy . . .'

'The flowers are heaven.' I buried my face in them. 'Now tell me about being so happy.'

'I'm going to be married.'

'Well . . . *Stella!* Who is he?'

'You've met him at the Botticelli, though you may not remember. He was always rather shy and never joined in with all the crazy stuff. His name is Johnny Hammerstein.'

I could not recall Johnny Hammerstein.

Stella said: 'He has fair curly hair and glasses, and he's thirty-four. I suppose that's a bit old for me, as I'm just eighteen, but if you love each other it shouldn't matter, should it?'

'Not a bit, if you are quite sure about loving each other.'

'Sure, sure – so sure!'

'Tell me about him.'

'He's an American army psychiatrist – and—' her face fell a little, 'he's a Jew.' She smiled again. 'But he says our babies can be Catholic.'

'He can't say fairer than that. Is he here in Florence?'

'He's stationed quite near. He'll be here tomorrow. He gets lots of days off. Oh, Joy, I do love him so much . . . and I'm so sorry for him! Don't you think it's very terrible to be Jewish and know what your people have suffered all these years? Johnnie suffers with every persecuted Jew – even though no one of his own has been in a concentration camp. You know those ghastly pictures in your Information Centres – those dreadful death-camps—'

'I should,' I said rather grimly. 'I put those dreadful pictures in our windows. I've had nightmares ever since. But people ought to see them.'

She covered her face with her hands. There were childish bead bracelets on her plump wrists.

'Praised be the Blessed Virgin my Johnnie is American—'

I said: 'And when you're married you'll be American too. You'll have an American husband, and an American passport—'

She forgot her anguish and rolled over on the bed hugging my pillow. 'And I'll have lots of American babies. A little baby of my own – just think of it!'

'When are you going to marry Johnny?'

'As soon as he has his permission from his Colonel. Will you be my matron of honour?'

'I'd love to be your matron of honour, sweetie. What are you doing about a trousseau?'

She abandoned the pillow, and sat up and gazed at me with rapturous eyes.

'There's an American girl in Rome who's been getting it for me from the P.X. So cheap, and wonderful value. Johnnie asked her to fix it up some way – and she has. Look, this is one of the slips.' She flicked up her skirt and showed me her plain little artificial silk slip – cheap and good value, certainly, but entirely devoid of the frivolity one associates with the word trousseau. 'Johnnie's not very well off,' added Stella. 'We'll have to live pretty quietly while he works up a practice. But I don't mind that. I think I must be the luckiest girl in the world – all my dreams are coming true.'

From an ancient overworked bag she drew a dark-looking sausage, smelling powerfully of garlic, a pen-knife and piece of stale bread.

'Have some,' she invited. 'It's good, nyum-nyum.'

I recalled that Number Seventy-Six had become a repository for odd bits of food during Stella's sojourn there. Curious edible horrors were always coming out of her bag like white mice and worms from the pockets of small boys.

'I couldn't,' I said, hiding a shudder. 'You munch while I read my letters.'

'Yes, do read your letters. I'll be quiet as a little mouse. But you don't know what you're missing with this sausage!'

Piet had written to me from Corpus Christi, the Fleet Air Arm training base.

I said: 'This is wonderful! Piet's best friend, Ronnie, is here – based somewhere near Florence in the South African Air Force. They were at the same school and they went into the war at the same time. Piet writes: "Here I am, still training, and that lucky little so-and-so, Ronnie, is in the thick of it already, in the same country as you and Dad." He's given me the address—'

'Is Ronnie a fighter pilot, too?' asked Stella, who knew all about Piet.

'No, an air-gunner.'

'Are you sorry Piet isn't here instead of Ronnie?'

I held the schoolboyish scrawl limply in my hand and looked across the red-tiled roofs to the towers and spires of yesterday.

'No. I'm glad the Fleet Air Arm's a long training. I'm glad Piet's in America. I don't want him here.'

There were letters from South Africa – Mother's 'little chats' giving me all the news of my home and friends – and some long letters from my Uncle Wilfred. I glanced at them and then began to read. Presently I folded them and put them away to enjoy at my leisure. They were not letters but literature. They were the pure gold of his sifted memories of 'Lang Piet'. There were skilfully written stories, sketches and full-length portraits of that tall old patriarch and his long and varied career, and each had been recorded by his son, Wilfred, against the wide South African background of the Transvaal, the Cape or the Thousand Hills of Natal.

> 'There may be other instalments,' wrote my uncle. 'When memory and the spirit move me, I'll write a few pages about Lang Piet and send them to you to use if and when and how you please . . .'

And finally there was a letter from Mrs. Millar, of Eyre and Spottiswoode, the publishers of 'Pack and Follow', which was having a stormy passage into print, owing to the paper shortage and flying-bombs that had knocked out a number of printing presses.

> 'Thank you for the photographs of Piet. I think we'll use the small boy one as being appropriate to his age in the book . . . I am now passing the proofs of your book, which I hope will go to press within the next week or two. Publication, I

hope, about August or September, according to whether the printer and binder do their best or their damnedest.

'Yes, Hitler's pennies from heaven did make a mess in the old town. Sometimes, when I look at its shabby streets, all with missing teeth, I wonder whether it will ever again be the town we once knew. But perhaps its heart is in its people. However, I hope we can put some paint on it before you see it again.'

I gave the letter to Stella. 'You see, we have our troubles as well as Italy.'

She looked through it. Then she said: 'You don't sing so loud about them.'

When we went down to dinner we found the Mess fairly empty. Many of the Army liaison personnel had gone. We joined Miss Hutton at her table.

She said: 'The Fifteenth Army Group is on the move. Army transport have been pouring through Florence during the last few days.'

After our meal I walked home with her through the ruined riverside blocks to her lodging on the other side of the Arno. I had a letter to post in the main army post office – a note to Ronnie, telling him where to find me and asking him to come and see me next time he was in Florence on leave.

'It's to a South African boy,' I said, as I slipped it into the letter-box. 'My son's great friend. I'm so thrilled to know he's here somewhere.'

'But the South Africans have gone from the town,' said Gladys Hutton. 'There are no more orange flashes to be seen. I'm sorry they have gone. They were such well-behaved boys – friendly and courteous. And they were the first troops over the river when the city was liberated. I wept for joy when I saw them . . .'

The night was still and fragrant. The Corsini Palace brooded, majestic and aloof, upon the Lungarno, and, from one of its open windows, we heard a Piano Concerto. Probably Anna. I could imagine Donna Rezia sitting listening to her daughter, her big tortoiseshell cat on her lap, her mischievous eyes grown sad, her hands folded – '*Pazienza* – one must have patience.'

'Let's cross by the Ponte Vecchio,' said Gladys. 'It's only a little out of our way, and its such a lovely night.'

On the only remaining historic bridge we paused to gaze at the river, mysterious in the starlight, going its way indifferent to ruin and change.

Then, suddenly, the horizon blazed in flash upon flash of pale blinding light, and in the distance we heard the long sombre booming of the guns.

Gladys put her thin hand on my arm, and we stood quiet and half afraid.

Mark Clark's great offensive had been launched. The last Battle of Italy had begun. Away to the north of us the Allied planes were going forth to pulverize their vital targets – British, American and South African bombers were flying across the Plain of Lombardy towards the enemy lines.

Was Ronnie there? – I wondered – the little fair-haired boy who had ridden soap-boxes on wheels with our own six-year-old Piet; who had broken his arm aquaplaning behind their home-made speed-boat and explored the ocean-bed at Kalk Bay in their Heath Robinson diving outfit. Was Ronnie there now – with that look in his eyes – that extraordinary bright look that had shone on their faces every time they talked, or even thought, of being 'in it at last'? Was he flying into the night with the thunder of the guns and the roar of the planes shaking the very stars in the luminous Italian sky?

Yes. In the spring of the year, in the spring of his manhood, Ronnie was there.

But I only knew it when they sent my letter back to me.

CHAPTER FORTY-FOUR

END OF A LEGEND

On 12th April, in the hour before the dawn of victory, President Roosevelt died, and a great statesman, fighter and humanitarian was lost to the world. On 21st April the Allies liberated Bologna and swept on towards the River Po.

Outside our Information Centres the crowds surged and swayed. Everywhere news was 'breaking' and our news in picture panels had hard work keeping abreast of the tide of events sweeping down on us from inside Europe.

George reported from Bologna that the mobile exhibition was mobbed daily by the news-starved population and that he had opened up three Information Centres, which we must hasten to service from Florence.

In a few days he was back, standing by for the liberation of Milan, which would be the signal for the section to go forward as a whole. A British Army Sergeant, who had been a publicity man in private life, was handling Bologna, and American Marjorie Fergusson, as academic and delightful as ever, had been sent from Rome in readiness to take over the Florence branch from Ken Carrick.

The first suggestion that the moment was at hand came to us when Emmanuela's dark young Partisan came into our office greatly elated to tell us that Milano was in the hands of '*i Partigiani*'.

Emmanuela had undergone a remarkable change in the past few weeks. Perhaps it was the spring that made the sap rise again in dead young veins, or maybe it was the mounting excitement of the Allied advance and the imminent freeing of her city, or, more likely, a combination of the two. At all events, she now had a faint colour in her cheeks, there was life and gloss in the ash-gold of her hair, and her eyes no longer seemed blind to her surroundings. Often she laughed, and when Emmanuela laughed, her laughter rippled over her whole supple body.

'*Senta! Senta Roberto!*' she cried to the young artist, to all of us. 'Milan is held by the Partisans!'

Roberto, whose long neck was swathed in a coarse grey woollen scarf, because he had a sore throat, forgot his discomfort and cheered.

The Boss came in and spoke a few words to the Partisan.

'It's not official,' he said to us. 'We can't put it out as news.' He went back to his room, neat, brisk, sure of what not to do. To do or not to do, in his work he was always confident of his ground, no matter how violent the earth tremors.

Next evening the dark young man came again. He was quivering with excitement and his words stormed across the pictures and notes on Emmanuela's desk in a torrent that brought her to her feet, white-faced, with eyes blazing in a terrible pent-up triumph.

'Mussolini is dead!' she cried. 'The Partisans have killed him and hung him up by his heels! They have killed Farinacci and many other Fascist leaders – and they have killed la Petacci – Mussolini's mistress! She hangs beside him. It is the end – the end of Fascism!'

I got a line and rang through to Caserta to ask Bertie if he had received the news. It had not yet come through. But a few hours later it was confirmed by Fifteenth Army Group Headquarters, who announced that the Allies had entered Milan and Venice.

Next day, May Day, Hitler, the arch-antagonist of Bolshevism, took his own life in the Reich Chancellory, while the Battle for Berlin raged on every side.

Doenitz, Commander-in-Chief of the German Navy, and Hitler's successor in the hour of Nemesis, announced that: 'The Fuehrer has fallen at his command post. My first task is to save the German people from destruction by Bolshevism. If only for this task the struggle will continue.' A strangely sweet May Day message to be intercepted by the Russians already closing in on the Berlin bunker wherein lay the charred remains of the Dictator and Eva Braun, and Goebbels, the clubfoot, with his beautiful wife and their children.

That night, outside the window of our main Information Centre, just opposite the P.W.B. hotel, the crowds gathered with torches to play them on the photographs of Mussolini, la Petacci and many Fascists lying in the Piazza Loreto in Milan, where the people came to spit on them and stone them.

They were a grim record of a grizzly event. Yet the children of the gay and gentle Florentines were held on high that they might see and remember the end of il Duce who had led their country into the abyss.

As I passed to go back to the Mess I saw Giovanna standing leaning against her bicycle on the fringe of the crowd. There was a puzzled frown between her wide-set eyes as she stared up at the pictures. She was a student, and history was her subject. Here was a dramatic human facet of history, the personal touch in the welter of disaster. Here was the end of one who had shaped the course of history. Presently she shrugged her shoulders, mounted her machine and pedalled away towards the Duomo. I wondered what she was thinking, what it all meant to her. What, after all, was the end of Fascism? Was it not the beginning of something else? For is not every ending a beginning? In the window of our Information Centre was the past. In the eyes of Giovanna, and millions like her, was the future – not theirs alone, but that of their lovely land.

And, while it was my job to catch events on the wing and pin their tortured image on our great news panels, strange things were happening in the woods on the hill above Caserta, where dwelt the little souvenir dachshund, Fritzel, and all those lean distinguished young Generals I had met that night less than a month ago.

A special hut had been constructed among the trees, and the Army, Air and Naval Chiefs-of-Staff at A.F.H.Q. had been secretly warned to stand by for an emergency meeting of the utmost importance.

On the afternoon of 28th April the negotiations of Generals Lemnitzer and Airey bore fruit, and an Allied plane landed on a flying field near the Swiss border. The weather conditions were stormy and dangerous for flying, but so urgent was this mission that the pilot took a chance, and his judgment was rewarded when he landed near Caserta with the mysterious passengers who had joined him on the border.

These were met on the airfield by Lemnitzer and Airey and taken to the hut in the woods.

Shortly afterwards, at six o'clock, those few who were to be present at this preliminary meeting with the strangers arrived at the hut. My husband, representing the Naval Commander-in-Chief, was there, and it was from him that I subsequently received an impression of those final surrender negotiations between the two German envoys and the Allied officers.

The Germans were Lieutenant-Colonel Victor Von Schweinitz, representing Von Vietinghoff-Scheel, the Commander-in-Chief of the German Forces in Italy; and Major Eugen Wenner for Waffen S.S. General Wolff. Both wore civilian clothes.

On the Allied side, the Supreme Commander, Field-Marshal Alexander, was represented by General Morgan, a wiry determined officer, who was also a man of the world and a sound judge of character.

It was interesting that General Morgan, General Airey and my husband all happened to be German interpreters, and could understand the occasional low-voiced and often acid exchanges between the two envoys.

'But, of course, we gave no sign,' said Bertie. 'Everything

was done through an interpreter – the German Baron who had been responsible for getting Lem and Airey into touch with Wolff in the first place. He was a nice fellow, an anti-Nazi who had escaped to America and taken American citizenship when Hitler came to power. The two emissaries were typical of what they represented.'

What they represented was very different. For there was that curious situation in Germany of two separate armies – the traditional Army under the control of the General Staff, and Hitler's own personal S.S. troops – and both were infiltrated by the spies of the Gestapo. Hitler's men were the time-servers and gangsters, and, like all gangsters, were the first to quit when the end was in sight.

'Vietinghoff's Colonel was tall and very correct, a German officer of the old school. The S.S. Major was a dark, hard-faced little thug, who would have done well as Al Capone's First Lieutenant. There didn't seem much love lost between them, because, when the S.S. man tried to take the lead, the Colonel shut him up with a sharp "*Halt dein Maul!*" '

It soon became evident at that first meeting that the Colonel had not come to Caserta prepared to accept unconditional surrender. But when he began to raise objections to the terms, General Morgan brought him firmly to heel.

'We are not here to argue,' he said. 'We are here to read the terms of surrender and assure ourselves that you understand them fully. Anything that is not clear to you will be explained. If you are not prepared to accept the terms *as they are* negotiations will cease immediately.'

Next day, at two o'clock on 29th April, the 'Instrument of Local Surrender' was signed in General Morgan's office at the Royal Palace of Caserto. It was to take effect at noon on 2nd May.

The fiercest battles of the war had been fought in Italy, and the Surrender of those defeated forces was the beginning of the ultimate disintegration of the proudest armies in history – the armies that had swarmed across Europe with the legend of Invincibility bright and terrible about their names.

Five days later, on 7th May, the final submission was made at Rheims.

It was Victory in Europe. Peace there will never be.

The Americans have a remarkable concertina system. They

expand and contract their organizations in a flash. And no sooner had the personnel of P.W.B. finished rejoicing at the news of Victory over Germany than they were flung into consternation at the speed with which they found themselves being shipped off home.

That was why I discovered Stella weeping in her slit of a room. Her round childish face was swollen and streaked with tears. The end of the world had come.

'Sweetie,' I said. 'Whatever is it?'

'Our permission to marry hasn't come through yet ... and ... any m-moment n-now ... Johnnie'll be sent back to America ... *without me!*'

On the little wooden chair beside the dressing table lay the big Leghorn straw hat she had been trimming with blue ribbon to wear on her wedding day. In her suit-case were neatly folded the plain little slips and pyjamas and pants from the P.X. with sweet-smelling cachets between the artificial silk folds, and the three pairs of nylons that were the joy of her heart.

'Oh, I'm s-so m-miserable!'

I sat down beside her and stroked her tumbled hair as she plunged her face back into the sodden pillow.

'Johnnie'll get the permission in time – you'll see.'

'I've no money,' she wailed. 'How could I ever g-get to America except as Mrs. H-Hammerstein?'

It was certainly a problem.

Outside the evening was mild and beautiful, and the birds were loud in their twittering. A horrible thought crossed my mind. Was Johnnie really trying all he knew for that permission? Or was Stella – like many others I knew – to be hastily discarded? Was she perhaps just 'one of those things' – an Italian interlude?

Then I heard quick steps leaping upstairs and hurrying along the corridor, and the door burst open. One look at Johnny Hammerstein's face reassured me, and I was ashamed of the moment of suspicion that had just passed.

'Honey-child – my little Stella – I've got it right here! And the Army Chaplain will marry us tomorrow!'

I don't think Johnnie saw me standing by the window, and I doubt if he'd have cared. He saw only the crumpled figure on the bed.

I heard a little moan from the pillow, and then she raised her tousled head as he sat beside her and took her in his arms, rocking her like a baby. She was sobbing and laughing, and her blotched tear-smudged face was radiant.

'I'm so happy . . . Johnnie . . . Joy . . . I'm so h-happy!'

Next afternoon they were married by a Roman Catholic Army parson, and they had their small unpretentious reception at an Army Welfare Club. Stella wore her big Leghorn hat with the blue ribbons and a blue linen summer dress. She carried a bouquet of rose-buds, and happiness transfigured her as she stood beside the kind spectacled Jewish psychiatrist who would take her to America and allow her to bring up her babies in the Roman Catholic faith.

On the following day the advance guard of our section set off for Milan – George Bowman, an American Sergeant, and Emmanuela.

As she took my hands and said 'Till we meet again!' I saw in Emmanuela's eyes a joy so intense that I caught my breath. She was going home.

But what would be her home-coming?

CHAPTER FORTY-FIVE

BEGINNING OF A JOURNEY

KEN CARRICK came into my office, which seemed quite large and very quiet now that George and Emmanuela had left. It was nearly six o'clock and Hedy had gone home.

Ken straddled a chair and rocked it and screwed up his eyes.

He said: 'We're going to Milan at the end of the week – Roberto, too – then I'm going through to Trieste. I'd like you to come on, but women aren't allowed. The situation in Venezia Guilia is still very confused.'

I said: 'I'm sorry. I'd like to go to Trieste.'

'Well, I suggest you hang on in Milan till things straighten themselves out a bit. P.W.B. will be operating there for a short time still, and when I'm in Trieste I'll have a better idea of the chances of getting you there.'

'There's another thing,' I said. 'I've volunteered for the Far

East. But in my application I stipulated that I wasn't available till you could spare me.'

He nodded, and went back to his room, where I could hear Marjorie Fergusson's clear deliberate Italian as she discussed some point of intellectual propaganda with one of the locally employed staff.

Anyone wishing to go on to the Far East with P.W.B. had been invited to apply. I had done so because it seemed to me that soon my husband and son would be engaged in the cruel fight against 'the yellow dwarfs of the Eastern Sea', and I, too, wanted to be where things were happening. The pendulum was swinging towards Japan.

I heard Marj Poole's high heels tapping across the stone floor.

'Are you busy?' she asked.

'Just finishing,' I said. 'Sit down.'

She perched on the edge of my desk and her wide amber eyes rested thoughtfully on the notes I was putting away. Her work with the Partisans was done, and I guessed that she was wondering how soon she would lose her volatile George.

She said: 'I've just heard I'm to go to Genoa tomorrow. But it won't be for long. After that . . .' She gave a little interrogative shrug of her shoulders.

I said: 'If you want to go with P.W.B.' – and George, I thought – 'there's only one safe bet. It's Trieste. But they don't want women there yet. But you know how these things are – when the situation seems more stable they'll probably lift the embargo. Ken is going on to Trieste, and he'll need most of us there. Why don't you have a word with him?'

She slid off my desk. 'Is he in the office?'

'I think so.'

Just as I was about to leave I saw Roberto standing in the doorway. His face was flushed and blotchy and he held his hand to the muffler round his neck.

'I don't want to go to Milan,' he said in Italian. 'I want to go home.'

'You look ill,' I said.

He croaked a reply. '*La gola.*'

'Let's look.' I pulled him over to the window and made him sit down while I peered into his throat.

'Wait there,' I said, and went into Ken's room.

'Roberto is very ill. We must get a doctor,' I said.

It was always difficult to get medical attention for locally employed staff, but Ken Carrick had a keen sense of responsibility towards everybody in his section. A doctor was found for Roberto.

When the physician had given his verdict we knew that Roberto would have his wish, and that we would go to Milan without him. So here, too, there was the touch of the 'monkey's paw'!

Roberto was taken to an isolation hospital, where he was very ill with diphtheria for many weeks. They submitted the unfortunate young man to many indignities, and, worst of all, shaved his mane of thick artistic black hair, leaving him with a head like an ostrich egg. And when, at long last, poor Samson returned to Rome with a stubble of coarse dark hair instead of the lock that had fallen so romantically across his brow, Delilah mocked him and cried out that he was like '*i Tedesci*' now! So the tears of reunion were more bitter than those of parting.

Ken and I left for Milan in the weapons' carrier soon after sunrise.

The air was golden and fresh, as yet untouched by the languor of the day. Just as we were about to leave I saw Giovanna's bicycle swoop into the empty early morning curve of our street. She had a mass of roses in the basket on the handlebars. The dew was on them and they were as pink as her cheeks. Her flaxen plaits swung forward over her shoulders as she jumped down and parked her machine against the kerb. Then she picked up the flowers and pressed them into my arms. She tried to say something in English – a few words of farewell and good wishes, but she was quickly tongue-tied and, with a characteristic toss of her head and a look of blushing chagrin, she broke into Italian.

There was always such a tumult of the unexpressed and inexpressible in Giovanna – such a hunger for history, such a thirst of philosophy, such a yearning after music and the plaintive song of poetry, and, in the presence of Art, such a silent awe. I understood this Florentine Giovanna, for I, too, had been a student with all the glory of the day before me, and a wealth of intangible rapture and unaccountable melancholy within me. But I had not grown to maturity in the heart of the whirlwind. Giovanna and her generation needed the spirit of the phoenix. In her it was strong-winged and bright.

Scarcely waiting for me to thank her for the roses, she plunged on to her bicycle again and was gone.

It was only as Ken drove the weapons' carrier through the gates in the city wall that I found her little scribbled pencil note among the flowers.

'Oh, my dear Miss Packer, I must pass many, many examinations. I will burst! And I can not more see you. Truly; I was always in a hurry, but I was very glad to see your fair curls and your eyes full of intelligence.

'Oh Miss, I have – no, *am* – twenty years old today!

'I remember you, when you are looking for a word and you are lifting your little head rebel and volitive. Now you go far and I will never see you. But I will remember you so – looking for a word.

'I can say you not more.

'Many, many *wisches* (?)

'Your GIOVANNA.'

So I left the city of the past – Florence of Dante and the great Medicis, of the Palazzo Corsini and the ghosts of lovely ruined bridges, of Donna Rezia and Gladys Hutton – and in my arms I held the roses of the future, of Giovanna who was twenty years old when 'peace' came to Italy.

On a mountain pass the weapons' carrier broke down, and a very black American Negro in the Engineering Corps helped to put it right. He told us that he had learned to be a mechanic in the Army, but it didn't suit him, he would rather play the saxophone in a jazz band.

'But you're obviously a very skilled mechanic,' I said, to comfort him.

'Lady,' he said, 'you're telling *me*! It isn't the work I mind. It's getting my hands black.'

The first person we saw at the P.W.B. hotel in Milan was *il Sergenti* of the Botticelli.

Cookie's lizard eyes flickered upwards.

'Say,' he said to me wearily. 'You aren't by any chance going to ask me for a room to yourself?'

'Not if Colonels are doubling up.'

He grinned and gave me my allocation.

It was a room along a little alleyway perched up on the flat roof of the hotel. It was an inferno that hot summer. But it *was* a room to myself and it was a room with a view.

In the evenings some of us used to sit on the roof outside it and look straight across the ruins that surrounded the Cathedral Square to the Golden Madonna and the Twelve Apostles on the gothic spires of the Duomo. Thousands of doves and martins dwelt among the saints in the eaves and niches, and towards sunset the rose-pearl sky was darkened by the pattern of their flight, and the still air was fanned with the beat of wings and filled with high twittering.

We used to watch those little whirling birds as we waited for the miracle when the last rays of the setting sun fell full upon the Golden Madonna, so that she stepped forward in a blaze of glory before submitting to the shadows of approaching night.

George Bowman was in charge of our diminished section now that Ken Carrick was in Trieste, but, outside the job, which he took in his stride, he was a lost and restless young man. With Marj Poole in Genoa, George had no one to trip into his office suggesting tea, no one to take to the opera, no one to knock on his door of a morning and wake that deep sleeper in time for him to get to the Mess for breakfast before it closed down. He had nobody to sew buttons on his uniforms or mend his socks and generally look after him with playful maternal solicitude. George felt lonely and neglected as he sat on the roof in the evening and gazed at the Golden Madonna and her host of swooping birds. When he took off his glasses to wipe them, I observed that the red mark across the bridge of his nose was no longer raw and angry, for Marj had made him change the heavy steel frame for a light one in imitation tortoiseshell. His eyes, for the moment naked and unmagnified, looked baffled, and he sighed gustily as he said:

'It's always rather gloomy – winding up an operation.'

'P.W.B., you mean?'

He cast me a sharp glance, and grinned. 'P.W.B., of course.'

'I know,' I said. 'People lose interest.'

George said: 'It'll be a good thing when we move on to Trieste. Ken's determined to have you and Marj in his section.'

'When – and if – they allow women.'

'When Ken makes up his mind he usually gets what he wants.'

Our work in Milan was soon to be taken over by civilian organizations, and it was established that Emmanuela would continue to be employed by one of them.

Emmanuela no longer walked like one pressed upon by heavy invisible currents; she no longer raised lifeless eyes from her work. She was a woman of flesh and blood, daily more confident of herself and more careful in her appearance. She took the bombed areas in her city for granted, for she had many standards of comparison, and she was satisfied that Milano had been luckier than it knew. She had found friends from 'that other life' eager to welcome her, and nowadays there was always someone waiting to take her out after working hours.

There were lovely places to go for anyone who could borrow a jeep. Here, in the north, the German retreat had been so rapid that there had been no time for the detailed destruction of every route that had been such a heartbreaking feature in the south. And, quite often, we went out to Como or Maggiore or Garda and ate a late supper at some little inn, sitting out of doors on the lake-shore under pergolas of grapes or honeysuckle. A breeze came up from the water and cooled the hot summer air, and the moon was pale and serene over the Alps. We used to see the South African occupation troops, burned brown by the sun, strolling along the waterfront under the forested hills with the dark-eyed Italian girls so many of them married and took back to their own South Africa.

In general we found the Milanese rough and uncouth after the cultivated Florentines. They stole our photographs out of the showcases on street corners or from the windows of our Centres, and they pinched the publications from P.W.B. libraries without a moment's compunction. Emmanuela said she was ashamed of them – and laughed. Then her face assumed the air of intent gravity it so often wore when she talked of her country and its problems.

'Honestly,' she said. 'Don't you agree that it's a good sign that they want our stuff? It shows they are interested. The Milanese are always interested in ideas and movements.'

I said: 'When it comes to the unauthorized movements of part of our displays – for which I happen to be responsible – then I am interested, too.'

She laughed silently, and the ripple of her amusement trembled over her body. Presently she said:

'My city is still very much alive. Don't you notice that? The people move at a different pace here. When there is a *risorgimento* in Italy it will come from Milan.'

'It has suffered much less than the south.'

She shrugged. 'I'll tell you a thing. These people are tougher than they are in the south. They also love the arts and music. To have sung or conducted at the Scala in Milano used to be the world's first hall-mark for opera – but the Milanese are practical too. This is an industrial centre. It is the heart of our commerce. Everything begins and ends here – Fascism – Communism . . .'

Death to Fascism and to all Fascists! was the watchword in Milan. 'Epuration' was the official term for the purge which was taking place in Italy, not only through the courts trying war criminals, but at the shadowy hands of those brought up in the tradition of Vendetta.

Every night, soon after twelve o'clock, I woke in the heat of my little room to the sound of shots, and knew that once again the Partisans had taken the law into their own hands and that next day we would read of the bodies of notorious Fascists found dead in the ruins round the Duomo.

One evening George came to me on the roof. The golden miracle had blazed and faded and dusk was falling. He had a letter in his hand and he was beaming from ear to ear.

'Ken Carrick has permission for you and Marj to go to Trieste. And Hedy is to go there direct from Florence. I'm to make arrangements to get Marj over from Genoa, and we leave as soon as possible.'

'I'm delighted to hear it.'

'So am I,' said George. 'I've been wanting to go to Trieste. Listen, I've got bags and bags of gin – let's have a drink on it!'

A few days later we crossed the verdant thigh of Italy in a three-tonner, and spent the night in Venice, where I discovered Suzanne, who was waiting to get to Trieste in the News Division. Since she had lost her *protegée*, Stella, she had acquired a little Corgi, and, in much the same way that she had smuggled Stella into Number Seventy-Six at the Botticelli, she now smuggled Brownie into Messes and billets where dogs were frowned upon. She had cut off her long dark hair. 'It's cooler off than on,' she said. But the metamorphosis had in no way lessened the exoticism of her presence.

'I must hear all about Stella's wedding,' she said. 'There's a little man I'm supposed to be meeting, but I'll give him the slip and we'll dine together and swop news.'

'Brushes them off,' Figaro had said. So another of Sue's 'little men' fumed somewhere in Venice that summer night while we dined on a terrace overlooking the Grand Canal, where army ducks roared to and fro past the pink Palace of the Doges and the soaring Campanile.

Presently we saw a gondola go by with a young couple reclining in the stern – a fair lieutenant with spectacles and a girl with soft dark hair and a naughty-nineties figure.

'George and Marj,' said Sue. 'And the boatman's serenading them!'

The gondola slid out of the traffic of the Grand Canal and into the quiet network of waterways where little arched stone bridges link narrow streets, curved like scimitars, and where tall creeper-covered houses and palaces with carved doors and Juliet balconies dream of carnivals gone by.

In a gondola, on a summer night, time is but the dwindling silver lantern of the rising moon and movement is a phantom of itself. Sound is the swish of starlit water, the song of the gondolier and the murmur of a lover's voice. It was very late when Marj slipped into the room we shared and undressed quietly in the dark. Before she crept into bed I saw her standing by the window silhouetted against the setting moon. There was silence save for the slap-slap of water against the mildewed wall of our hotel, and her little sigh as she turned and adjusted her mosquito net.

CHAPTER FORTY-SIX

FLASH POINT

As we followed the winding cliff road to Trieste* I realized that all the historic charm of Florence on the Arno would never

* *Trieste and northern environs assigned to Italy in 1954 by treaty and southern sector to Yugoslavia.*

long compensate me for the sight and smell and sound of the sea.

Indian regiments were encamped in the wooded coves, for General Freyberg's New Zealanders had recently left and their place had been taken by Thirteenth Army Group under General John Harding. The General and his staff lived in a castle built into the rocks above the Adriatic. Yachts leaned upon the bright ruffled surface of the water and sunburnt soldiers aquaplaned behind those speed-boats the New Zealanders had refrained from taking away as souvenirs.

In the harbour of Trieste lay two British cruisers and a minesweeper. A familiar thrill went through me at sight of the ships, so stern and menacing yet reassuring, policing the seas and protecting the coast. George, too, was excited.

'Might be my young brother's minesweeper,' he said. His younger brother, Kenneth, who had set aside his medical studies for the duration to serve in the Navy, was in command of a minesweeper somewhere in the Adriatic. George was very devoted to his 'young brother', and was elated at the prospect of possibly seeing him. In fact, George was in a mood of high elation in any case, with his eyes gleaming behind his spectacles and his good-tempered mouth breaking into its incorrigible smile.

'Trieste is going to be bags and bags of fun,' he said.

The heat was intense, but fresh, after the closed-in city of Milan. We found that P.W.B. – which had now changed its name to Allied Information Services and was known as A.I.S. – shared a requisitioned hotel with the Allied Military Government until other accommodation could be obtained. Our offices were in a large open square, almost opposite the hotel.

When Ken Carrick took us into our section and introduced us to the locally employed staff my heart sank, for I realized that this job was going to tax my ingenuity to the uttermost, and, for the first few sickening days, I was afraid that it was quite beyond me. I had to keep reminding myself of what my husband had said: 'It's the beginning of a new job that's difficult. See that through and you'll do the rest on your head.'

The beginning in Trieste was formidable.

Many interests converged upon the Venezia Giulia Peninsula and the port of Trieste, whose commercial position at the head of the Adriatic had served the old Austrian Empire, and later the Italian Kingdom, and might equally well be claimed by the Yugoslav State which had come into being after the 1914–18 war. It was the port for the whole of Central Europe. Many languages and dialects were spoken in the area – Italian, Slovene, Croatian and the Triestini dialect. The people of the port regarded themselves as 'Triestini' – not Italian or Austrian and certainly not Yugoslav – and they wanted to see Trieste a free port. 'Trieste for the Triestini!' was their slogan.

In the Allied race for Trieste the Yugoslav forces of Marshal Tito had won by a short head and established themselves in the town before the New Zealanders linked up with them. To persuade them to withdraw behind the Morgan Line, which had been set by that same brusque General 'Monkey' Morgan who had taken the Surrender at Caserta, had been a delicate operation successfully accomplished. A complication was added by the fact that the British Naval Commander-in-Chief had insisted upon retaining the control of one small enclave in the Yugoslav sphere, and this was the Port of Pola at the tail of the Venezia Giulia Peninsula.

So, in one way and another, Trieste was a 'flash point', and we were all expressly warned that in our work, our behaviour and our conversation, we were to remain strictly impartial to the various conflicting elements.

The business of our section in A.I.S. was fundamentally the same as it had been in Florence. We must put out a news service in pictures, project democracy, and, in every way in our power, help to back up A.M.G. and Allied Welfare Services in their task of rehabilitation, and, above all, we must promote goodwill. We had outposts in Udine, Goritzia and Pola, and these we serviced with the material and displays it was my job to plan and see prepared. My supreme problems were languages, and the fact that one man's meat was often another man's poison when it came to propaganda in the different parts of Venezia Giulia. So our displays could not all be interchangeable. Output for Trieste had to be captioned in Italian and Slovene, for Udine in Italian only, for Goritzia in Croat and Slovene, and for Pola in Italian and Croat. Thus I was in charge of two Italian, two Slovene and two Croat interpreters who were seldom on speaking terms with each other.

As I knew from my experience of South Africa the development of a young language, or the revival of one gradually dying out, is an immensely sensitive subject, and we had to be meticulous in observing our bi- and tri-lingual obligations. A language is a symbol of independence, and the Croats and Slovenes, who had once been content to accept German or Italian as official languages, now insisted upon full equality for the Slav tongues indigenous to the area. But, as often happens in the early process of lingual development, there are bound to be spelling pitfalls. To take an example; the Afrikaans spelling of 'kopje' – a word well known in the Boer War and meaning a small hill – is now spelt phonetically, 'koppie'. And it was much the same with Slovene and Croat. Every caption on every picture had to be passed by a linguistic expert after the interpreter had done his or her work. But, nevertheless, indignant individuals used to storm into our offices to complain about some accent or letter, and the air would be loud with argument and abuse as the interpreter was attacked and fought back.

Every rise or fall in the temperature of the political situation was reflected in our office – in the faces and demeanour of the interpreters and artists. On the border there were constant 'incidents'. Our vans were shot up on the way to Pola through the Yugoslav Zone, our Centre in Goritzia was burned to the ground in a riot, and stories were squashed just as we were about to put them out after much labour because, for some subtle reason, it had become 'inadvisable' to use them. There were always rumours. Italians were disappearing in hundreds on the Carinthian border and no one knew what had happened to them; Yugoslavs were said to be infiltrating into Trieste. The Navy, who were sweeping mines at the risk of their lives so that the ports of the Adriatic might once more be opened to shipping and much needed UNRRA supplies, were shot at from the shore.

After one such incident it was necessary for my husband to fly to Trieste to clear up the matter.

I went with him overland to the port of Pola through the 'free corridor' in the Yugoslav Zone. We were in a naval car, flying the little white ensign and escorted by two motor-cycle outriders with the necessary permits. Suddenly two young Yugoslav Partisans sprang from behind a rocky outcrop and fired their guns 'across our bows'. Our car stopped, and the outriders, who were already well ahead, turned and roared back. The youths, who could not have been more than sixteen or seventeen, made a great show of examining our papers, and then signed to us to carry on. There was no official barrier where they had ambushed us. They were young and over-zealous, and they had grown up on the principal of shoot first and ask afterwards.

My husband said: 'On the border the guns are always loaded.'

Here, in Venezia Giulia, was the spirit of the border country – defensive and suspicious, with the perpetual threat of some hasty or foolish individual action setting the whole place ablaze.

And, while ignorant boy Partisans were shooting off their guns high, wide and handsome on the Pola Road, George Bowman was preparing a special exhibition to be shown at the opening of our Pola Centre. It was headed 'ALL MEN OF GOODWILL PULL TOGETHER'. When I returned, I told him somewhat acidly that I thought the attitude of today was not so much 'pull together' as 'pull the trigger'.

The harbours round the coast were choked with derelict ships, bombed or scuttled, but in Trieste, practically in the town itself, the two cruisers were very much alive.

The Triestini loved the warships. They felt safe when those guardians of the peace were anchored in their port. And the merry easy-going girls loved the sailors. The ships added glamour for all of us. And for me they were reminiscent of the happiest days of my life when I had arrived in strange far lands – China, Turkey or Greece – and seen those grey emblems of home safe under the emerald sugar-loaf of the Peak, or against the domes and minarets of Istanbul or the bare blue mountains of Athens.

There was a hot evening when the whole town gathered in the Main Square on the waterfront to see the ships' companies 'Beat the Retreat' to the martial music of the Marine Bands. When the White Ensign, flying from the balcony of A.M.G. Headquarters, was furled at sunset to the solemn and moving strains of the 'Last Post', I thought of the days from which this ceremony was a survival – the days when English soldiers patrolled the outposts of Empire, and at sunset retired into the confines of their fortress. So it must have been on the Eastern Frontier of my own South Africa, when the fierce sun sank below the horizon of the thornveld, and the bugler, far from home, sounded those lovely and melancholy notes on the distant border of Kaffir Land.

Suzanne had arrived in Trieste with her Corgi, Brownie, and the Navy fell in love, as one man, with the little feline girl who was always to be seen with her pencil, her grubby notebook and her dog. Sue was a reporter in the Allied Information News Service, and she felt that the Navy was 'good copy', and the Navy was only too anxious to be co-operative. The line was drawn, however, when she decided that she ought to go out minesweeping for a day and give the woman's angle on 'queer fish'.

Often she and I went sailing with officers from the cruisers, when everybody enjoyed themselves enormously except poor Brownie, who was always as sick as a dog. And on Sunday evenings we used to go on board to supper and the pictures, or perhaps to 'the Little Brown Jug' along the coast to swim and dine out of doors, or – if it was a Saturday night – to dance. Sometimes we were unfaithful to the Navy and two officers with a jeep at their command drove us down to the fishing village of Muggia, where we sat on the waterfront eating spaghetti and drinking the cheap harsh red wine of the district, while we watched the fisherfolk strolling on the terrace for their evening promenade when girls meet boys and the older folk exchange the gossip of the day.

The summer heat reached its zenith, relieved only by brief storms when the Bora lashed the Adriatic and sent the fishing boats skipping back into harbour. I had the measure of my work, and days and nights passed swiftly – too swiftly, for now Piet wrote that a few weeks more would see him fully trained and 'ready to have a smack at the Japs'.

Then, on 6th August, the world was shaken by an event more cataclysmic than any that had gone before.

The first atomic bomb in history had been dropped by the Allies on a Japanese city.

Hiroshima – the name that will never again be spoken without a shudder of fear and shame – dissolved in the heat that was of hell. Men, women and little children, old and young, innocent and guilty, were annihilated without trace, save for here and there the shadow of their presence in the moment of doom.

Three days later, the lurid Satanic toadstool billowed once again in the Japanese sky, and the people of the God-Emperor and the Rising Sun knew that, for them, it was either the end of the war or the end of their world.

On 15th August Victory in the East was announced.

In Trieste there were great celebrations and wild rejoicing among soldiers and sailors, who saw visions of at last returning 'in safety to enjoy the blessings of the land with the fruits of their labours'. A dance was given in our hotel. The girls wore their gayest dresses and officers of the Army and Navy gathered in force.

But I made an excuse to be absent and walked alone to the waterfront.

The night was breathless, the sea lay warm and quiet beneath the stars, a vagrant flutter of wind rose suddenly and scattered papery leaves from trees that so short a time ago had been young green. Peace or war, the seasons took their course of the joys and woes of human-kind. Too little of the great count of universal suffering was stilled by the bells that pealed for Peace, and, for many wives and mothers that night, they rang too late. But for me they came in time. And when, at midnight, their resonant music burst forth from every tower and steeple, echoing among the hills and drifting far out to sea, I gave thanks that at last the dark shadow of the Stranger had been lifted from the lives of those I loved.

CHAPTER FORTY-SEVEN

MALTA OF THE GEORGE CROSS

THE War was over, they said. But Trieste remained a sore spot beneath the mask of Peace. It was necessary to go on spreading the gospel of goodwill and Allied unity in Venezia Giulia; cruisers must remain stationed in the port, and mine-sweepers must continue to sweep the waters of the Adriatic.

So A.I.S. settled down and resumed its work, and one bright day Lieutenant Kenneth Bowman brought his minesweeper into the harbour of Trieste. It was a great day. It was George and Marj's wedding day. And the face of George – who had hitherto regarded matrimony as the shadow of the noose – was as bright and shining as his highly-polished Sam Browne.

Towards evening, as the first breath of a Borina shook the golden vine leaves over our heads at the 'Little Brown Jug', and filled the sails of yachts in the bay, we waved George and Marj good-bye and they drove away in the weapons' carrier for a honeymoon in Venice.

A few days later, in the office, heavenly Hedy slipped the cover over her Olivetti typewriter for the last time, and said, with her seraphic smile:

'I have my trousseau to make ready.'

So beauty walked forth at the side of a tall dark Guards Officer who had haunted our office of late and would haunt it no more.

Kenneth Carrick was promoted to Major, and we heard that George was now a Captain. Suzanne was given leave to spend a fortnight in Paris with her relatives, and, in her absence she consigned Brownie to the tender care of the Navy. But since Suzanne was the Cat Who Walked By Herself, and all places were alike to her, I presently received a letter from her post-marked London.

> 'I landed absent-mindedly in London instead of Paris. But I wasn't sorry, for it turned out that my father was getting back from Singapore that day. So I went to meet him at Waterloo, where I had to be introduced to him by another prisoner, as I couldn't recognize him. After which I stayed in London for ten days . . .'

One morning Bertie telephoned me from Caserta.

'Joy-Joy, great news! I'm to take the C.-in-C.'s staff back to Malta next month, and the Governor has given permission for me to have my wife in the Island. We'll have an official house and stewards and various obligations . . . You must resign from A.I.S. . . .'

When I went to see Ken Carrick about it he looked up from his desk, screwed up his eyes and said:

'When will you be going?'

'In about six weeks' time.'

'You must be very thrilled about Malta,' he said. 'I'm glad for your sake and the Admiral's.'

Before I left he presented me, on behalf of the Section, with a souvenir more precious than silver or gold. It was a small album, with a vellum cover, designed and painted by our artists. In it were snapshots of all those with whom I had worked –

British, American, Italian, Croat, Slovene and Triestini – and each picture bore a signature and a friendly message. The inscription on the fly-leaf in English, Italian and Slovene, made me extremely happy. Here it is:

'Gospej Joy Packer
osobje oddelka 'Displays and Publications Sections' urada A.I.S. v Trstu v spomin lepih dni skupnega dela ter ji tem potom isrăza svoje obcudovanje za njeno neizčrpno energijo in domišljijo.
Trst *1945'*

And what it means – as my mother-in-law said to the oculist – I shan't tell you!

Under Ken's photograph he had written, 'I said photographs would haunt you'. And indeed, when I went into his office for the last time, and gave him my lists of displays, planned as far ahead as the tide of news permitted, I did feel rather like Alice in Wonderland when the whole pack of cards which had taken on so fantastic, and, even at times, so alarming a character:

'... rose up into the air, and came flying down upon her;
' "wake up, Alice dear!" said her sister. "Why, what a long sleep you've had!"'
' "Oh, I've had such a curious dream!" said Alice, and she told her sister, as well as she could remember them, all these strange Adventures of hers that you have just been reading about ...'

We flew to Malta* in a luxuriously converted Dakota lent my husband by American Admiral Glassford, who was in charge of the United States Naval Forces in the Mediterranean – a generous and friendly gesture which seemed to me to embody the ideal spirit of Allied Unity and Goodwill!

The Island of the George Cross welcomed the return of the Commander-in-Chief's staff with eager enthusiasm. It was a symbol of peace and prosperity to come, for the fortunes of Malta are inextricably interwoven with the presence of the Royal Navy. Malta is our Mediterranean Fortress. She belongs to the Services, and the Services belong to her, which is why the

* *Malta now has Dominion status.*

Maltese cherish the tradition of a Military Governor. Only a soldier can understand a Fortress.

We lived in a tall white house overlooking St. Julian's Bay – a villa built on a hillside, with great bare rooms and little balconies above a rocky garden, a villa just like the one we had lived in nearly twenty years ago when Piet was a very young baby lying in his basket on the flat roof in the bright winter sunshine.

Opposite was the Convent School, and a bright-eyed little Maltese girl called Joyce used to run in to see me sometimes after lessons with a message from her mother or her aunt. Her mother and aunt were the same Angela and Carrie who had looked after us in those long ago days of our son's babyhood, and now they did my mending or embroidered underwear for me with their skilful convent-trained fingers.

My husband's stewards and cook were the Maltese who had staffed the Villa Masoni in Italy and they were all very well content to be home again, and soon all their wives were expecting the inevitable increase in the family.

Chief Petty Officer Corney drove my husband's official car and took unofficial charge of our garden.

The Island was wonderfully clean and bright after the chaos of Italy and bore its terrible scars with the pride of a veteran whose empty sleeve tells a tale of courage. The shops were restocked in the towns, and in the country the herds of goats were building up again. There was new paint on the dghaisas and on the flat Maltese carts drawn by the sleek brisk trotting horses, and in the gold of mid-day the women sat in their doorways and laughed and talked and scolded at their swarms of children without rancour, for the Maltese are loving and indulgent parents.

Gone was the black faldetta of the traditional islander, for, in the bad days, the Maltese women had cut up the voluminous canopies they had been wont to wear in the street and had made them into black-out curtains. Gone were the wretched lean horses harnessed to the spindly carrozins. They had been killed and eaten during the siege in company with the goats, and now, with a shortage of cars and petrol, the horse had come back into his own. He was given a substantial ration of fodder at a controlled price, and his owner recognized him to be an engine worth tender care.

The fatal spiral of modern times afflicted Malta – high cost of living and soaring wages – but even in spite of these things, the Island of the George Cross was in the process of regeneration.

We met many old friends and acquaintances again, and soon it was borne in upon me that, for all of us, there is never any war save our own. Malta had suffered and starved. Her cities and churches and palaces lay in ruins and she had lost much of her noble heritage of the Knights of the Order of St. John of Jerusalem; but she had gained her Geroge Cross and a new pride.

As Londoners will always focus the war upon the Blitz, so Malta will remember it as 'the Siege'.

One day, towards the close of the year, Bertie telephoned me from his office above the sea in the fortifications of Lascaris.

'I'm bringing a friend home to lunch. He arrived half an hour ago in a destroyer from England. Expect us about one o'clock.'

'Darling, who is it? . . . Hullo – hullo . . .'

The friend who came home with my husband was a tall bronzed young man in sailor's uniform with the badges of a Petty Officer and the wings of the Fleet Air Arm on his sleeve.

'Piet!'

'I wanted to surprise you, Mom—'

He stayed with us for a fortnight – a new Piet, with an American accent, a great admiration for the United States, and a young restless uncertainty about the future. He was sore because the expiration of Lease-Lend had cut short his training as a pilot within a few weeks of passing out. 'And we were so mad keen,' he said. He had even bought and cherished the little gilt pilot's wings in anticipation of the great day that never came.

'You have them,' he said. 'I have no right to them. You can wear them as a brooch.'

I took the badge and put it away in my jewel-case.

'When you're demobbed,' I said, 'what do you want to do?'

'I don't know.' He looked at his hands – strong-boned and sensitive. 'I suppose I'll study to be an engineer. It's always fascinated me – knowing how things work.'

Piet sailed for England in a warship, and very soon afterwards was repatriated with a draft of other young South Africans.

They arrived in Cape Town on Christmas Eve. So my

mother had her young grandson back home in the house under the mountain in time for Cookie's Christmas turkey.

A few weeks later we received a cable. 'Request permission study medicine. Piet.'

'What do you think?' I asked Bertie.

He did not answer immediately. I said: 'Maybe it's in the blood. Your father was a doctor and so was mine, and both my brothers are surgeons. He has the hands for surgery . . .'

Piet's father stood on the little stone balcony and stared down at the sparkling blue waters of St. Julian's Bay. Out at sea a warship went about her lawful occasions.

'He has great humanity,' he said. 'He'll make a good doctor.'

On New Year's Eve we went to the Warrens, who lived in a narrow house built into the massive walls of the mediaeval city of Imdina.

'The Warrens' – Ella and Kay – are as much a part of the Island as the Navy. We had known these two sisters, the daughters of a retired British Naval Officer, twenty years ago, when a season in Malta had been a merry-go-round of picnics and sport, with Grand Opera in Valetta when the Italian companies came on tour, with carnival, amateur dramatics, and dances on board the warships. Kay and Ella were everywhere, always on the look-out for new talent for the Malta Amateur Dramatic Club, which was their special interest. Now they still sought talent, only it was for plays produced under the aegis of the British Council, with mixed Maltese and British players. The Warrens belonged to the Island now even more than they had done before. They were bound to it by the shared suffering and hardship that had broken down so many old and foolish barriers.

Ella and Kay had served Malta and the Navy throughout the years of danger, they had endured bombs and the siege, and welcomed the first decimated convoy to bring relief to the starving people. They had heard the bells ring out above the ruined cities as Lord Gort — a great soldier and a great Governor – presented his Island with her George Cross, and they had listened to his address that had brought tears of pride to weary eyes: 'Battle-scarred George Cross Malta, the sentinel of the Empire in the Mediterranean, stands firm, undaunted and undismayed, awaiting the time when she can call "Pass Friend, all is well in the Island Fortress!" ' They had seen the surrendered Italian Fleet 'anchored under the guns of Malta'. And, in the archives of the Public Library, may one day be found Ella Warren's personal diary of their day-to-day life in that time of stress.

It was sunset when we came to the house in the city walls.

Kay said: 'You must see our view before the light goes. You know it's the best part of the house.'

She led us to a window alcove and stood there for a moment with the cold breath of evening ruffling her white hair.

Ella joined us, with her soft step and her sleepy eyes that saw so much. The Plain of Malta was rose-red in the sunset; the little sandstone villages were washed with golden light, and we could hear, in the clear air, the barking of the watch-dogs on the flat roofs and the thin tinkle of goat-bells as the children drove the flocks homewards. Then suddenly the bells began to peal in the double towers of Malta's many churches, for there is always this music of bells in the Island. Away in the creeks the buglers sounded 'Sunset' and ensigns were hauled down on board His Majesty's Ships.

The last day of 1945 faded and died – the last day of the war years.

As dusk merged towers and spires with land and sea, making all things one, Ella said in her soft voice:

'There's something I'll never forget about the war – and nor will Bertie. It was the time, after Salerno, when we all thought the old *Warspite* was lost . . . when she made it after all. As long as I live, I shall remember seeing her come into the Grand Harbour, slowly and dreadfully scarred, listing heavily, but with the sailors on deck and the band playing . . .'

In the gloom I slipped my arm through my husband's. To bring the 'Old Lady' to safe anchorage that day had meant more to him than a duty accomplished, for he had loved her.

'The Old Lady had a heart of oak,' he said, half to himself.

When we turned into the room where a fire burned in the hearth, the first stars faintly pierced the night – the last of 1945.

EPILOGUE

GOOD-BYE GREY MISTRESS

THE 'Old Lady' had served her country well. Even so, the time came when it was decreed that she should be delivered into the hands of the ship-breakers.

In that ignoble hour the sea rose to her defence. As they towed the proud old warrior to a shameful end a mighty storm arose and freed her from her captors, casting her at length upon the rocks of the Cornish coast.

One day my husband took me to that lonely place to see her for the last time. It was cold and grey, with a biting wind. There seemed no life on the headlands, no human being, no signpost to lead us to her. Then we saw an old countryman plodding painfully into the gale. We stopped our car to speak to him. His speech was slow and lilting, and he raised his voice against the weather. His words were Biblical in their simplicity.

'Prussia Cove? It's yonder' – he pointed the way he had come – 'down a small turning to the cliff. . . . Aye, the old *Warspite* do lie there. I mind the night she came – broadside on and terrible to see. There was a high wind and powerful seas, and none could hold her. She broke the tow and took the ground close by . . . Then, on the high tide, she rose again and came into the cove.'

We left the car at the head of the cliff and walked down the steep path between the fishermens' cottages. Nets were drying on the boulders, and lobster-baskets were piled between the rocks. The wind blew icily into our faces and made our eyes water.

There she lay – all that was left of her – close in shore in the grave of her own choosing, stripped by wind and weather and the hand of man down to the bone, right down to her heart of English oak.

I stood beside my husband and we looked in silence at the great hull, shorn of all its majesty. No towering superstructure here, no guns to give tongue against the enemies of Britain.